Also by Nick Bunker

An Empire on the Edge: How Britain Came to Fight America

Making Haste from Babylon: The Mayflower *Pilgrims and Their World*

· YOUNG ·
BENJAMIN FRANKLIN

· YOUNG ·
BENJAMIN FRANKLIN

The Birth of Ingenuity

NICK BUNKER

ALFRED A. KNOPF
New York
2018

THIS IS A BORZOI BOOK PUBLISHED
BY ALFRED A. KNOPF

www.aaknopf.com

Knopf, Borzoi Books, and the colophon are registered trademarks of Penguin Random House LLC.

Jean-Antoine Houdon's marble portrait bust of Benjamin Franklin at the age of seventy-two, made in Paris in 1778–79. Philadelphia Museum of Art: see page 441.

Library of Congress Cataloging-in-Publication Data

Names: Bunker, Nick, author.
Title: Young Benjamin Franklin : the birth of ingenuity / by Nick Bunker.
Description: First edition. | New York : Alfred A. Knopf, 2018. |
"A Borzoi Book."
Identifiers: LCCN 2017057711 | ISBN 9781101874417 (hardcover) |
ISBN 9781101874424 (ebook)
Subjects: LCSH: Franklin, Benjamin, 1706–1790—Childhood and youth. |
Statesmen—United States—Biography.
Classification; LCC E302.6.F8 B8833 2018 | DDC 973.3092 [B]—dc23
LC record available at https://lccn.loc.gov/2017057711

Jacket illustration by Michael Halbert
Jacket design by Kelly Blair

Manufactured in the United States of America

First Edition

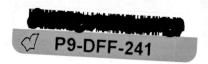

In Memory of Henry Chapman Mercer (1856–1930)

Founder of the Mercer Museum, Doylestown, Pennsylvania

An ingenious American

Contents

· YOUNG ·
BENJAMIN FRANKLIN

Prologue

THE ENIGMATIC SEER

Behold, all alive, one of the ancestors of modern America!

—AUGUSTE RODIN, 1910, ON THE BUST OF FRANKLIN BY JEAN-ANTOINE HOUDON[I]

Before we share the story of his origins and early years, we begin with a glance at the man as he was late in life: Benjamin Franklin, the affable sage, in the Paris where he played the role of diplomat. With his long hair, his paunch, and his spectacles, he delighted his hosts in France with a manner that conveyed serenity as well as charm. Some of us can do gravitas, and some of us can do joie de vivre, but the Franklin of 1780 could do both. It was a rare combination, and all the more exceptional because it seemed to come so easily.

As America's envoy to the court of Versailles, Franklin could hush the chatter in a salon merely by pausing for a long while before he replied to a question. An oracle at peace with himself, or so it seemed, Franklin was always friendly and polite but also rather distant and reserved. Here was a sage who could be funny when he chose, but somehow never lose his aura of gentility.

Partly the secret lay in his build, stricken though he was by arthritis and the gout. In his prime, Franklin had been broad-shouldered and muscular, an inch or two under six feet tall. Even now at seventy, leaning on a cane, he struck one French observer as "a very big man with an excellent figure." Although Franklin would lounge for hours over breakfast, reading the news from the war with the British, the long legs that stretched out across the floor were still firm and shapely: "a very handsome leg," one visitor recalled.[2]

Besides the long pauses, which made the big American seem so august and sublime, Franklin had another way to be inscrutable. Unlike most public men of advancing years, he rarely bored his listeners with tales of past achievements, and least of all did he speak about his boyhood and his youth. This was true of his correspondence as well as his conversation. When we turn to his letters, surviving in the thousands, we meet a Franklin who took the utmost pride in his grammar, his spelling, and the rhythm of his prose, but we will mostly search in vain for intimate details of his early years. Instead they show us a practical, up-to-date Franklin, for whom history—including his own—always seemed to matter far less than the future.

And so besides the dignity and the gravitas, Franklin also had a touch of mystery. By saying so little about his past, he maintained his aura of reserve, and he did it so well that it has endured until the present day. After a lifetime's study of the man, scholars sometimes come away feeling that Franklin will always slip through our fingers. "He kept a kind of inner core of himself intact and unapproachable," wrote Edmund Morgan, the historian from Yale, in one of the finest books about him. In Franklin's own era, those who tried to grapple with the sage often found him even more elusive. Whether they loved or hated Dr. Franklin, they could simply never pin him down.[3]

Where had he come from? That they knew—first Boston, and then Philadelphia—but it was hardly much to go on. What were his origins? Who were his family? How had he become the genius he was? Today when we look for answers to these questions we simply open his autobiography, written in fits and starts over the space of twenty years. There we find a very different Franklin, a man who loved to delve into his roots; but in his lifetime he chose to keep the book from the public eye. Not until 1791, the year after his death, did the first edition of his memoirs appear in print. Even then it was only a French translation and it was incomplete.

As far as the outside world was concerned, his career had begun with a flash and a bang in 1751, when—at the age of forty-five—he published the first edition of his scientific papers, *Experiments and Observations on Electricity,* with his startling theory that electricity and lightning were identical. After that Franklin was rarely out of the news, as he played his many parts as scientist, politician, ambassador, and rebel. His earlier life was something else entirely: provincial, obscure, and all but impossible to reach.

In the Philadelphia of the Revolution, there were aging citizens who remembered Franklin the printer, bent over the proofs of *The Pennsylvania Gazette,* but that was a very long time ago and the details were hard to recover. Three decades had gone by since he ceased to be the paper's editor. Although everyone knew Franklin as the author of *The Way to Wealth,* with its maxims and its jokes culled from his annual, *Poor Richard's Almanack,* even that was something whose origins were lost from view. In its heyday in the 1740s, the almanac had a circulation of ten thousand, but it was a product people kept for a few years and then discarded: how could they know that one day the author would be famous? As for his early journalism, written when he was a teenager in Boston, it had been forgotten long ago. Bylines had yet to be invented, and so his youthful columns disappeared into the archives, dusty and anonymous, to be rediscovered only in the nineteenth century.

With his memoirs still hidden away so discreetly, Franklin's public image was very different from the picture we now have of him. For us he will always be the teenage runaway made good, a whimsical fellow with his gadgets and his jokes. In his lifetime, when they encountered the elderly Franklin what most people saw was a mountain of a man, whose sense of humor took a distant second place to his weighty achievements in science and public affairs. It was as if they had beheld another Moses: a prophet from Sinai, bearing his tablets of stone, wrapped in a cloud that concealed the sources of his energy.

From time to time, however, Franklin would meet a shrewd observer who could see behind the mask of serenity. Among the many portraits that survive, perhaps the best is the marble bust made in Paris in 1779 by a French sculptor, Jean-Antoine Houdon, whose powers of insight were superb. With that unflinching realism for which the French are famous, he shows us a hero with a hinterland: a patriarch whose wisdom is the product of hard labor.[4]

At first sight the bust gives us a classical figure, a philosopher king of the kind that Plato hoped to see ruling his ideal city. The dignity is there and so is the reserve. In the firmness of his gaze, we see the Franklin who had been an athlete in his youth: an excellent swimmer and a fine boxer who knew how to fell an opponent with an upper cut to the jaw. But if we walk around the bust, and peer at it closely, the image becomes as subtle and complex as the man it sought to portray.

Houdon did not mean to flatter or to be a toady. Instead the artist gives us what he found before his eyes: an old man with a sagging chin. The long hair is an old man's hair, falling over Franklin's collar like a clump of dry seaweed on a rock. Although his jowls are heavy with flesh, in places the cheeks have sunk into hollows to reveal the skull beneath, as if to signify the imminence of death. Most skillfully of all, Houdon has shown the mouth tightly set, with pursed lips and a sense of strain. Perhaps the oracle is deep in thought; or perhaps he is trying to suppress a fit of anger.

While Franklin hoped to be seen as the affable sage, a hero who bore his grandeur with ease, the artist gives us someone else entirely: a Franklin who has achieved his gravitas only by way of a long campaign for self-control. More than a hundred years later, another French sculptor, Auguste Rodin, hailed the bust as a masterpiece in which Houdon captured aspects of Franklin that the sage preferred to conceal. In what he called Franklin's "long apostolic hair," Rodin found the homespun wisdom of Poor Richard; in the "large, obstinate forehead," the sculptor had shown courage and self-reliance, but in the eyes, the mouth, and the sheer bulk of Franklin's mighty head, Rodin also saw "the hard commonsense of the calculator." With his jowls and his furrowed brow, this is the Franklin who had been a tradesman.[5]

In a century when to count as a dignitary you were supposed to be born to grandeur, and to show no signs of strain, Franklin was an oddity: a man who had risen to fame after an early career filled with the daily grind of business. The successes of his life required long years of effort: with his science, with his books or in the printing shop, always on a deadline, where the work was exhausting and repetitive and subject to the foibles of the market. Many printers went bankrupt, and most of those whom Franklin knew died young. For businesspeople in the 1700s, an age without a safety net, life could be more precarious than we can readily imagine. A storm in the Atlantic, a crisis in the markets in London, a war in the West Indies, or a failed harvest of tobacco—any one of these could spell commercial disaster. If you were in business in colonial America, calamity lay just around the corner.

In the bust that Houdon made, we see a survivor of adversity who always knew how close he had come to failure. In his years of stardom, when people told him what a genius he was, Franklin would enjoy the compliments but remain aloof: partly because he had diplomacy to do, but also because he knew that his career might easily have ended in oblivion. Time and again in his early life Franklin had seen the sorry fate of other young men, his friends or his rivals, who had fallen by the wayside, victims of smallpox, alcohol, or promiscuity: or simply destroyed by bad luck when the market turned against them.

Why had he gone on to be a success, while so many others dropped down into ruin? This became the central theme of Franklin's memoirs, but he did not wish to have it explored by his readers until he was safely in the grave. Witty he might be, but Franklin was also a deeply serious man, conscious of the task he had to fulfill in building a new American republic. It would not have been helpful to give his rivals or his enemies, and not only the British, too many clues to the secrets of his past.

In his youth he had made embarrassing mistakes. Franklin listed in his memoirs those he was willing to confess. His life had also contained long detours and delays, so that he had to wait far too long to find his true vocation as a scientist. In his century, a man or woman of forty was already far advanced in middle age, but not until Franklin was turning forty-one could he begin his sustained experiments with physics.

With his pioneering work with electricity, Franklin became the American heir of Sir Isaac Newton, helping to engineer another scientific revolution, not quite as profound as Sir Isaac's but close enough and still immensely fruitful. In the process, Franklin gave birth to the systematic study of science in America, as a program of disciplined research by a team and not a mere hobby for clergymen or lawyers working alone in their spare time. But as Franklin also knew, the pursuit of science placed severe demands on its practitioners.

First he had to master the technical literature. Next he had to find the apparatus, or build it for himself; and then, as he made his observations, Franklin had to devise a new scientific language to make sense of what he saw. After four years of trial and error, and thousands of hours of concentrated thought, Franklin produced his masterpiece, his electrical essays: but how many people truly understood the scale of his achievement?

Only Franklin knew the obstacles that he had overcome, and they were not a subject for casual talk around the dinner table. Like a veteran who comes back from a war but does not wish to speak about it, because he fears that the civilians will never understand what combat means, he did not wish to dwell in conversation on the rigors of his early life. Another thing was this: Franklin also knew how old he was and that the world of his youth bore little likeness to the civilized America in which his fellow rebels had come to maturity.

George Washington, the Adamses, John Hancock, and the rest: they were all far younger. Whatever they had seen by way of wars and politics and hardship, they had never known the world he had experienced as a boy. When Franklin was born in 1706, the last of the Stuarts still occupied the throne of England, and the colonies were only a few generations old, often raw and uncouth, with traces of barbarism. In the Boston of his childhood, every day in the street he would see men still in the prime of life who had helped to hang the Salem witches. As for Philadelphia, in his youth it was not far away from being a frontier post. When Franklin first entered the city, at just seventeen, people could still remember a time when settlers lived in caves by the Delaware.

If the world of Franklin's boyhood seems remote, the England that his family inhabited feels more like something lost forever in a mist. Fascinated though he was by his ancestry, Franklin gives us in his memoirs only a brief account of his father, Josiah, and the rest of his forebears. This would not pose a problem if the Franklins had been just another poor, downtrodden family from some quaint little hamlet where nothing much happened from year to year. If that were so, the tale of the English Franklins would tell us very little about the sources of Franklin's genius.

In fact, when we investigate his origins, we find that long before he was born the Franklins were already talented people on the move. Excellent craftsmen, and highly ambitious, they emerged from a part of rural England where, even in the seventeenth century, there were clusters of science and technology, and local people of learning with whom they came to be friends. There and in London, where they went to work, the Franklins laid the foundations for Benjamin's career in America. Reading books and hearing preachers, plying their trade and acquiring the skills they needed, as time went by the Franklins built a family endowment: not a trust fund consisting of cash or stocks and bonds but instead a repertoire of ideas and expertise. In 1683, when Josiah Franklin arrived in Boston, he was a refugee, political and religious, in search of asylum at a time of crisis in the mother country. With him on the boat, Josiah carried a cultural legacy that he would bequeath to his children: a legacy defined by the word "ingenuity."

If Franklin had a favorite noun, it was this one, a term that conveyed in the eighteenth century a far richer meaning than it carries today. In one form or another, the words "ingenious" and "ingenuity" appear seventeen times in his memoirs, used by Franklin to describe his father, his uncles, and all the other people he respected. When Franklin spoke of ingenuity, he had in mind a quality of being with as many facets as he had himself.

It was a hybrid virtue, a blend of many different ingredients: intellect, of course, but also imagination and skills with the hand and with the eye as well as with the brain. Ingenuity required not only diligence and learning but also an element of playfulness and sociability. Once achieved, it could be a source of happiness as well as a way to make money. Everyone would want to meet ingenious people, because they were fascinating, fun to be with, and filled with curiosity. Their ingenuity might also take them up the social ladder, because the qualities they had, of wit, variety, and flair, were those that a gentleman was meant to possess: and a lady, too, if only she were given the opportunity to shine.

Adopted from the Latin, the word had been current in English for centuries, but suddenly, in the 1650s and the 1660s, a moment arrived when ingenuity became the height of fashion. When Josiah was a boy, at the time when Newton was making his earliest discoveries, it seemed that an age of ingenuity was dawning, an era of progress and invention, with the English poised to take the lead—or so it seemed to them—as the world's most ingenious people. And so the word was endlessly repeated, in books and pamphlets and in poetry. Josiah brought it with him to the colonies, where the pursuit of ingenuity became the guiding principle of Benjamin Franklin's career.

None of this came easily in an era when, however brilliant they were, people from the social rank of the Franklins had the odds stacked against them by a culture of deference, on both sides of the Atlantic, that only the most determined men and women could surmount. The Franklins always strove to be ingenious. For a while they were so successful that they briefly won acceptance as members of the gentry. Even so, in England their luck ran out, so that their quest for advancement ended in frustration. In America Josiah Franklin had to work still harder to secure his family's future. On arrival he was treated as a nobody. In Boston it took Josiah more than twenty years to win the esteem his brothers had fleetingly enjoyed at home.

All of this left its mark on his son. In Benjamin Franklin's early life, his principal emotions were ambition and the fear of failure. He wanted to be ingenious and he wanted to be a gentleman: in his eyes the two things went together. Desperate to be successful, Franklin pushed himself hard, waging long battles against the temptations that ruined so many young people. By the time he came to Paris, Franklin knew how to pretend that he was always serene. But as Houdon the sculptor saw so well, behind the charm of the affable sage there lay a life with many layers: an odyssey complete with episodes of guilt and phases of anxiety.

This portrait of the scientist as a young man begins with an incident of strife that occurred a hundred years before his birth. It took place in the heart of Shakespeare's England, where the Franklins were a family of upstarts.

Part One

Beginnings

Chapter One

His Ingenious Kin

Seventy miles from London and beneath the turrets of a Norman castle, there stood the town of Northampton, spilling down a gentle slope toward the River Nene. In the early 1600s, it was a borough mainly built with wood and thatch, prosperous but overcrowded, and squalid with the smell of tanneries and leather. Most of its citizens earned their living making shoes, and so the fields around the town were filled with herds of cattle. The wealthiest men in the region were the graziers, whose cows and sheep had come to dominate the county.

With many people hungry for some land of their own, its price was increasing rapidly, and few slices of real estate in the English Midlands were as precious as the valley of the Nene. To the south of the town, the ground rose up from the river toward a village by the name of Houghton Magna. It was here, in the course of a dispute about the tenure of the soil, that the Franklins left their earliest traces in history as anything more than brief entries in a parish register.

The village had a splendid site, with a distant prospect of the castle. The houses were sturdy, built of stone, so that a few of them can still be seen today; but the most attractive feature of the place was the earth on which they stood. Fertile and easy to plow, the soil at Houghton Magna was "the best . . . in all Northamptonshire," in the words of a surveyor at the time. Anyone who knew his land could see how good it was, and among the men who hoped to settle in the village was a blacksmith in his early thirties. His name was Henry Franklin: the great-grandfather of the sage of Philadelphia.[1]

More than a hundred years later, living in retirement in Boston, one of Henry's grandsons composed a family history: a remarkable document, colorful and rich in anecdote, of a kind that seldom survives from the working folk of England at this period. The author was Franklin's uncle, another Benjamin, writing at the age of sixty-nine. His manuscript begins with old Henry, whom he revered as a man of principle who defended the villagers against an overbearing clique of landlords.

As Benjamin Senior admitted, he had only "a dark idea" of his ancestor's biography. Indeed his account of old Henry is garbled and mistaken when it comes to dates and details. However, the records that remain from the area are excellent, and they show us that the gist of the tale was correct. A resilient man, eager to rise in the world, Henry Franklin was something of a local hero, fit to inspire his descendants with an example of courage. Far into the eighteenth century, his story would help to fashion the view the Franklins took of themselves as people who refused to be done down by those who claimed to be their superiors.[2]

Henry Franklin was born in 1573, four miles from Houghton Magna in the parish of Ecton, another hillside village above the River Nene. There he plied his father's trade as a smith, making plowshares, horseshoes, bolts, hinges, and iron rims for wagon wheels. Away from the forge he was also a husbandman; or as we might say, a small farmer, owning a few dozen acres of land and some animals. In 1595—a year of plague and famine, when the laboring people of England were at their lowest ebb—he married Agnes Jones. She had a brother called Michael.

His descendants remembered Henry as a dour, unsociable person, but he made friends with Michael Jones and they became partners in business. In about 1604, when James I had recently become the king, the two men bought some land at Houghton Magna, fine tillage for grain with a share of the hay from the meadows. And then the trouble started. The events that followed will lead us into the world from which the Franklins arose: a society whose harsh realities gave them their yearning to do better, but also taught them how to be pragmatic as they strove to climb above their circumstances.[3]

In the sixteenth century, most of Houghton Magna had belonged to the Treshams, a renegade crew of Roman Catholics, led by an elderly patriarch, Sir Thomas, who suffered the persecution to which his faith was subject. For the crime of clinging to the old religion, he was sent to prison and made to pay huge fines. Being one of the richest of the graziers, of course he tried to make his tenants foot the bill. Not only did he raise the rents as high as they would go; Sir Thomas Tresham also hit upon the technique of enclosure. In London, which was growing fast, city dwellers wanted beef and mutton and the nation also needed wool to feed the textile trade. It made economic sense, or so the Treshams thought, to sweep away small farmers and replace their fields of grain with oblongs of grass, fenced and hedged for their vast flocks of sheep.[4]

In 1601, Sir Thomas's eldest son joined the Earl of Essex in his disastrous rebellion against Elizabeth I. To save the young man from the scaffold the family had to raise more money; and so they began to dispose of their estates, including Houghton Magna, which so far they had left unenclosed. At the end of 1604, the Treshams sold their holding in the village to investors led by a fellow Catholic, one Ferdinando Baude. He set about at once to fence in the fields: including the tract of land that Henry Franklin had recently acquired.

As often happened at the time, the title deeds at Houghton Magna were ambiguous and open to dispute. And so there were arguments aplenty: about who really owned each acre, and the rights they had to graze their animals or sow their crops. Soon Ferdinando Baude met with stiff resistance from the peasantry, who broke down his hedges and continued to plow their land. The villagers were "every day more obstinate," he wrote. And among the awkward squad at Houghton Magna, none were more stubborn than Franklin and Jones.

Mr. Baude hired ruffians who beat up Henry Franklin; and when that tactic did not work, he took him and Michael Jones to court, accusing them of fraud in the way they bought their piece of soil. As Mr. Baude saw it, he was on the side of progress, with his plans for what he thought was "a lawful and reasonable improvement," while the likes of Jones and Franklin were nothing more than malcontents. "Covetous and troublesome"—those were the words Baude used about them: the earliest description we can find of any member of the Franklin family.[5]

Now Henry was not the surrendering sort and neither were his friends on the farms at Houghton Magna. The villagers found their own attorney, a Puritan with a seat in Parliament, and meanwhile they also turned for support to the people of Northampton, a Puritan town where a Catholic landlord could expect to be vilified. And then, in November 1605, the nation reeled back aghast at some horrifying news: the Gunpowder Plot against King James, with Catholics like Mr. Baude to blame and the Tresham family among the plotters.

Early in 1606, at what must have seemed to be an ideal moment, Jones and Franklin issued their legal defense against the lawsuit from the enclosers. In doing so they tried to occupy the moral high ground of virtue and the common good. In Henry Franklin's eyes, the scheme to fence in the fields was nothing but a plot by powerful men to "prejudice the common wealth," throwing the poor off the land, by what he and Jones called "the decay of tillage, and subversion & decaying of many houses . . . and the diminishing of people."

Eloquent though they were, Henry and his business partner failed to win their fight for justice. The details are obscure, but one thing we know: Jones and Franklin lost their bit of land at Houghton Magna. It appears that for a while Henry lost his liberty as well. In 1743, when Benjamin Franklin was trying to research his ancestry, he received a letter from his father in which Josiah added some more information. According to Josiah, Henry Franklin went to prison "on suspicion of his being the author of some poetry that touched the character of some great man." The man he libeled must have been Mr. Baude or one of his cronies.[6]

The times were hard, the economics cruel, and when Henry was defeated he was only one of many people dispossessed. Across a broad swathe of the English Midlands, the landlords went to work, enclosing the fields. Tenants were evicted, houses torn down, and livestock took the place of people; until at last, in the spring of 1607, in three counties in the region the peasantry could take no more. Taking up their bill-hooks and their scythes, they rose in a futile rebellion that ended with the bloodiest form of retribution.

The authorities crushed the Midland Rising, hanged its leaders, and mounted their heads on the gates of the nearest town. In an effort to prevent more trouble, King James appointed a board of inquiry to investigate the enclosures. From the tattered records the board left behind, it is clear that the evictions at Houghton Magna had been some of the most destructive. When the members of the board came to Northampton, and summoned Ferdinando Baude to give evidence, he refused to appear: because he feared that a mob would lynch him in the streets.[7]

It seems that Henry Franklin never joined the armed rebellion. Which is just as well, since if he had done so the Franklins might have vanished forever. The desperate truth was this: the landlords had won the day, and soon enough the government chose to take their side. The inquiry of 1607–8 was the last occasion when the English crown made any serious effort to halt the process of enclosure. In the years that followed, the Stuart kings fell in love with economic projects of the kind that Mr. Baude had called "improvement." As a way to enhance the wealth of the nation, and to raise some revenue, the monarchy issued a host of permits and royal patents, not only for more enclosures but also for schemes to drain marshes, plant new crops, dig canals and mines, breed silkworms, and to found plantations, in Ireland or America. In these new outposts in the west, King James and his successors hoped to bring the benefits of progress to the heathen and the Irish, and of course there were profits to be made as well.[8]

Eighty years had yet to pass before Josiah Franklin left for the colonies. In the meantime his forebears had to find a way to prosper at home, surrounded by powerful landowners whose estates grew ever larger as each decade went by. In this new environment, it made little sense to try to win an outright battle with the men of property. Instead, if a blacksmith wished to be successful, he would have to find ways to make himself useful to people of rank. And this is precisely what the Franklins did. Putting their talents to work for the local gentry, whom they could serve as craftsmen, secretaries, and surveyors, the Franklins acquired an education, a higher social status, and—eventually—the money to give their children a better start in life.

After the affair at Houghton Magna, Henry Franklin stuck to his trade as a blacksmith. For fifteen years or so, his name drops out of the archives—it seems that he moved away, to the nearby town of Desborough—until in the 1620s he reappears at Ecton doing another property deal in partnership with Jones, whose career as a farmer had flourished in the meantime. In 1628, when King Charles I imposed the notorious Ship Money—in other words, a tax to finance his navy—the authorities made a list of the yeomen affluent enough to have to pay it. At Ecton the wealthiest was Michael Jones. Two years later the villagers chose Henry Franklin as the parish constable. This we know because again he was assaulted, this time by a man he was trying to arrest.[9]

And so by the time Henry died in 1631, the Franklins were firmly planted at Ecton with their forge, their plot of land, and their successful in-laws. As yet the Franklins were still a long way from affluence, but they were headed in the right direction. Henry had a son called Thomas, born in 1598; and it was Thomas Franklin, Benjamin Franklin's grandfather, who made the decisive breakthrough in the family's affairs.

In the 1640s, the Franklins began in earnest their ascent toward gentility. Mostly they owed their achievements to their talents, but they also acquired the powerful friends they needed. As their luck would have it, the village of Ecton had come to be controlled by a family of landlords who were unusual, highly intelligent people, less inclined than most of their class to bully their inferiors. In time they became the patrons of the Franklins in religion, in politics, and best of all in ingenuity. Far from being poor, Ecton was a thriving parish close to the highway; and far from being dull and isolated, the village was about to advance to the leading edge of the science of the era.

The Mathematical Divine

In 1758, when he had recently made his home in London, Benjamin Franklin began what would become an American tradition. That summer he went to Northamptonshire in search of his ancestors, taking with him his son William. At Ecton they found the parish register and the family graves. They met the rector and his wife—"a good-natured, chatty old lady," as Franklin described her—who supplied a brush and a basin of water to scrub the headstones clean of moss. Beyond the churchyard wall, Franklin saw the fine rectory house and the village his forebears had known, with a landscape that had barely altered since the 1300s.[10]

Ecton had never been enclosed, and so, like the spokes of a cartwheel, three open fields, each a mile wide, still lay in a circle around the ancient church of St. Mary Magdalene. In medieval fashion, each one was divided into narrow strips, with just enough space for a plow and a team of horses to turn at each end. To the north, the ground rose to a hilltop with another panoramic view across the valley. To the south, the earth dropped away into meadows where the village boys played bowls, except in those years when the grass was flooded by the Nene.

The soil was not as rich as Houghton Magna's, but it was fertile even so and in the town of Northampton they had a ready market for their crops. Because of all this, in the 1600s the minister at Ecton drew a handsome income from the tithes, three times larger than the average for a clergyman at the time. It was also a peaceful village where the farmers rarely quarreled with the lord of the manor. In 1629 they fell out about grazing rights, but the two sides reached a compromise, the fields were left unfenced, and the deal survived for another hundred years.[11]

Nor did the residents come to blows about religion. By the 1640s the village had become a bastion of a quiet, unusually tolerant form of Puritan belief. In an age of bigotry, Ecton stood out as a place where people could be holy without being fanatical. Although the Franklins were always Puritan, enemies of anything that smacked of old Catholic ways, they did not have to fight to defend their creed, and from the records that remain it seems that the English Civil War passed them by entirely.

It had not always been that way. At one time the Franklins had been in danger for their choice of faith. In 1546, soon after Henry VIII broke away from Rome, the authorities in Northamptonshire had begun to find artisans and farmers studying the scriptures for themselves. They described these early Protestants as "meddlers with the Bible." The Franklins must have been among the meddlers, because Uncle Benjamin told a story dating from the reign of the Catholic queen, Mary Tudor, about a trick the family used to deceive her officials when they came in search of heretics. Although the first Bibles in English had only recently appeared, Henry Franklin's father* had acquired a copy, which he fastened to the bottom of a stool. To read the word of God, he would flip the stool over and balance it on his knees while he turned the pages. One of his children stood at the door, watching for the clerical police. When they came by the old man would put the stool back on its legs, and the family pretended to be law-abiding.[12]

And so the Franklins had to be cautious: but not for very long. In the country close to Ecton, many of the landed gentry were going their way and abandoning the old Roman religion. Across the valley to the south there stood the village of Whiston, where by the 1570s the principal landlords, the Catesby family, had become ardent Puritans, picking as their chaplain a preacher who hoped to sweep away all that was left of Popery in the region. In 1574, the Catesbys bought the manor of Ecton, which gave them the right to choose the rector of the parish. With that the village became a Puritan enclave where the Franklins could be as prayerful as they chose; and they were all the safer because the Catesbys had acquired some allies in the world of politics. In 1560, one of the Catesby daughters had married a lawyer, Sir Christopher Yelverton, who stood at the peak of his profession. He was a Puritan too. In time he became one of the highest judges in England, and in Parliament he served as speaker of the House of Commons.[13]

The Yelverton estate was seven miles from Ecton, and from there Sir Christopher's web of patronage spread out across the county. His alliance with the Catesbys would endure for many decades, and in time it proved to be very fruitful for the Franklins. As it happened, the Catesbys and the Yelvertons had a taste for science. It led them to promote young

* Or perhaps Henry's grandfather: the dates of the generations are not entirely clear.

men of learning: and these were the people who took Ecton to the forefront of ingenuity.

In the famous words of Sir Isaac Newton, if he saw further than other scientists it was because he stood upon the shoulders of giants. In the generation just before Sir Isaac, the giants of English science included a mathematician, Samuel Foster, whose father was the parish minister at Whiston. After graduating from Cambridge University, Foster became the protégé of the Yelvertons, who did all they could to help his career. In 1636, he took the post of professor of astronomy at Gresham College in London, where he applied the new discoveries, logarithms and the like, to the problems of navigation and the mapping of the stars. Foster had a scientific friend, John Palmer, another Cambridge graduate, and he was the man—"the famous Palmer," as Benjamin Franklin described him in the 1750s—who became the friend and mentor of the village blacksmith and his family.[14]

At Ecton in 1641, the post of rector fell vacant. By now the civil war was approaching and in the county of Northampton, where so many of the gentry were Puritans, politically at odds with King Charles, it seemed that the moment had come to complete the English Reformation, by filling the pulpits with clergymen who shared their opinions. To occupy the rectory, the Yelvertons and Catesbys chose Mr. Palmer, who was only twenty-eight. He would be the Ecton pastor for more than thirty years, a fair-minded man who tempered authority with kindness. His prestige was all the greater, not to mention his wealth, because John Palmer married Bridget Catesby.

By way of his theology, Palmer belonged to the Presbyterian wing of the Puritan movement. In other words, he was a moderate, an opponent of King Charles but otherwise conservative, and so although he disliked the authority of bishops he did not intend to turn the world upside down for the sake of being zealous. Next to Bridget and the Bible, the pursuit of science counted as the principal love of Palmer's life. By the age of twenty, he was already taking daily notes of wind and weather and poring over books by maritime explorers. At Ecton he made the church tower his observatory, while the rectory became his studio for designing instruments for mariners. There with Foster's help he compiled a catalogue of eclipses, using his equations to forecast the arrival of each one.[15]

A man abreast of all the latest inventions, John Palmer owned a telescope and a "minute watch," with which he took down the details of twelve eclipses of the sun and moon. On these occasions he would always

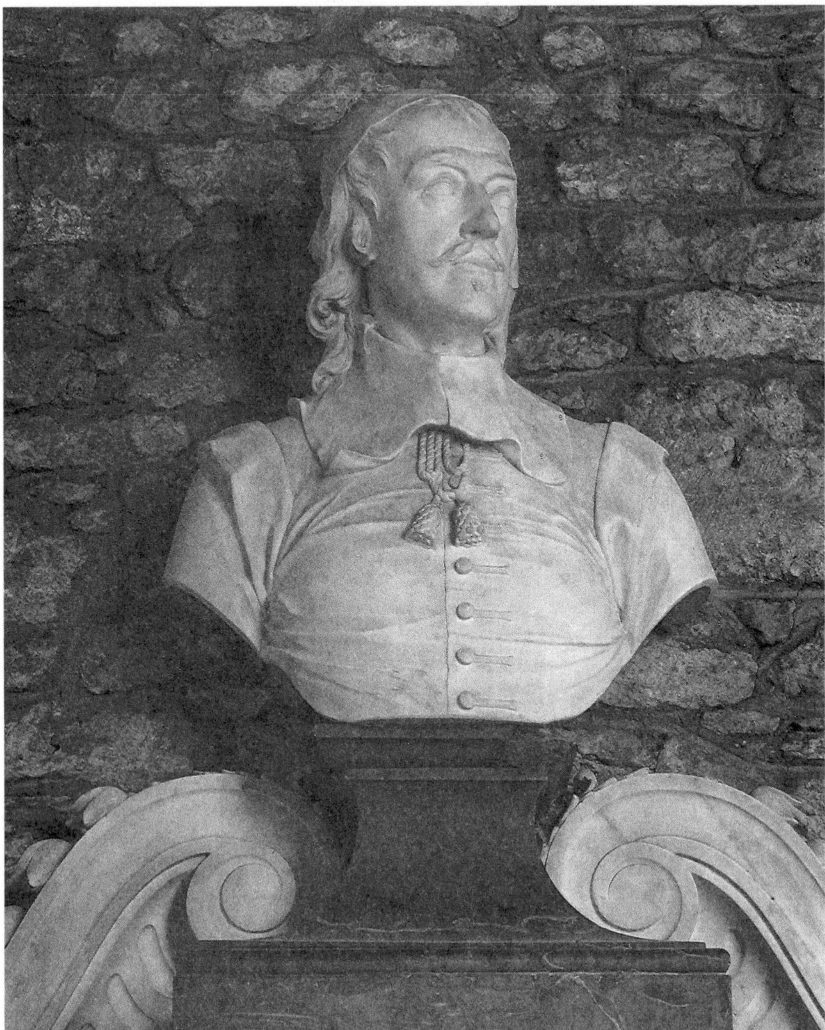

From the church of St. Mary Magdalene at Ecton, Northamptonshire, the monument to the Franklin family's friend and mentor, the scientist Archdeacon John Palmer (1612–79). Based on an earlier portrait, it was carved in about 1732 by the Flemish sculptor J. M. Rysbrack: who also created the monument to Sir Isaac Newton in Westminster Abbey.

have an audience, eager to see if the event occurred just as the rector had predicted. A case in point was the gathering at Ecton on the morning of March 29, 1652, when right on cue, at 9:21, the sun disappeared from view. "I observed the great eclipse," Palmer wrote, "in the company of half-a-score gentlemen and ministers my neighbours." To measure the depth of the darkness they went indoors and tried to read a page from a book.[16]

Somewhere in the gaping crowd you would have found the Franklins. Of this we can be sure, because when Palmer needed help with things mechanical, the man to whom he turned was the blacksmith, Thomas Franklin. By the time Palmer took up his post, Thomas was a hefty fellow in his mid-forties: good-looking, suntanned, but "inclined to corpulence," according to Benjamin Senior. To hide his baldness, Thomas always wore a cap. He was a Presbyterian too, with a list of Bible texts that formed his personal liturgy. His wife, Jane, led her women friends in midweek sessions—two hours, every Thursday—at which they sang hymns and discussed last Sunday's sermon. While their piety was bound to recommend the Franklins to the rector, Thomas also had the skills to assist him with his scientific work. Two of John Palmer's account books have survived, to show us how closely he and the blacksmith cooperated. Two pages record Thomas Franklin's debts to the rector for tithes and rent, but much of the time he settled them by doing jobs for Palmer at the smithy.[17]

Old Thomas was one of those people we all need at a moment of crisis: the sort of person who can mend anything broken, after years of solving problems in his workshop. In his spare time he practiced surgery—he cured his son Benjamin's swollen leg with a poultice and ointments he concocted—and he could do carpentry and turn wood on a lathe. Thomas Franklin could read and write, with fine calligraphy. He knew history and he could make guns. He could also build the wonderful clocks that English blacksmiths loved to assemble from iron teeth and cogwheels fashioned in the forge. Best of all, his son remembered, Thomas had "some skill in astronomy and chemistry, which made him acceptable company to Mr Palmer."

By now the English had a word for clever people such as this. In 1658, Palmer brought out a book, *The Catholique Planisphere,* in which he described his own invention, a new kind of astrolabe, mounted on a tripod so that the user could carry it about to fix his latitude at any spot on land or sea. It was, Palmer wrote, a device "very useful for mariners, and for all ingenious men, who love the arts mathematical." That was the word: "ingenious." When he spoke the language of ingenuity, John Palmer caught the spirit of the decade.

The civil wars were over, King Charles had been beheaded in 1649, and Oliver Cromwell was left to govern the nation with all the discreet charm of a military dictator. Among his supporters there were men and women who felt that with their new republic the English were about to enter a golden age. They were, said one pamphleteer, "an ingenious and industrious people." Led by Cromwell, his major-generals, and the Puritan clergy, they hoped to guide the rest of the human race along a path of godliness, science, and prosperity.[18]

In the Midland counties, these ideas found a spokesman in a veteran of Cromwell's army, Captain Walter Blith. From his home a day's ride from Ecton, the old soldier beat the drum for progress, calling himself "a lover of ingenuity." His magnum opus appeared in 1652, dedicated to Cromwell and filled with new ways to plow or plant trees, new species of grass, and new methods for preventing floods. "If we can but bring ingenuity into fashion," wrote Captain Blith, "this very nation might be made the paradise of the world."

Far from being empty words, the captain's bold agenda struck a chord with his neighbors. Cromwell died, a Stuart king returned in 1660, and it became apparent that if England wished to be ingenious, it did not also have to be a Puritan state. A monarchy would do just as well; and under Charles II and his successors the cult of ingenuity grew stronger. In the year of his restoration the Royal Society came into being with a mission to educate the nation in the ways of science. Few people were more receptive than those who dwelled in Northamptonshire.

In 1712 a local clergyman by the name of John Morton produced a pioneering book, a natural history of the county, in which he catalogued in loving detail its plants, its animals, its landscape, and its geology. He gave examples of local people of ingenuity—clergymen, physicians, and landlords—who had made improvements in the valley of the Nene. Among them Morton mentions craftsmen who took old workshop skills and developed them as far as they would go, partly as a way to make a living but also just for the pleasure of creating something new and magical. For example, only two miles from Ecton the Franklins had a rival, Samuel Warren, "an ingenious blacksmith" who doubled as a hydraulic engineer. The Earl of Northampton used vast quantities of water, to fill his ponds and cascades and to feed his kitchen and his laundry. But the nearest spring was a mile away. So Warren built a chain of aqueducts, pipes, and a water wheel, to ensure that the earl would always have his fountains and clean linen.[19]

In the work of blacksmiths such as Warren and the Franklins, we can find a foretaste of the scientific movement that the sage of Philadelphia would strive to create in the colonies. Fed by new ideas from London, the English cult of ingenuity put down ever deeper roots in the Midland counties until it underwent another transformation, as scientists and artisans worked closely together with people of business: in other words, the cult of ingenuity gave birth to the Industrial Revolution. It began in the years around 1760, at about the time when Franklin took his summer break at Ecton, where he found the roots of his own ingenious ways among the sort of people who had made that revolution feasible.[20]

Of all the English Franklins, the cleverest was his uncle, Thomas Franklin Jr., born in 1637, only five years before Newton, whose origins could also be found among the farmers of the Midlands. When Benjamin Franklin came to visit, the rector's wife had a fund of anecdotes about Thomas Junior that he found enthralling. He and his uncle were two of a kind, eager to use their talents for the public good. In fact, the likeness between them was so uncanny that when William Franklin heard the stories told at Ecton, he fancied that perhaps his father was Thomas Junior reincarnated. He noted the fact that Thomas Junior had passed away precisely three years before his nephew was born. "Had he died on the same day," William said, "one might have supposed a transmigration."

Thin and dark haired, Thomas Junior had a hot temper and he could be abrasive but he was also an excellent craftsman. Trained as a blacksmith, like Samuel Warren he became an expert with water, devising a system of sluices to prevent the Nene from wrecking the meadows. He taught school, he dealt in tobacco, and he played the organ. Inheriting his father's writing skills he also worked as a scrivener, drafting wills and leases. In 1665, when John Palmer became Archdeacon of Northampton, with the job of making sure that the clergy and the laity did as they were told in matters of religion, he chose Thomas Junior as his clerk. Chiefly, however, Thomas made his living as a surveyor, acting on behalf of the Catesbys, the Palmers, and other landowners eager to enhance the value of their estates. A cache of his letters has been preserved, dating from the 1670s and 1680s. They show us Thomas Junior hard at work collecting rents, overseeing the harvest, and shipping coal for kitchen fires around the countryside.[21]

Later in America his nephew would invent the famous Franklin stove, more correctly described as an iron fireplace, designed on scientific principles to heat a room efficiently. If the Franklin stove had its own genealogy, part of it lay in Thomas Junior's career as an engineer in rural England. "He was looked upon by some . . . as something of a conjuror," the rector's wife remembered, and his magic included the creation of bells for churches. Not far from Ecton there was a patch of clay and

Archdeacon Palmer's brother-in-law, the Whig landowner Thomas Catesby (1632–99), who employed Franklin's uncle Thomas Franklin Jr. as land agent and surveyor on his estates at Ecton and Whiston, Northamptonshire. With Catesby is his wife, Margaret, on their monument at the Church of St. Mary the Virgin, Whiston.

sand ideal for shaping molds in a foundry. And so in the 1680s Thomas Junior became the partner and friend of a bell founder, Henry Bagley, who moved his works to Ecton and took the Franklins into the business of casting bronze.

For the makers of bells, it was a golden age when—after decades of neglect, as churches fell into disrepair during the years of civil strife—suddenly the clergy and their congregations found that they had money to spend. And so the firm of Bagley & Franklin turned out scores of bells, to be hauled up muddy lanes by teams of horses bound for parishes many miles away. When the cathedral at Lichfield installed a new ring of ten bells, the largest of which weighed a ton and a half, they ordered them from Mr. Bagley. By the time Benjamin Franklin arrived in the 1750s, the foundry at Ecton had long since disappeared, but a set of chimes survived, placed in the church tower by Thomas Junior; and before he left the village, the great American heard them play a patriotic tune.[22]

And so, long before Franklin was born in Boston, his forebears in seventeenth-century England had already been ingenious, as they followed careers that required not only fine craftsmanship but also a talent for business. Like every family with aspirations, the Franklins gazed southwards down the highway to London, where the skills a boy could learn were still more advanced and earnings were much higher than in the countryside. Old Thomas Franklin had six sons, and while Thomas Junior would inherit the forge, the younger boys had to find their own vocations. Beginning in the 1650s, all five of them—including Franklin's father, Josiah—were sent to the capital to enroll as apprentices. Their timing was perfect, as they arrived in the capital in the age of Cromwell and then of Charles II, ready to catch a rising tide of creativity in the mechanical arts.

Fascinated as he was by chemistry, old Thomas selected a demanding trade where his sons could develop capabilities beyond his own. Four of the boys were to train as dyers of silk, led by Samuel, the second son. It was a shrewd choice of occupation, and one that would have its consequences in America. In the art of coloring, a young man could become still more ingenious, as he acquired not only a host of practical skills with the eye and with the fingers but also what amounted to a scientific education in the curious behavior of alkalis, acids, and the fabrics to which they were applied. Eighty years later, the everyday grind of Josiah and his brothers would come to fruition in Philadelphia, in Franklin's experiments with electricity.[23]

Chapter Two

Coats of Many Colors

The decisive turning point in the lives of the Franklins can be given an exact date and almost a precise location. It took place ten years before the Great Fire of London. On July 24, 1656, at the age of fourteen, Samuel Franklin—good-looking and "very ingenious," it was said—came to the hall of the Dyers' Company to sign his indentures as an apprentice. The hall stood somewhere close to the River Thames, at the heart of the city, and so it was destroyed by the flames and its site was lost. If its address could be found today it would merit a plaque to commemorate Samuel's arrival, because this was where the Franklins set off on the journey that would lead to the birth of American science.

To secure an apprenticeship for Samuel counted as a fine achievement in itself. To win his son a place in a sought-after trade, Thomas Franklin Sr. had to find a master craftsman prepared to take on the boy. In return there was always a fee to be paid to the employer, which for a trainee dyer of silk would be at least £10. In England at the time, it would take a skilled artisan six months to earn that kind of money, and so it was a hefty price for a country blacksmith to afford.

Even so Thomas Senior found the cash for the master's fee: not once but five times, for all his younger sons, hard evidence that he had been a constant worker at the forge. After Samuel, he sent John Franklin to Dyers' Hall to swear his own indentures in 1660. Next to come were Joseph and Benjamin, Joseph as a carpenter and Benjamin as yet another colorist. The last of the boys to arrive was Franklin's father, Josiah. In London in 1671, at the age of fourteen, Josiah Franklin became an apprentice dyer of silk.

Samuel died young and never qualified; but the others—John, Benjamin, and Josiah—all reached the end of their seven years of training. With that they became freemen of the Dyers' Company. This was just as much a mark of social status as it was a means to earn a living. As members of the company, they were also enrolled as freemen of the City of London, which gave the Franklin boys the right to vote in local elections as well as the prestige that came with the mastery of a difficult vocation.[1]

The dyeing of silk was a booming business, but only a fit and strong young man could endure the burdens it imposed. In the second half of the century the market for silk in England more than doubled in size, so that in the 1680s it was estimated that more than forty thousand families earned their keep from weaving or handling the fabric. To make dresses, robes, and drapery, the silk had to be colored and this required subtlety and imagination. Hence the high wages the dyers could negotiate. In exchange they suffered a daily ordeal of stink and heat and scummy residue.[2]

It was a filthy way to make ends meet, so horrid that the dyers were confined to the poorest parts of London, where their pits and vats caused the least offense. The waterfront was the usual location, and this was where the Franklins plied their noxious trade. "My practice was upon raw silk in the skein, both black and colours, for about 30 years," wrote Benjamin Senior in his family history, "and afterward I dyed garments . . . and stuffs and cloths for about nineteen years more."

In retirement in New England, the old man wrote a manual for dyers, listing the tints he knew, and in combination with other sources from the period it tells us how he and his colleagues spent their days. The colors came to more than a hundred, from amaranth to scarlet, and from celandine to strawberry. Each shade was a mixture of many ingredients: among them antimony, madder, or verdigris, hardwoods from the Amazon, or spices from the Orient. Did the silk need to be yellow? If so, the dyer would turn to "the urine of laboring men, kept till it be stale." Alternatively, if crimson were required the dyer could make do with a less appalling mixture.

First he had to boil the raw silk, clean it with Thames river water—because it was oily, and made the soap froth and bubble—dry the fabric, soak it with alum, and smear it with more soap. Then he would make a liquor of cochineal, arsenic, and tartaric acid, boil it up with water, and immerse the silk. After that more drying, beating, a rinsing in hot suds, a soaking with more river water, and more beating and more drying. Add saffron and lime juice and the crimson would turn to Spanish carnation.

If wheat bran went in, and Brazilwood as well, the silk would take on the color of blood.[3]

Despite the smelly pits and boiling vats, the dyers of silk were proud of their trade and, because they were doing a form of chemistry, they won the respect of people of science, including members of the Royal Society. A dyer of silk had to be *inquisitive,* always looking for new methods or new sources of color. Careful too, extremely so: because, if he failed to pay attention, he would ruin the expensive stuff he had to beautify. He would have to be tough and determined as well, and capable of working fast. He was paid by the piece and not by the hour.

In England Josiah spent thirteen years acquiring these habits of ingenuity, and in time he passed them on to his son. Although in Boston he had to find another career, Josiah never lost what Benjamin Franklin called his "mechanical genius." In his autobiography, he remembered his father as somebody who was "very handy in the use of other tradesmen's tools." Along the way Josiah learned carpentry, the craft his brother Joseph had practiced, helping to rebuild the city after the Great Fire. Fifty years later in Boston, Josiah knew the trade so well that in 1722 he signed up a boy as an apprentice in joinery.

At about the same time, Josiah took the teenage Benjamin to meet craftsmen of all kinds—bricklayers, turners, braziers, and more—in the hope of finding the career for which his son had the most aptitude. "It has ever since been a pleasure to me to see good workmen handle their tools," Franklin recalled in his memoirs. "It has been useful to me, having learned so much by it . . . to construct little machines for my experiments." As everyone knows, he chose not to build houses or to make brass kettles; but even so his father's mechanical talents were essential for his future.

As a printer Franklin made his own ink and sized his paper with gum and soap, drying it carefully overnight before it could bear the mark of lead type. These were skills akin to the dyer's, and they would give Franklin the practical expertise he required as an electrician. For the vocation of science he needed something else as well: a love of books and what they had to teach. Here was another thing that London could supply and that Josiah conveyed to his children.

It was a city of words that the Franklins were eager to absorb. Under Cromwell, provided they did not insult the regime the printers could publish more or less anything they chose; and even when Charles II came home from exile and more rigid censorship returned, books continued

The London the Franklins inhabited, from a 1666 map by Wenceslaus Hollar showing the area—all in white—destroyed by the Great Fire. The silk dyers' workshops were located along the northern bank of the Thames to the west of London Bridge, and also in Southwark. Little Britain, where Benjamin Franklin

A MAP or GROVNDPLOT of the Citty of London and the Suburbes thereof that is to ſay, all which is within the Iuriſdiction of the Lord Mayor or properlie calld London by which is exactly demonſtrated the preſent condition thereof ſince the last sad accident of fire. The blanke ſpace ſignifeing the burnt part & where the houſes are expreſt, those places yet ſtandīg.
Sould by Iohn Overton at the White horſe in little Brittaine, next doore to little S. Bartholomew gate 1666.
Artilery ground
Moore Fields
Spittle Fields
Lothbury
Old Jewry
Tower street
Thames Street
Tower hill
East Smithfield
The Tower
Part of Southwarke
Annotations of the Churches, and other remarkable places in this Map.

had his lodgings in 1724–25, was untouched by the flames, and it can be found immediately to the northwest of the gate in the city walls marked "C," with Smithfield to its left. In 1726 Franklin lived on Duke Street just off Lincoln's Inn Fields, the open space shown surrounded by buildings on the far left of the map.

to pour from the presses. Most of the output was religious, but the Franklins were avid readers of sermons, tracts, and sacred poetry. They had all the more reason to study books such as these because—for an old Puritan family like this—the Restoration period gave rise to new dilemmas that they had to try to resolve as best they could.

At Ecton before the death of Cromwell, in matters of belief their lives had been pious but uncomplicated, given that the Franklins, the rector, and the local gentry all shared the same Presbyterian creed. With the return of the king and his bishops, Mr. Palmer and his friends had to think again about their faith: but in a new, more troubled atmosphere.

FOR PEACE AND GOOD ORDER

In the autumn of 1662 Jane Franklin passed away. She had brought up her offspring with the Hebrew prophets and the psalms, in a cottage with Gospel verses painted on the walls. Her last seven years were full of affliction as she wasted away with tuberculosis. Despite her suffering, she never lost her attachment to the Book of Malachi, with its forecast of the coming of a Messiah. Although when she died Josiah was not yet five, her teachings remained a vivid memory that he shared with his son in Boston.

In 1739, when Benjamin Franklin was starting to inquire into his origins, Josiah sent him some family anecdotes, telling him that his parents had taken "great care . . . to breed us up in a religious way." These are simple words, but there was nothing straightforward about the plight of old Puritans in the 1660s. In every county with a strong Puritan element, the return of Charles II created a messy, ambiguous situation, in which men and women often had to make compromises that they found distasteful or dishonest. John Palmer and the Franklins found themselves in just this situation.[4]

In politics and faith, Palmer had never been a radical. Outraged by the execution of Charles I, he never cared for Oliver Cromwell, whose religious policies he disliked, because—as a Presbyterian— Palmer did not favor a free-for-all, where every congregation worshipped independently, which was Cromwell's way. But neither did Palmer want to see the bishops come back and make the old Anglican Church compulsory. The same thing was true of his landowning friends and kinsmen in their corner of Northamptonshire, the Catesbys and the Yelvertons. In the civil wars, they had stood up for Parliament; but even before Charles I met his end on the scaffold, they had been obliged to retreat into private life. Sir Henry Yelverton, a member of the House of Commons, lost his seat in 1648, bundled out of the chamber by Cromwell's men in the military coup known as Pride's Purge.[5]

And so when Charles II came back to claim his throne, in theory the people of Ecton had little to fear from the monarchy. Because the rector and his friends had never been followers of Cromwell, John Palmer could stay on as the parish minister; and perhaps that should have been enough for the Franklins. Sadly, there was a complication: Palmer would have to abandon his Presbyterian faith, and so would his parishioners. In time this would lead to an important outcome: the departure of Josiah for the colonies.[6]

There was a new Sir Henry Yelverton, son of the old politician, and he threw in his lot with the Royalists. In 1660, as the king prepared to return to England, young Sir Henry had gone hurrying about to rally the county to his side. With his own career to make, Yelverton was eager to be rid of the Cromwellians, whom he blamed for the long years of strife in which, as he put it, the people had been "torn in pieces by deceitful men." Keen to see an end to conflict, Sir Henry wanted everyone—including Mr. Palmer—to line up in support of King Charles, in the hope that the nation would at last be reunited.

The catch was simply this: all of them would have to accept the king's new Book of Common Prayer, hateful though it was to Puritans because of the traces of Catholicism that it still contained. It took a while for matters to come to a head, but at last—in 1662—the moment of decision arrived. On August 24, the feast of St. Bartholomew, every clergyman in England had to agree to use the new prayer book or face the loss of his position. Under pressure from Sir Henry, John Palmer signed his name, but many of the kingdom's Puritan clergy refused to do so. They numbered about two thousand.

On "Black Bartholomew's Day," as it came to be known, the Puritan ministers found themselves ejected from their parishes. While for the laity the consequences were less severe, even so it was a painful experience that spelled the end of an era of religious freedom. By now Jane Franklin was close to death—her funeral took place in October—but her husband lived on for twenty more years, obliged to be an Anglican against his conscience. The old blacksmith was sixty-four: a little late to change his ways. "And for Mr Franklin, I wish it were in my power to help him, but I fear he is but a partial conformist," Sir Henry told John Palmer.

In the end, Thomas Franklin swallowed his doubts and carried on going to Sunday service but only grudgingly. He did so "for peace and order's sake," Benjamin Senior recalled.[7]

The story was all too familiar, in an era when old Puritans deeply resented a state religion that rested on the force of law. Left with bitter feelings of exclusion, many of them gave themselves a new identity, calling themselves "dissenters" and forming their own unofficial assemblies. These "conventicles," as they were known, met on Sundays in fields or farmyards, and in doing so they committed a crime. New laws came into force, known as the Clarendon Code, which made conventicles illegal and barred the dissenters from holding public office.

In Northamptonshire, however, where there had always been so many Puritans, the conventicles continued to flourish. Undeterred by the threat of prosecution, they drew their inspiration from some of the ejected ministers who refused to be silenced. As archdeacon, John Palmer had no choice but to enforce the Clarendon Code, with Thomas Franklin Jr. sitting by his side to take down the names of nonconformists. Often in poor health, Palmer would have preferred to be answering the letters he received from the Royal Society seeking his views about mathematics, astronomy, and the state of agriculture in his county. Instead he had to soldier on, trying not to be too severe. All the while he was shoved about by his superior in the church, the pompous old bishop of Peterborough, who issued John Palmer with a series of reprimands, urging him to be more rigorous.[8]

Like the enclosure affair at Houghton Magna, this period of oppression lingered on in the Franklin memory long after the family had come to live in Boston. In his autobiography, Franklin tells us that his father and his uncle Benjamin had been among the nonconformists who joined the conventicles. The two boys were dissidents, members of a movement that linked the Ecton area with disobedient preachers in the capital. In his jurisdiction in 1669—when Josiah was twelve—Archdeacon Palmer counted more than thirty conventicles, with at least two thousand participants. Among them there were "far more women than men, many children and servants," Mr. Palmer wrote. Most likely, Josiah attended the biggest of the assemblies, which met six miles from Ecton at a barn near the town of Wellingborough. The London connection came about because the dissenting clergy often went to live in the city—where it was easier to hide—and then made forays back to the countryside. The conventicles at which they preached included the one at Wellingborough.[9]

And so by the time he became an apprentice, Josiah was already a rebel, if a peaceful one. On the waterfront in London, where the Franklins learned their trade with silk, he and his brother continued down the path of nonconformity. Because the rents were low, these were also the districts where the dissenting preachers chose to settle. By the river Thames the Franklin boys entered a religious underground: a twilight world of gatherings held against the law, where a young man could become a radical in politics as well as faith.

Exclusion and Despair

At his death in 1727, Franklin's uncle Benjamin left behind a minor masterpiece. Preserved today as a manuscript in Worcester, Massachusetts, and all too rarely examined by historians, it consists of a cycle of poems charting his spiritual life from youth until old age. Benjamin Senior read an enormous amount and it shows: many of his poems are pastiche, as he imitates the famous writers of his age. Even so there was nothing naive about his writing.

The longest poem in the cycle, "The Reflection," an autobiography in verse, runs to nearly five hundred lines, with careful little notes in the margin giving names and dates. While the meter is clumsy and the style roughly hewn, "The Reflection" takes us deeply into the mind of the Franklins. We see the author and his brothers as they were in the seventeenth century, engaging with the public issues of their time and creating their endowment of ideas.[10]

By the 1770s, when Franklin composed his own memoirs, the world had changed and his uncle's kind of piety had become a museum piece. Even so, his account of his life contains many echoes of Benjamin Senior's adventures in Restoration London. Both men had to live the life of an ambitious artisan, at the mercy of the market, beset by the lure of vice, and always at risk of failure. While the uncle prayed to a Presbyterian God and the nephew believed in Virtue, with a capital V, they both saw life as a journey for self-improvement in which it was all too easy to wander off the path.

For Benjamin Senior, life in the city begins with a catastrophe. At sixteen he swears his indentures at Dyers' Hall. Three months later the Great Fire sweeps through the capital. Like most Londoners, he blames the disaster on arson by the Catholics, but soon enough he finds another meaning in the destruction of the town. A book appears, *God's Terrible Voice in the City*, written by a Presbyterian minister, Thomas Vincent, who sees the calamity as a punishment for wickedness: alcohol, idleness, and the slighting of the Gospel.[11]

Terror grips Benjamin Senior's heart, as he reads the book and recalls his mother's warnings of damnation. His quest for salvation begins, but his poems hint at episodes of drink and fornication. Ill-treated by his boss, he is accused of theft. By now, his brother John Franklin is out of his apprenticeship, and he helps Benjamin clear his name, but only after weeks of anguish as they wait for the case to come to court.

The innocent youth moves to a new master dyer, qualifies, and finds a spiritual mentor, in the shape of another Presbyterian pastor, Nathaniel Vincent, Thomas Vincent's younger sibling. As the city lies in ruins after the Great Fire, the Vincent brothers bring the word of God to the people who have lost their homes. After that, Nathaniel goes to prison; but by 1672, when temporarily the authorities relax the Clarendon Code, he has his own chapel, down by the river, close to the workshops where the dyers color silk. Benjamin Senior joins his congregation. He remains a member for the next twenty-five years, taking shorthand notes, as Vincent builds a reputation for his sermons that extends as far as Massachusetts.*

All the while, as he tries to resist temptation, Benjamin Senior feels the force of what he sees as tyranny. The bishops and the king begin another purge of dissenters, seeking once again to put an end to the conventicles. As he studies his Bible, in search of a parallel, Benjamin Senior reads the Book of Esther, the ancient Jewish parable of faith in conflict with the state. There he finds a prophecy of what is taking place in England, where the godly and the pious lie in danger of betrayal by Charles II. In the young man's mind politics becomes an obsession, as he sees his quest for redemption mirrored in the traumas of his country.

Across the sea in Europe, the Protestant cause lay in grave danger, as the Dutch lost battle after battle to the armies of Louis XIV of France. At home, there was the prospect of a Papist king of England, who would surely bring about the triumph of the Vatican. Although King Charles remained officially a Protestant, he never produced a legitimate heir and so the crown was likely to pass to his brother, the Catholic James, Duke

* Nathaniel Vincent exerted a deep and lasting influence on the Franklin family. In Boston in 1722, when Benjamin Franklin was apprenticed to his brother John's printing firm, they reprinted three of Vincent's sermons from Benjamin Senior's notes, with a preface describing his character and his preaching style.

of York. At Westminster, Parliament stood prorogued; and in the eyes of the king's opponents, this seemed to prove that the monarch was bent like his father on ruling entirely by royal decree, with the aim of becoming a despot as absolute as King Louis at Versailles.

Or so it appeared to Franklin's uncle. In "The Reflection" and his other poems, Benjamin Senior gives us his version of the crisis that occurred in the England of the late 1670s: the crisis which, as it unfolded, gave the Franklins their political philosophy. As he narrates in poetry the history of his time, Benjamin Senior shows us the emergence of a party—the Whigs—who would become the heroes of the Franklin family. Their leader was a member of the aristocracy, Anthony Ashley Cooper, Earl of Shaftesbury, who had served his time in the corridors of power. Around him a Whig coalition began to form, embracing not only the dissenters, but also dukes and bankers, and gentry families from the countryside, people like the Catesbys of Ecton, who had felt deceived by the king's snub to Parliament. From his pulpit in Southwark, Nathaniel Vincent gave sermons full of Whiggery, and the Dyers' Company became another stronghold of Shaftesbury's supporters.[12]

Civil liberties, the right to jury trial, the Protestant succession, freedom of worship for dissenters, and taxation only with Parliament's consent: these would be the doctrines of the Whigs. They also came to be the Franklin creed. For the rest of his days Benjamin Senior remained an ardent Whig, keen to lend his pen to the patriotic cause. In the reign of Queen Anne, when the Whigs ruled the nation and their hero the Duke of Marlborough led his armies to defeat the French, old Benjamin would write an ode in honor of his victories. He and Josiah had been Whigs from the beginning, in the late 1670s when the party first began to develop their ideology.

At the heart of Whiggery there lay a simple notion: that freedom was in danger from an evil coterie of autocrats and fellow travelers of Rome. And so in 1677, Uncle Benjamin wrote another poem inspired by the Old Testament to which he gave the title "Israel's Oppression and Deliverance." Immensely long, and very obscure—he felt he had to wrap his meaning in a veil of allegory—the poem likens the Protestant dissenters to the Hebrew slaves in Egypt. They lie at the mercy of Pharaoh, the tyrant: by whom the author means King Charles. Hard reading though it is, the poem gives us the authentic voice of a Franklin, anxious that his faith and the kingdom are in peril. The following year, a story broke that seemed to prove that Benjamin Senior was correct.

In the summer of 1678, while walking in the park Charles II was accosted by an informant, bearing news of a conspiracy against the realm. Led by the French and the Jesuits, the conspirators intended to murder the king, and after that, they would place his Catholic brother on the throne: or so it was alleged. At that moment, there began one of the most shameful episodes of English history, the saga of the Popish Plot: a witch hunt of a kind, with many more victims than those who died at Salem.

The affair will be linked forever to the name of the chief informer, Titus Oates, a turncoat and a pedophile, whose evidence sent scores of martyrs to the gallows. But in the eyes of the Whigs, it seemed that the moment had come to assert themselves. If Oates was telling the truth, and the Jesuits, the French, and their Catholic friends in England were planning a rebellion, then the firmest of countermeasures were required.[13]

Taking the Popish Plot as their opportunity, in Parliament the Whigs began a campaign against James, Duke of York, with the aim of excluding him or his heirs from the throne. The consequence was this: the Exclusion Crisis, a long and complicated business, dragged out over three acrimonious years. At last in 1681 it came to an end, with a victory for Charles II and his brother, so that James the Catholic was assured of his succession to the crown.

During the Exclusion Crisis, the Whigs brought their political ideas to a new height of sophistication. Even so they were defeated, many of them went into exile, and this was how Josiah Franklin came to be in Boston as a refugee. It was something the young man could never have predicted when he completed his training as a dyer of silk.

The Banbury Connection

Two weeks after the revelation of the Popish Plot, with the streets of London filled with talk of wicked Catholics and a French invasion, Josiah returned to Dyers' Hall to sign the register of freemen. It was August 27, 1678. Although he was still four months short of twenty-one, he already had a wife and a baby daughter. The previous year, Josiah had married an Ecton girl, Anne Child, from another farming family, known to the Franklins for half a century. Free from his indentures he could go where he wished, and he chose the Oxfordshire town of Banbury, a day on horseback to the west of Ecton.[14]

Like a miniature version of the City of London, the borough of Banbury ruled itself, with a charter, a mayor, and a platoon of aldermen who steered their own course in matters of religion. With a tradition of Puritan sympathies, it was a borough where, protected by the aldermen, you could go to the official, Anglican church on Sunday morning and pray at the dissenting chapel in the afternoon. It made an ideal home for Josiah, where he and his brothers could perhaps aspire to join a local elite whose Whig opinions they shared.

The Franklins had known the town for many years. Josiah's mother, Jane, had come from Banbury, and in about 1667, when Thomas Franklin was nearly seventy, too old to work his forge, he had retired there to live. The old man had fallen out with his eldest son, leaving Thomas Junior with the smithy at Ecton. Later John Franklin had followed his father to Banbury, setting up in business as a dyer.

The town had a small textile trade, weaving cloth for lining suits and making colorful uniforms and stockings. There John began to prosper. A gentle spirit, kind and fraternal, he was a man "of very pleasant conversation," said Benjamin Senior, "and did, when he pleased, insinuate himself into the good opinion of persons of all qualities." Successful and popular, sought after by young women, he shared his good fortune with his siblings.[15]

John Franklin brought his sister Hannah over from Ecton to keep house; he invited Josiah up to Banbury to join him in the dye works; and then he stepped in once again to save their brother from a catastrophe. Working in London in wretched conditions, Benjamin Senior suffered one ailment after another: dropsy, scurvy, and some strange industrial complaint that left his arm half paralyzed. His emotional life was turbulent as well, as he sinned, repented, and sinned yet again.

Often he felt at the mercy of Satan; and in 1679, when the young man fell ill with a fever, he took it to be a punishment from God. As the fever reached its climax a spiritual doctor appeared, in the shape of a preaching friend of Nathaniel Vincent who joined in tearful prayers above the sickbed. At last the fever broke, and Benjamin felt his terror of damnation ebb away. Soon afterward John arrived from Banbury, and took him home to the town for ten months of convalescence. It was a typical Franklin thing to do—the brothers were very close—and in Banbury they grew still closer. John had found a wife, another Anne, who brought with her some money, and he and Josiah began to raise large families. In the years that followed, John and Josiah and their two Anne Franklins took eight children between them to be baptized at Banbury Church.[16]

A page from the Freedom Book of the Dyers' Company of London. The signature of Josiah Franklin, Benjamin Franklin's father, can be seen three quarters of the way down, recording his completion in the summer of 1678 of a seven-year apprenticeship as a silk dyer and his admission as a freeman of the company.

In his autobiography, Franklin said that he had been born and bred "in poverty and obscurity." In writing that, America's favorite son was telling the truth—yes, he grew up in a crowded tenement in Boston, the son of a workman—but behind his simple words there lies a story with far more nuance. The fact of the matter was this: in the England of the 1680s and 1690s the Franklins did extremely well, they were far from poor, and they found new friends among people who could never be described as obscure.

At some unknown date, but no later than 1682, John Franklin became a trusted ally of Banbury's leading Presbyterians. Merely by making their acquaintance, the Franklins climbed another rung of the social scale. Better still, they found a well-born partner for Benjamin Senior. The woman he married, Hannah Welles, took the Franklins into an alliance with an extended family of gentlefolk: an alliance that would help to lift the Franklins into the town's inner circle of godly politicians.[17]

At Banbury the dissenters found their spiritual leader in a clergyman, Samuel Welles, Hannah's father, whose connections were exceptionally good. A moderate Puritan of Palmer's kind, Welles had married into the landed gentry, taking as his wife one Dorothy Doyley. Her brother Edward Doyley, a colonel in Cromwell's army, had taken part in the conquest of Jamaica in 1654, fighting the Spanish so bravely that he became the island's first English governor. Eight years later, Samuel Welles lost his post as vicar of Banbury on Black Bartholomew's Day, but when the Franklins settled in the town he was still preaching in private under the patronage of the aldermen.[18]

Mr. Welles was, said Benjamin Senior, a man "of cheerful disposition, and of a large and liberal heart." He and Dorothy produced ten children, Hannah being the youngest, and when the old man died she was still single. As the niece of a colonial governor, she would make a splendid catch for a tradesman with ambition. So John Franklin became a marriage broker, in the hope of easing his brother's emotional turmoil. In 1682, the widowed Mrs. Welles and her daughter moved to London, where Benjamin Senior had found a job in one of the largest dye works in the capital. The following year he married Hannah Welles.

It was a love match but also a coup for the Franklins. By marrying so well, Benjamin Senior entered the upper echelon of London's dissenting community. Dorothy Welles lived with the young couple in the city, where her Doyley cousins counted among their friends the foremost preachers of the period. Benjamin and Hannah did not have much money, and his career had many ups and downs. But the milieu they inhabited—dissenting and Whig, but also commercial—was the kind of environment in which the Franklins would always feel most comfortable, on both sides of the Atlantic. In Banbury meanwhile, John Franklin continued to prosper, with the prospect of rising to become a member of the borough's ruling class: but only if the Whigs were not destroyed.[19]

Chapter Three

Coming to America

In the spring of 1682, at last old Thomas Franklin passed away, surviving his friend John Palmer by three years. Born late in the reign of Elizabeth, in a decade of plague and hardship, Thomas had lived to be eighty-three and to see an age in which his children were thriving. And yet, at the hour of the old man's death, the Protestant cause in which he believed seemed to lie in danger of obliteration.

The previous year, the Dyers' Company of London had chosen as their leader a linen draper called Samuel Shute, a dissenter and a rampant Whig. In the summer of 1681, Shute and a fellow Whig won election as the sheriffs of London and Middlesex. In doing so, they provoked Charles II to mount a direct attack on the city, its preachers, and its guilds, including the dyers, that formed so hard a nucleus of Whiggery.[1]

The king's officials had arrested Lord Shaftesbury for treason. In November, a grand jury chosen by Shute and his fellow sheriff slung out the charge and the earl walked free; but this gesture of Whig defiance served only to antagonize the king. His Privy Council told the magistrates to enforce the law against conventicles. On the waterfront they raided the meeting house where Benjamin Senior sat at the feet of his favorite preacher, Nathaniel Vincent. As Mr. Vincent went to prison, the king's attorneys began a legal assault on the metropolis. Just before Christmas, the lord mayor and the sheriffs were served with a writ of *quo warranto.* In plain English, this meant that Charles II intended to revoke the city charter, and to end the independence of London from the Crown.

While Vincent survived to fight another day—he too was rescued by a friendly grand jury—the Whigs as a party were driven into abject retreat.

Not only in London but up and down the country, including the counties of Oxford and Northampton, in 1682 the authorities struck at the roots of Whiggery, seeking to penalize men and women who were seen as agents of sedition, with among them the squire of Ecton, Thomas Catesby. North of the border the authorities created an army, the Highland Host, with firing squads to shoot those Scottish Presbyterians who would not come to heel.

In the middle England of the Franklins, the bishops drew up new lists of dissenters, with the aim of making the following Easter another Black Bartholomew's Day, this time with laypeople as the target. Meanwhile in London the writ of *quo warranto* proceeded through the courts, bringing ever nearer the subjection of the city to the king. Again Nathaniel Vincent was thrown into jail.[2]

It was during this dangerous period that Josiah Franklin made his plans to leave for America. Ninety years later, when his famous son described Josiah's departure, he did so in a passage in his autobiography so brief and so laconic that it has rarely been awarded the attention it merits. What Franklin wrote was this: "Josiah, my father, married young, and carried his wife with three children unto New England... The conventicles having been forbidden by law, and frequently disturbed, induced some considerable men of his acquaintance to remove to that country, and he was prevailed with to accompany them thither, where they expected to enjoy their mode of religion with freedom."

Since the 1930s, biographers of Franklin have tended to ignore this plain statement of the case. Instead they have mostly preferred another narrative, portraying Josiah as an economic migrant, driven out of England merely by a lack of business opportunity. This version of the story has only one item of evidence to support it: a cursory remark by Benjamin Senior, to the effect that Josiah left Banbury "things not succeeding there according to his mind." This might be taken to mean that Josiah Franklin left the town for one reason only: because in Oxfordshire he could not make a career on his own as a dyer of silk. However, the language is simply too vague and ambiguous—"things not succeeding there"—to carry so heavy a weight of interpretation. It need not be construed as a reference to problems in Josiah's business life.*

* If Josiah had simply wished to set up on his own as a dyer of silk in a better market than Banbury, he would have had far less hazardous options than a voyage to America. More likely, he would have returned to London or he would have moved to Coventry or

The bulk of the evidence points very clearly in another direction. It falls squarely into line with Franklin's account of his father: an exile for the sake of faith and politics, not a poor man in search of better pay and prospects. The conventicles had been "forbidden and disturbed," no question: that is a matter of historical fact. And by the end of 1682, it was indeed the case that "considerable men" were looking for places of safety in America. Among them was Lord Shaftesbury. In 1669, when the settlers of Barbados wished to create an outpost on the mainland, the Whig earl had helped them finance their new colony in South Carolina. Together with his friend the philosopher John Locke, he drafted the colony's first constitution. Thirteen years later, while temporarily locked up in the Tower, Shaftesbury briefly thought of going into exile in Charleston, only to opt for the Netherlands instead.

As a dyer in Banbury, of course Josiah Franklin had no direct connection with a Whig as exalted as the earl, but the Franklins knew a local family that did: a family that shared the earl's belief that America might offer a political safe haven. Banbury had recently chosen as its mayor a merchant in textiles, an old Puritan alderman named James West, whose son was as close as could be to Lord Shaftesbury. The young Robert West was a lawyer and a Whig, deeply engaged in London's underground.

In the summer of 1682, Shaftesbury had hired Robert West to defend a fellow Whig accused of treason; and the earl's confidant, John Locke, gave West a room in his house in Oxford. Meanwhile Robert had his own designs upon America, where an opportunity arose to create a refuge for rebellious Whigs. That same year, the colony of eastern New Jersey came up for sale, and it was bought by a consortium of twelve investors who hoped to build a town on the Raritan River. While eleven of the purchasers were Quakers, the twelfth was Robert West, the Banbury Whig.[3]

Since Josiah did not write a memoir, we may never know precisely how he decided to leave England. However, the Franklins certainly knew the West family—they too were Presbyterians, close friends of Mr. Welles the preacher—and so the Wests must have been the "considerable men" who encouraged Josiah to sail to the colonies. Nobody else at Banbury is known to have taken an interest in America. Josiah's motivation is equally plain. As 1682 drew to a close, many Whigs and dissenters felt driven to

---

Norwich, the leading provincial centers for the English silk trade, where dyers were very welcome.

desperate measures. For some, it seemed that they were left with little choice but armed insurrection; or failing that the path of exodus.

Up Out of Egypt

For Josiah, the point of no return arrived in the middle of 1683. Step by step, the king and his ministers had carried through a purge of their opponents. In London, there were more arrests, of booksellers, preachers, and members of Parliament. Nathaniel Vincent was jailed for three months and told that next time, he would be hanged or expelled from the kingdom. And then, in the summer, Charles II seized his chance to destroy the topmost tier of the Whig opposition.[4]

Shaftesbury had fled to Holland, where he died; but before he passed away, the earl had left behind a plot for a coup d'état. An audacious plan, it called for the assassination of the king and his brother at Rye House in Hertfordshire, as they returned from the races at Newmarket. The plot never came to fruition, but it was treason nonetheless, and it gave the king his moment of opportunity.

Addicted to meeting in taverns, where wine was the fuel of sedition, the Whigs could never keep a secret. One of the plotters, a Baptist, suffered a fit of conscience or of terror and went to the Privy Council with the story. This was in the middle of June. His evidence led straight to Robert West of Banbury. Clapped in irons and threatened with torture, Mr. West began a hunger strike. For three days, he stuck it out; and then, to save his neck from the gallows, he revealed the names of the Rye House conspirators.

There followed the usual orgy of violence by the state. The men who led the Rye House Plot went to an appalling death. The first to go was the Earl of Essex, who slit his throat in the Tower; though some said it was murder, committed by the warders. Next it was the turn of Lord William Russell, beheaded by a clumsy fellow who required three blows of the axe. After that, the authorities executed Russell's comrade, Algernon Sidney. In the century that followed, Americans would come to regard Mr. Sidney as a prophet of liberty, revered by Thomas Jefferson as one of his forerunners.[5]

It was a brutal time, when it seemed that dissenters and Whigs were to be stamped out forever. And at just this moment, so full of disaster, Josiah Franklin and his family traveled down to London from their home in Oxfordshire. This was something his brother, Benjamin Senior, would

This Tory broadsheet from 1683 tells the story of the Rye House Plot against King Charles II, with the Whig Lord Shaftesbury conferring with his accomplices. The images show the fate of the conspirators, including the beheading of the Whig martyr Lord William Russell.

never forget: that Josiah had passed through the city "at the time when the noble Lord Russell was murdered."

It would be foolish to suggest that the Franklins had anything directly to do with the Rye House Plot. The point is simply this: that Josiah felt that he had no future in a kingdom where the causes in which he believed were approaching their apocalypse. The Whigs were defeated, so were the dissenters, and that was why he had to leave for the colonies. In the closing days of May, to add to their first two children, Elizabeth and Samuel, his wife had given birth to a girl—another Hannah—but this did not deter the couple from their expedition.

The weather was foul that summer, with weeks of heavy rain; but down the Franklins came to the capital, arriving in July, the season when cargoes were loaded onto ships bound for America. Those sailing for Virginia that year were filled with frontier supplies—lead shot, saddles, and gunpowder—but the vessels going to New England contained items more relevant to Josiah. The Franklins must have sailed on one of two ships, the *Richard* or the *Endeavour,* which made for Boston in August. In their holds, there were goods of the sort a civilized town required: not only spices, pewter, playing cards, and clocks, but also many rolls of silk, some of it raw and undyed.[6]

At the age of twenty-six, Josiah was about to begin his new life in the New World. Although his reasons for leaving England were political and religious, he still had to select a destination. And so he chose to go to Boston, where—if the residents had a taste for silk—he might stand a chance of making a living as a dyer. However, in London and Boston alike it was politics, not commerce, that supplied the year's main talking point. One of the ships that sailed from England that summer took with her a legal document whose arrival caused an uproar in Massachusetts.

Not content with attacking the freedoms of London, King Charles and his advisers also intended to revoke the charters of companies such as the dyers, and those of Whig boroughs such as Banbury. The American plantations came next upon their list. Each colony had its charter or its patent from the Crown, giving it a constitution and a degree of self-government. A case could be made that by harboring smugglers, pirates, Whigs, and traitors, the colonies abused the liberties they enjoyed. And so, beginning with Bermuda, the Privy Council issued writs of *quo warranto* against the colonial charters.

Among the most offensive, from the Crown's point of view, was the old charter of Massachusetts, a place where Whigs existed in profusion. Dating from 1629, it gave the Bay Colony an array of privileges including the right to choose its governor. In June, as the Rye House Plot obsessed the capital, the judges at Westminster signed the writ against the Massachusetts charter, with a view to imposing far tighter control by the king. Soon the writ was on its way to America, carried by HMS *Golden* of the Royal Navy.[7]

We will never know what the Franklins took with them to America by way of worldly goods; but he and Anne possessed an intangible asset that ought to have spoken more loudly than money. The couple resembled the first generation of Puritan exiles who had left the old country during a similar crisis in the 1630s, and come to Boston looking for a city on a hill. In Massachusetts, the Puritan clergy kept in touch with their brethren in London; they knew about the Rye House Plot; and they were expecting a horde of new arrivals from England. They also knew that the writ of *quo warranto* was crossing the Atlantic.

In October, Anne and Josiah came ashore in Boston and HMS *Golden* sailed in as well, carrying the writ. Here again Josiah and the people of New England had something in common: on both sides of the ocean, liberties were being swept away. In Banbury that autumn, James West and the aldermen had to agree to surrender their borough charter, and soon after that he and his Whig allies lost their seats on the town's ruling council. In London the dyers suffered a similar fate, forced to give up their old charter and to accept the supervision of the Crown. With their situations apparently so similar, the Franklins could surely expect a friendly welcome from Americans whose freedoms were in danger.[8]

Or so it might have seemed; but until the very recent past, Boston has rarely been an easy place in which to be accepted as an immigrant. Dissenters and Whigs though they were, the Franklins were latecomers to a province already fifty years old and set in its ways. By now Massachusetts had acquired its own hierarchies, almost as conceited as those of the mother country. Far from being greeted as a hero in New England, Josiah found himself rejected: like so many immigrants in centuries to come, he and Anne were sent to the bottom of the heap.

The Winning Side

To begin with, the godly folk of Boston would not permit the Franklins to join a place of worship. Only in 1685, two years after his arrival, did Josiah's name appear on the books of the town's Third Church, the Old South Meeting House. Even then he and Anne were merely junior members, forbidden to take Communion. By Boston standards, their pastor Samuel Willard was a fair-minded fellow who opposed the pogrom at Salem. Even so, Mr. Willard clung to the old "New England Way," obliging every worshipper to pass an exacting test of holiness before becoming a full member of a church. It took nine more years for Josiah Franklin to qualify. Although he had left England for the sake of his principles, it was only in 1694 that the Old South allowed Josiah to share the bread and wine.[9]

We know all too little about Josiah's first decade in America, but one thing we can say for certain: on arrival he underwent a humbling downgrade in his status. As a dyer of silk who had finished his apprenticeship, Josiah had ranked as a citizen of London, free to vote and to practice any craft he wished within its walls. In Massachusetts this meant very little; because, as he discovered, despite their imports of raw silk, the citizens of Boston had only the most basic of textile industries. While he and Anne strove to be accepted as Christians, Josiah also had to find a new career. He became a maker of candles, a business as unpleasant as the dyeing of silk but without the high wages he might have earned in the empire's capital.

As a tallow chandler, Josiah would have to boil down potash, lime, skin, bones, and animal fat to produce many gallons of jelly, through which to pass the twisted skeins of cotton that formed the wick. In the long Boston winters everyone needed candles, and so Josiah always had customers. They wanted candles made from consistent tallow and a reliable wick, to ensure that the flame would be steady. Quality, in a word; something the ingenious Josiah could supply, taking a measure of pride in his new line of work.

Even so it was not the same thing as coloring silk in many shades, to be sold to the drapers of Banbury or London. In time Josiah added soap to his product range, and the Franklins perfected a recipe that saw them through the first half of the eighteenth century; but soap and candles could not satisfy the instincts of a craftsman so skillful. Nor would they take the Franklins swiftly up the social ladder. As they built their future in America, they had to endure what amounted to another long apprenticeship.

Their progress was methodical but slow, and it had its episodes of grief. At about the same time as he and Anne joined the Old South, Josiah signed a lease on a small clapboard house in Milk Street, opposite the church. That summer, Anne gave birth to a fourth child, Josiah Junior, who would grow up to be a seafarer. Soon another daughter arrived, a little Anne. She was born in 1687, the date when Josiah passed another milestone: for the first time he featured on the list of Boston's taxpayers, having made enough money to do so.

In 1689 he went a step further and opened a shop on Cornhill, Boston's leading thoroughfare, just around the corner from his home. That same year, the first Mrs. Franklin died in the heat of the summer. Anne's age at death is unknown, but she passed away in July soon after the birth of her son Joseph. A few days later, the little boy died as well. With five young children to care for, her husband needed to marry again, and soon he found a second wife: Abiah, the mother of Benjamin Franklin, whose origins were almost a mirror image of Josiah's.

Before the wedding she was Abiah Folger, born into a Puritan clan whose roots lay in the English textile city of Norwich, full of weavers and dyers of the kind among whom Josiah spent his youth. In 1635 or so her grandfather joined the Puritan exodus to America, coming over with his son Peter, Abiah's father, settling first in the Boston area, then on

Martha's Vineyard, and finally on Nantucket. There, like Thomas Franklin Jr. far away at Ecton, Peter Folger earned his keep as a surveyor and also taught school. Like Josiah with his conventicles, he was an independent who did not care to be told what to believe. In the 1670s he fell afoul of the law, refusing to pay a fine for contempt of court. And so he spent more than a year in a shed built for hogs that served as the Nantucket jail. Like Benjamin Senior in London, Peter Folger was a poet. In his sty he composed a polemic in verse against religious coercion, defending the rights of Baptists and Quakers to worship as they thought they should.[10]

By 1688 his daughter was in Boston at the age of twenty-one. There Abiah Folger joined Mr. Willard's church; in November 1689 she married the widowed Josiah; and she bore him ten more children. They came every two years or so until 1708, while Josiah slowly grew his business. Eighteen months after the marriage, he put up a small shed, eight feet square, behind the Milk Street property: presumably to house his vats and coppers and his store of tallow. That was in the spring of 1691. The seasons flowed by, his candles sold well, until at last—seven years later—there came a moment of public recognition.

In Boston, the reins of civic power lay in the hands of the town meeting. In 1698, they picked Josiah to serve a yearly term as a tithing man. His duties involved inspecting inns and taverns and keeping good order, like his grandfather Henry so long ago at Ecton. At about the same time, Josiah hoisted a sign—the Blue Ball—above his premises: another symbol that at last he was a man to be reckoned with.

It had taken fifteen years since his voyage from the Thames; and during his hours of toil with wax and soap, Josiah must often have wondered how much easier his life might have been if he had lingered on in Banbury. His situation had its share of irony: because, as things turned out, the Franklins need never have left the mother country for the sake of conscience. If Josiah had remained at home like his brothers, in time he would have found that they were on the winning side.

Although the 1680s were a decade of turmoil, they had ended with the triumph of the Whigs. At home Charles II died in 1685 and his brother James II took his place, only to lose his crown to yet another of England's coups d'état. Over from Europe there came a Dutch prince and a Protestant, William of Orange, married to James's daughter Mary. He landed his army on the English coast; by the spring of 1689, he was calling himself King William III; and in Parliament his Whig allies engineered what came to be known as the Glorious Revolution. King James had left for

Paris and then for Ireland, forming a Jacobite party and an army to wage war against England with the aid of their ally, Louis XIV.[II]

Far to the west, Massachusetts greeted the new government with glee. In the interim, since the dark days of 1683, the colonists had lost their old charter and endured a period of coercion from the king's officials. And so they rejoiced at William's arrival on the throne. Staging their own revolution, the people of Boston kicked out the men they saw as lackeys of King James, and began to reclaim their heritage of freedom. Whigs for the most part, they knew that the future would be challenging—there would be war with the French fur traders to the north—but it was a war for a Protestant cause to which they adhered.

In America and in the mother country the Whigs had been victorious, but it was the English members of the Franklin family who stood to benefit the most. In the Northampton area, the landlords were Whigs almost to a man, including the Catesbys to whom Thomas Junior was so close. With their patronage to help him, the 1690s were to be a decade in which he could attain new heights of prosperity. In London the dyers of silk clung equally firmly to the cause of King William; and when Parliament passed a Toleration Act, Benjamin Senior was free to hear as many sermons as he wished from his mentor, Nathaniel Vincent. His chapel now enjoyed the protection of the law.

In Banbury meanwhile, where the Whigs were firmly back in power, a career in politics seemed to lie in store for John Franklin. By now he had become a man of property, owning his house and some land and a cottage that he let to a tenant. After the Glorious Revolution the Wests and their friends regained control of the borough and packed the corporation with their fellow Whigs. In September 1690, they chose the genial John Franklin as one of Banbury's constables: the first step on the path that might take a man to the rank of mayor.

And then disaster struck. While mounting his horse, John suffered a painful injury in his groin. He lanced the swelling with a dirty needle. A few days later, in June of 1691, John Franklin passed away—"much lamented of rich and poor," said his brother Benjamin—leaving a son, five daughters, and a widow. Thomas Franklin Junior came over from Ecton to wind up his brother's affairs, and the children were scattered far and wide. While the boy went on to become a dyer in a market town, the girls were sent out to make lace or to be ladies' maids: and that was the sorrowful end of the Franklins of Banbury. Eighty or so years later, when Benjamin Franklin was living in London, he did his best to help his poor

English cousins and their offspring, but some of them had disappeared entirely.[12]

Ingenious though the Franklins were, their prospects in England were all too fragile without a much larger endowment of land to guarantee their status, and a much bigger fleet of children to ensure that their name survived. In London, where the death rate was far worse than in Oxfordshire, Benjamin Senior and his wife, Hannah, produced ten babies in the space of twenty years. Only two survived past infancy. Victims of the cruel demographics of their age, the Franklins were doomed to disappear in the mother country. Their fate was all the more poignant because it followed one last period of success.

In the years after 1689, Thomas Junior enjoyed a degree of esteem from his neighbors that none of his forebears had commanded. At Ecton the bell foundry must have been making a rich return, because in 1698—the year the Blue Ball went up in Boston—his partner Henry Bagley built not a shed but a splendid stone house that still stands in the village. Meanwhile Thomas had also found a new patron, an aristocrat whose influence extended far beyond the confines of Northamptonshire. As Franklin put it in his autobiography, Thomas Junior "was much taken notice of and patronised by the then Lord Halifax." All too easily overlooked, this is another remarkable detail; because the peer in question was one of the most powerful politicians of the age.

In the 1690s, Halifax was not yet a nobleman in his own right—he was still merely Charles Montagu—but he had married a Yelverton lady, the widow of an earl. The couple took up residence a few miles from Ecton in the village of Horton, from which Charles would travel back and forth to Westminster. A trusted servant of King William, Montagu belonged to a Whig cabal, the Junto, that led the nation for six years, but his lasting achievements lay in finance. Not only did he help to found the Bank of England. Montagu, or Lord Halifax as he became, also enjoyed the doubtful distinction of inventing the National Debt, by issuing bonds to pay for the king's long war with France.

To pay the interest on the loans, the Whigs required new taxes and reliable men to collect them. Here was a task for which Thomas Franklin, land agent and surveyor, had all the necessary skills. When Parliament created a new levy on landed property, His Majesty's Treasury chose Thomas Franklin as the inspector for Northamptonshire, a role that meant that he could be called a gentleman. The first and the only member of his family who could claim that title in England, he worked hard to justify his status.

Riding to and fro, measuring the land, Thomas raised far more money than the Treasury expected, and they paid him a bonus for his pains. At election time he said thank you by voting for the Whigs. Meanwhile his patron Halifax grew ever more powerful. As the war against Louis XIV dragged on and the land tax became a permanent levy, Thomas Franklin did his bit to help, serving as clerk to the county's tax commissioners.[13]

It was just the kind of quality—a flair for administration—that his nephew would display in America in the years to come, when Franklin ran the postal service for the colonies. The two men also had something else in common: a talent for attracting powerful friends, whom they could impress with their technical expertise, their honesty, and their willingness to undertake long hours of work. But in the England of 1700 or so, these qualities were far from sufficient to guarantee a permanent place among the gentry.

As the fate of the Banbury Franklins had shown, you needed more than ingenuity; you also needed genteel lineage and real estate, and Thomas had nothing of the former and all too little of the latter. Nor did he produce enough children. He fell out with his family friends, the Palmers, in a legal quarrel about the tithes of Ecton; and then, having lost that battle, Thomas Franklin expired in January 1703. He died without a son and so his dynasty died with him.[14]

Eight years later, his widow Eleanor joined him in the churchyard, where Franklin found their headstones beneath the tower where John Palmer had gazed at Orion. Eleanor and Thomas had a daughter, Mary, who married, sold the family acres, and moved away. Living to be eighty-five, she met her famous cousin when he visited Northamptonshire, but by then the graves and the chimes in the belfry were all that was left of her father's ingenuity. If Eleanor had borne a son, the Franklins might have gone on rising to become a leading voice in the county. As it was the family baton had to pass across the Atlantic, to Boston where Josiah was inching forward year by year.

He always kept in touch with his English relatives. So Josiah knew what his brothers had achieved. He also knew what he might have accomplished if he had stayed at home, to take the place of John and Thomas when they died. Did Josiah feel resentful or embittered? His American career must have been frustrating, and—as we shall see—in Boston the Franklins had their squabbles. So many children, in a small house, so many candles to make and so much soap to boil: it would be enough to give anyone a fit of temper.

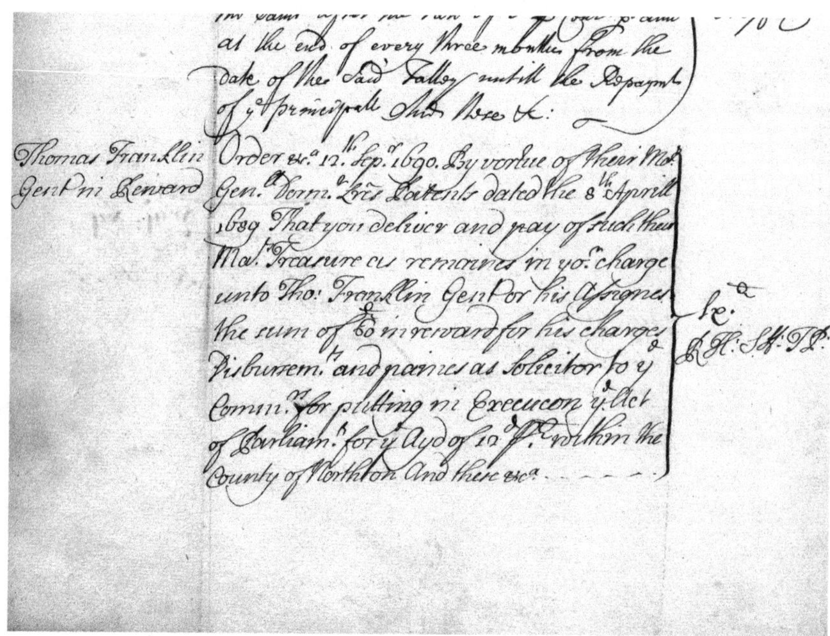

at the end of every three months from the
date of the said Talley untill the Repaymt
of ye principall And Inte &c:

Thomas Franklin
Gent in Reward

Order &c.a 12th Sep.r 1690. By vertue of their Mats
Gen.ll Dorm.t Lres Patents dated the 8th Aprill
1689 That you deliver and pay of such their
Mats Treasure as remaines in yor charge
unto Tho: Franklin Gent or his Assignes
the sum of 60li in reward for his charges &
Disburem.ts and paines as Solicitor to ye
Comm.rs for putting in Execucon ye Act
of Parliam.t for ye Ayd of 12d within the
County of Northton And these &ca.

From the records of His Majesty's Treasury, a minute from September 1690 referring to Thomas Franklin Jr. as a "gentleman." Initialed by the Lords of the Treasury, who reported directly to King William III, the entry grants Thomas Junior £60 for his success in collecting the land tax in Northamptonshire.

When he wrote the epitaph for his parents, Franklin described Josiah as "pious and prudent," a devoted husband to Abiah, the two of them living lives of "constant labour and industry." These are little more than clichés, too conventional to be relied upon. Fortunately, we have just enough evidence, by way of anecdotes, and details in the Boston archives, to give us a picture of Josiah. Neither bitter nor disappointed, he was a stoical character, resilient and philosophical.

Like his son he had a fine physique. A cheerful, healthy fellow of medium height, Josiah would pick up his net and go fishing for herrings on his few days away from the workshop. He had what Franklin remembered as "a clear, pleasing voice," and he kept up the Puritan custom of singing psalms in the evening. Like the poet John Milton's father, who did the same in London, Josiah would accompany the psalms with tunes on his violin.

And of course he was ingenious. Josiah had built up a store of resources—skills with his hands, ideas from books, and his habit of curiosity—that he could draw upon to give his life a meaning. For example: his passion for geography. Somehow Josiah obtained four large maps that hung in the parlor, where his children memorized the names of seas and rivers. They had a family library as well. And although most of the books were dry and theological, they included one title—*An Essay Upon Projects,* by Daniel Defoe—that kept alive Josiah's contact with the inventive England of his youth.

It was an odd thing to find in a Boston tenement. A very rare book, published in 1697—long before Defoe became famous as a novelist—the *Essay* never sold well. A technical book for businesspeople, it emerged from the same climate of ideas that produced Charles Montagu's financial innovations. Hence it contained clever schemes for banks, insurance companies, a pension fund for widows, and a college for the children of the commercial classes. Sophisticated though its contents were, the essay was one of the first books Benjamin Franklin read as a child.

For the rest of his life, until he wrote his memoirs in the 1770s and 1780s, the language of Defoe would remain a constant feature of Franklin's journalism and his projects for the betterment of life in America. An author in love with opportunity, Defoe spoke directly to people like the Franklins, whose origins and milieu in London were very similar to his. According to Defoe, lasting achievement had to rest on what he called "the honest basis of ingenuity and improvement." Those words from Defoe's essay on projects would become an intrinsic part of Benjamin Franklin's vocabulary of ambition.[15]

As a first-generation arrival, in Boston Josiah had to be content to do only modestly well. This could never be said about his youngest son. Early in 1706, when Josiah was approaching forty-nine and his wife was thirty-eight—a couple past their prime, by the standards of the age—Abiah gave birth to a boy who would never be satisfied with second best.

Part Two

A Boston Boy

Chapter Four

His Happy Childhood

On the day before the Sabbath the mail came in from the frontier, where the settlers went in fear of murder or abduction by their enemies, the Abenaki and the French. In 1706, Queen Anne's War with France was at its height. In Europe, things were going splendidly for England, as the Duke of Marlborough swept the army of King Louis from Flanders; but in the town of Boston, the elite were squabbling about how best to take part in the fighting. At noon the snow began to flurry in the streets, and that night it fell heavily. The following morning—Sunday, January 6, according to the old calendar of the first half of the eighteenth century—Abiah Franklin was delivered of a boy. Pastor Willard baptized him on the same day. Such was the custom, for fear that an infant might go to an early grave.*

Benjamin Franklin was born in a season of animosity in Boston, a place where the people wished to obey their English queen but could not abide the officials she chose to rule over them. Although Josiah kept aloof from party politics—that winter, he was trying a new way to make candles, with rushes from Nantucket—it was never easy to ignore the feuds that beset this angry town. The wilderness lay close at hand, drink and violence were just around the corner, and loyalty to England sat side by side with deep resentment of authority. In January 1706 the town's loathing had for its object Governor Joseph Dudley. In the past he

* Throughout this book, for the sake of consistency dates are always given according to the old Julian calendar, as it was used in Great Britain and America prior to 1752. According to the calendar we employ today, Franklin's date of birth was January 17.

had antagonized his fellow colonists by supporting King James, and he remained a man who knew how to be unpopular.[1]

Shortly before Christmas, Dudley had engaged in an affray that captures the heated atmosphere of the Boston where Franklin came into the world. On the road into town, the governor had met two wagon drivers who blocked his path with a cart full of wood. Dudley stepped down from his carriage, struck one of the men with his sword, drew blood, and threw both of them into jail. When Franklin was six days old, the governor's council held a session filled with anger and recrimination, as Dudley accused Pastor Willard of taking the side of the carriers.

There followed a typical New England quarrel about the rule of law, the powers of the governor, and the independence of the judiciary. Ten months later, to Dudley's dismay, the judges acquitted the defendants, and one of Willard's friends added his powerful voice to the chorus of disapproval of the governor. At the Second Church in Boston, the pulpit belonged to the Puritan eminence of New England, Increase Mather, who shared it with his son Cotton. They had many reasons to loathe Joseph Dudley. Not only was the governor a friend to Anglicans; the Mathers also disagreed with his risky strategy of all-out attacks against the French in Canada. And so that fall Cotton Mather composed a pamphlet bewailing what he called "the deplorable state of New England." Under Dudley, he wrote, the colony had become "the very scene of . . . all that's miserable."[2]

Perhaps the pastor's rhetoric was overdone; but by nature Bostonians were voluble, and their language was often extreme. By this time the town's seven thousand inhabitants could walk on streets paved with cobblestones, buy a weekly paper, *The Boston News-Letter,* and take their pick of eighty taverns in which to read it with their rum. They could worship in any one of six churches. Fine new houses were going up, built not with wood but with brick. Each year the shipwrights launched dozens of ships. If the colonies had a metropolis, this was it; but although the local economy was growing, misery was all too visible as well. Prices were rising because of the war. Taxes were increasing too, and when Benjamin Franklin was four years old a shortage of bread caused riots in the streets.

In the background there lay tensions that would persist in Boston for as long as it remained a colonial town. On one side there stood the popular party, always looking back to the old Bay Colony charter of 1629, which had given Massachusetts something close to independence. Ranged against them was a mercantile elite, allied with Governor Dudley, who preferred the new charter granted by King William. Although it made the governor a royal appointee, it left some elements of democracy—town meetings, elected juries, and the colony's House of Representatives—and these became the battleground for party strife. In the middle were the clergy—Harvard men like the Mathers, who wanted law and order, but not at the price of diluting their Puritan creed—and also people like Josiah Franklin.

All Josiah looked for was peace and quiet, in which to make his living and to keep his conscience clear. Again he took after his late brother John in Banbury. Benjamin Franklin remembered how his father strove to be an honest broker, hoping to pacify his neighbors when they came to him for help in settling their disputes. As Franklin put it in his memoirs, Josiah "was also much consulted by private persons about their affairs, when any difficulty occurred, and frequently chosen an arbitrator between contending parties." It may have helped that Josiah did not drink hard liquor.

Three times Josiah served as a tithing man; in 1700, he was a clerk of the market, making sure that traders gave good measure and took away their trash; and two years later he was chosen as a constable. He became a supplier to the town, selling candles to the almshouse and to the artillerymen who guarded the harbor. At last there came a moment when Josiah could feel that he commanded the kind of respect his father and his brothers had enjoyed in England. It occurred in 1708, on the 9th of September, twenty-five years after he landed in America. That evening, the tenement in Milk Street hosted a prayer meeting attended by a few of the town's most powerful men.

They listened to a biblical text read by no less a dignitary than Samuel Sewall, landowner, merchant, and luminary of the Old South. A close friend of Mr. Willard and the Mathers, Sewall had been among the justices who hanged the Salem witches. In 1697, stricken with remorse, he made an apology in church. Nine years later, he was one of the judges who freed the wagon drivers accused of assaulting the governor. Here was a pious man, endlessly self-critical, whose approval spoke volumes about the esteem that the Franklin family had won at last in Boston. When he recorded the prayer meeting in his diary, Sewall awarded his friend the same polite honorific that Thomas the blacksmith had been given at Ecton: the judge called his host "*Mister* Josiah Franklin."

Josiah had passed another milestone, and he did so at a time when Massachusetts had many reasons to be optimistic. In the year of Frank-

Josiah Franklin's friend and fellow member of the Old South Meeting House, the Boston merchant, politician, and philanthropist Judge Samuel Sewall (1652–1730), painted by Nathaniel Emmons, 1728.

lin's birth, Parliament in London had made the laws to ensure that when the queen expired, her successor would be a Protestant, the Elector George of Hanover; and to keep the Scots within the British fold, they also passed the Act of Union, making England and Scotland a united kingdom. In celebration, the people of Boston changed the names of two of their principal streets to Hanover and Union. And then, four weeks after Josiah's prayer meeting, news arrived of another military triumph.

At the battle of Oudenaarde, the Duke of Marlborough had crushed the French again. Cotton Mather preached a sermon thanking God for victory, and although the war still had five years to run, the Protestant side seemed to be assured of success. For decades the Franklins had lived their lives beneath the long shadow that Louis XIV cast over the Atlantic. As at last the shadow lifted, Josiah entered a new, more comfortable phase of his career.

His eldest daughter was already launched in life, married to the master of a ship; Samuel, his eldest son, was out in the world in the old family trade as a smith; and Josiah Junior, the first Franklin born in Boston, had run away to sea. As one by one the children found their feet and left the tenement, so Josiah's finances improved. Blessed with the friendship of Judge Sewall, he could borrow money from people who could see that his credit was good. Early in 1712, he took out a mortgage from another member of the prayer meeting. At Banbury his brother had owned his own home, and now at last Josiah could leave Milk Street and do the same.

Aptly enough for a Whig, Josiah Franklin bought a corner property on Union and Hanover. In a letter written very late in his life to his sister Jane Mecom, one of Abiah's daughters, Benjamin the scientist remembered their new home as "a lowly dwelling." Even so the plot was big enough for a wooden house, a workshop, and extra space that could be let to tenants. The Blue Ball came with the family and hung above the premises.

In his autobiography, when Benjamin Franklin referred to himself as the youngest son of a youngest son he wrote of this as though it was a handicap; but in reality, the date and circumstances of his birth were more favorable than he cared to say. Although he was born in wartime, he had the good fortune to live out most of his early life in an age of international peace. In the spring of 1713, when he was seven, the war drew to an end with the Treaty of Utrecht. Two years later, King Louis XIV died at last; and when the despot vanished from the scene, the British and their navy were free to turn their attention to the scourge of piracy. Other than that—and by the end of the 1720s, the pirates had been cleared from the ocean—the guns fell silent in the North Atlantic.

For almost thirty years, a system of treaties preserved the balance of power between Great Britain and France. Many points of rivalry remained—in the Baltic, in India, and on the Abenaki frontier—but until the 1740s neither country felt obliged to fight the other. Far to the south, the British in the West Indies kept up a long cold war with Spain, as each nation vied for the profits of a slave economy. But even there no genuine hostilities occurred until 1739. By the time the Caribbean became a battleground, Benjamin Franklin was already thirty-three.

For the making of the affable sage, these long years of peace were essential. To acquire his training with words and ideas, Franklin needed a society where vigorous debate was a habit; but he also had to make a living. For that he required a stable economy where trade could flow uninterrupted. In the America of his early life, both conditions were fulfilled. Although Boston remained a troubled place, beset by inflation, and riven by party quarrels, no terminal crisis took place. There was just enough conflict to make for colorful journalism, but not so much as would wreck the prosperity everyone wanted to see.

And so Franklin came to adulthood in an era of equilibrium. In the absence of war, people and ideas could pass freely over the ocean, enriching the atmosphere of the towns along the coast. For the Franklins, crossing the Atlantic became almost routine. The family ceased to be landlocked yeomen from middle England. Instead they underwent a maritime rebirth. By the time Franklin was seven years old, his brother Peter, born to Abiah in 1692, had followed Josiah Junior to sea. Both young men shipped back to London, where in the twilight years of Queen Anne they were entertained as guests by their uncle Benjamin.

The Franklins had always been adventurous; and after Utrecht they became even more so, as immigrants came flowing in to diversify the culture of the colonies, creating new relationships across the sea. Among the children of Josiah and Abiah was a daughter Mary, who reached the age of twenty-two in 1716, when she married an Irish mariner. He was Robert Holmes, the son of a Presbyterian minister from Donegal who had found a parish on Martha's Vineyard. Two years later Holmes became a pioneer of the Irish diaspora, when he skippered one of the first shiploads of settlers to sail from Ulster to America. The dark side of the boom in Atlantic commerce lay in the slave trade, which prospered as never before now that the ocean was safer to travel. The Franklins were among the Bostonians who played their part, sharing in the money to be made from human bondage.[3]

Although Judge Sewall hated slavery—he called it "man-stealing: an atrocious crime"—his friend Josiah clearly had no qualms about the business. In the August of 1713, the Franklin name appeared for the first time in an American newspaper, when Josiah advertised the sale of five Africans from the sign of the Blue Ball. Here was yet another aspect of life in Boston, and one that would leave a stain on the career of Benjamin Franklin. In colonial America the press and slavery were deeply intertwined. Every paper ran advertisements for slave sales, or offered rewards for runaways; and so Franklin would carry the smell of the trade on his hands for as long as he remained a publisher. Eventually—it has to be said that it took a very long time—Franklin would come to see that Judge Sewall was correct. In his youth and early manhood, he and his father took it for granted that Africans could be the objects of a callous transaction on the street. As yet, the evils of slavery did not trouble the conscience of the average Whig.

In the house at Hanover and Union, Benjamin Franklin grew up in an environment of the kind the government denied to slaves. He had two parents legally married and members of a church. He lived in a town that gave him the freedom to explore and to learn, with a mother and father who had nothing to fear from their neighbors. In his fifties, secure and happy, with his older children leaving home, Josiah could offer the boy more attention than he might have done when he was still establishing his business.[4]

From his father, Franklin acquired the ingenuity of a literate English craftsman; from his brothers and from Boston, the yearning for travel and the sea; but it was his mother who educated his feelings. By the time he was born, Abiah Franklin had raised so many children that she knew what she was doing when she had another. She had lost one son in a terrible accident: Ebenezer, at sixteen months, drowned in 1703 in a vat of soap and water. Precisely what she felt by way of grief or guilt, we will never know. And then she lost another boy, a Thomas, who died an infant three years later, as Benjamin might so easily have done.

Somehow Abiah survived the pain, and her youngest son would be the beneficiary. We know so little about Abiah that we cannot give a full account of the way she raised the boy, but we can at least be confident of this. It appears that she did everything a parent should, giving him the right combination of attachment and liberty, now and then a touch of discipline, but mostly the time and the space for him to play creatively. This is more or less what Franklin said himself, on the few occasions when he is known to have shared any secrets of their relationship.

The Whistle and the Wharf

In his later years Benjamin Franklin gave two accounts of his childhood. One is very famous, contained in his autobiography, while the other is familiar only to Franklin connoisseurs. In his memoirs he touches briefly on Abiah, praising his mother for her "excellent constitution." He notes the fact that she fed all her children from the breast, which might or might not be significant, in Freudian terms. Franklin also quotes Abiah's epitaph, in which he called her "discreet and virtuous." Then he hurries on to more masculine topics, as though too embarrassed to linger on a subject as sentimental as a mother's love. But in private—although this was very rare—Franklin could be more open about Abiah.

In France in 1779 he befriended a medical student, Pierre-Jean-Georges Cabanis. In their long conversations, which Cabanis turned into a portrait of his mentor, Franklin dwelled on his earliest memories of Boston. All of them were happy. "He lacked for nothing in his childhood," wrote Cabanis: a comment that gives the lie to any notion that Franklin was reared in poverty. In the few childhood anecdotes preserved in his letters, Franklin refers to the games he enjoyed as a boy, blowing bubbles with soap suds out of a tobacco pipe, or keeping six pigeons as pets in a box nailed to the wall of the house. But he never said much about his mother: except to Cabanis.[5]

It seems that he trusted the young French biologist more than he did any American of his period. Franklin bared his soul to Cabanis, as he did to almost no one else. After their meetings in Paris, the Frenchman came away convinced that Abiah was the principal source of the virtues that her son displayed. "It seems that his mother was a woman full of wisdom," he wrote. One story seemed to sum up her qualities better than any other.

At about the time the family left Milk Street, there was a fair in Boston, held on a public holiday. To mark the occasion his parents filled Benjamin's pocket with halfpennies. On the way to the fair he met a boy making wonderful sounds with a whistle. Benjamin handed over all his coins, took the whistle, and hurried home, where he ran about the house, "blowing hard enough to break the windows." His brothers and sisters laughed at the little boy when he told them how much he had given for his new toy. Benjamin burst into tears.

Mrs. Franklin gently pointed out that if he had been more careful and paid a fair price, he would have had money to spare for a drum, or a little cart to pull along. Benjamin—he was six years old, or thereabouts—stood there deep in thought. "My friend," said Abiah, "when you buy a whistle, you should always know what it's going to cost. Here's my advice: every time you really want a thing, say to yourself first of all: *how much is the whistle worth?*" Franklin told Cabanis that he never forgot his mother's wise maxim. At moments of passion—or "*violent désir,*" as the Frenchman put it, as a Frenchman would—Franklin would pause, and ask himself what price he might have to pay for the loss of self-control.

It was a lesson in the elements of prudence, just right for a boy who would go into business. At first, however, Josiah hoped to educate Benjamin to be a minister. By the time he was five the boy was reading the Bible. Soon he was deep into Bunyan, and not just *Pilgrim's Progress,* but Bunyan's collected works, books written out of the religious strife of Josiah's England. At seven he was composing his own little poems, which Josiah sent back to Uncle Benjamin in London. Since the Franklins had always tried to make friends with clergymen, it was natural enough to think of preparing the boy for Harvard and a clerical career. So in 1714, when he was eight, Benjamin went to the Boston Latin School to be drilled in the basics of English and Latin grammar. He rose straight to the top of his class.

And then Josiah Franklin had second thoughts. Harvard was expensive. The college also produced too many graduates—twenty or so, in an average year—for the churches of New England to digest. So in 1715 he took the boy out of the grammar school and sent him to a private academy, run by George Brownell, who taught practical subjects to boys and girls. It was a "writing school": a place to perfect a boy's calligraphy and spelling, and learn how to write model letters, do sums, and keep accounts. At Ecton, scrivening had been one of the talents of Josiah's brother Thomas. And so Benjamin had to learn the trade. The one thing he did not master was the arithmetic—an odd little failing in a boy so clever. It was one he would later have to correct.

All too soon, it was time for Benjamin to earn his keep. At ten he left Mr. Brownell's school and became his father's assistant. He made soap and candles, cut wicks, filled molds, served customers, and ran errands. He hated the work but stuck at it for two years, while Abiah intervened on Benjamin's side to negotiate periods of relaxation. To build up his physique, he told Cabanis, "she let him play freely . . . in winter in the snow and ice, and in summer on the seashore and in the water."

Play was essential, and he was allowed to have plenty of it. As a boy Franklin would mess about in boats and canoes and swim for hours, eat prodigiously, and then go swimming again, growing faster and stronger all the time. In his teens he made fins and flippers—the fins like a painter's palette, ten inches long—to pull himself along more rapidly. The weight of the fins made his wrists ache with fatigue. Even this was excellent training. Whatever kind of artisan he became, he would need hefty forearms to drive a saw or carry heavy loads.

All of this took place close to his front door. Across Hanover Street to the north there were two taverns, the Green Dragon and the Star, but just beyond the smell of ale and rum there lay a saltwater lagoon, the Mill Pond. Twice a day, at high tide in the Charles River, water flowed over floodgates into the pond, before draining away through the wheels of a flour mill and into a creek that led down to the harbor, a short walk from the Franklin house. As is the way in Boston, the pond was emptied long ago, and the land has been reclaimed. Today the site of the pond is dominated by railroad tracks, a hotel or two, and the concrete box of a stadium where the Bruins play ice hockey. The Mill Pond was Franklin's playground as well, and the location for his first experiments.[6]

Besides his pigeons and his bubble pipe, he also had a paper kite. On the Mill Pond he devised a creative way to play with it. While he swam, he tied the kite to a stick thrust into the bank. One day it occurred to Franklin that if he floated on his back, holding the stick, and the wind was in the right direction, the kite would pull him across the pond while he gazed up at the clouds. And so it did: this was, he recalled, a "singular mode of swimming." Abiah's response is not recorded. Franklin told Cabanis that occasionally she urged him not to waste so much time in the water, but she did so without any threat of punishment. Benjamin was fit and strong. That was the important thing, for a mother who had lost two of his brothers.

It seems that his father punished the boy only once, and it happened because of another escapade by the lagoon. The pond spilled over into a salt marsh beneath the heights of Beacon Hill. As Boston grew, people with money began to build stone houses on the hill and by the marsh. One day, some workmen left a heap of stones near the pond, close to a spot where Franklin and his friends liked to fish for minnows.

"By much trampling we had made it a quagmire," he remembered. And so, in the spirit of Daniel Defoe, the young Benjamin undertook a project to improve the fishery. At this period wharves were starting to appear along the banks of the pond, built of crisscrossed timber laid in the mud, where in the twenty-first century archaeologists would find their remains. Franklin went one better. He decided to build a wharf from masonry. In the evening, when the workmen had gone home, he organized his friends to fetch away their heap of stones, and make a jetty where they could stand to cast their nets and lines. When the workmen turned up the following morning, to find that their materials had vanished, suspicion soon fell on Benjamin Franklin. "Several of us were corrected by our fathers," he wrote in his memoirs. "And tho' I pleaded the usefulness of the work, mine convinced me that nothing was useful which was not honest."

Here was another lesson in elementary ethics. It was only one of many. Beneath the Blue Ball, Josiah and Abiah did their best to fill their home with the language of faith, honesty, and virtue. Franklin recalled how his father would invite friends and neighbors round for supper, and then begin a conversation on "some ingenious or useful topic, which might

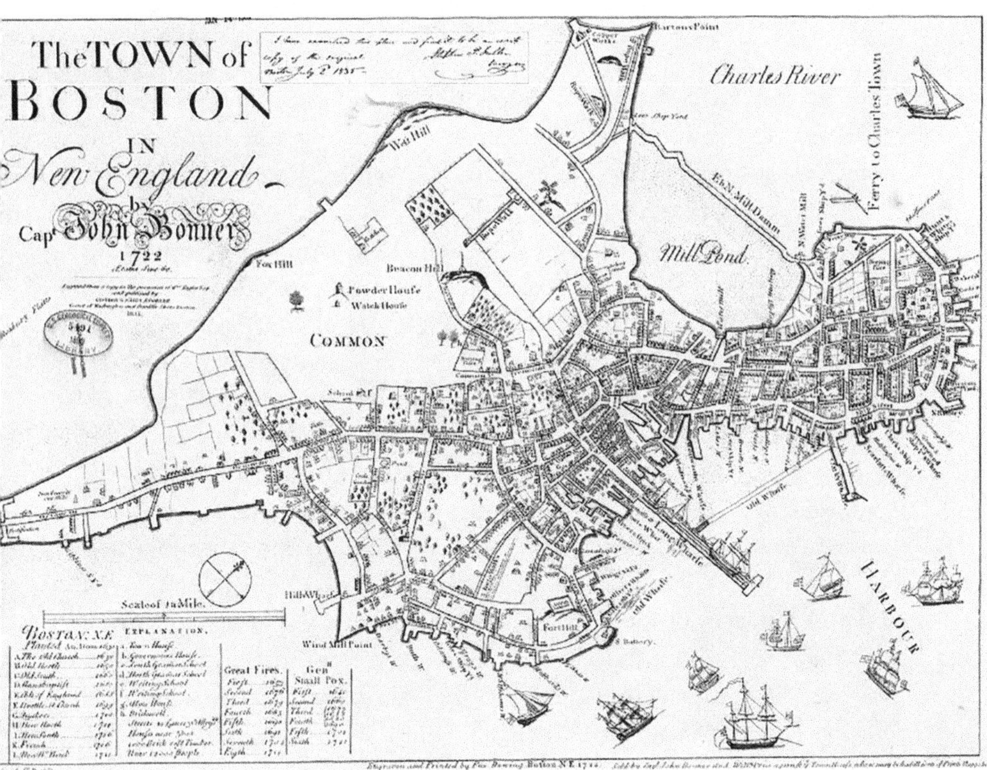

Boston in 1722, when Benjamin Franklin was sixteen, with his playground the Mill Pond and—beneath it—the stream that ran down into the harbor close to the Franklin house at Hanover and Union Streets.

tend to improve the minds of his children." The food would lie forgotten as they listened to edifying parables about the meaning of goodness, justice, and prudence. According to Franklin, this was how he came to be a plain, frugal man of simple tastes, paying little heed to the dishes that he ate.

Or so he claimed in 1771, when he started to write his memoirs; but as so often with Benjamin Franklin, the truth about his eating habits and his education is more complicated than he liked to make out. Although he could be austere when he had to be, he had a taste for luxury as well, as anyone can see who reads an account of his years in France. The Franklin who devoured the best cuisine that Paris had to offer was scarcely indifferent to food. Nor was he a child who simply listened to his parents and believed the moral lessons he was given.

In starting these conversations over supper, Josiah was treading on another piece of slippery ground. At the age of five, Benjamin had dreamed of being a soldier. Much later, bored with soap and candle wax, he talked about copying his brothers and running off to sea. In the meantime, he found another way to be rebellious. The Franklins, he recalled at the end of his life, were "always subject to being a little miffy."* As a child his miffiness took the form of a sharp tongue and a talent for mockery. According to a story that Franklin left out of his memoirs, he once made fun of Josiah's habit of saying a long grace before a meal. As they were salting fish for the winter, Benjamin suggested that they bless the whole barrel, since it would be "a vast saving of time."[7]

Franklin was hugely precocious. And when Josiah encouraged ethical discussion around the dinner table, he was inviting his son to be provocative at a point in history when debates about morality and God were moving in new and hazardous directions. Things had changed since the days when as a child at Ecton Josiah learned his faith from a Gospel text painted on the cottage wall. In his memoirs, Franklin tells us that as a boy in Boston he too was "religiously educated as a Presbyterian." That being so, he learned the language of Calvinism: a string of words that he lists for us—Eternal Decrees, Election, and Reprobation—that were supposed to encapsulate the Presbyterian creed. By 1715, when Franklin left the Latin School, the meaning of these phrases had come to be fiercely contested. It was no longer clear that a Presbyterian had to accept all the notions that lay behind them.

At one time—in the middle of the 1640s—everyone who claimed to be a Presbyterian would have also been a Calvinist, a believer in the doctrine of Double Predestination. It was a harsh and divisive idea. Even before God created the world—or so an orthodox Calvinist would say—he had assigned in advance every human soul to one of two groups, the Elect or the Damned. From this point of view, the Christian life consisted of no more than a long, painful endeavor to discover whether one was either saved for Heaven, or predestined to the flames of Hell. In the Boston of Franklin's boyhood, this kind of Calvinism still wielded a powerful influence, upheld by pastors such as Mr. Willard or Cotton Mather; but here and in England, it underwent a process of erosion.

After the Glorious Revolution, the Toleration Act had given English dissenters of the Franklin kind a degree of religious freedom. The new

* By about 1620, according to the *Oxford English Dictionary*, the word "miff" had entered the language to mean a fit of ill humor. By 1700, "miffy" was being used to mean peevish or irritable.

law was meant to be a modest compromise, leaving intact the power of the Church of England. However, there were people who took it to mean that they could think as they wished and worship as they wanted: or perhaps not worship at all. To the horror of most of the clergy—dissenters and Anglicans alike—the 1690s witnessed the start of four decades of intense debate in England about the basic tenets of the Christian faith. Transmitted to the colonies, the arguments advanced on either side supplied the raw material for Franklin's schooling in ideas.

In England, the Presbyterians came to be divided, between those who clung to Calvinism in its old form and those who harbored doubts about Predestination, that concept so severe and so alarming. They also had to cope with something else: scandalous writers who dealt heresy. In London in 1695, an Irishman called John Toland brought out a book, *Christianity Not Mysterious,* in which he attacked conventional religion with a vitriol rarely seen before. In the Dutch Republic, Toland had steeped himself in the ideas of one of the era's most radical thinkers: an exiled French Huguenot, Pierre Bayle, whose books would become some of Franklin's favorite reading.

"We hold that reason is the only foundation of all certitude," John Toland wrote, echoing the words of Monsieur Bayle. Toland was a deist: or in other words, he believed that the universe probably had a Creator, but not the Christian God of the Bible. As his influence spread in London, so Toland set in motion a debate—"the deistical controversy"—that would rack the brains of intellectuals, including Benjamin Franklin, until the 1730s. Only then did Franklin lose interest in metaphysics, and turn his mind in more fruitful directions—eventually, to electricity.[8]

Deists, Whigs, and Tories

"Deistical notions grow epidemical," wrote Cotton Mather in 1712. Or so the pastor feared, as he heard reports that even in New England people had their doubts about the truths of Scripture. A few months earlier, outraged by the works of Bayle and Toland and their kind, the most eminent clergymen in England had said much the same thing. Assembled at Canterbury, the Anglican clerics condemned what they called "the late excessive growth of infidelity," and the disrespect they encountered from freethinkers and libertines.[9]

Whether Anglicans or Matherites, the ministers tended to overstate the problem. The Christian faith still reigned supreme, with a powerful arsenal of concepts and authority; and indeed in America an evangelical revival lay only two decades around the corner. But that was not the way the men of God saw their situation. In the years when Franklin was growing up, the ministers *felt* insulted and beleaguered. As they fought back against what they saw as defamation of the Gospel, so the clergy became reactionaries, inviting ridicule, which—when the moment came—someone as acute as Franklin would be only too happy to provide.

If the deists so upset a pastor like Cotton Mather, it was partly because they refused to be pinned down. "Deist" could be taken to mean many things: so many that often the epithet was just another word for atheism. A deist accepted that God was probably a necessary being, because if the universe was governed by physical laws, then it must have a creator of some kind. Beyond that, however, the deist could not be specific; because it was impossible to show that this creator had to be the Jehovah who revealed himself to Moses. Worse still, deists would claim to uphold Christian ethics, while keeping their most radical ideas hidden in a mist of double meanings. And few deists were more evasive than Pierre Bayle, a scholar who knew how to bury an alarming notion deep in the undergrowth of footnotes. Even today experts cannot agree whether or not he denied the existence of God.

In 1697, Bayle had begun to publish his masterpiece, the *Historical and Critical Dictionary.* A vast compendium of learning, in time it became a fixture of Franklin's bedside table. In the 1730s and 1740s, he sold copies from his store in Philadelphia, and twenty years after that he liked to have Bayle close at hand. Against the dogma of belief, Bayle rallied the forces of scholarship, exposing inconsistencies and errors in the text of the Bible. Like Toland, he appealed to reason as the test of truth. Bayle looked for answers to ancient questions: Why does God allow calamities and evil? If he gives human beings a leaning to be sinful, how can it be just to condemn them to hell? Bayle worried away at the issues, until his readers saw revealed what they took to be the flaws in Christian logic.

Among his disciples, Pierre Bayle counted not only John Toland, but also the young Lord Shaftesbury, grandson of the Whig conspirator. With the help of allies such as these, Bayle's ideas became common currency in London. On both sides of the Atlantic, they opened up divisions in the ranks of the clergy who knew that they had to defend their faith but could not agree how best to do so.[10]

Should they cling to old certainties, and condemn anybody who deviated from them? Or should they reach out to their opponents, and try to find common ground where everyone could agree? This was never easy. By the time Queen Anne died in 1714, in England the Presbyterian ministers were deeply divided and confused. So were the Anglicans. Even the essential doctrine of the Holy Trinity had come to be a matter for dispute. In Boston meanwhile, Cotton Mather and his friends feared that a tidal wave of blasphemy would soon come hurtling in from Europe.

It was all the harder to build a consensus at a time when arguments about religion were thoroughly political. In theory, it was possible to hold deistical ideas and yet remain conservative in every other way. But the politics of England were so deeply polarized that every debate about God also became a party fight. From the left, the Whigs and their constituents, including the dissenters, applauded the new king from Germany, who filled his government with Whigs. On the right were the Tories, pledged to defend the Anglican Church, who pointed out that George I had only a dubious claim to be the monarch. Each party accused the other of heresy or worse. The Tories alleged that the Whigs were deists, whose ideas would undermine the sacred basis of morality. From the other side, the Whigs—insofar as they agreed with each other, which was seldom, since they were divided into factions—would tend to brand the Tories as closet Jacobites, secretly in league with the Church of Rome.

Angry though it was, the strife of Whigs and Tories had one very positive outcome: it left no room for complacency. All the leading English writers—Defoe, the journalist Joseph Addison, the poet Alexander Pope, and his friend Jonathan Swift, to name only the most famous—had to take their stand in these debates. Addison was a Whig, so was Defoe, while Swift and Pope were Tories. And so, paradoxically, the rage of party in Great Britain gave birth to some of the finest prose and poetry in English. Nine weeks away across the Atlantic, their writings found eager readers in the colonies. The young Franklin was among the most enthusiastic.

By virtue of their history, Bostonians were usually Whigs, committed to the House of Hanover, but they had their own agenda too. The people of Boston were always looking for arguments—from whatever source, Whigs or Tories, clerics or philosophers—that they could recycle for use in their political controversies. Whether they wished to uphold authority, in the church or in the state, or to assert their independence from the royal governor or from the likes of Cotton Mather, they found their ammunition in the books that came from England.

By the time Franklin finished his year at the Latin School, this habit was firmly entrenched in Boston. The shelves were groaning with books, at a moment when Franklin was ready to begin reading prose and poetry meant for adults. As he studied the best English authors, he steeped himself in the controversies, religious and political, that energized their work. He also become an expert with the written word. But to set him on the path to fame, Franklin needed more than natural talent. He also had to find people to point him in the right direction. Soon he encountered the mentors he required, the first of whom was a member of his family.

Shortly before the boy's tenth birthday, his schooling began a new chapter when the Franklins received a visitor from London. Among the immigrants who came to America was his uncle, Benjamin Senior, sailing in on the schooner *Nantucket.* On October 8, 1715, he stepped ashore in Boston, an old, bewildered man to whom the passing years had been unkind.

Chapter Five

Mr. Pemberton's Method

We think of Franklin as the master of the positive. Here was a man who made a brilliant success of his life and believed that if they followed his advice, everyone else could do the same. And yet his finest writing often had to do with failure. He wrote many paragraphs about ruined lives, flawed men and women, and people who simply disappeared one day, leaving a trail of creditors behind them. The first of the many failures he encountered was his uncle Benjamin. At the age of sixty-five, he arrived in America alone: a man almost broken by debt and by bereavement.

Ten years earlier, he had lost his wife, Hannah—"my heart's desire, mine eyes' delight"—and then in 1709 his daughter died as well, the eighth of his children to precede him to the grave. Long ago old Benjamin had left a well-paid job and set up on his own in the west end of London, selling dyed silk and printed calico from a shop in a fashionable spot near Drury Lane. By 1710 the business was in trouble; Benjamin Senior could not pay the rent, and so he began to slide toward insolvency.[1]

"In solitude as left alone, my low dark state I much bewail'd," he wrote. At last Uncle Benjamin accepted defeat, sold up everything he had, left his precious library with a lawyer, and boarded the ship for New England where he installed himself with the Franklins. Although he had a son in lodgings in the town—Samuel, a cutler, who had followed family tradition and served his time as an apprentice in London—he preferred to squat with Josiah.[2]

Uncle Benjamin came as a houseguest and stayed four years, trying and failing to find a job, and talking politics incessantly. Here was an

English Whig who consoled himself for his hardships by turning the Hebrew psalms into rhyming couplets. When he came to a psalm thanking God for helping the Israelites in battle, the old man added a note in the margin: "King William's deliverance from Popery and slavery, 1688—and a second deliverance by King George."

Although Josiah shared his brother's politics, the old man soon became a burden and the miffiness became extreme. The brothers fell out; and in 1719, when Samuel married and set up a household of his own, Uncle Benjamin went to join him. But these had been four of the most important years of his nephew's life. As he sat composing verses in the corner, the old man was a constant reminder that across the sea there was a city called London, where there were books to be authored and adventures to be had.

In his memoirs, Franklin awarded his uncle his highest accolade: "he was an ingenious man," he recalled. From England, Benjamin Senior had sent the boy a little poem, warning him against becoming a soldier—the military life was "a dangerous trade . . . the nurse of vice," he wrote—and in Boston he offered more of what he thought of as wise counsel. He taught the boy his form of shorthand, so that he too could take down sermons. Franklin did not practice and he soon forgot the technique, but his uncle's form of verbal ingenuity left a permanent impression. A man in love with words, Benjamin Senior strove to be a communicator, and he conveyed this aspiration to his nephew.

In London the old man had never ceased to go to chapel, and the Presbyterians he heard were some of the finest preachers in the city. While the deists were at odds with the theologians, a small revolution was occurring in evangelism, as the ministers Uncle Benjamin admired looked for new ways to spread their message in the capital. Once again, it was Daniel Defoe who captured what was happening and made it available to the widest audience. In 1715, a few years before he wrote *Robinson Crusoe,* he brought out *The Family Instructor.* A self-help book for Christian tradesmen and their wives, it had a preface written by one of Benjamin Senior's friends in the clergy, a celebrity preacher by the name of Samuel Wright.

The book soon became a best-seller. Franklin admired it immensely, and he mentioned it in his memoirs even though by the 1770s it had long since become an outmoded relic of the past. What Franklin liked about it was its literary quality. Full of lively dialogue, *The Family Instructor* consisted of everyday stories from London, each one a domestic drama intended to teach a lesson about vice and virtue, or temperance and chastity, or about the duties of masters and servants to each other. Moralistic though it was, the book was also moving and enjoyable because, in the words of the preface by Mr. Wright, "the substance of each narrative is real . . . not ill contriv'd to take hold of the hearts of those who are loose and ignorant."[3]

It would be hard to think of anything more Franklinesque. Edifying parables, written in direct and vivid language—it was the kind of thing Franklin tried to achieve in his journalism, in *The Way to Wealth,* and in his memoirs. It was a style of writing to which Benjamin Senior could introduce him. But if Franklin was going to be a scientist as well as a writer, he would need a clear, logical mind. And neither Defoe, nor Wright, nor Benjamin Senior could think with the clarity Franklin would display in his work with physics.

It must have helped that somebody taught him chess. At some point in his boyhood, Franklin learned to play the game—in later life it became an obsession, and he played it very well—but he never tells us who gave him the lessons or when they occurred. But Franklin did have a teacher of logic; or at any rate, a teacher who rammed home the message that a thinker needed to be clear and precise. The teacher in question was Ebenezer Pemberton, the eccentric pastor of the Old South Meeting House.

When Samuel Willard passed away in 1707, Pemberton stepped up to occupy the pulpit, and so his sermons were the first that Franklin heard. Ebenezer was an odd man indeed, who would sometimes appear in the pulpit wearing a blond wig. Prone to fits of anger, he once flew into a rage with his most eminent parishioner, Judge Sewall, almost wrecking their relationship. His rival Cotton Mather detested Mr. Pemberton, calling him a man "of a strangely choleric and envious temper." But others disagreed. In a clergyman who died too young, they saw the vestiges of greatness.

Above all they praised him for his intellect. When Ebenezer Pemberton preached, he put his points across not with windy rhetoric but with relentless chains of inference, so that he sounded more like a lawyer than a man of God. "He was a master of logic and oratory," said his best friend, Benjamin Colman, the pastor at the new, more liberal, and swiftly growing church in Brattle Square, who gave his funeral sermon. Mr. Pemberton, he recalled, always made his case for the Gospel with "perspicuity, distinctness and exactness of method."[4]

Today, his homilies make for tedious reading, but at the time they broke new ground in Boston as models of accessibility. We know exactly what Pemberton said and how he spoke, because one of his parishioners took notes, and some of his sermons appeared in print in Boston and London. Never pedantic or obscure, Ebenezer Pemberton avoided the academic vices of speaking in jargon or piling up citations for the sake of appearing to be learned. Everything had to be clear and lucid, so that his listeners could follow each step as his argument developed.

Down in the pews at the Old South, Franklin began to understand the meaning of "method," a word that would become another of his favorites. He also encountered a form of Christianity more generous than the older, more rigid doctrines of Calvinism with which pastors like the Mathers were still obsessed. At Harvard, Pemberton had been a hard-reading man, up through the night at his studies. By the time of his death, when he was forty-five, he had amassed a library of a thousand books. However, the remarkable thing about his collection was not so much its size as its open-mindedness. As well as reading deeply, Pemberton had read very widely, in science and politics as well as in theology. Nothing less would have satisfied his flock.[5]

By this point in the history of Boston, people expected more from a minister than tirades against depravity. In the 1710s, a pastor could not hope to keep his audience merely by invoking the grim old Jehovah of the past. Although Pemberton knew his Calvinist theology—he owned all the usual manuals, and it seems that he still believed in predestination—he had to offer something more than hellfire. And so in his sermons God underwent a change of heart, gradually becoming a benign creator who offered salvation as broadly as he could; and in this new, more accommodating deity, Pemberton found his answer to the puzzles of the age.

He knew about Toland, he owned a volume of Bayle's dictionary, and he had studied the deistical controversy. But most of all Pemberton admired a new religious party in England, who had come to be known as the "latitudinarians," or more simply the "latitude men." The name said it all about the views they held. Although they were Anglican ministers, duty bound to uphold the king's Book of Common Prayer, they hoped to find a middle ground with dissenters, by giving everyone some latitude to differ about the finer points of doctrine.

Long ago at Ecton in the 1660s, when the Franklins were wrestling with their consciences, the local squire Sir Henry Yelverton had enlisted the intellectual support of the latitude party as he tried to persuade his neighbors to enter the Anglican fold. Eager to prevent any more strife about religion, Sir Henry urged his friends to read the elegant prose of the party's leader, John Tillotson, a rising young star of the Church of England. As the years went by, Tillotson drew ever closer to the Whigs, for whom he acted as a sort of house theologian. After the Glorious Revolution, when it fell to King William to select a new Archbishop of Canterbury, of course he gave the job to the trusty Mr. Tillotson the Whig.

Today the name of Tillotson has almost been forgotten; but in the eighteenth century, people of letters, including Ebenezer Pemberton, revered his latitudinarian sermons as masterpieces of the English language. In Boston, Pemberton studied them closely and he passed them on to his congregation, with among them the Franklins. "I am of the old opinion," John Tillotson once wrote, "that moderation is a virtue": by which he meant that instead of going to extremes, Christians should focus on the things they had in common. Surely they could all agree that God meant to be merciful, a benign creator who wished to see his children being good and kind, loving one another and living happy lives. His benevolence was obvious, in the orderly cosmos that God had made. Provided everyone accepted that, said the Whig archbishop, matters of detail could be safely put aside, and only madmen or fanatics would be left unredeemed.[6]

From a portrait by Peter Lely, this is John Tillotson, the Anglican "latitude man" who served as Archbishop of Canterbury in the 1690s. His sermons were regarded in the eighteenth century as models of English prose, and read and admired by Benjamin Franklin.

In a homily that found many readers, Tillotson had said that the law of God "requires nothing of us, but what is recommended to us by our reason." At the Old South, as Pemberton preached on the book of Isaiah he quoted the archbishop almost verbatim. Drawing up a list of the virtues every human being should display—justice, self-denial, temperance, and charity—Ebenezer made the very same point: that even if they were not commanded by the Gospel, our reason would tell us that they marked out the path to happiness.[7]

Many years later, and far more famously, Franklin would say precisely the same thing. It was an optimistic creed, ideal for people who hungered for advancement; and if the ideas of the latitude men were pushed just a little further, they could be made to sanctify all kinds of material success. When Pemberton died and his friend Mr. Colman gave his eulogy, he set out the same Tillotsonian agenda: a creed that could be followed by Anglicans and Puritans alike. If we are sober, diligent, and self-controlled, in any walk of life, we are doing what God demands. He gave us minds and bodies so that we could set them to good use. Or as Benjamin Colman put it, "we were made for diligence . . . he that gave us being, gives us business."

Again, these were words that Franklin would echo in his own writings. By the time he was eleven, it seems that these opinions had come to be shared by at least two members of his family. Mr. Pemberton died in February 1717, and two weeks later Colman gave his sermon of commemoration. In April, Uncle Benjamin left the Old South and joined Mr. Colman's congregation at Brattle Square. In July, he was followed to the same meeting house by his nephew James Franklin, the third son of Josiah and Abiah.

Times had changed again, and the Franklins were moving with them. With the Atlantic at peace and trade beginning to flourish, the family were coming to inhabit a new world where commerce might loom larger than the words of scripture. In this new situation, the teachings of Tillotson and Colman made the very best of sense. Worldly, loose, and flexible, their kind of Christianity did not require heroic feats of prayer and Bible reading. Instead, their disciples could simply be diligent at their trade: a message that must have appealed to the young James Franklin, who was just embarking on his business career.

Early in 1718, the family passed another milestone, when James turned twenty-one, celebrating the occasion by setting sail for England. A printer by profession, he was off to London to buy the equipment he needed to start his own firm. As yet, although Americans could make a printing press, their paper mills were few, and the colonies had no mines of lead to supply the quantities of type—as much as half a ton—that each machine required.

Just as old Thomas Franklin had financed his sons' apprenticeships, so Josiah found the money for James to buy his apparatus. A press and the kit to go with it would have cost at least £100 in sterling, or about £200 in Boston's depreciated currency. The scanty records that survive suggest that in 1718 Josiah signed an IOU for something close to that sum. He also gave his son his first assistant. When James came home later that year, he took on the bookish young Benjamin as his own apprentice.[8]

His Brother James

If we know too little about Abiah, we also know much less than we would like about James Franklin. Born in 1697, he must have had some schooling, because he proved to be a competent writer, with a flair for poetry as well as prose. It seems that he was also close to Benjamin Senior. Not only did they both attend the church at Brattle Square: James also learned his uncle's craft of printing calicoes and linen. As for his trade, he probably acquired it in the workshop of the Boston printer Bartholomew Green, the man who turned out the *News-Letter* every week. Green was a member, alongside Josiah, of the private prayer meeting linked to the Old South. But even the source of James's training cannot be known for sure.

And so, for lack of information, James has come to be seen as something of a thug: the irate, resentful older brother, who bullied and beat the young Benjamin when he became a rival, and ended up by driving him out of Massachusetts. But Franklin himself was never quite sure about the rights and wrongs of the affair—"perhaps I was too saucy and provoking," he conceded in his memoirs—and there is another way to tell James's story.

He was another ingenious young man, brave and innovative. Purely as a newspaperman, James Franklin had perhaps more audacity than his brother. He was also more original. What he lacked was staying power, and the young Benjamin's deeper intellect. His master stroke was this: James took an English model—the outspoken, combative, and entertaining newspapers printed in London—and he brought the concept to the colonies. Founded in Boston in 1721, his weekly journal, *The New-England*

Courant, is rightly remembered as the most distinguished landmark of early journalism in America.

On arriving back in Boston with his printing press, in the spring or early summer of 1718, to begin with James had to play it safe. He started as a jobbing printer, taking on routine assignments for which Mr. Green lacked the time. The first books James is known to have produced were as dull as tedious could be: a sermon, and a catalogue for the sale of a clergyman's library, commissioned in August by the bookseller Samuel Gerrish. A close friend of Judge Sewall, Mr. Gerrish belonged to the private prayer meeting that Josiah attended. A few doors away from the Old South the judge and his friends would come to his bookstore to sip their coffee and do business.

Grim though they were, these early products of the Franklin press showed that James knew his trade: the design was clear, the type set immaculately, and the white space was just right. But this was not the stuff of fame and fortune. If James were to thrive, he could not rely forever on the circle of middle-aged worthies who surrounded the Old South. He had to find something more lively to print, and in England he had seen how he might do so.

On his trip to London, James had carried with him a letter from Judge Sewall, addressed to the judge's cousin, Samuel Storke, a merchant who dealt in whale oil, pelts, tobacco, and sugar. A keen Presbyterian, he belonged to one of the chapels at the eastern end of the city, where Benjamin Senior had lived for ten years or so. And so in meeting Mr. Storke, James Franklin reentered the London his uncle had inhabited, the city of Defoe, with its dissenting preachers, and its pious merchants: the city that had done so much to shape his family's view of the world. It remained a town politically divided, between parties and factions who feuded in the pages of the press.[9]

During James's spell in the capital, Defoe was just starting to write *Robinson Crusoe*—the first edition would appear early in 1719—but he was also a columnist for a startling imprint owned by one Nathaniel Mist. It went by the name of the *Weekly Journal.* Mist was a Tory and a Jacobite, but he did not let his politics stand in the way of good writing. Although Defoe was a Whig, Mist hired him nonetheless, because he needed the very best of journalists. His newspaper belonged to a new breed of weekly paper, published on Saturdays, that fought each other hard for circulation.

With six pages to fill, the weeklies had lots of space. They crammed it with news and comment, poems, essays, jokes, and puns, and tales of highwaymen and adventures at sea. The first journal of the kind had gone on sale in 1714, but when Mist launched his paper he swiftly came to be the market leader. Mist catered, said one of his rivals, to "the lower class of readers": which was another way of saying that his paper was great fun. At every opportunity, Nathaniel Mist attacked the Whigs in the government with satire or with allegations of corruption. Time and again, he went to prison for seditious libel, but he knew that politics alone would not sell papers. While James Franklin was in London, Mist ran a column describing what he offered every week: "an agreeable miscellany of subjects, out of which every person may pick something to entertain themselves."[10]

This was the model James would adopt when, at only twenty-four, he founded *The New-England Courant*. We can be sure that he knew Mist's paper and the other London weeklies, because later James plundered their columns for material. Having seen this kind of journalism, he could not devote his Boston career to setting up in type the platitudes of dreary Harvard men. He had to do something equally outrageous, even at the risk of going to jail himself. And if that meant offending the obvious target, the Puritan clergy of Massachusetts, then offended they would have to be.

However, the time would need to be right for the *Courant* to make its debut. James would need to have a running story, some troublesome controversy in Boston that would give his paper a theme. He would also need a team of writers with enough imagination to make the *Courant* sparkle every week. And this was where his brother Benjamin would come in, with his precocious love of books and his talent with his pen.

Boyhood Heroes

In his spare time away from the Mill Pond, the candles, and the soap, the boy had consumed Josiah's small library. Most of the books had to do with divinity, but the young Benjamin, who could not stop reading, was done with that before the age of twelve. Having learned the lesson of the whistle, he spent his pocket money on the works of Bunyan, which he loved; but soon he had finished those as well. He traded them in for popular history: forty or fifty cheap, pocket-sized books by an English writer, who gave himself the pseudonym Robert Burton.

Actually, the author was Nathaniel Crouch, an English bookseller who had built his business with anti-Stuart propaganda. Whig and sensational, filled with xenophobia, his vast output consisted of stories "filled with wonders, rarities and curiosities," in the words of his obituary. His were patriotic books in which the heroes were always Protestant—Drake, Raleigh, Cromwell, and so on—while the villains were traitors and Papists, in league with the atrocious kings of Spain and France.

It was the kind of writing that Franklin had to absorb sooner or later, because the attitudes that motivated Crouch were deeply ingrained in the culture of New England. If the boy was going to be a journalist, he would have to switch back and forth between the language of the street, the chapel, the law courts, and the drawing room. Variety was one of Franklin's hallmarks—like Defoe, or Dickens, or James Joyce, he could write in a multitude of voices—but it could only come from experience. He would have to listen hard, to people from many different walks of life. He would also have to read cheap throwaway stuff as well as the classics; and few books were more throwaway than those of Mr. Crouch.

Fortunately, soon he found something more sublime. Apart from Bunyan and Defoe, the author Franklin recalled with most affection from his boyhood was a writer from the classical world: Plutarch, the Greek biographer, whose accounts of ancient heroes were also in Josiah's collection. "I still think that time spent to great advantage," said Franklin in his memoirs about the hours he devoted to Plutarch's *Lives,* a book that helped to shape his politics as well as his prose.

At the Old South, Mr. Pemberton would quote from Plutarch when he wished to conjure up examples of justice, courage, and humility, or to explain how a town should be governed. Here was another kind of patriotism, very different from the ideology of Crouch. In the stories of Solon, who gave laws to Athens, of Brutus the slayer of a tyrant or Cicero the orator, a reader could find a definition of virtue that went beyond the narrow notions of a bigot. Thirty years later, when in 1749 he wrote the syllabus for what became the University of Pennsylvania, Franklin urged the students to study Greek and Roman history. It would teach them many things—not least how to govern a republic, a new Athens on the Delaware—but most of all it would teach them morality. In Plutarch, Livy, and the rest, the college men would find "the causes of rise and fall of any man's character . . . the advantages of temperance, order, frugality, industry, perseverance."

It was much the same list as Pemberton had given from the pulpit; but Plutarch had something that the pastor lacked, a flair for energetic prose.

The only complete translation of the *Lives* was the one coauthored in the 1680s by the poet and playwright John Dryden. This is the one Franklin must have read. Dryden's prose was superb: learned but informal, sprightly and vivid—or, as it would be described by Samuel Johnson, "airy, animated, and vigorous"—with the main verb dropped into the sentence in just the right place to keep the reader moving forward with vigor.

If Franklin could master not only this kind of prose but also the narrative style of Defoe, then add the authenticity of speech from the waterfront, he would become a writer who could keep his audience in touch with any subject. But as yet, he was too young to be a journalist. Instead, like Robinson Crusoe, the boy still yearned to be a sailor; and just like Crusoe's father, Mr. Franklin was appalled by the idea.

In 1716 Josiah Junior had briefly returned to Boston, then left again and vanished forever, lost it was thought on a voyage to Asia. His father had been furious when the young man first went to sea, and he had no intention of allowing Benjamin to disappear in the same fashion. Another of his sons, John Franklin, trained as a tallow chandler, had recently married and begun making soap and candles in Newport, Rhode Island. This left the young Benjamin as the obvious successor in the family business at the Blue Ball. But he so clearly loathed the craft that his father knew he had to find him an alternative. It was at this point, in about 1717, when the boy was eleven, that Josiah took the boy around the town to watch artisans at work, in the hope that one of their trades might appeal.

Eventually Josiah settled for the obvious solution, by putting Benjamin out to be apprenticed to his cousin, Samuel the cutler. He did a spell as a sort of intern in Samuel's workshop, helping to make cutting tools, but Samuel demanded the usual London payment of a hefty fee for taking him on. Josiah refused, and Benjamin came back to the house on Union and Hanover. Then James arrived home from England, to find his youngest brother still without a trade, and still longing for the ocean. The boy liked the thought of printing rather better than the prospect of a life boiling soap. Even so he had to be coaxed or cajoled into becoming James's assistant.

Sixty years after the first of his uncles swore his indentures as a dyer in London, Benjamin Franklin became yet another apprentice, signing up to work for his brother. James insisted on nine years of service, rather than the usual seven, and eight of those would be unpaid. Benjamin's reward would come by way of literature.

Chapter Six

For the Love of Books

The perils of the ocean were all too plain to see in the fall of 1718, a season of storms and piracy. Eight miles out from Boston, on a slice of rock above the sandbanks, George Worthylake and his family tended the lighthouse that marked the way into the harbor. They were pious souls. On the first Sabbath day of November, they came into town to hear their pastor preach, only to capsize on their journey home. It was, said *The Boston News-Letter,* "an awful, lamentable Providence," the loss of six people by drowning, but the accident caught the journalistic eye of James Franklin.

His youngest brother had been writing verses since his infancy. So James set Benjamin to work to tell the lighthouse story in a ballad—"wretched stuff," Franklin recalled, but good enough to make some money—and then sent him out to hawk the printed version in the street. The ballad sold very well; and in March of 1719, the brothers tried to do the same again. Off the Carolina coast, two sloops of the Royal Navy had caught up at last with Blackbeard the pirate. With swords and pistols, they fought it out, killed Blackbeard, sliced off his head, and carried it home to claim their reward. When the news reached Boston, here was another story too good to miss.

Benjamin wrote a sea shanty about the incident, and it was printed too. But neither this nor the grievous tale of the Worthylakes met with his father's approval. At the time, the devout Josiah was hoping to be chosen as a deacon at the Old South—the ballot was in April, when he lost by a mile, polling only ten votes out of forty-one—and he did not care to see his youngest son indulge in vanity. Poetry was a waste of time, and men who followed that calling were usually beggars, Josiah told the boy. Doubtless he had in mind the tiresome old poet Uncle Benjamin, who was still intruding on his hospitality. However that may be, this was the moment—when he had just turned thirteen—at which young Franklin turned his back on a poetic career, after heeding his father's advice. Or so he claimed in his autobiography.

As so often with his streamlined version of events, Franklin's memoirs make things sound rather simpler than they were. He never shared his father's contempt for poetry. Far into his thirties he remained an avid consumer of the best of English verse. It was only when electricity became his passion that he ceased to keep up with the latest poems from London. Although he did not hope to be a professional maker of rhymes, until then in his hours away from the printing press he would turn for relaxation to Milton, Pope, and Dryden and their followers.

Because nobody reads their work today, except when forced to do so for a college grade or seminar, it is hard to conceive how much these poets meant to Americans in the eighteenth century. Not only were they seen as masters of rhythm, meter, and the purity of diction; they were also regarded as fountains of wisdom and enlightenment. In Milton, his readers beheld a poet who had clung to his vocation, even when laid low by poverty and blindness. And so women and men in the colonies, including Franklin, would make extracts from *Paradise Lost* or better still Pope's *An Essay on Man*, when it appeared in the 1730s, and compile them to form a personal philosophy, sometimes as a substitute for the Bible.

This kind of thing became a habit with Franklin, almost from the moment that he entered his teens. He began to live a double life, on the waterfront and in a small room lit by the candles his family had fashioned. By day, he was the printer's boy or the athlete, swimming in the Mill Pond and learning how to box. By night he was a scholar. Making friends with the bookstore apprentices, he could borrow what he wanted, so long as he returned the books by store opening time.

Ashamed of his poor start with sums at school, he pored over the standard English textbook, Edward Cocker's *Arithmetic,* and rapidly absorbed what it contained. Still in love with the sea, he studied books of navigation, picking up some geometry but never fully mastering its puzzles. Meanwhile, at the printing shop on Queen Street, between a schoolhouse and the Boston jail, James Franklin had assembled a coterie of friends who included a tanner by the name of Matthew Adams. Another member of the church in Brattle Square, Adams loved books, and he shared them with his protégé, the young Benjamin.

From his reading, from Mr. Pemberton's sermons, and from the talk around Josiah's supper table, the boy picked up the Boston habit of controversy. He also acquired a new acquaintance, John Collins, talkative, eloquent, and especially good at mathematics. Together they pondered the lofty questions that fascinate boys at puberty. Was it right that women and girls should be given an education? As their curiosity deepened about the females who surrounded them, the two boys debated the issue with enthusiasm. Girls were incapable of study, said Collins, and so sending them to school was wasteful and improper. Franklin argued the opposite; and as a way to hone his arguments, he wrote them down.

Like warring academics, he and Collins exchanged letters seeking to demolish each other's reasoning. Josiah read one of his son's, and he offered a critique of its prose. As a printer, Benjamin could spell and punctuate to perfection—throughout his life even his briefest, most casual notes were never slovenly—but he had yet to master the finer points of style. Franklin recalled that his father told him that he "fell far short in elegance of expression, in method and in perspicuity."

If these were Josiah's exact words, they were highly revealing. These were the very qualities—"perspicuity," and "method"—that Pastor Colman had singled out for praise in his eulogy of Mr. Pemberton. The Franklins had clearly been listening carefully. Josiah had intended his son for the church, and if he could not go to Harvard and become a minister at least he could speak or write like one. Here was the point that Josiah intended to make: that style, correct and orderly, could serve as an emblem of gentility. At Ecton and Banbury, the Franklins had yearned to be gentlemen, and—briefly, before the death of Thomas Junior—they had attained their goal. In America, they hoped to do the same: to be rightfully seen as the gentlemen they were, with their cleverness and their powers of application. And just at this moment, the young Benjamin Franklin discovered an author who could show him precisely what it meant to be polite.

Somehow—presumably, by way of Matthew Adams—he came upon the writings of Joseph Addison, some of whose essays Franklin knew almost by heart. There was a time, which persisted until the age of *Little Women,* when every schoolchild in America was supposed to know the work of Addison, because he was regarded as a model of good taste. You could not do better, or so it was thought, than the style of *The Spectator,* where Addison displayed his skills at their finest. It began as a daily magazine, founded in 1711 by Addison and his friend Sir Richard Steele, but soon their articles were bundled up into bound volumes, one of which Franklin read in Boston.

Franklin adored *The Spectator.* In its pages the boy discovered a flexible style that could lift him out of provincial life and make him an elegant man of letters and wisdom. Although it was a London paper, *The Spectator* had little else in common with the buccaneer journalism that James Franklin had seen in the empire's capital. While Nathaniel Mist and his weekly rivals were fiercely partisan, slugging away at each other with satire and invective, *The Spectator* posed as a journal of intelligent neutrality. As the title suggested, Addison and Steele pretended to rise above the din of party strife. Like people with the best seats in a theater—Addison also wrote for the stage—they surveyed the foibles of mankind from a vantage point of calm, good-humored objectivity. *The Spectator* claimed to be the voice of reason. It aspired to be urbane and civilized, always up-to-date with the latest affairs but never once succumbing to fads and foolishness.

Of course, the pose struck by *The Spectator* contained an element of make-believe. Far from being neutral, Addison belonged entirely to the Whigs; indeed, in 1716 the king appointed him as one of the realm's two secretaries of state. His politics were those the Franklins shared. Addison owed his political career to the Junto, the club of Whig grandees led by Charles Montagu, the Lord Halifax who had been the patron of Franklin's uncle Thomas. Later, in Philadelphia, the young Benjamin would borrow the name of Montagu's cabal and apply it to his own Junto, the club he founded for ambitious tradesmen.[1]

However, Addison's politics were not the thing that most appealed to the boy. What Franklin admired was his style, his method, and his metropolitan tone of skepticism and cool self-assurance. "There is nothing," wrote Addison, in the volume that Franklin read, "in which men more deceive themselves than in what the world calls Zeal." A man who was born to be a newspaper columnist, Addison could take an idea such as this—not very new, and really quite banal—and make it sound like the deepest of philosophy.

Addison would come at his subject from all angles, using all the weapons of irony and paradox. Throwing in anecdotes from history, Greek and Latin tags or lines of verse—most often from Milton or Dryden—he would display just enough scholarship to lend him authority but not so much as to be pedantic. Best of all, from Franklin's point of view, Steele and Addison would fill their pages with fictitious characters with names like Abraham Thrifty, Jack Modish, or Rebecca Nettletop. With a London accent, but in the different dialects of coachmen, milliners, jilted fiancées, and gentlemen of leisure, these invented citizens staged their own controversies. Addison made them nag away at the meaning of virtue, or the merits or the evils of ambition. They also had things to say about sex. Endlessly his characters talked about the rights and wrongs of chastity or wenching, the vagaries of gender, and the oddities of marriage.

Reading *The Spectator*, Franklin learned how to write with a flair that Pemberton or the Mathers could never manage. An exercise in ventriloquism, *The Spectator* showed him how to take the messy, mundane realities of life in Boston and make them into sparkling prose. In the miffy little world of the Franklins, there were incidents for a young writer to explore. One such occurred in the March of 1720—the boy was just fourteen—when his half-brother Samuel passed away. Born in Banbury, and raised as the last blacksmith in the clan, Samuel Franklin died in Boston at only thirty-eight. He left behind him four children, his widow, Elizabeth, and a sordid narrative of marital woe.

Only six months earlier, Uncle Benjamin had finally quit the Blue Ball. In the elegy he wrote for the blacksmith, the old man heaped abuse on Elizabeth, calling her a feckless gossip—"careless, sluttish, lazy and unfaithful"—and he implied that Josiah was to blame for his son's poor choice of a spouse. Like the saga of the Worthylakes, Samuel's early death was a tragedy; but in this family tale of adultery the young Franklin found excellent material. When the moment came, he would invent characters like Addison's and make them play the parts of Elizabeth and Samuel in his own first forays into journalism.[2]

In the meantime the boy had to perfect his style. He took items from *The Spectator*, and read them over and over again. He made brief notes and then—after a gap of a few days—he rewrote each one, comparing his effort with the original. "This was to teach me method in the arrangement of thoughts," Franklin remembered. As a way to extend his vocabulary he did it all again in verse, which called for a wider supply of words to fit the meter and the rhyme.

In its own way, it was a discipline as rigorous as mathematics, but the young Franklin did not make do with Addison alone. In search of new ways to win debates, he fell in love with Socrates as well as *The Spectator*. From the Greek thinker, he could learn how to trounce an opponent like John Collins without ruining a friendship with a show of bad temper. Some fifty years later a young admirer in England, the daughter of an Anglican bishop, would pay him a supremely flattering compliment, when she looked up from her book and exclaimed, "Mama! Socrates talks just like Dr Franklin!" She had been reading Xenophon's *Memoirs of Socrates,* filled with examples of the Socratic method of crushing the other party to a dispute by gently asking questions until the flaws in his reasoning are plainly disclosed.[3]

It was the very same book that Franklin studied in his teens, as he strove to master the Socratic technique for politely coming out on top. As he told his French friend Cabanis, "it was Socrates he wanted most to resemble," not only as a thinker but also as a human being. He aspired to be wise, modest, and generous, full of intellectual finesse and yet devoid of arrogance. Even in Paris, at nearly eighty, these were virtues Franklin did not always exhibit: he could also be devious and disorganized, and he tried to seduce other men's wives. And in his boyhood he irritated his neighbors almost as much as Socrates upset the Athenians.

Gradually, his reading opened a rift between the boy and his family. It grew still wider with the years and could never be entirely closed while his parents were alive. Reading obsessively, Franklin came to inhabit a world of blasphemous ideas about God and the cosmos that would horrify even the liberal clergymen at Brattle Square. In the eyes of Abiah and Josiah, these ideas would have been still more alarming—the stuff of mortal sin—if they had known precisely what their son believed, and where the logic of Socrates had led him.

In his sermons at the Old South, Pemberton had told the boy that religion had to measure up to reason. With his diluted form of Puritan belief, the pastor had dissolved old certainties; and so, following his advice, Franklin put the Christian God to the test of dialectic. He convicted God of failure. Full of what he read and bursting with intelligence, he chose to discard Josiah's Presbyterian creed.

In middle age, Franklin would find this aspect of his early life deeply embarrassing. As a man of substance, admired in America but increasingly at odds with the British, Franklin did not wish to be perceived as a libertine. For political reasons, he could not afford to be seen as a man who did not care for faith or conventional morality. And so he tried to suppress any evidence that at one time he had been so skeptical.

Even posthumously, in the pages of his memoirs where he dealt with the subject, Franklin preferred to be evasive about it. But when all the evidence is gathered in—and this is not an easy task—there can be no doubt about the truth. By the time he was nineteen, and working as a printer in London, Benjamin Franklin had become a defiant atheist. Later he changed his mind, acquiring in his mid-twenties a new personal religion, including belief in a Supreme Being, which owed a debt to Archbishop Tillotson as well as to the English poets; but he never recovered Josiah's form of Bible Christianity.

CRAZY WITH PHILOSOPHY

It took a while for the teenage Franklin to lose his faith. The process began in the traditional way: he skipped Sunday service at the Old South. Once indentured to James, he went into lodgings with James's other apprentices, away from Josiah's watchful eye. On the Sabbath, while everyone was at the meeting house, Franklin would find an excuse to shut himself up in the printing shop with his beloved books. Much of what he studied was austere and technical—*An Essay Concerning Human Understanding* by John Locke, and a French textbook of reasoning, *Logic, or the Art of Thinking* by Antoine Arnauld—but he read books like these with as much excitement as his uncle had found in Bunyan and the scriptures.

Ambitious though they were, the Franklins had never been purely career-minded people, narrowly focused on the main chance. Not Josiah, with his bold decision to leave Banbury on grounds of conscience; not Benjamin Senior, with his religious angst; not Thomas Junior, falling out with the Palmers at Ecton; not even the polite John Franklin, trying his hand at surgery and killing himself with a dirty needle. The family had a reckless streak. They courted controversy, and they loved travel and the sea. If they were miffy, it was because they were passionate as well.

We remember Franklin as the apostle of hard work, temperance, and self-control. This is the way he *hoped* to be remembered. But when a human being writes so much about prudence, virtue, and sobriety, it may be because he or she would prefer to be wild, intemperate, and rash. This seems to have been true of Franklin as a young man. In adolescence—when, for obvious reasons, his battle with his instincts was hardest to win—he became obsessed with philosophy. It was his way of coping with the troubling emotions that also made him yearn to be a sailor.[4]

His early reading in philosophy did many things for Benjamin Franklin. Like boxing, swimming, and building the wharf, it gave him an outlet for his energy. Like chess, it trained his mind; but it also started him thinking about politics, not as a professional career—he was never very good with speeches and elections—but as a means to human progress in pursuit of an ideal. Soon he fell under the influence of books by a strange but prolific English Baptist, Thomas Tryon. If Franklin was always a connoisseur of failure, intrigued by men and women who went astray, he also loved to meet eccentrics: people whose lifestyles and notions were unusual. And Tryon was certainly that: an eccentric but also a highly original thinker, with a vision of an alternative social order, built from a marriage of ingenuity and faith.[5]

Tryon was yet another London apprentice, from a generation slightly older than Josiah Franklin's. He grew up to become an English version of a Hindu holy man. Indeed Tryon wrote an imaginary dialogue in which a Brahmin priest became the spokesman for his ideas. Although some of his thinking resembled Defoe's—like Defoe, he urged his countrymen to devote themselves to "improvement," trade, and manufacturing—at heart Thomas Tryon was a mystic. At twenty-three he underwent a form of conversion. The path to wisdom lay by way of self-denial, he was told by God. And so, to cleanse his soul of vice, Tryon took to eating only bread and fruit and drinking only water.

Like the young Franklin, he was "mightily addicted to reading and study." In 1683, the year of crisis when Josiah left for the colonies, Tryon had published his masterpiece, *The Way to Health,* whose title Franklin would later borrow and adapt for a famous piece of writing of his own. In the book, Tryon designed an ideal commonwealth, whose citizens would live lives of charity, peace, and honest industry. Of course they would give up meat and alcohol. For Tryon, the drinking of wine and the eating of flesh had their roots in humanity's worst inclinations, or what he called "the high lofty spirit of wrath and sensuality." There had to be another way—"meek love," said Tryon—and he hoped to see it come to pass in America. He wrote to the Quakers who were sailing to Philadelphia, urging them not to hold slaves or hunt game.[6]

Somehow Tryon's work found its way to Franklin. In Plutarch, the Boston boy had already come across vegetarian ideas, because Plutarch the Greek was a moralist, a disciple of Plato and Pythagoras, and so he denounced all forms of luxury and wrote essays against the slaughter of animals. Tryon went a step further and produced a cookery book for vegetarians, containing recipes for porridge, onion soup, boiled cauliflower and cabbage—"for they purge by urine"—and his dish of choice: hasty pudding, made with milk, flour, water, and a dash of ginger.[7]

Entitled *The Way to Save Wealth: Shewing How a Man May Live Plentifully for Two-pence a Day,* the book became Franklin's dietary manual, with a host of austere menus to follow. He practiced hard, mastered the régime, and offered his brother a deal that James could not refuse. What if, every week, James paid him just half the money he spent on his board at the lodging house? Out of that, the apprentice would feed himself. Using Tryon's methods, Franklin soon found that he could survive on even less—he spent only half of what James gave him—and he used the spare cash as a fund for buying books. Better still, he could eat his biscuits, bread, and water at his workbench in the printing shop, reading all the time, while his colleagues wasted precious minutes going out for meals.

In his memoirs, Franklin dwells only briefly on this episode, as though it had been just an adolescent fad. But in his conversations in Paris with his young friend Cabanis, he insisted that it was Plutarch—an author whom French intellectuals revered—who inspired his vegetarian phase. This suggests that he never really dismissed it as a passing whim. Instead he always thought of it as his first serious essay in virtue. It seems that his mother agreed. Franklin told Cabanis that when his friends mocked him for refusing to eat meat or fish, Abiah replied that her son was *"un fou de philosophe"*—"a crazy philosopher"—and then she added in an undertone, "He's learning that with willpower, we can achieve anything."

He was also learning how to dismantle Christianity. In 1721, when he was just fifteen, Franklin read a course of lectures about science and religion that began to undermine his faith in the Bible. Because in his memoirs Franklin was a little vague about the details, it is impossible to say exactly which lectures they were. A little digging reveals that they must have been the work of one of two English clergymen: Samuel Clarke, who gave his lectures in 1704, or his brother John, whose turn came later. But since their views were identical, it does not really matter which of the brothers Franklin read.

Samuel Clarke was a controversial figure, rector of one of London's most fashionable churches. A scientist as well as a cleric—he belonged to the small elite who had fully grasped Newton's calculus—Mr. Clarke was widely suspected of heresy. He was said to be an Arian; or in other words, he denied the divinity of Jesus Christ. Although they meant to be defenders of orthodox belief, using Newton's model of the solar system to prove the existence of God, the Clarkes had an unfortunate tendency, often seen among clergymen who venture into physics. They tended to raise more questions than they answered; so that readers came away more baffled than they had been before.[8]

So it was with Franklin, who pored over what the Clarkes had to say. As he put it later, with a degree of understatement, they "wrought an effect on me quite contrary to what was intended." After reading their work, he became ever more doubtful about religion. In their lectures, the Clarkes had tried to bridge the gap between the deist and the Christian by invoking the essence of Newtonian physics. Gravity, said Newton, was a universal force, defined by equations, and sufficient to explain the motion of the planets. But gravity must have a cause, said the Clarkes; that cause was God; and if gravity acted everywhere, as it must, so too did God; and if God was universal, then his providence must be everywhere as well, by the Sea of Galilee, among the rings of Saturn, or in a pew in Boston or in London.

Were these arguments for God a plausible option? Possibly, thought Franklin, but not if they were coupled with the notion that the deity chose to come to earth in Roman Palestine. The boy could not subscribe to the teachings of Josiah's Christian church. "In short, I soon became a thorough Deist," he recalled in his autobiography. Then he moved on from the Clarkes to more compelling philosophers, who gradually led the young Franklin into the depths of apostasy. One of the authors he read was Lord Shaftesbury, the English accomplice of the skeptic, Pierre Bayle. Courteous and discreet, Shaftesbury sought to mend the holes in the fabric of belief by turning the Christian God into something different: not the Jesus of Calvary, or the Jehovah of Mount Horeb, but instead an aesthete and a gentleman. Here was a God that Franklin felt more inclined to worship.

In our love of beauty, wrote Lord Shaftesbury, we feel elevated, edified, and pious. Sin and evil are ugly; we perceive them as such; and when we do so we follow the best promptings of our nature. Human beings have a moral sense—this must be true, because instinctively, we know right from wrong—and it is identical with our sense of what is beautiful or hideous. But if this is so, said Shaftesbury, there must be a benevolent creator. Only an artistic God, who has made the moon and stars, the rainbow and the rose, could endow us with a soul that appreciates their beauty, and also feels the beauty of goodness.[9]

Put in this way, Shaftesbury's notions might sound shallow or naive. Be that as it may, his lordly vision of cosmic benevolence did not seem superficial to Franklin. It cannot be said too often that the Boston boy was vastly precocious. He simply would not stop until he had drilled down to what he took to be the bedrock of truth. This disposition began in Franklin's teenage years. It came to its fulfillment in his work with electricity; and it explains why, as a boy, he devoured the writings of philosophers such as Shaftesbury.

Intensely serious, even when he made a joke, Benjamin Franklin was not a man who could cease his exploration halfway. Like Tolstoy, the thinker whom sometimes he seems to resemble, Franklin had to arrive at a personal statement of his philosophy about God, about human nature, and about the place of human beings in the universe: a statement of belief that he could endorse without reservation. This statement might have to be secret, since otherwise it would open him to ridicule or worse. But just such a statement he had to find. It was what he was looking for when he read books with such a frenzy. Years afterward, in Philadelphia in the 1730s, Franklin would take Shaftesbury's ideas, develop them with the help of Tillotson and the poets, and make them into the personal creed, vague though it might be, that would carry him through to the end of his days.

Once he had accomplished that—and when he had made enough money, and acquired enough leisure, to permit him to do as he pleased—Franklin could move forward, and become a scientist. But all of this took many years of effort. In the meanwhile, Franklin had yearnings and emotions to deal with, a business to build, and other, more subversive notions to contemplate. Although he deeply admired Lord Shaftesbury, the English thinker who influenced Franklin the most in his youth was someone far more radical, who could never be described as naive. This was Anthony Collins, an ultra-Whig, whose writings were profane. By adopting his ideas, Franklin made himself a pariah in Boston.

The Gospel of Free Thought

John Locke the philosopher had many disciples, but none more controversial than Anthony Collins. Born into wealth, the son of a lawyer, Collins married an heiress from a banking family. Schooled at Eton and Cambridge, he served as a justice of the peace and displayed, like Thomas Franklin, the skills with tax and finance that Whigs such as Collins regarded as their forte. And yet this defender of good order in the state was also a cynic who dealt in heresy and scandal.

In 1713 the London hangman publicly burned his most notorious treatise, *A Discourse of Free Thinking.* Copies of the book found their way to Boston, where Franklin read it. In its pages he discovered some of the most radical ideas that Europe had to offer at the time. Anthony Collins adopted the philosophy of Bayle; and since the early 1700s, he had also been a close friend of John Toland. When the *Discourse* appeared, Collins and Toland were leading a club of freethinkers who met in a London coffeehouse, where they acquired their reputation as atheists.[10]

As an old man in Paris, Benjamin Franklin made it plain to Cabanis that he had found Collins fascinating. The date at which he came across the book cannot be fixed precisely, but a brief allusion in his memoirs suggests that it was soon after he had finished with the Clarkes. In other words, it was in 1721 or so, when he was still less than halfway through his teens. Although this was very, very young for Franklin to be delving so deeply, the books he had read, by John Locke and others, had prepared him to assimilate what Collins had to offer.

Collins's favorite word was "absurdity." By that, he meant anything we cannot prove, from the evidence of our senses or with logic and with mathematics. Here he was following the teachings of Locke, but he went far further than Locke had dared to go. For Collins, history amounted to an endless struggle to free the minds of human beings from what he called "the dictates of . . . crack-brain'd enthusiasts." By this, he meant mystics, zealots, and the vast majority of clergymen. "Priests are hired," Collins wrote in the *Discourse,* "to lead men into mistakes." Superstition was the source of all evil, he believed. He devoted many pages to the nonsense to which religion gave rise: the stock in trade of self-seeking pastors, men who loved their stipends more dearly than the truth.[11]

At one point, Collins took issue with the King James translation of the Bible, calling it "a pious fraud." This, it seems, was the feature of the *Discourse* that caused most offense. At times, he inserted notes of caution, so that he could pretend that he was only vilifying false images of God, while remaining a Christian of a kind. Few of his readers would agree that Collins was any such thing. In his catalogue of absurdities, he included not only the belief in witchcraft—he was outraged by the idea of witch trials—but also every sacred dogma of the Church. Original sin, hellfire, and the Holy Trinity: none of them survived his test of reason. As for the soul's immortality, Collins quoted Cicero to raise grave doubts about its likelihood.

If any section of the *Discourse* came to be a favorite with Franklin, it must have been the closing pages. At the climax of the book, Collins made a list of nineteen enemies of superstition, heroes who epitomized the virtues of free thought. The list began with the boy's beloved Socrates—"the divinest man that ever appear'd in the heathen world," said Collins—it included Plutarch, and it ended with John Tillotson. Perhaps it was as well that the archbishop had been dead for nearly twenty years, because he would have been horrified by the use to which Mr. Collins put his sermons.[12]

"We are to govern ourselves by our natural notions," Tillotson had said; but Collins wrenched the words from their context, making them part of his tirade against the clergy. On his list, he placed Tillotson next to the infamous Thomas Hobbes, whose name had become a synonym for disbelief in God. Nailing his colors to the mast, Anthony Collins praised Hobbes the philosopher as a "great instance of learning, virtue and free thinking." This was more or less a confession by Collins that he was an infidel too.

What did Franklin bring away from the *Discourse*? For one thing, Collins took a wrecker's ball to his Christian faith, which was already very shaky. One sentence in the book seems to have made an especially deep impression on the boy. In describing the qualities of Socrates, Collins says that he "had the common fate of free-thinkers, to be calumniated in his life-time for an Atheist." After reading that, Franklin might respond in two different ways.

Either he could embrace the fate of Socrates, and go about the town of Boston causing trouble, teasing his neighbors about their beliefs. This option was the more courageous. It was also the one more likely to end badly, as it had for Socrates, martyred with a dose of hemlock. Alternatively, Franklin might choose to be an entertainer. He could make his freethinking take the form of satire, hiding his radicalism behind a mask of irony. This second course of action was the safer bet, if one could keep the humor flowing.[13]

In his youth, Franklin switched back and forth between these two strategies, until he discovered which one was more effective in the era of King George I. Soon enough an opportunity arrived for him to display his ingenuity. While he was eating cabbages and musing on philosophy, his brother James had been hard at work, building his business. The moment was approaching when James could apply in America the lessons he had learned in London about the trade of journalism.

The Island of Insania

In the March of 1719, as Franklin sold his pirate ballad on the street and Josiah ran for office at the Old South, another election took place in Boston. Victory went to a group of populists, who swept the board in the poll to choose new men to manage the town's affairs. Led by a physician, Elisha Cooke Jr., the popular party repeated their success two months later. In the ballot for the colony's House of Representatives, the Cooke-ites won all four seats from Boston.

Until Cooke's death in 1737, his electoral machine held sway in Massachsetts. Although he was a Harvard man, Dr. Cooke had the common touch; and this—together with his money—was the secret of his success. Cooke wrote well, and he drank heavily. With his dealing in real estate he made himself perhaps the richest resident of Boston. Here was a fellow who knew how to win elections by campaigning hard for popular causes. When the time came, he could also dole out the beer and the tax breaks to those Bostonians who turned out to vote.[14]

Elisha Cooke made public affairs entertaining. In doing so, he opened the way for James Franklin to launch *The New-England Courant*. In the atmosphere that Cooke created, the *Courant* could flourish, at least for a while, filling a need for sharp, irreverent opinion of a kind to dismay the likes of Cotton Mather or Judge Sewall. Moreover, in the New England of the 1720s there were genuine issues that had to be debated. Although his enemies saw Cooke as a drunken demagogue, in fact he had important things to say; and in his better moments, he said them with eloquence and wit.

A forerunner of Samuel Adams, whose father was one of his supporters, Dr. Cooke yearned to take the colony back to the days before the 1680s, when Massachusetts had enjoyed something close to independence. Since this was out of the question, he made do with campaigns against specific grievances inflicted by the British. In the forests of Maine, where Cooke owned tracts of land, the king laid claim to the tallest trees as masts for the Royal Navy. Tyranny, said Dr. Cooke; and even worse, the British were bent on nailing the Americans to a cross of gold. As the currency for payment of taxes, or to settle debts the colonists owed in London, the British insisted on nothing but hard cash: best of all gold sovereigns, or failing that the Spanish silver dollar.

Time and again, the politics of money, banking, inflation, and so forth have loomed very large in the history of America, and for Benjamin Franklin, young or old, they were always a subject he found fascinating. His exposure to the issues had its origins in the New England of the early 1720s, where, after a period of buoyancy, the economy had slumped back into recession. The problem was partly this: in Boston they had too little of the bullion that the British demanded. As a remedy, Cooke wanted to issue paper money, backed either by a new institution, a land bank that could issue mortgages, or by the revenue he could raise from taxes. This was something the royal governor of Massachusetts, Samuel Shute, simply refused to allow.*

Shute had arrived in 1716, only to find that Cooke and his allies could reduce him to impotence. Although the governor had powers of veto, so that he could block any Cooke-ite measures he disliked, he could not be sure of his salary, because the House of Representatives always had the power of the purse. On the frontier another war was looming with the Abenaki, but Shute could not obtain the resources he required: the House refused to vote the money. He wrote a stream of letters home to London, complaining about Elisha Cooke.

In the eyes of some members of the colony's elite, including Cotton Mather the pastor, it seemed that Cooke the drunkard was leading Massachusetts to disaster. When the British read the governor's dispatches, surely they would lose their patience with the colony? The king might impose direct rule, doing away with what the province still possessed by way of autonomy. In print and in private letters, Mather fumed at the doctor and his friends, calling them "idiots and fuddle caps," who would arouse the wrath of George I. By this time *Robinson Crusoe* had appeared in London and also made it to America, where readers adored the novel quite as much as did their English cousins. And so, in a clumsy attempt to be witty, Mather wrote a pamphlet to which he gave the title *News from Robinson Crusoe's Island.*[15]

It appeared in the summer of 1720. A few weeks earlier, Governor Shute had outraged the House by blocking their choice of Dr. Cooke as speaker. Mather intervened on the governor's side, depicting Massachusetts as "the Island of Insania." The people receive a visit from Crusoe, warning them about the consequences of their folly. It was a heavy-handed joke, and it met with a far funnier rebuke from Elisha

* By coincidence, the governor was the nephew of the earlier Samuel Shute, the Whig who in the 1680s led the London company of dyers to which Josiah Franklin had belonged.

Cooke. He wrote his own little piece and called it—what else?—*More News from Robinson Crusoe's Island.*

In time the crisis subsided, to become a stalemate, in which Dr. Cooke and his followers blocked most of what Shute wished to do, while in London the authorities had too much else to occupy their minds to bother with a clash with a colony so remote. But while it lasted, the fracas between Cooke, Mather, and the governor helped create the market James Franklin required for *The New-England Courant.* In Boston, the people he wanted as his readers were eager to have a newspaper that engaged in this type of affray, but with a lighter, still more entertaining touch.

While Mather and Cooke were at each other's throats, James had begun to diversify his business, but only slowly so. A new publication—*The Boston Gazette*—had recently appeared on the scene to compete with the *News-Letter.* For seven months, until he lost the contract in August of 1720, James Franklin printed the *Gazette;* but although this must have been commercially worthwhile, the paper broke little new ground. It was mostly the same old stuff, of the kind the *News-Letter* contained: endless diplomatic news from Europe, lists of ship arrivals and departures, and advertisements for hardware, molasses, and African slaves.

In amongst the verbiage, however, there were brief reports about a financial crisis in London. By the end of November, Bostonians knew that at last, after a summer of rampant speculation in its stock, the South Sea Company stood upon the brink of ruin. With a grandiose scheme, first to take over Britain's National Debt, and then to pay a rich dividend from its trading in the tropics, the company had drawn in the greedy and the gullible. The scheme was absurd and the promoters dishonest. Soon enough the South Sea Bubble burst, threatening to bring down the banking system. As the markets fell, and stories spread of misconduct in high places, the Whig administration seemed likely to collapse. With a general election drawing near in England, this left Mr. Shute as the lamest of lame ducks. Appointed by the Whigs, the governor could not expect to retain his post.

In Boston, which relied so heavily on credit from London, 1721 seemed likely to be a year of deeper economic hardship and yet more political controversy. For the Franklins, the situation could not have been more helpful. They had a talent for being in the right place at the right moment—the Franklins were a family that made its own luck—and now the time arrived for James to seize the publishing initiative.

With Cooke and Mather still in the news, the paper money question now more relevant than ever, and with the fate of the Massachusetts charter still hanging in the air, he would have no shortage of material. James Franklin began the new year with a burst of activity to replace the business he had lost from the *Gazette*. In 1719, he had printed only eight books and pamphlets, and in 1720 only five. In 1721, James printed more than twenty, some for booksellers and some his own commissions from the author. It was a risky way of doing business, but the books were highly topical. Plunging into economics, James Franklin published three pamphlets in defense of paper money, written by an ally of the Cookeites, Dr. John Wise, a pastor and a forceful writer, and an old foe of the Mathers. Calling himself "a freeborn Englishman," Wise spoke the political language that the Franklins knew so well from the London of the Whigs.

To make his own position clear, James revived a minor English classic, reprinting a user's manual of Whiggery with the title of *English Liberties.* Written in 1682 by Henry Care, a pioneer of London journalism, it was partly a simplified legal textbook, defending trial by jury and the like, but it also contained a brief history of England with Magna Carta as the central episode. For Benjamin Franklin, the book would become another constant companion. It amounted to a source book of ideas that he would draw upon until the 1770s, when Americans replaced it with better treatises of their own. In Philadelphia, Franklin sold *English Liberties* from his store, finding readers among local politicians who needed a digest of principles.

When James Franklin invoked the ghost of Henry Care, he also made a statement about the kind of journalism he intended to pursue. Another prolific writer, Care had been known in his heyday as "ingenious Harry," a comedian as well as a political commentator. "Everything is big with jest," he once wrote, "if we have but the wit to find it out." By the time he died in 1688 he had established in England the image of the journalist as maverick: courageous, funny, and inventive, and unafraid to go to jail for libel.[16]

Care's work had been the inspiration not only for Defoe, but also—with a delay of thirty years—for the combative weekly journals that James had seen in London. In response to the South Sea crisis, the English weeklies revived the legacy of Henry Care and went on a crusade against the government, with Nathaniel Mist in the front rank of satire. Some of the most outspoken writers were a team of radical Whigs on *The London Journal* who opposed the men in power and produced a series,

Cato's Letters, that came to be immensely popular in the colonies: and especially with the Franklin brothers, who would raid them for copy.

Their articles traveled to New England, where the British papers arrived in the spring of 1721 with the full story of the Bubble and its aftermath. In Boston, where James and his printing press were now so well established, with a store, a clientele, and friends who were eager to write, the time had come at last to launch a colonial equivalent. If James aspired to be the Cato or the Mist of Massachusetts, all he needed was a story that would run and run: a story as engrossing for his readers as *Robinson Crusoe* or the South Sea Bubble had been for their counterparts in London.

The story James required was about to break. There had been a pestilence in Spain and France, a sickness so fearful that the British had begun to close their harbors. In April the disease arrived in Massachusetts, carried in on a ship of the Royal Navy. Governor Shute declared an epidemic. It was smallpox; and while for many it brought death or disfigurement, there were some people, including the Franklins, for whom affliction spelled opportunity. The *Courant* was about to be born.

Part Three

The Breakout

Chapter Seven

The New-England Courant

By the middle of 1721 the governor was in despair, and in Boston the people were counting their dead. At the end of July they reckoned up the total: eighteen already, and each week the burials became more frequent. Out at Cambridge, Mr. Shute dissolved the House of Representatives. Time and again, Elisha Cooke and his party—"a few designing persons," as the governor described them—had stood in his way, as he did his best for the public good. This time they had gone too far, when they blocked his plan to crack down on the smuggling of French silk, which he believed carried the taint of infection.[1]

In Boston, the onset of the smallpox led to yet another feud in a town addicted to dispute. Once again Cotton Mather was in the thick of it. Eight years earlier the minister had lost his wife and three of his children to an epidemic of measles; and so he had scanned the scientific literature in search of a means of protecting the town from disease. In 1716 he came across the practice of inoculation, used by doctors in Turkey and described in a paper from the Royal Society in London. Take a person with smallpox, and from the pustules on their skin remove some fluid. If the pus were conveyed to the blood of a healthy individual, the outcome would be a mild fever, followed by immunity.

When the smallpox arrived in Boston in April, Mather urged his medical friends to use the new technique. Two blocks from the Franklin house, there lived a surgeon and apothecary named Zabdiel Boylston, expert at speedily cutting a malignant breast from a woman. Late in June, he began to inoculate, with some success, starting with his son and two African slaves. He found himself an object of hatred in the streets.

The Puritan minister Cotton Mather (1663–1728): tireless preacher, prolific writer on history, science, and much else, and pastor of Boston's Second Church. Frequently the object of satire in *The New-England Courant,* Mather cast a long shadow in Boston. From a painting by Peter Pelham, ca. 1728.

Undeterred by threats of a lynching, Boylston stood his ground and carried on inoculating. On July 17 he placed a notice in *The Boston Gazette,* where it ran beneath an account of the political crisis in London. His intention: to defend a procedure that came, as he put it, "well recommended from gentlemen of figure and learning." With that the smallpox controversy began: a matter of insults, animosity, and even violence, that would last the length of the epidemic and draw to a close only the following spring.

The notice aroused the wrath of Dr. Cooke. He summoned Boylston to a public hearing on July 21, to be vilified by his rivals, the physicians of Boston. Cooke and his friends ordered the surgeon to cease the inoculations, and then they took to the press to slander him in print. They called him rash and negligent, and accused him of spreading the infection. The author was a Scotsman, William Douglass, the only medic in Boston who had qualified at a British university. Of this he was inordinately proud. A doctor who met him in the 1740s called Douglass "the most complete snarler I ever knew."

Only one body of men dared to defend Boylston: the clergymen, led by the Mathers and Benjamin Colman. All his life, Cotton Mather had studied science and astronomy but also spoken of the Christian duty to "do good"—he had written a treatise, *Bonifacius,* on that very subject—

and in the practice of inoculation he found an excellent example. On the last day of July the *Gazette* ran an open letter from the pastors in which they came to Boylston's rescue. He was a "good Genius," they said. Inoculation was safe, a conclusion reached by "men of piety and learning after serious thought." With that turn of phrase, Cotton Mather and his friends exposed their weakest flank: their arrogant reliance on their rank and title.

In the wake of the South Sea Bubble, authority was under siege on both sides of the Atlantic. In this climate of disrespect, no one could hope to win an argument, whatever it concerned, merely by affirming that something must be true because a learned minister from Oxford or from Harvard said it was so. Especially when the voters were against them. Two days later Boston went to the polls. Again they sent Elisha Cooke and his allies to the House of Representatives, where Dr. Cooke would be the Speaker.

And then on Monday, August 7, at threepence a copy, at last *The New-England Courant* entered the fray. Sold from James's store or home delivered by young Benjamin, it was just two sides of a sheet of paper, but it promised to be all things to all people. As the masthead put it, the *Courant* would be a "Jack of all Trades."

The Compass of Truth

To begin with there was nothing courageous about the *Courant.* At first James Franklin merely swam with the tide, flowing as it was in favor of Dr. Cooke and the anti-inoculators. As it happens, Dr. Douglass was a neighbor of the Franklins, living across the street at the Green Dragon. The Franklins had their own doctor, who had failed to relieve Uncle Benjamin from a chronic dose of eczema; but James also knew the conceited Scot, doubtless as a customer for books. In the first issue of the *Courant,* Douglass wrote a column sneering at the pastors, calling them "profoundly ignorant."

This set the tone for the first three weeks of James's paper. Its pages were filled with satirical abuse, aimed at Boylston and his allies, attacks that became more personal as each issue went by. By now the schools were closed for fear of contagion, and the death rate was increasing rapidly. There were fifty burials in August and more than 130 in September. In a Boston where people met warily in the streets, watching each other for the first signs of fever, the *Courant* played upon the fear that hung over the waterfront. It was only human to look for somebody to blame. So the *Courant* made a scapegoat out of Boylston and the ministers, for spreading what the paper called "the artificial pox."

What did Benjamin Franklin make of all this? Fifty years later, when he came to write his memoirs, although he told the story of the *Courant* he did not mention the smallpox controversy. By then, Franklin had long been a convert to inoculation. His silence implies that he felt uncomfortable about the memory of his and James's role in the affair. Certainly, Franklin was fully involved. The only reason we know who wrote each article is that he kept a personal file of the *Courant.* He marked each issue with the authors' names, suggesting that he set them up in type himself. But he was still only fifteen; and his brother James had a temper. It was commonplace for masters to beat apprentices. James often used his fists on his brother; and frequently Josiah had to intervene. So whatever Franklin thought about the *Courant*'s campaign against inoculation, he had little choice but to lend a hand.

As the weeks went by, the campaign became so abusive that readers began to fall away. In the fourth issue James had to climb down a little, with a column by a clergyman from Boston's only Anglican church, King's Chapel: it was anti-inoculation, but politely so. Beneath it, James printed some verses of his own, mourning "the loss of youth" and putting the epidemic down to vengeance by the Lord for the sins of the people. Indeed the poem was so pious that it reads ironically, as though really James was making fun of that kind of theology.

The truth was surely this: James Franklin did not care one way or the other about the rights and wrongs of the smallpox debate. It was merely a fertile source of copy. In launching the *Courant,* it seems that he had two goals in mind: not to get rich—if that had been his aim, he would have gone into real estate—but to make a splash. First and foremost, he wanted the *Courant* to be a metropolitan paper, like the London weeklies, with the same variety of content, writing as good as Defoe's, and a circulation that extended way beyond Boston, as far as Long Island Sound and up into New Hampshire.

Of course James Franklin had his own opinions. They were very clear, from the many clues he left in the pages of his paper. The authors his brother knew—Addison, Defoe, the English deists, and John Tillotson—had made their mark on James as well. Time and again, their names or long quotations from their writings popped up in the *Courant.* It was

James's way of saying what he wanted to be: a cool, modern man of wit and style, who had been to London and risen above the prejudice and bigotry of Boston.

If the Franklins were artisans, they could be gentlemen too: this was the point he intended to put across. In London, if you wished to be genteel you were supposed to be broad-minded. And so James—like *The Spectator*—tried not to be pigeonholed as a creature of party politics. "Let impartiality be your constant motto, and truth be the compass by which you steer," said the *Courant* on November 20, and much of the time his paper fulfilled that ideal.

Loosely aligned though he was with Cooke, James Franklin did not wish to be the doctor's megaphone. And so he never made personal attacks on the royal governor. James also steered clear of the paper money question, and the wrangling about the Maine lumber trade: tedious subjects, long since done to death. Instead, it was religion that kept coming back as the *Courant*'s favorite topic. Not that James held any strong views about God. It was simply that by making fun of ministers and dogma, he could show what a sophisticated gentleman he was. And it made his readers laugh.

All the time, James tried to push back the boundaries. In his first few issues, he gave space to a writer who could be labeled a subversive. John Checkley kept a store, selling medicine, books, and tobacco, and in his spare time he enjoyed making fun of Puritans. An Anglican who worshipped at King's Chapel, he had refused to swear allegiance to the king: which meant that Checkley was what the British called a "non-juror." In other words, he was more or less a Jacobite, like Nathaniel Mist in London. In Boston, that was quite enough to put him beyond the pale of respectability.

Soon enough, Checkley was fired from the *Courant*, but the fact that he had been there at all was bad enough in the eyes of the orthodox. James Franklin had to try to get the balance right: to be polemical, but not to be shrill; to be satirical, but not just sarcastic; and to make the *Courant* entertaining, not only for mechanics and gentlemen, but also for ladies and mechanics' wives. He turned for help to his club of companions, of whom the cleverest was Nathaniel Gardner.

Gardner was a tanner, like his friend Matthew Adams, who had given young Benjamin the run of his library. That autumn, as the smallpox continued—in October, more than four hundred people died—so

Nathaniel came to the fore in the *Courant.* He was another fine writer, steeped in Defoe and Addison. Gardner was especially good at writing parodies of hellfire sermons given by the pastors.

In the autumn, they relaunched the *Courant,* to escape from the crude invective of the first four issues. They gave themselves a name—"a most generous club of Honest Wags"—and issued a declaration of their principles. Their mission? To provide "nothing but what is innocently diverting," even when they wrote about inoculation. The *Courant* would contain "a full and methodical account of foreign and domestic affairs," and something amusing in every edition. "Give us but the hint," wrote Nathaniel Gardner, "and we will furnish you with a charmingly various as well as copious supply."

Of course, wit and variety were more easily promised than achieved. When there was nothing else to write about, inoculation kept recurring as a theme. Often the *Courant* had to rely on long extracts from the English weeklies, especially *The London Journal,* the voice of Mr. Cato and the radical Whigs. Time and again, the writers of the *Courant* plagiarized the British authors they loved.

In November a storm blew up that might have sunk the *Courant* before it was five months old. With the smallpox controversy still raging, Mather chanced to meet James Franklin in the street. "The plain design of your paper," said the pastor, "is to banter and abuse the ministers of God." A fair point; and then, within forty-eight hours of their encounter, under cover of night someone tossed a makeshift hand grenade through Mr. Mather's window.

The fuse went out, but attached to the bomb was a note: "COTTON MATHER, You dog, Damn you; I'll inoculate you with this." At this awkward moment, when he might have been accused of complicity in the crime, James kept his nerve and did not apologize for something for which he was not responsible. Instead he printed a full report of the outrage, and advertised the governor's reward for the name of the culprit. In the next issue, he set Gardner to work with another parody of Mather's learned style.[2]

In the fall the *Courant* had begun to hit its stride. At its best, it was bright and lively, with a blend of satire, crime, and human interest—a horrid murder in Rhode Island, or a man who castrated himself in Connecticut—together with tabloid items from the English papers. Much of the content was trivial, but it was never boring. And in amongst the jokes James had a serious purpose: to open a window for his readers, to let in the sunlight and fresh air, and to expose hypocrisy and deceit. As Gardner put it in the *Courant:* the paper existed "to promote enquiries after truth, quicken and rouse the slothful, and animate and inspire the dull."

Among the readers it aroused, the one we remember was Benjamin Franklin. He listened with mounting excitement as James and his friends preened themselves on the paper's success. Soon it occurred to the boy that he could compose columns as sparkling as Gardner's. Starting in the fall of 1721, the *Courant* had been running a series on *The Spectator*'s old theme of the battle of the sexes, featuring a cast of jilted bachelors, cuckolds, henpecked husbands, and "boisterous wives" with names like Fanny Mournful. Having worked so hard to master Addison's style, and having seen so much miffiness in his family, surely he could do as well, or better, with some ventriloquism of his own?

There was just one obstacle to overcome. If James was a bully, he was unlikely to welcome his brother as a rival with the pen. So the boy had to bide his time. His moment arrived in the spring of 1722, when Benjamin had just turned sixteen. The *Courant* needed new material. At last the epidemic was over, and the quarrels about inoculation had faded away. Despite the threat of war with the Abenaki, in Boston for the moment all was quiet. During the winter, James had once again copied his London models, Mr. Mist and the others, by pursuing a crude vendetta against a publishing rival: the town's postmaster, who edited *The Boston Gazette.* But this was another well of inspiration fast running dry.

And then one morning, when the printers unlocked the workshop, they found on the floor a paper, unsigned and written in a hand that had been artfully disguised. It was a brilliant comic sketch. Gardner and the others praised it to the skies, trying to guess who the author might be. Their new star writer had arrived.

Silence Dogood

"The venomous itch of scribbling is hereditary," the *Courant* had said in January. Meant as another insult to Cotton Mather and his father, the comment was an apt description of the Franklins too. The anonymous item was Benjamin's work. Like James's columns it carried a sharp edge of satire aimed at the pious heart of Boston. More pieces of the same kind—ironic, facetious, and just the right length—soon appeared on the doormat in the same clandestine way. The first one was printed in the *Courant* of April 2.

Unaware that his brother was the author, James began to publish the sketches as a series running every fortnight until October. There were fourteen in all. Written with flawless grammar and syntax, and with diction almost as wide as Addison's, they were polite in their style but often very impolite in their content. That was the point. Purporting to be letters to the editor, they carried the fake byline of a clever, very nubile widow lady in her twenties, her name being Silence Dogood.

Although her husband had been a country clergyman, and although she claimed to be "an enemy to vice, and a friend to virtue," somehow she had acquired a talent for the double entendre, extending to jokes about erections.* That was another big part of the fun. All his life Franklin loved hoaxes. Although sometimes the sketches made a political point, they were really one long charade, an exercise in literary cross-dressing, written by a youth with many things on his mind, with sex among the uppermost.[3]

All the vices of Boston were exposed. Drunkenness, always the curse of the town; hypocrisy, likewise; and the dark underworld of the waterfront. The best of the series came toward the end, on September 24, when Silence described a moonlight stroll. Out she goes, for a break from her books and her prayers, into a night-town filled with immorality. In the very first sketch, Franklin had dropped a hint that her mother was another kind of lady of the night—she was "put to hard shifts for a living"—and here the innuendo reappears.

On the street, Silence runs into some drunken ramblers, speaking in "a confusion of tongues," who accuse her of being a female of bad character: why else would a single woman be out so late? Next she encounters a gaggle of seamen, arm in arm with their harlots, spouting the jargon of the sea and staggering toward the Common for some fornication on the grass. Full of rum, Jack and Betty fall over, leaving Mrs. Dogood to reflect on the benefits conferred by prostitutes. Night walkers are agents of charity, she writes, who minister to "the health and satisfaction of those who have been fatigued with business."

In this, the last but one of the sketches, Franklin took his teenage fascination with sex, worked it over in the style of Addison, and added firsthand observation of what occurred by night in a seaport filled with whores and mariners and widows left destitute by husbands lost at sea. In Boston the Common served as a brothel in the open air. No other

* On May 22 for example: "Women are the prime cause of a great many male enormities."

writer dared capture the town's underside in this way. In London that year, Defoe brought out his novel about a young woman alone in the city, "put to hard shifts" of petty crime and adultery and something close to prostitution. We cannot say exactly when Franklin read *Moll Flanders,* but in later life he knew and admired the book. In the Dogood letters he covered the same territory: another sign of just how precocious he was.[4]

Up to a point, the letters resembled Gardner's columns, reading like another homage to *The Spectator,* but they had something else that was very new. Hidden just a little way beneath the surface, there lay the author's boyhood and his own obsessions. From behind the mask of Mrs. Dogood, he explored issues of his own that had nothing much to do with Puritan guilt. Being Franklin's other self, Silence had many things in common with the boy.

She too was a Whig, calling herself "a mortal enemy to arbitrary government and unlimited power." Indeed one sketch was just a long quotation from the series, *Cato's Letters,* that had run in *The London Journal.* Like Franklin, she had been apprenticed to a trade. In her teens, like him she had spent much of her time alone, "reading ingenious books." And her fictional father and mother had sailed as immigrants from England, like Josiah and Anne Franklin forty years before. In Silence's case, the male parent met an untimely end on the ship, lost overboard at the moment of her birth, leaving his widow penniless in a new continent.

Something made Franklin wish to write about the lives of newcomers to the colonies, arriving without friends or a career, just as Josiah had done. He also wanted to write about how it felt to be excluded. Franklin was the tallow chandler's son who had been denied a place at college. That was something he always resented; and so Harvard appeared in the fourth of the Dogood letters, as a target of satire for its vanity. Rich parents sent their sons to college, said Mrs. Dogood, only to have them come home "as great blockheads as ever, only more proud and conceited." From one point of view, the Harvard sketch was no more than a clever pastiche of a piece by Addison, in which *The Spectator* made fun of the Bank of England. From another, it was a cry from the heart by a gifted boy shut out of academia.

Because the sketches were brief and meant to be read just once, then cast aside, and because the author was still so young, none of his themes was fully explored. Franklin merely played with them, showing off his cleverness while revealing something of his adolescent self. But there was one thing no one could fail to notice. By running the series, the *Cou-*

rant insulted Cotton Mather again, and with the worst possible taste. The title alluded to the pastor's tract, *Bonifacius,* with its message that we should all "do good." With that, they were making fun of the minister. As for "Silence," that was nothing better than a snide little joke with which they were mocking the afflicted.

The previous September, Mather had lost not only his beloved daughter Abigail to a fever, which may have been the smallpox, but also her daughter, a newborn girl. Over their coffin he preached a sermon in praise of patience in the face of tragedy. The sermon was published late in 1721 as *Silentarius,* or *The Silent Sufferer.* And that was how Mrs. Dogood came to be called "Silence," in a vicious allusion to the pastor's grief. It was a way for the *Courant* to hit Dr. Mather where it was most painful.

When you are running a newspaper, and trying to be popular, you cannot make the omelette without cracking eggs. And if your star writer is still in his teens, the outcome is likely to be all the more messy. Even so, this was a cruel form of journalism. It is scarcely surprising that when Benjamin wrote his memoirs he was stricken with what seems to have been another fit of embarrassment. Although he referred to the sketches, he left out the name of Silence Dogood, and so these early writings could not be identified as his. Not until 1868 did a scholar confirm that the Dogood columns were his work.

As an old man, Franklin tried to make amends to the Mathers, in two letters to Cotton's son Samuel. Written eleven years apart, in 1773 and 1784, they praised Increase and Cotton for their piety and scholarship. Both letters contained an anecdote about a meeting with the pastor. According to Franklin, as a youth he went to see Cotton Mather, chatted with him in his library, and then turned to leave along a passageway. "Stoop! Stoop!" cried the minister, but even so the youth hit his head on a low-hanging beam. Mather drew a pious moral from the accident. "You are young and have the world before you," he said. "Stoop as you go through it, and you will miss many hard thumps." It was a lesson he took to heart, Franklin claimed: "I often think of it when I see pride mortified, and misfortunes brought upon people by their carrying their heads too high."[5]

A charming little story: but did it really happen in quite the way Franklin described it fifty years or so after the event? He does not tell us what reason he might have had to visit Cotton Mather; the incident does not appear in his memoirs; and it seems that Franklin never mentioned it to anybody else. Perhaps the anecdote was entirely faithful to the facts.

Or perhaps—and I think this is more probable—Franklin took a nugget of truth, a fleeting encounter with the Boston pastor, and then developed the tale to create a diplomatic piece of partial make-believe intended to please Samuel Mather by showing what an amiable man his father had been. Nor were these letters the only occasion when the elderly Franklin went out of his way to be charming to the Mathers. In about 1789, while revising his memoirs, Franklin inserted a vague little sentence that looks like another attempt to apologize to the family for the insults the *Courant* had heaped on Cotton Mather's shoulders.

What Franklin wrote was this: that his boyhood reading of Mather's *Bonifacius* "perhaps gave me a turn of thinking that had an influence on some of the principal future events of my life." Relying on this rather flimsy statement, many scholars have argued that Cotton Mather was the inspiration of Franklin's career in public service. Maybe: but more likely not. In the 1740s and 1750s, when Franklin was entering politics, helping to create in Pennsylvania a militia and a college, and working on a host of patriotic projects, he wrote a vast amount: pamphlets, columns, memos, and letters in their hundreds. In those that have survived, not once did he refer to Cotton Mather or his books.[6]

So Franklin's statement about Mather's influence may have been another diplomatic fib, meant perhaps to appeal to readers from New England. As an envoy in Paris, Franklin knew how to tell a gentle fib when a fib was required: that is what ambassadors do. There is one thing of which we can be certain. Whatever Franklin felt about Cotton Mather after the pastor's death, the *Courant* was never anything but scathing about him in his lifetime.

As each issue of the *Courant* hit the streets, the moment drew nearer when Franklin would have to break out of Boston. You could not write so well, and so satirically, without upsetting powerful people: not only Cotton Mather, but also Josiah's old comrade in prayer, Judge Sewall, who sat on the governor's council of advisers. And a terminal breach was all the more likely if the Franklins were determined to get themselves into trouble.

The two brothers shared the Franklin trait of miffiness. Being the man he was, James had indeed felt envious when at last, toward the end of the Dogood series, his brother revealed that he was the author. As Benjamin grew in prestige with James's friends, the miffiness increased between the siblings. Bored and frustrated with being an apprentice, Benjamin wanted his freedom. In the meantime, however, he and James made common cause by turning their miffiness outward, in defense of the freedom of the press. Toward the end of 1722, they seized another chance to be outstandingly offensive; and again it had to do with Christianity.

Leaving Home

By the autumn of that year, Governor Shute had almost washed his hands of the tiresome citizens of Massachusetts. "I must assure your lordships," he wrote home, "that the people here pay little or no deference to any opinion or orders that I receive." When the Abenaki attacked a frontier post, Mr. Shute made his declaration of war, only to find that Dr. Cooke and the House of Representatives insisted on meddling with every detail of the campaign. Meanwhile the press were annoying too, upsetting not only the governor but also the House. The time had arrived for the Franklins to be taught a lesson.[7]

In June, the *News-Letter* and the *Gazette* had offended Elisha Cooke and his colleagues by printing election results without their permission, and by making some small errors in the process. The editors were summoned before the House and made to say sorry. Not to be outdone, five days later James Franklin ran a brief story in the *Courant* implying that the authorities had been too slow to send a ship to sea to chase away some pirates. On June 12, the Suffolk County sheriff arrested James and put him in jail. The orders came from Sewall and the governor's council, but with the approval of Elisha Cooke.

For a month while James was in prison, permitted on grounds of poor health to pace about in the yard, he left the *Courant* to be put out by Benjamin. He too had been hauled up before the councilors, who demanded to know who had written the story. Despite James's bullying, Franklin sided with his brother, told them nothing, and was sent away with a warning. He went back to the printing shop filled with resentment at the way James had been treated. The incident only made the brothers still more audacious.

For one thing, they felt emboldened by a matter of detail: that Dr. Cooke and the House had intervened to save the *Courant* from a punishment worse than jail. According to Sewall and the governor's council, the newspaper made a point of insulting the government, the churches, and Harvard College. Or as they put it, the *Courant* tended "to fill the readers' minds with vanity, to the dishonour of God and disservice of good men." That being so, they wanted it placed under strict censorship: but the House refused to do any such thing. All they wanted from James was an apology.

The council's empty threat must have been deeply gratifying to James Franklin, and all the more so because of the pompous language in which it was expressed. He knew that his role models in the London press, Mr. Mist and the others, only saw their circulation jump each time they were arrested. And soon enough, in September in New Haven, an incident occurred that gave him a perfect opportunity to be still more controversial.

This time it was a scandal at Yale, and something far more serious than a routine tiff among the faculty. From about 1714, heretical ideas had begun to circulate among the ministers who taught at the college. They studied the same modern authors—Locke, Bayle, Shaftesbury, and Tillotson—that the teenage Franklin read in Boston. While he lost his faith, at Yale the clergy did something almost as atrocious. Led by the principal, Timothy Cutler, seven ministers publicly left the Congregational Church, proclaiming their intention to become Anglicans. Worse still, they meant to go to London to be ordained again, and this time by an English bishop.

The affair came to be known as the Yale Apostasy. When the *Courant* broke the story, in the issue with Mrs. Dogood's ramble in the dark, the pastors of Boston were appalled. A century on from the *Mayflower,* it seemed that perhaps, after so much struggle, the Puritan mission to America was doomed. At the Old North, the Mathers led a day of prayer and fasting; but by now Increase Mather was eighty-three, so frail that his voice could barely be heard. The worst of it was that the traitors from Yale had made it plain that—in their opinion—the Puritan chapels were not really churches at all, but merely voluntary gatherings, with nothing by way of law or tradition to support their claims to holiness. So all their ministers were counterfeit, including the Mathers, because they had never been anointed by an Anglican. This was deeply insulting.

For the *Courant,* it was another story that would run. On October 8, in the last of the Dogood letters, Franklin struck a rather lofty, dismissive attitude toward Cutler and the renegades—"there are too many blind zealots among every denomination of Christian," he wrote, with all the gravitas of a youth not seventeen—before ending the piece with two long passages from Addison. For the next three months, the Yale affair became an obsession with the *Courant,* as Gardner and the Franklin brothers came at the subject from all angles. Veering back and forth between opposing points of view—pro and con the Cutlerites, the Anglicans, or the meeting houses—they extracted the maximum by way of entertainment.

For instance, they pointed out that if Cutler was correct, all the weddings he and his comrades had conducted must be null and void. Hence the husbands and wives were entitled to divorce, and their children were technically bastards. Sarcastically written, in a style similar to Mrs. Dogood's, the piece may well have been Franklin's. Even after Cutler left for England, the *Courant* would not let the matter drop. Instead of making fun of Yale, they went back to sneering at Harvard. With each issue, the *Courant* became more barbed and more daring, until—early in 1723—at last they went too far.

Late in December, with Mr. Shute still squabbling with Cooke and the House of Representatives, the politics of Massachusetts took an ugly turn. Someone fired a gun through the governor's window. The bullet missed, and perhaps the shot was an accident, but it brought matters to a head. Shute had been planning a long vacation at home, to consult his superiors and—perhaps—to urge them to revoke the colony's charter. Without warning, he sailed for London on New Year's Day, in the frigate that had brought the smallpox, leaving his province in disarray. It was "a cloudy and tempestuous time," Judge Sewall wrote in his diary. The *Courant* made it even more vexatious, when on January 14 they printed issue 76, their most scurrilous assault upon religion.

Probably by Gardner, it read more like a blasphemous item by one of the London deists, Toland or Anthony Collins. The writer posed as a Christian, claiming to be offended by people he called "hypocritical zealots." When they paraded their holiness in public—keeping the Sabbath, saying their prayers, and quoting from the Bible—it was all just subterfuge, to help them cheat their neighbors out of money. Few people in Boston could have read the column without a sharp intake of breath, so outspoken were the things the writer said. "Whenever I find a man full of religious cant and palaver," the author wrote, "I presently suspect him to be a knave."

Whom did he mean? Judge Sewall, and his circle of friends? The Mathers, and their congregation? Or simply *every* pious tradesman or his wife, people like Josiah or Abiah? There was worse to come. The writer rounded off the piece with a few lines that might have put an English journalist in prison. "Religion itself suffers extremely by the dishonest practices of those who profess it," he wrote. "Their cheating tricks have a tendency to harden such as are disaffected to religion in their infidelity and strengthen their prejudices against it. Why, say they, such and such zealous religious men, they will lie, cheat and defraud, for all their high profession; and so they presently conclude, that Religion itself is nothing but a cunningly devised fable, a trick of state, invented to keep mankind in awe."

The last nineteen words—from "Religion" to "awe"—were modeled on a passage by John Toland. Calling religion "a trick of state" put the *Courant* in the worst of company, with atheists and libertines. In the same issue, at last the *Courant* came out firmly against the governor, warning its readers that Shute would destroy the liberties of Massachusetts. Perhaps this was a political maneuver by James Franklin, an attempt to ally himself more closely with Elisha Cooke; but if it was, it proved to be a failure.[8]

Judge Sewall and the council were furious. Within hours of the paper's appearance on the streets, again they demanded the right to censor the *Courant*. And this time—although by only the narrowest of margins, when the matter came to a vote—the House of Representatives agreed. Jointly they condemned the *Courant*, calling it profane, a journal intended "to mock religion, and bring it into contempt." On January 16, they banned James Franklin from publishing this or any other newspaper, except under strict supervision.

To which James could give only one reply. He ignored the ban. The following Monday he published issue 77; and then he left town for a place of refuge sixty miles away. Just three weeks after Benjamin turned seventeen, once again he was left in charge, but facing the threat of closure if the *Courant* continued in his brother's name.

What should he do? Like their role models in the London press, Henry Care or Nathanuel Mist, young Benjamin carried on regardless. On the 28th, in defiance of the law, he put out *Courant* No. 78, with a front page filled with a rousing defense of the paper. The writer was certainly brave, because he finished with a gibe at Speaker Cooke. In Boston, he wrote, there was something called "the Canvas Club" made up of "men of power and influence," who would try to crush anyone who spoke up against them. That had to mean Elisha Cooke and his friends, with their smoke-filled rooms and their political machine.[9]

Could the *Courant* be any more insolent? They could. With Benjamin at the helm, and James still on the run, the *Courant* went still further in No. 79. At the top of the page, he quoted from Henry Care's *English Liberties*, calling his brother's prosecution nothing but an act of tyranny.

Beneath it, he ran a fictional story about a judge in Anglo-Saxon England who had gone to the gallows for unjustly hanging someone by the name of "Frankling." Ponderous the wit might be, but the message was very plain.

Reaching into the past, to the politics of London in the age of Charles II, Franklin took his stand with the Whigs of yesteryear. Again he turned to Henry Care for ammunition. The remainder of issue 79 was a long, insulting letter to a dignitary—unnamed, but almost certainly Judge Sewall—accusing him of flouting the sacred principles of Magna Carta.

This sort of thing could not continue. Sooner or later the sheriff was bound to arrive to enforce the ban, at least within the line of Suffolk County. So in February, when James came back to Boston to turn himself in, the Franklin brothers and their friends held a council of war in the printing shop. One suggestion was this: to evade the ban by changing the name of the *Courant*. Legally, this could not work. Anyway James objected: presumably, because his circulation was doing well, and his business might suffer if it seemed that the *Courant* had been neutered.

The better option was to make Benjamin the publisher. Even this might leave them in breach of the law. Because Benjamin was still an apprentice, with three years left to run of his term of service, James was responsible for everything he did. So they hit upon another ploy. James would end the apprenticeship by signing the back of his brother's indentures, and if the authorities tried to censor the *Courant* Benjamin would show them the document. Secretly, however, he signed another set of articles, binding himself to James until 1726, when he would reach the age of twenty.

With that accomplished, the next issue of the *Courant* hit the streets on February 11, with the words "printed and sold by Benjamin Franklin" in large type along the bottom. The following day, James surrendered to the sheriff, bringing along two friends—not his father Josiah, who must by now have been utterly distraught at the way his sons were behaving—and they posted his bond for bail.

For the next four months, while James waited for his case to come to trial, the *Courant* came out under Benjamin Franklin's name. Gradually, the passion ebbed away from the paper. The tone became more moderate. Not so the rivalry between the brothers. They quarreled again. Benjamin knew that their relationship was reaching its end. In later life, again he felt the nag of conscience about his rift with James, just as he had about his insults to the Mathers, worrying—as he put it in his memoirs—that he had been "too saucy and provoking" to his brother.

Perhaps he was: but he had to make his exit. He was a marked man in Boston, where he had offended all the people in power. In his autobiography, Franklin says that he "made himself a little obnoxious to the governing party": a phrase that can only mean Dr. Cooke. It must have been issue 78 that did the damage. Worse than that, he was seen as the architect of the paper's onslaught on religion. And so he became an adolescent copy of the Socrates whose life he had hoped to emulate. Suffering the fate of the philosopher, he was pointed at with horror in the streets. People called him an infidel, or even—and this was almost unspeakable—an outright atheist.

It was time to go. In May, a grand jury dismissed the charges against James Franklin, and so the *Courant* could continue, less angry, less political, but still funny and sometimes obscene. Benjamin tried to find a job with another printer—there were four more in Boston—but James had been around to see them, and persuaded them not to hire his brother. Since Benjamin had James's signature releasing him from his apprenticeship, he could make a run for it without being pursued, or so he thought; but first he had to get aboard a ship. Josiah and James had kissed and made up, which meant that his parents were unlikely to help. His old debating friend John Collins came to his rescue. Collins arranged his passage with a Dutch skipper bound for New York, telling him a tale that Benjamin had made a girl pregnant and was trying to escape a shotgun wedding.

To pay his fare, Franklin sold a portion of his library. On or about the 25th of September 1723, in a week of heavy rain, with his chest full of clothes and the rest of his books he slipped aboard the Dutchman's sloop, the *Speedwell.* The wind was in their favor. The *Courant* came out again the following Monday, with an off-color sketch about the most intimate parts of a woman's body. By then the young Franklin had put three hundred miles between himself and Boston.

He was alone, all but penniless, and he was not eighteen. At home, despite his quarrels, his fads, and his daring ideas, he had lived a life protected by routine, in a structured town with an array of familiar institutions. He was about to venture into an adult world without maps, where an apprentice was all too liable to go astray.

Chapter Eight

The Crusoe of the Delaware

New York did not detain him long. The city had an eminent printer, William Bradford, a prosperous man in his early sixties, well supplied with staff and with no vacancy for Franklin. If you need a job, you might try Philadelphia instead, the old man told him. There he had a son in the same trade, Andrew Bradford, who had recently lost a talented worker, a poet-cum-printer by the name of Aquila Rose. In August, Rose had succumbed to a chill after a mishap with his boat in bad weather. His death left a gap at the Bradford firm in the City of Brotherly Love. So off Franklin went in the hope of taking Rose's place. To get to Philadelphia, the young athlete planned to walk across New Jersey in the cold and the rain of October.

The first stage of the journey should have been easy. It was just a question of leaving the lower end of Manhattan in a small boat in the morning, and then passing westwards around the back of Staten Island to reach the Jersey shore. Then a squall blew in from the sea, ripping their sails off the mast, and the gusts of wind grew into a gale. A heavy swell was running, driving the vessel in the wrong direction, away to the east. A trip that should have taken no more than half a day became instead an odyssey of thirty hours that all but ended in catastrophe. As the afternoon wore on they approached a rocky beach somewhere in Brooklyn, only to find that the surf made it far too dangerous to land.

Seeing people with canoes at the water's edge, Franklin and the boatman tried to call for help. But, as he put it in his autobiography, with the waves still beating at the stones all their efforts were in vain: "the wind was so high . . . that we could not hear to understand each other."

Darkness fell, and the gale continued. They spent the night on the water, huddled in the bows against the spray. It was not until late the next day, rowing hard at the oars, that they entered the mouth of the Raritan River, docking at the harbor town of Perth Amboy: hungry, thirsty, and worn out, but still alive.

In his memoirs, Franklin recalled his journey to Philadelphia in far more detail and with far more emotion than he gives to any other episode. Only rarely, there or in his letters, does Franklin show that he is scared, or even mildly anxious. He can be funny, charming, and enthusiastic; he can be flirtatious (very); and in the 1770s, as he falls out of love with Great Britain, we can feel his anger grow with each exasperated letter that he sends from London. But with Franklin *fear* is very hard to find: except in this account of his journey in the autumn of 1723. As far as we know, he had never left the Boston area before. This first experience of danger left a mark on his soul that remained with him all his life.

One detail stands out with a peculiar intensity. On the boat, Franklin has a fellow passenger: a Dutchman, soused with rum, the only stuff they had to drink. As the squall blows them off course, the drunken man falls overboard. Benjamin Franklin, muscular but agile, leans out of the pitching boat and hauls him back by his hair. From out of his pocket, the man takes a book, which he wants Benjamin to dry off while he sleeps away the liquor. It turns out to be Franklin's childhood favorite, Bunyan's *The Pilgrim's Progress.* Rendered into Dutch, it was finely printed on good paper.

It was an odd discovery to make at such an alarming moment: odd or even uncanny, as though it were some kind of omen or a symbol. It was all the more striking because—unusually for him—Franklin had no books of his own. He had sent his chest around to Philadelphia by sea. In his memoirs, Franklin makes sure to be very precise in his description of the Dutchman and his expensive copy of John Bunyan. He mentions the book's illustrations, more skillfully engraved than any he was used to. It is not too hard to see why the appearance of *The Pilgrim's Progress* on the boat made such a deep impression, or why he wished to write so much about it.

In Boston he had been outrageous, but only verbally. In other ways he had lived a sheltered life, with a family to whom he could turn if need be. For the first time, Franklin found himself wandering in the dark, like Bunyan's Pilgrim in quest of the heavenly city. As a lover of books, he saw his adventures through a literary lens. By now, however, although Franklin still admired Bunyan's skill as a writer, he had ceased to think of life in Bunyan's terms, as a pilgrimage where the only reliable guide was the Gospel. And so the sight of the book was something Franklin found deeply significant: a last glimpse of home, as it were, as he left the pieties of Boston forever. At this point in his memoirs, suddenly he mentions other, more up-to-date writers whose narratives felt closer to his own experience.

After praising Bunyan's style, Franklin moves swiftly on to speak still more highly of the English novelists: Defoe of course, but also Samuel Richardson, the author of *Pamela,* the literary sensation of the 1740s, telling the story of a young woman who had to fight off seduction by her employer. As we read about Franklin in his teens, he wishes us to think of him as though he were another Crusoe or a Pamela: a young hero, cast adrift from the family home, often in peril, and at risk of deceit and abuse by adults with their own vicious agenda.

Later, when he reaches London, a city full of moral danger, the parallels with *Pamela* become more relevant. As he describes his adventures on the way to Philadelphia, Franklin wants us to think about *Robinson Crusoe.* His story echoes Crusoe's brushes with calamity. Indeed Franklin writes in a style so close to Defoe's that he must have intended us to see the connection. Here were two runaways, at odds with their parents, with only their ingenuity to save them from ruin. The difference between them is this. An orthodox man when it came to religion, Defoe made his hero a devout believer in Christian providence: but this was a factor that Franklin, young or old, could never count on with Defoe's degree of certainty. In his memoirs or his letters, he would acknowledge his belief in something he called Providence and then skip swiftly forward to tell us what he did to help it on its way.[1]

That evening Franklin struggled into bed, feeling very feverish. Rather than say his prayers he drank pints of cold water, something he had read about: it was supposed to be a cure for fever. After sweating through the night, feeling healthy once again Franklin crossed the river by ferry at dawn, landing at South Amboy. Ahead of him lay forty miles of wilderness.

The Skeptical Doctor

It was Thursday, October 3. Again it was raining heavily. From the Raritan what passed for a highway carrying the mail across New Jersey followed the route of an old Indian trail. It took Franklin up a long slope, through a belt of stunted little pines three miles deep. From the top of the ridge the trail dropped him down into a boggy plain where the going was difficult: loose sand, or thick, muddy clay, with streams often crossing the path and only a log or two to serve as a crude kind of bridge.[2]

It was like that for most of the day: hard walking, dark skies, a landscape of little value for the farmer. There was almost no one to greet or from whom to ask the way. Forty years after the English had named it Middlesex County, this tract of land remained almost devoid of settlers. That afternoon, tired and bedraggled, Franklin reached a little inn by the wayside. It was somewhere near the town of Cranbury, almost in earshot today of the traffic thumping down I-95. Then the country was so desolate that even in 1800 there were still barely a dozen houses in the neighborhood.

There at the inn Franklin spent the night, "beginning now to wish that I had never left home." So it had been with his fictional cousin, Robinson Crusoe, as he made his weary way to London, filled with "many struggles with myself," in the words of Daniel Defoe. At Cranbury, Franklin found himself under interrogation, as any stranger would be in a place so bleak, if he was very young, dressed in working clothes, and had no horse and no belongings. His landlord guessed, correctly, that he was a runaway, an apprentice or an indentured servant—only a runaway would look so wretched—and Franklin was afraid that he would be detained. Next morning, he rose early. He hurried down the track as fast as he could go, his pockets stuffed with his spare shirts and stockings. Gradually, the countryside grew softer and more inviting; and gradually his luck began to change.

Fifteen miles on, in a district where the native people of the Lenape still inhabited the woods with their maize and their canoes, the soil became more fertile. Here the farmers were more numerous. The harvest had been poor that year, but there were signs that the country had excellent prospects. At a place called Crosswicks, the trail ran between groves of trees with beyond them wide fields, cold and bare in the fall but ready for wheat in the spring. Franklin was approaching the land of the Quakers. Since the 1680s, they had been settling in the region, in search of a Utopia of peace and love and fruitful economics. On the road beyond Crosswicks he would have passed a small brick building mentioned in the records from the period. It was probably the first time he had seen a Quaker meeting house.[3]

It may be that until this moment Franklin had never even spoken to a

Quaker. In Boston, the Society of Friends was legal but frowned upon, like so much else in that prickly town. But as he trudged along the road, there came a moment when at last he crossed an invisible line. At a tree stump or by somebody's barn, Franklin passed beyond the orbit of New England, and he entered the world the Quakers had created.

With its northern end in New Jersey, and its center in Philadelphia, the region of the Quakers reached out as far as the Susquehanna River in the west. To the south it laid its fingertips on Maryland, where they grew tobacco. It was a much looser world, less predictable, and far more diverse than New England. It was also a world where Franklin would feel more at home than he ever had in Boston. As if to make the point, the first person he recalls that he met in Quaker country was a kindred spirit. He was a clever man who gave him a friendly welcome and to whom Franklin awarded his highest praise. His new acquaintance was "ingenious."

Turning west toward the Delaware on October 4, with still thirty miles to go to his destination, Franklin walked along the street of a little place called Farnsworth's Landing. It was just ten houses or so, at a spot where a ravine cut a slot through the bluff by the river and took a traveler down to the water's edge. Today it is known as Bordentown, a charming little suburb for commuters, with a riverfront that is perhaps the only place on Franklin's route where one can still see the terrain as it was when he came by. The township had an inn, where he could find a bed. It was kept by John Browne, a medical man. Dr. Browne had traveled in Europe but somehow he made his way to the frontier, where he built a practice among the Quakers.[4]

Browne and Franklin hit it off at once. As Franklin ate his supper, they talked. John Browne could soon tell that his guest was a well-read individual. A friendship sprang up between them, lasting fourteen years until the ingenious doctor died from "a stoppage in his urine." Those words come from the obituary Franklin ran in *The Pennsylvania Gazette*, calling his old friend "a gentleman of singular skill in the profession of surgery." Like Franklin, the doctor was a freethinking man—"much of an unbeliever," Franklin recalled in his memoirs—and like the young Franklin he was controversial: which is clearly what made Browne so appealing.

All his life, Franklin loved to come across clever but eccentric people, flesh-and-blood equivalents of his vegetarian mentor Thomas Tryon. He kept them stored in his memory to form his own cabinet of human curiosities. This became an essential part of Franklin's modus operandi.

Only by meeting unusual men and women, with views and ways of life that deviated from the norm, could he extend his horizons and cultivate his own ingenuity. Time and again, Franklin would seek out people of that kind and record their quirky doings for posterity.

In John Browne's case—as so often in the eighteenth century—the quirkiness took the form of poetry. Toward the end of his life, the doctor decided to turn the Bible into doggerel verse. Being an unbeliever or a deist, of course he tried to make the stories sound ridiculous: that was what the skeptics were up to in London. The difference was that Browne was doing so at the western edge of the empire, amid the Lenape and the Quaker farmers, people used to living with no authority but their own. The doctor could say what he pleased, with no danger of censorship or prosecution. And that was one of the things Franklin liked most about the Quaker hinterland. Although he was never a Quaker himself, he knew that in their midst he could be as skeptical as Browne, without suffering the death of Socrates.

So he slept Friday night at the doctor's inn. Next morning Franklin walked down the riverbank to Burlington. He was looking for a seat on one of the boats that carried wheat downstream to the wharves of Philadelphia, for shipment out to feed the slaves in the West Indies. He missed the boats due that day, the 5th, and found shelter for the afternoon with a kind old woman who sold him gingerbread. She cooked him a little offal, the cheek of an ox. He gave her some ale in return.

Saturday night saw him gazing down the Delaware, with his stock of money now reduced to a Dutch silver dollar and a shilling in copper pennies. He saw a boat come by, with on board a few people, including a woman with an infant. They took him in. He put his muscles to the oars—the wind had died away—and at midnight they took refuge in a creek. With the broken rails of a fence, they made a fire against the cold. They woke to find themselves in sight of journey's end.

At breakfast time on Sunday, October 6, filthy, exhausted, and again very hungry, Benjamin Franklin arrived in Philadelphia, passing the place where today the suspension bridge is named in his honor. Looking awkward and ridiculous—his own words—he stepped ashore and found himself gazing up a thoroughfare far broader than any he had seen at home. It was Market Street, one hundred feet across. Even today, when so much careless modern building has wrecked the riverfront that Franklin knew, we can see a little of the Philadelphia he entered. The wide streets, the spacious grid: they still survive, laid out as they were by the Quakers.

What Franklin saw was a raw, unfinished city, very different from Boston. Here by the Delaware, life had far less definition than it did in New England. Although in early Massachusetts the wilderness was never far away, even so the colony had a perimeter, guarded by a militia, it had a charter, and a royal governor—however disliked he might be—and some of its towns had a hundred years of history. And so they had sheriffs, juries, county courts, and a settled code of laws. In theory, Pennsylvania had the same: but in fact, although it had a constitution, based on a charter granted by its Quaker proprietor William Penn in 1701, there were still a host of decisions yet to be made in a colony with vast potential but an ambiguous status quo.

It was a rather peculiar province. On the one hand, no one who arrived there in the 1720s could fail to see that one day Pennsylvania might be very prosperous. If they survived the sea crossing from Europe, newcomers entered what one of them called "a precious land . . . a good and free country," where wages were high, the soil fertile, and rents and taxes and the price of soil were low. In the woods that surrounded Philadelphia, even the pigs dined on apples and peaches, and every farming family had its garden and its orchard. It was a place, said another immigrant, where "whoever is willing to work can become rich."[5]

So they might: but could they agree about who owned the land, how to govern themselves, and how best to share the benefits of progress? There were 45,000 settlers, more or less, but fewer than two thirds of them were English or Welsh. The remainder were German, or Scots-Irish people from the north of Ireland, or African slaves. To whom did they owe allegiance? They were supposed to be loyal subjects of King George. But in practice the Crown took little interest in people whose only purpose in life, from a British point of view, was to send their grain and pork to the sugar islands. In 1712, tired of endless squabbles with the locals, who simply would not pay the rents they owed him, William Penn had tried to sell Pennsylvania to the government in England. A deal was struck, but then fell through. And so the opportunity was lost to bring the province firmly within the British fold. In time this led to a messy situation in which nobody really knew who owned the colony, or who was the rightful governor.

When Penn died in 1718, he left two wills—not his fault, the poor man, because the old Quaker hero had been broken by two strokes, and he could scarcely hear or speak—but from his incapacity, the consequence arising was chaotic. With Mr. Penn consigned to the grave, to whom did Pennsylvania belong? To the children of Penn's first marriage, or to those of his second? For the time being, in London his widow, Hannah, acted as the colony's proprietor, hoping to hand it on to her sons; but their title to the province would remain in dispute until 1731. While the lawyers in England argued the rights and wrongs, Pennsylvania did the best it could. Even so, the 1720s were years of strife as rival parties vied for control of its fate.[6]

As for Philadelphia, it was an odd sort of place: no college, no state house, no militia, no cannons by the shore—like Thomas Tryon, the Quakers would not fight or arm themselves—and little by way of a city government. Although Market Street had aspirations, when Franklin arrived it was still paved with nothing but dirt. It ended abruptly after three blocks. Times were hard in Philadelphia, thanks to the same recession that blighted the affairs of Boston. Many lots were vacant and many houses stood empty. The wide streets and the grid were only part of the story: the rest was squalor. Wooden shacks and narrow alleys, wells and water pumps too close to privies, poverty by the waterfront, immigrants from Ulster and the Rhineland, mostly coming in as bonded servants to be bought and sold, and also the Africans relied upon, but also feared and despised: all of this was Philadelphia too.

Beyond 4th Street, a new arrival saw the fields and the orchards, with their herds of swine, and a hint of blue hills in the distance. Somewhere behind the hills, where no one had mapped the rivers or the colony's boundary, there rose the smoke from the fires of the Lenape, soon to be dispossessed. Beyond them there lay the distant hunting grounds of the Iroquois, with whom the colonists had recently signed a treaty of alliance. For Franklin, coming off the boat, the town was his equivalent of Crusoe's island: the wide, flat plain between the two rivers, the Delaware and the Schuylkill, where his ingenuity would have to leave its mark.

Once again his timing was perfect. With its lack of definition, its open borders, and its ambiguities, Pennsylvania would prove to be ideal for a young man eager to make his own way. And besides: in his first winter in the city, the economy began to recover. Not that Franklin could have expected that on his arrival in this confusing town. He was just another runaway, close to destitution.

HIS PHILADELPHIA STORY . . .

Up he came from the wharf, lonely and dirty, but determined to do some good even so. Almost as though he wished to strip away any legacy he had from his family and Massachusetts, so that he could feel like Crusoe that he had done his best entirely alone, he gave his copper coins to the people on the boat. They took the money only with reluctance, so manfully had Franklin done his share with the oars.

Taken in 1855, this rare photograph shows an early-eighteenth-century Philadelphia house—at the corner of Chestnut and 2nd Streets—of the kind that Franklin saw on his first arrival in the town in 1723. It can be compared with Peter Cooper's painting of the city in about 1720, reproduced elsewhere in this book.

Having nowhere to go, since it was Sunday and the Bradford printing shop was closed, he wandered aimlessly up Market Street. He saw some bread, and found the baker's shop. The shop was open, which he would have found very odd: in his hometown, the Sabbath was obligatory. Here in Philadelphia it was a matter of choice. And when Franklin asked for some food, he was still more perplexed by what occurred.

By the Delaware, his Dutch silver dollar was a rarity, with a purchasing power far greater than he had expected. In return for threepence, which would have bought only a loaf in Boston, Franklin came away with three puffy rolls, of a size he had never seen at home. With a roll beneath each brawny arm, he drifted up the street, chewing away on the third, then circled back down to the wharf. He drank from the Delaware, and saw the poor woman from the boat. He gave her and her child the rolls he did not require. By now the Quakers were drifting by as well, on their way to their Sunday gathering at their meeting house: which, as it happened, was opposite the Bradford premises. He followed the Quakers—why not? he had nowhere else to go—and while the Quakers meditated, the young man fell asleep.

And then he relied on the kindness of strangers. One of the Quakers woke him when the meeting was done. In the street another one found him an inn: not the first one Franklin saw, the Three Mariners, a house of ill repute, but instead a ramshackle old tavern by the waterfront, called the Crooked Billet. There he began to recover from the rigors of the journey. Exhausted, and suspected yet again of being a fugitive, as he tells us in his autobiography, Franklin ate and slept and then he ate and slept again. On Monday morning, October 7, refreshed and a little less untidy, he went looking for work without any breakfast. Soon enough he discovered that despite the high ideals with which it had been founded by the Quakers, the colony had its darker side.[7]

The following year another brilliant man arrived in Philadelphia, not from Boston but from Germany. He wrote his own account of the town that made this very point with brutal candor. In the eyes of Johann-Christoph Sauer, son of a Lutheran pastor, the city of brotherly love was a Babylon as sinful as anything in Europe. Or perhaps it was even worse: Sauer was appalled by the sight of brothels like the Three Mariners. In later years, Sauer would become a printer too, serving the German people in Pennsylvania. He never aspired to be an English gentleman; and so although he could never write as stylishly as Franklin, often his tales of what he saw are more informative and more direct.

"A gathering place for . . . restless and eccentric people": that was how Sauer described the Quaker colony in 1724. Although he admired its fertile soil, its woods, and its religious liberty, the province contained "so many scheming people that one can hardly believe what intrigues are here thought of." Franklin did not use language such as this, but his first encounter with Philadelphia was very much the same. It was a slippery place where you had to be wary.[8]

On that Monday morning, Franklin made for an address on 2nd Street. Here beneath the sign of the Bible—the holy book, painted on a board—Andrew Bradford sold chocolate and printed the town's newspaper, the *American Weekly Mercury*. That week, its lead story was the trial for treason of a Jacobite in London, but the paper also advertised rewards for the recapture of runaways. So Franklin was putting himself in danger, by venturing into the printing shop. And yet he received a welcome so warm that it had to be a matter for suspicion.

William Bradford had come down to the Delaware, making better time on horseback than Benjamin had achieved on foot. He greeted Franklin like a long-lost friend. His son Andrew Bradford gave the boy something to eat, and then he made what seemed to be a helpful suggestion. A new printer had set up in town, Samuel Keimer, an immigrant from England. Perhaps he needed a likely lad like Franklin? So off they went, to find Keimer's home on Market Street, and to see what he might have to offer.

By sunset Franklin had a promise of a job with Keimer, but it was not the job he would have preferred. He also discovered that in Philadelphia nothing could be taken at face value, including the sign of the Bible. It turned out that William Bradford—a Quaker in his youth, and then a keen Anglican, apparently so kind and so moral—had a sly and cunning streak. In taking Franklin to see Mr. Keimer, the old man had an ulterior motive, his purpose being to ask questions and to spy on a rival. Without revealing his identity, Bradford wanted to find out just how Keimer proposed to run his business; who his backers were; and where he stood politically.

Franklin listened while the game was played. Soon he decided that Bradford was nothing but "a crafty old sophister." In years to come Franklin and the Bradfords would become sworn enemies, as they competed in the printing trade. In the meantime Franklin had to work for Keimer. In making his acquaintance, Franklin collected another exhibit for his private museum of unusual people.

The printing shop was a shambles, with a broken press and only a meager supply of lead type, bearing little resemblance to the costly apparatus James Franklin had brought home from London. As for Samuel Keimer, he was an example of the restless people Sauer had seen flooding into Pennsylvania. At thirty-five, Keimer was a refugee from debts he could not pay and from a wife and family he did not love. He was poor and unkempt, with a beard that hung down toward his waist because a Bible passage had forbidden him to shave. By an odd coincidence, Keimer had grown up by the Thames in the 1690s in Southwark, the district where Franklin's uncle was coloring silk. Indeed, Keimer's mother had been another follower of Nathaniel Vincent, the minister whose sermons had meant so much to Benjamin Senior. But while the Franklins strove to be respectable, the pursuit of faith had taken Mr. Keimer into the realm of the extreme.[9]

In 1707, aged nineteen and apprenticed as printer, Keimer fell in with a cult known as the Camisards, because it was their custom to wear a linen smock, or in the dialect of southern France, a camisa. Otherwise known as the "French Prophets," the Camisards were Huguenots who had fled from persecution by King Louis XIV. Once arrived in London, the Prophets dealt in religious ecstasy, receiving the Holy Spirit by way of what they called "agitations": fits of weeping, trembling, gasping, and hiccups, followed by a trance, from which they would awake to speak in tongues. Among city people eager for faith they made a few converts, whose number for a while included Samuel Keimer.

Taking the name of "Jonathan, of the Tribe of Asser," he began to grow his beard. Around his neck he wore a long green ribbon: so that at the moment of the Second Coming, Jesus Christ would recognize him as a Camisard. For a time Keimer did rather well as a printer, with his own paper, the *London Post,* and he got to know Defoe, some of whose work he published. Sadly, he made the mistake of flirting with the Jacobites at the time of their failed rebellion of 1715, and so the Whigs sent him to prison for seditious libel. After that, he was jailed for insolvency. By 1718 he had broken with the Camisards. He broadcast the fact to the world in his own autobiography, *A Brand Pluck'd From the Burning:* a book that Franklin must have seen, but never mentions.[10]

Some time later Keimer shipped up in Philadelphia, where early in 1722 he ran a notice in the *Mercury* in which he offered "to teach his poor brethren, the Male Negroes, to read the Holy Scriptures." There he was far ahead of his time—seventy years had yet to pass before people of color were allowed to have a church of their own, in this city so devoted to religious freedom—and so the project came to nothing. Keimer found himself living in poverty, inhabiting his rented house and shop on Market Street with barely a stick of furniture.

When Franklin first saw him, Keimer was struggling to complete an elegy in memory of Aquila Rose, the gifted young poet who had worked for the Bradfords. Dead before the age of thirty, leaving a widow and a baby son, Rose had been immensely popular in Philadelphia, where he was given almost a state funeral at Christ Church, the Anglican place of worship. As if to pay his own tribute to Aquila, whose untimely end had brought him to the city, Franklin did what he could to help. He repaired Keimer's press. A few days later, the strange old Camisard summoned him round to his shop to print the finished version of his poem.

And so their complicated relationship began. When the mood took him, Samuel Keimer would amuse his new employee by performing the agitations of his former brethren. In time, Franklin formed the view that Keimer had "a good deal of the knave in his composition," a judgment for which we have only Franklin's evidence. It is just as plausible to think of Keimer as a visionary of a kind, the sort of visionary who sometimes emerged from the dissenting chapels of eighteenth-century London: someone who looked for God in the taverns, the prisons, and the squalor of the streets, and yearned—like William Blake, whose background was similar to Keimer's—to build a new Jerusalem beside the Thames. With no hope of fulfilling his dreams in England, Keimer turned to Philadelphia, but once there he had to live by his wits. Did this make him a knave, as Franklin described him? Although his style and his methods were unconventional, Keimer survived in the town for nearly ten years as a printer and publisher, which suggests that he was more talented than Franklin cared to admit. To begin with, Keimer was also somebody Franklin found indispensable.

Besides giving Franklin a job, Keimer could also give the young man another kind of opening. Keimer rented his little house from an Englishman who lived in another little house next door, a carpenter named John Read, married to Sarah. At first Franklin had roomed with the Bradfords, but Keimer did not care for that, seeing how duplicitous his competitors could be. So the young man came to lodge with the Reads, and there he met his future partner: their daughter Deborah, whom later he would take as his wife.

. . . And Deborah's

She first saw him on the Sunday morning, as he walked up Market Street eating his bread roll. When he came by, tall but ragged, his pockets bulging with spare linen, she was standing on her father's doorstep. No doubt she was on her way to prayer. All her life Deborah knelt in the pews at Christ Church. Although Franklin looked silly, he caught her eye. In time he found her attractive too. Deborah Read was only nineteen or so, but behind her she had her own heritage of talent.

At this point we come to perhaps the most difficult problem to face anyone who writes about Franklin. We know far too little about his wife and about their relationship. In the eighteenth or the nineteenth centuries nobody took the trouble to gather up Deborah's letters, other than some of those she wrote to him. It seems that no one preserved her belongings, her family history—even her date and place of birth—or anything more than a few anecdotes about her. Because of that, and because in the 1750s they parted when he went to live in London, causing some embarrassment for Franklin devotees who would prefer every aspect of his life to resemble a scene by Norman Rockwell, she has suffered a humiliating fate at the hands of some of his biographers. They have sneered at Mrs. Franklin, damned her with faint praise, or made fun of her atrocious spelling. Often they just ignore her, as if she were irrelevant.[11]

The best that is usually said about Deborah Read Franklin is that she was frugal, honest, and hardworking; the worst, that she was plain and plump and dowdy, with a fearsome temper and a foul mouth. Her husband did not help her cause. In the second section of his memoirs—composed in 1784, when she was ten years dead—he described her in terms that made her sound like a hired hand. "She assisted me cheerfully in my business," Franklin wrote, "folding and stitching pamphlets, tending shop, purchasing old linen rags for the paper makers etc etc."

With those hasty "etceteras," Franklin dismissed the woman he had chosen as his partner. Then he hurried on to write about himself, telling us next to nothing about Deborah. He also made a curious omission. He forgot to mention this: she kept his firm's accounts—six bulky ledgers still survive in the library of the American Philosophical Society in Philadelphia, almost entirely in her handwriting—and on two occasions he granted her a power of attorney over his affairs. The first one, granted in 1733, may have been only temporary. The second one was signed by Franklin in 1757, just before he sailed for England, and it left her in permanent control of all his assets in America.[12]

From this, it should be clear that Mrs. Franklin was far more than just "a fat, jolly dame, clean and tidy": another patronizing description offered by her husband, in a letter in which he likened her to a Toby jug. Deborah had a life of her own in Philadelphia. At Anglican Christ Church and elsewhere she was a woman who had many friends and commanded respect. In the absence of the documents we ought to have, the balance cannot be redressed entirely; but we can at least try to establish how the Reads came to be in Pennsylvania, and what kind of people they were. The trail of clues starts with a letter that Franklin wrote to Deborah in 1758.

After going to Ecton that summer in search of his genealogy, Franklin went further into the heart of the English Midlands, to the county of Warwickshire and the town of Birmingham, the industrial center from which Deborah's family had come. Britain was at war with France, and so the gunsmiths were hard at work, making muskets and ammunition for the redcoats. Every branch of trade was booming. Franklin toured the factories—"seeing all the curious machines," as he told Deborah—but he also saw her relations, who had reaped the benefits of life in England's most dynamic region. He came away overwhelmed: so many people, eager to see him, with so many names—Cash and Guest, Salt and Wheat, Wilkinson and Tyler—a baffling array, all of them somehow related to his wife. He called them "working people," but there was nothing poor or humble about them. Instead they were busy, proud, and comfortably off, and one of them was rich: Benjamin Tyler, Mrs. Franklin's first cousin, who had built his fortune in the button trade.[13]

It was the sort of thing Birmingham did to perfection: the mass production of buttons, pins, and needles, as well as the more skillful trade of

A building Deborah Read Franklin knew well: the Slate Roof House on 2nd and Sansom Streets, Philadelphia. Occupied at one time by the colony's founder, William Penn, in 1704 it was acquired by the Quaker merchant and politician Isaac Norris (1671–1735) and remained the Norris family's town house until the 1730s. Mrs. Franklin and Isaac's daughter Deborah were close friends from childhood. This picture was taken not long before the house was demolished in 1867.

making guns and clocks and tools, and the forging of the iron and steel from which they were created. Benjamin Tyler owned a factory with many hands, and he counted among his acquaintances the town's leading men of business. He invited Franklin round to supper, where Tyler boasted of the money being made in Birmingham, as the nation embraced the cult of engineering.

If the Franklins had an endowment of ingenuity, so did Deborah's family. Her mother, Sarah White, was the daughter of a Birmingham whitesmith, meaning a craftsman with pewter, brass, and tin, another trade for which the place was renowned. By the time she was in her twenties, the town was rapidly expanding, and in 1700 Sarah White married a carpenter, John Read, a London man who built houses. Three years later, Sarah gave birth to a daughter, Mary, and then the Reads vanished from the parish registers of Birmingham, only to reappear eight years later in America. In 1711, John Read bought an empty lot on Market Street, Philadelphia, and there he put his home. In the meantime Deborah had been born, in about 1705, but whether in Britain or the colonies we cannot say. No record of her baptism has yet been found: perhaps because few scholars have tried to look for it.[14]

Why had the Reads crossed the Atlantic? All we know is that Sarah had an uncle, Caleb Cash, a shoemaker from Birmingham, who had taken his family to Philadelphia at some date before 1700. So the most likely story is this: Caleb wrote home about the opportunities available in Pennsylvania, and John Read decided to try his luck.

As well he might. In Birmingham, the workshops were already shipping hardware to the colonies—hoes, spades, and other plantation tools—and nails most of all, in vast quantities. Americans needed millions of nails for building ships and houses, and the slitting mills of Birmingham made the cheapest available. Early in the eighteenth century, the flow of goods across the ocean created close ties between the town and Philadelphia, and craftsmen from Warwickshire crossed the Atlantic to the Quaker colony. This was the movement to which the Reads belonged; and this tide of migration rose to a new peak when it was realized that Pennsylvania could fashion metal of its own.[15]

From the colony's earliest days, it had been known that within easy reach there were deposits of iron ore, especially in the upper valley of the Schuylkill, where the red stains were hard to miss in the water and the soil. So William Penn began to reach out to the ironmasters of the English Midlands in the hope that they would invest in his province. By

1710 or so, Quaker merchants from the Delaware were making long trips to the Birmingham area, looking to find heiresses to marry and hoping to do business.

Soon enough, in 1716, the moment came when steel and iron could be made in Pennsylvania. By a creek called Manatawny, fifty miles inland from Philadelphia, a blacksmith from the English Midlands—Thomas Rutter—built a forge and started to turn out iron bars. Two years later, a recent Quaker arrival by the name of Samuel Nutt opened a forge in Chester County. There was a war in the Baltic between the Russians and the Swedes; the British lost their sources of iron from the region; and so these new American ironmasters were given a chance to grow their business. Rutter and Nutt built blast furnaces, and bought many acres of the timber they required for charcoal. Mr. Nutt had come from Warwickshire, and he christened his forge and his furnace with English names taken from the towns he knew at home.[16]

Although John Read never did anything so ambitious, he belonged to the same diaspora of craftsmen from Birmingham and its hinterland of ingenuity. Once established across the sea in Philadelphia, he built houses with enough success to enable him to buy the adjoining lot on Market Street, where he erected the house that Keimer rented. By 1720 Read was doing business in style, dealing in land worth hundreds of pounds. He put up a brick house on 3rd Street, complete with sash windows and cellars, and placed a notice in the *Mercury*, offering to sell it in a lottery. Meanwhile Mrs. Read had a business of her own making ointments for itches and burns and selling them to her neighbors.[17]

The slump of 1721 seems to have hit John Read quite hard, because he ran no more advertisements in the press. Nor did it help when he lent money to a confidence trickster, William Riddlesden, wanted for fraud on both sides of the ocean. But while Mr. Read was running into difficulties, his relations in the town were looking to the future. In 1715, Sarah Read's cousin Mary Cash had married one John Leacock, a vestryman at Christ Church, who had arrived by way of Barbados. Like Sarah's father, Leacock was a whitesmith, working with pewter. Soon enough he branched out into iron. By the middle of the 1720s he was an investor in new forges on the Manatawny and elsewhere where his partners included Samuel Nutt, the iron Quaker.[18]

And so, when Franklin met and later married Deborah Read, he joined an extended family of craftsmen and manufacturers whose activities encompassed both sides of the Atlantic. This heritage was something he came to share. All too often biographers write about Franklin as though he did everything by himself. That is what he might have wished us to think, but the truth of the matter is very different. Almost from the moment he set foot in Philadelphia, he found people willing to help him and make friends, and best of all the Reads.

Although they had land, timber, and minerals, the Pennsylvania colonists never had enough of something else: and that was labor, especially when it came with skills. With his height, his muscles, and his talent with words and with his hands, Franklin was always going to be welcome. Young men like him were necessary. When he arrived in 1723, Pennsylvania was about to enter a remarkable phase of economic growth, which had more than two decades to run before the next disaster struck. With its steel and iron, its farmers, and its pluralism, the colony on the Delaware would make Franklin a new kind of American.[19]

Chapter Nine

Forgetting Boston

"I have some reason to believe our trade is on the mending," wrote a Quaker merchant in January 1724, as he urged his friends in England to send him nails and lead shot, calico, and blankets, to be sold in Philadelphia. Suddenly that winter people found they had some money in their pockets. In Jamaica the planters were thriving again, buying all the grain the colony could offer. Meanwhile in London the markets regained their confidence. As the South Sea Company crisis receded into the past, on both sides of the ocean the economy improved.[1]

With Franklin to help him, even Keimer could prosper in this new environment. Driven together by chance and by necessity, the two men found a way to earn a profit. They published little books that dealt with two of the period's favorite subjects—health and religion—in a quirky style that suited them both. From *The Curiosities of Common Water,* their readers learned of the benefits of drinking H_2O, "an universal remedy," fit to cure gout, kidney stones, dropsy, and sciatica. Another pamphlet, written by a pastor in Barbados, warned of the evils of alcohol, telling sad stories of people ruined by wine.[2]

For those of a more metaphysical bent, Keimer wrote a religious tract, which he called *A Parable.* It contained the most appalling heresy. No copy has survived; but his ideas so upset the Quakers that in December they bought space in the *Mercury* to make it clear that Keimer was definitely *not* one of their number. The following month, he and Franklin set out to annoy the Anglicans and the Presbyterians as well, by reprinting a scandalous book that had recently appeared in London. Written by a renegade Anglican priest soon after his release from a madhouse, it was called *A Free Gift to the Clergy*. The author insulted ministers of all denominations, calling them dunces, drones, and caterpillars.[3]

Although the books Keimer and Franklin published were eccentric or even outrageous, they found a wide market in freethinking Philadelphia. Here was a town where people wished to be challenged and provoked by writing that owed nothing to any kind of orthodoxy. The same had been true of some readers in Boston, but the *Courant* could only go so far before the authorities called the Franklins to heel. In Pennsylvania no holds were barred. The Anglicans were impotent politically; as yet, the Presbyterians were still a small minority; and as for the Quakers, they might huff and puff, but they could not ban anything Keimer and Franklin sold from their shop. Although in theory the English laws against blasphemy extended to the colonies, in practice the Quakers could not act as censors; it would have been against their principles.

By the spring of 1724, the two printers were thriving. Because the younger man had clung to his frugal Boston ways, saving his wages whenever he could, soon he had a wallet full of English silver. Franklin dressed with style; he owned a watch, in an era when that was still a rarity; and he built a social life in a town where young people were highly literate. During his own six years in Philadelphia, working as a printer and acting as clerk to the colony's General Assembly, Aquila Rose had gathered around him a circle of book-loving friends. Franklin joined their number. "I lived very agreeably," he recalled, "forgetting Boston as much as I could."

He saw no reason to rock any boats by writing to his parents. He kept in touch with only one old friend in his hometown: John Collins, his debating partner, who earned his living as a clerk in Boston's post office. Collins was sworn to secrecy as to his whereabouts. Even so, word leaked out that Franklin was in the Quaker capital. Soon it reached the ears of his brother-in-law, Robert Holmes, the Ulsterman who sailed his sloop up and down the eastern seaboard. By this time the little port of New Castle, forty miles down the Delaware, had become the principal landing place for immigrants arriving from the north of Ireland and so Holmes had connections in the town. From New Castle, Holmes wrote to Benjamin, telling him all was forgiven and imploring him to come back to Boston. Franklin sent a gracious reply, refusing to do any such thing and giving his reasons. Then he thought no more about it.

Life in Philadelphia was simply too enjoyable. Although he and Mr. Keimer were never really close, they took pleasure in each other's company. They had so much in common: a taste for the bizarre, a history of clashes with authority, and political views at the radical end of the spectrum. Later that year, Keimer brought out an American edition of a book that Franklin was bound to admire: *The Independent Whig*, a collection of London newspaper columns from the team responsible for *Cato's Letters*, the series that had so inspired the Franklin brothers.

First published in England four years earlier, *The Independent Whig* was fiercely anticlerical, but also very well written—forceful, pithy, and ironic, like the best material in the *Courant*. And so, although in this period Franklin was no longer a journalist but had to make do with setting in type the words of other men, his partnership with Samuel Keimer kept alive the flame of satire. His first six months in Philadelphia were some of the happiest in Franklin's life. With no commitments, well paid and with excellent prospects, how could he not have fun?

He was working for somebody who could never be accused of being dull. Besides growing his beard, there were two things Keimer liked best of all. One of them was eating—he was "a great glutton," Franklin remembered—and the other was disputation. He loved to argue, and in his hired hand he found a splendid adversary. And so while Keimer entertained them both with his comic impression of the Camisards, Franklin displayed his mastery of dialectic. The two men would argue about everything, but of course Franklin usually won, thanks to his skill with the methods of Socrates in Boston. Keimer admired the young man's expertise with logic; so much so, that it occurred to him that it could be put to good use.

Always looking for God, Samuel Keimer proposed that they should form their own religious sect. He would preach the doctrines and Franklin would crush their opponents with his intellect. From his reading of Tryon, Plutarch, and the deists, Franklin knew about the oddities of sects; he had no intention of joining any such thing; but he saw a chance to have some fun. And so he played along with the idea. When Keimer specified that members of the sect would have to do as he did, never shaving their facial hair and keeping the Sabbath on Saturday, Franklin made a stipulation of his own. They would have to eat vegetables only.

Keimer did not feel that this was sound theology. But Franklin convinced him that if he could abstain from meat and fish, he would emerge a better man. As it happens, by this time Franklin had already relaxed his own strict dietary rule, by permitting himself to eat fried cod. His lapse had occurred the previous autumn on the sea voyage down from Boston to New York. The sailors had landed some fish that were simply too tasty not to be consumed. Seduced by the smell of cod in the pan, Franklin ate the forbidden food. He consoled himself with the thought that cod were cannibals themselves, as shown by the fact that in their stomachs, the cod had smaller fish. Later, he had also eaten his slice of offal at Burlington: another breach of the code. But none of this did he reveal to Keimer.

Instead Franklin posed as a stern vegetarian. He demanded a menu taken from the works of Mr. Tryon, for whom the eating of fish was as culpable as chewing on a steak. Altogether there were forty recipes, close to vegan in their austerity. A woman from the neighborhood came in to cook them, until three months had passed and Keimer was reduced to despair. After so many pints of gruel and so much cauliflower, he longed for the taste of roast pork. So he ordered a pig, had it cooked, and invited Franklin and two women friends to share it for dinner. By the time the ladies and Franklin arrived, Keimer had eaten the lot.

Amusing though it was for a while, his relationship with Franklin had no future. It could only survive as long as Franklin failed to find another mentor, somebody far more powerful, an eminent man with a deeper appreciation of his talents. The fact was that Franklin needed a patron. On both sides of the Atlantic, that had always been the Franklin way.

It was the way things had to be in a deferential society, where the fabric of success was woven from threads of patronage and service, as lesser men attached themselves to the wealthy, in the hope of advancement in reward for being humble, clever, and industrious. In England, the Franklins had prospered not only because of their ingenuity, but also because they found benevolent patrons: John Palmer, Lord Halifax, and the Whig aldermen of Banbury. In America, although it took many years, Josiah had at last become a trusted friend of Judge Sewall, another patron of a kind. Only when he did so could he claim to have secured his status in Boston.

If Franklin were to do the same in Pennsylvania, he would need to acquire his own equivalent of Halifax or Sewall. And soon enough, it seemed that he had found the patron he required. The patron in question turned out to be a terrible disappointment: and this was important too. Far from being a good, kind man of God and science—in other words, another Archdeacon Palmer—his new patron in Philadelphia was a clever but volatile politician who could not be trusted. He deceived the young man, but in doing so he gave Franklin an education in the ways of politics.

At some point early in 1724—the date cannot be fixed, but it was probably in February or March, as he and Keimer were starting to turn a profit—Franklin made the acquaintance of the paramount official in the colony. One day, as they were upstairs in the workshop, through the window they saw none other than the hero of Pennsylvania, the governor himself, approaching them across Market Street. Popular, clever, and charming, and dressed to perfection, Sir William Keith was fifty-four and in his prime. With him was his friend John French, colonel of militia and the leading citizen of New Castle, a town where the Quakers did not rule the roost and so they had a little fort with artillery and a man could tote a gun and be a soldier as well as a merchant.

They knocked at the door. Keimer ran down, only to find that it was Franklin that Governor Keith wished to see. Mr. Keimer stared "like a pig poisoned," as Franklin recalled in his memoirs, when Sir William invited the young man to an inn nearby, for a bottle of Madeira and a business meeting. It transpired that down in New Castle, Keith and French had met Captain Holmes. They had read Franklin's letter and they liked the young man's style. We need an ingenious printer, the governor said, to do official business. We'd like to set you up on your own. Although Franklin had some doubts—how would they raise the money?—it was an offer he could not refuse.

In the months that followed, Franklin became an unwitting pawn in Sir William's games of political chess. The governor was a Scottish baronet: a title that sounds more impressive than it is. Sir William came from the lower reaches of the aristocracy of Scotland, an impoverished country where men such as he often had to live on borrowed money or the handouts they could scrounge from the government in London. The colonies offered an alternative, a field of opportunity where he might make his fortune. Because he was a Tory and a Jacobite, Keith had languished in obscurity for most of the reign of Queen Anne. But as she neared her end in 1714, with the Tories in office for a while, at last Sir William found his niche. He was sent to America to run the customs service from the Delaware down to Jamaica, and he did it rather well.

Like so many other Scots, Keith fell in love with the colonies; and so when the Whigs returned to power with George I, and fired him from his post, he longed to find another way to be an American. In London he met Hannah Penn, the acting proprietor of Pennsylvania, who was permanently resident in England. Deeply impressed with the gallant Sir William, she chose him to be the colony's chief executive. For a while he proved to be a very competent governor, farsighted and creative. But if he was gifted, he was dangerous too: a hungry man, deeply in debt, with a flawed agenda of his own.

"Capable to do mischief": those were the words the authorities had used about Sir William, when he was under arrest as a Jacobite. And mischief was the side of Keith that Franklin would eventually discover. More than sixty years later, when Franklin sat in the convention in Philadelphia that drafted the Constitution for the United States, he would warn his fellow delegates that the republic they produced must be made safe against the frailties of the human beings who would fill the offices of government. Sir William was a case in point: a man who promised far more than he could deliver.[4]

The Laird of Iron Hill

Ten miles or so from the town of New Castle, Delaware, the old turnpike highway to Baltimore passes beneath a patch of high ground. It does not look like much; but make your way up the winding road to the top, and hidden among the trees you will find some pits, with puddles of water at the bottom. The soil is streaked with red, and sometimes in the sunlight the puddles take on a deep ruddy color that explains why the pits came into being. This is Iron Hill. In the eighteenth century, the land hereabouts was known as Keithsborough, because it belonged to Sir William. Here the governor built a forge. The muddy holes are what remain of his mines for iron ore and his quest for riches in the earth.

At his worst, Sir William Keith could be a selfish opportunist. But at his best Keith was something else: a visionary who understood his colony's potential and did all he could to make it flourish. His inspiration was his friend and fellow Scotsman Colonel Alexander Spotswood, lieutenant governor of Virginia, who was trying to settle the western frontier and enrich himself in the process. In 1717, Spotswood had begun to develop iron mines and foundries along the Rappahannock. When Sir William arrived that same year as governor of Pennsylvania of course he wished to do likewise.[5]

But while Colonel Spotswood often found himself at odds with the Virginians, Sir William endeared himself to the people of the Quaker colony. He framed new laws, reformed the courts and the system of taxes, and worked with Spotswood to make a lasting peace with the Iroquois. His poetic friend and protégé, Aquila Rose, called him "great Keith," in an ode in praise of his achievements. Quakers supported Sir

William, because he defended their civil rights; the Anglicans likewise, because he worshipped at Christ Church, where Lady Keith's gravestone can still be seen next to the porch; and he also had a following among the Germans and the Irish, whom he urged to settle in the colony. When German settlers squatted illegally in the interior, Sir William turned a blind eye.

He could be enormous fun, just as he was when he and Colonel French took Franklin to the tavern. In the rural bliss of what is now Montgomery County, Sir William built a little mansion, Graeme Park, modeled on the houses that Scottish lairds inhabited, where he entertained his guests. In Philadelphia he was equally generous. One observer spoke of Keith's "sweetness of temper and carriage," which won him the affection of the people. Unlike so many other governors, in Massachusetts and elsewhere, he did not quarrel with the General Assembly. In 1721, the people's party—small farmers, tradesmen, and shopkeepers—won a landslide victory in the annual election. They became Sir William's coalition. As the economic slump grew deeper he saw it as his task to rescue them from hardship.

Early in 1723, when the recession was at its most severe, the governor set out his philosophy in a rousing speech to the legislature. "It is neither the great, the rich, nor the learned, that compose the body of any people," Keith told them. "Civil government ought carefully to protect the poor, laborious, and industrious part of mankind, in the enjoyment of their just rights, and equal liberties and privileges with the rest of their fellow creatures." It was the task of politicians, said Sir William, to secure the good of the whole community. These were more than merely empty words.[6]

He had already written to the royal authorities in London, seeking their support for a bold experiment in finance. Drawing upon ideas first conceived much earlier, in the Cromwellian England of the 1650s, and then revived in the colonies by the likes of Boston's Elisha Cooke, Sir William wished to found a land bank: or in other words, a scheme with which to make real estate an engine of recovery for the blighted citizens of Pennsylvania. Anybody who owned land or houses would be allowed to borrow on mortgage from the bank, up to a loan-to-value ratio of 50 percent. The loans would be made with paper money, but once it was in circulation it would oil the wheels of commerce. At last the people could afford to buy the food the colony produced so lavishly, and at last they could repay their debts.

Of course, all this would horrify a financial purist, someone wedded to bullion and hard cash, like Dr. Cooke's opponents in Boston. Surely prices would rise, and creditors would lose out, as their debtors met their liabilities not with silver dollars or with gold but with Sir William's dubious paper? Indeed: but in the dire circumstances of the time, the risk of inflation had to be taken. In the March of 1723, the assembly voted for the land bank and Sir William's paper money, and then in October, just as Franklin was taking his first footsteps in Philadelphia, they approved another tranche of the new currency. By Christmastime, the paper bills were flowing round the market. We can leave economists to argue about the rights and wrongs and wherefores and if nots, but the recession was over, and Keith could claim the credit for bringing back prosperity.[7]

As the new year began, so Keimer and Franklin started to make their profits, and John Read found a way to ease his own financial plight. As a house builder, Deborah's father could only stand to gain from Sir William's policies. When the land bank opened for business the previous spring, Mr. Read had taken out a mortgage on one of his houses on Market Street; and early in 1724 he mortgaged the other one as well.

Some fifty years later, when Franklin sat writing his memoirs, he found himself in a quandary about Sir William Keith. Fascinated as he was by economics, and himself an advocate of paper money, Franklin knew that in some ways Keith had been a fine administrator. "Several of our best laws were of his planning," Franklin wrote, seeking to be fair to a man for whose legacy he still had some respect. But he had also seen the governor's dark side. Try as he might, even half a century after their encounter Franklin could not prevent his anger at Sir William from exploding on the page. "What shall we think of a governor playing such pitiful tricks, and imposing so grossly on a poor ignorant boy!" This was one of the most passionate sentences that Franklin ever composed, but he had every reason to resent Sir William's memory. As they sipped their Madeira in the tavern, Keith was engaged in an intricate political maneuver in which the young printer was a piece to be manipulated.

For Sir William, the stakes were immensely high. From the earliest period of English adventures on the mainland of America, the era of Sir Walter Raleigh and then of the plantation at Jamestown, investors had hoped to find there a new El Dorado of precious metals. Their dreams had met with little but frustration; until at last, in New Jersey in about 1715, someone came across a vein of copper, which in time was developed into the Schuyler copper mine. By 1721 the mine was in full swing, shipping its ingots to Europe. Fired up by the prospect of mineral wealth, prospectors began to look for the red metal in every corner of Pennsylvania as well.[8]

Among them were Keith and his friend Colonel French, whose diplomatic missions into Indian country took them far to the west, across the Susquehanna River, where traces of more copper were discovered in land to which the Quaker colony laid claim. It might be a mine as rich as Schuyler's; and if such it proved to be, Keith and French intended to be the masters of its destiny. This they could achieve only if they clung onto power in Pennsylvania.

Sir William's problem was this: with his populism and his paper money, he had won the hearts and minds of the electorate, but he had also made some powerful enemies. None was more dangerous than James Logan, who served as the land agent in the colony for Hannah Penn and her family. A tough but brilliant man, who would come in time to be Franklin's scientific mentor, Logan had every reason to dislike the governor. A Quaker, born in 1674, Logan had been raised in poverty amid the strife of northern Ireland, where his family and friends suffered at the hands of the forces loyal to the Catholic King James. He loathed Tories and Jacobites and everything for which they stood.

Austere and abrasive, Logan was the ultimate meritocrat. He had taught himself Latin, Greek, and Hebrew; he immersed himself in Newton's mathematics; he studied botany, investigating the reproductive system of plants; and he also built a handsome fortune. With the help of a network of French trappers, Logan monopolized the fur trade in the west, shipping the skins to London for his own profit. At first he rather liked Sir William Keith, whose diplomatic skills he admired. But by the end of 1722 James Logan had come to detest the Scotsman as a schemer who hoped to make himself the overlord of Pennsylvania. "His designs are deep laid to serve himself," Logan told the Penns, warning them that Keith was bent on "absolute power."[9]

At best, Sir William would fill every official post with his cronies, and persuade the General Assembly to vote him an ever larger salary; at worst, Keith might convince the king that Pennsylvania should at last become a royal province, with Sir William as the Crown's representative. If so, then everything—vast tracts of virgin land, the iron, the copper, and the trade in skins—might fall into the hands of the Keithites.

Logan could accept Sir William's paper money, but only in small doses. As more and more of it was issued, he began to see it something

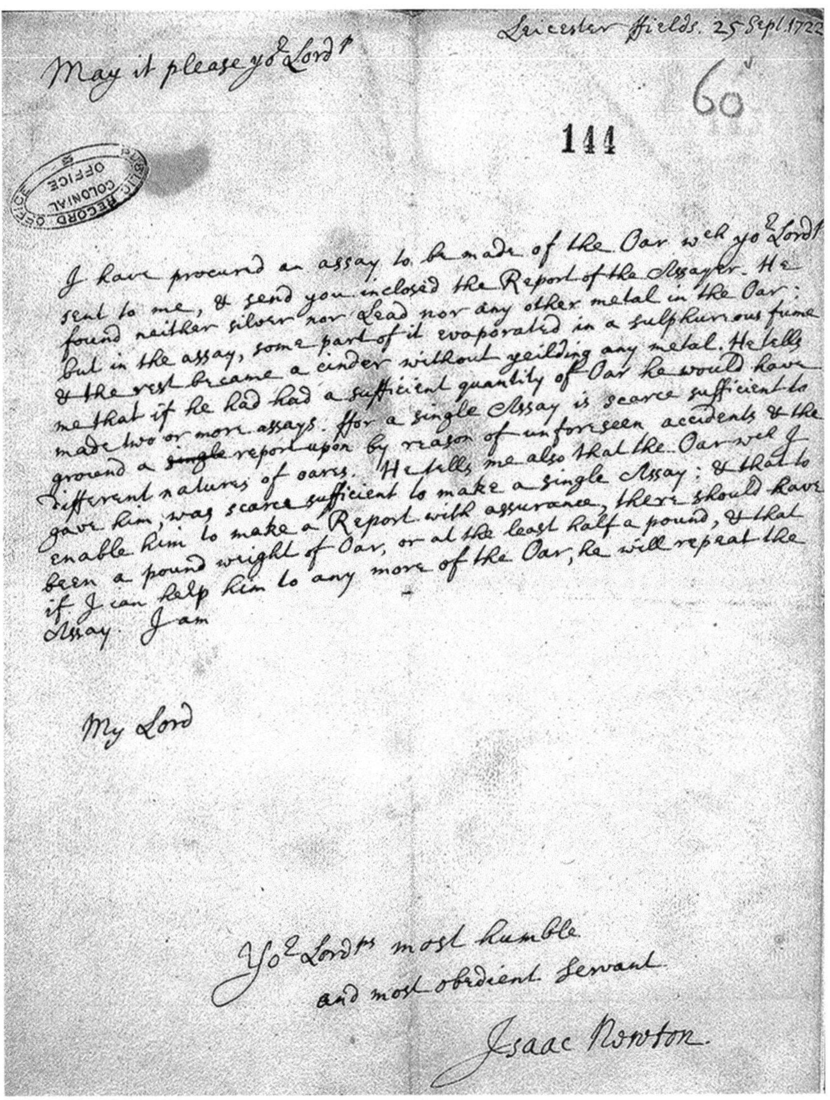

Leicester ffields. 25 Sept 1722

May it please yor Lord^p

60

144

I have procured an assay to be made of the Oar wch yor Lord^p sent to me, & send you inclosed the Report of the Assayer. He found neither silver nor Lead nor any other metal in the Oar: but in the assay, some part of it evaporated in a sulphurious fume & the rest became a cinder without yeilding any metal. He tells me that if he had had a sufficient quantity of Oar he would have made two or more assays. For a single Assay is scarce sufficient to ground a ~~single~~ report upon by reason of unforeseen accidents & the different natures of oares. He tells me also that the Oar wch I gave him, was scarce sufficient to make a single Assay; & that to enable him to make a Report with assurance, there should have been a pound weight of Oar, or at the least half a pound, & that if I can help him to any more of the Oar, he will repeat the Assay. I am

My Lord

Yo^r Lord^ps most humble
and most obedient Servant

Isaac Newton

From the colonial records in London, a relic of the mining craze of the early 1720s that followed the discovery of copper in New Jersey. As Master of the Royal Mint, Sir Isaac Newton is giving his opinion in 1722 on some rocks shipped over from Pennsylvania.

tantamount to fraud. James Logan spoke for the wealthiest merchants of Philadelphia: people dismissed by Sir William as "the lawyers and a few rich usurers." In their eyes and Logan's, Keith's paper money was nothing but a ploy designed to benefit debt-ridden men and to cheat their creditors. Sir William had borrowed heavily against his country properties.

If the feud between Keith and Logan had been merely personal, just another squabble between ambitious men, it would not merit much attention. In fact, the issues at stake were profoundly serious and classically American. The politics of money, the fate of the frontier, the conflicting interests of debtors and creditors, and a clash between a popular movement and a mercantile elite: before and after the Revolution of 1775, in almost every colony questions of the kind kept recurring, with many local variations, giving rise to sectional strife that could never entirely be resolved. In Pennsylvania, with its odd legal status, its diversity, its mineral wealth, and its rapid growth, the issues were especially complex and the personalities especially colorful.

And so it was here in the Quaker colony that Franklin acquired his first lessons in the adult realities of politics. In Boston, his brother James had run *The New-England Courant* for money and for laughs, chiefly at the clergy's expense. The paper was clever, but also rather shallow, and it owed too much to English models. It was funny, but it was futile too. For all its talk of politics, the *Courant* never thought about the subject seriously. The question it did not ask was the essential one: what was the best way to run a government in America, on the edge of the wilderness, where the issues were so different from those of Great Britain? In later life, Franklin would have to think deeply about that very thing. His training began when he met Sir William Keith.

In the spring of 1724, when the governor and Colonel French turned up on Keimer's doorstep, they were looking for ways to outwit James Logan, who was away in England playing what he thought was his trump card. Six months earlier, just before Franklin arrived in Philadelphia, Logan had set out for London, with the aim of seeing Hannah Penn and turning her against the governor. Logan wanted her to send an ultimatum, telling Keith to toe the line, rein in the paper money scheme, and do what Logan told him: if not, he would be dismissed. Since Sir William knew exactly what Logan was up to, he began to prepare for what might be the decisive battle of his life. In his own poker hand he held two aces: not only the General Assembly, where he was so popular, but also the town of New Castle and the area roundabout, including his mines at Iron Hill, in what later became the state of Delaware.

In the 1720s this tract of land still counted as part of Pennsylvania, but this was in dispute because the proprietors of Maryland claimed that it was rightfully theirs. In the Lower Counties, as the area was known, Keith had built a power base, from which—if he were ever fired as governor—he hoped to defy James Logan and the Penns. And so, to secure his position, he hatched a scheme to grant a city charter to New Castle, giving it a government of its own. This would happen in May, with Colonel French to be installed as the mayor. To produce the necessary documents, here and up in Philadelphia, they would need a printer: hence the proposition they had made to Franklin.[10]

There was something else as well. During his long years in London, Sir William had seen the machinery used by Whigs and Tories as they competed for control of the city. Caucuses and clubs, run from inns or coffeehouses, or the occasional use of a mob in the streets to riot or intimidate opponents: these were English tactics that Keith would adopt in America. He could also use the printed word as a weapon, just as it was in London where Defoe and Swift and so many other writers fought out the party strife of the day. To fight his corner, Sir William would need his own pamphlets—even a newspaper, maybe—when Logan returned from England and the struggle between them began in earnest. Here again, Franklin the printer might be very useful.

Everything was agreed in secret. Keeping Keimer in the dark about his true intentions, Franklin would take the next boat for Boston, carrying a private letter from Sir William, urging Josiah to help finance his son's new printing firm. In the meantime, the governor had the young man round for dinner now and then. Amid so much flattery, Franklin decided that Keith was "the best man in the world." Toward the end of April 1724, with James Logan expected home from England imminently, at last Franklin set off for Massachusetts. It was a difficult passage—they hit a shoal, sprang a leak, and again he had to use his muscles, helping to pump water from the bilges—but after two weeks they reached their destination. On their arrival, they found that it was business as usual in the Bay Colony, that peevish land of piety and violence.

The Prodigal Son

On the frontier, the war continued with the Abenaki, with ever more cruelty as each month went by. More pirates were caught at sea, their heads carried back to Boston for the reward. The president of Harvard died in his sleep, prompting Cotton Mather to revile the dead man as "an infamous drone." In the *Courant*, James Franklin was taking after his father and advertising African slaves for sale: "two very likely negroes (a boy and a girl), each about fourteen . . . enquire of the printer hereof."

To comply with the law, the paper still appeared above Benjamin's name, but it had lost its excitement. James had retreated to an older journalistic model. To fill most of his space, he merely recycled the politics of Europe, printing long accounts of the activities of kings and diplomats.

Three months earlier he had taken a wife. Even so James remained as miffy as before. Perhaps the couple were unhappy, because while Franklin was in town, the *Courant* ran an item about the plight of husbands who "have suffer'd shipwreck in their choice of wives." At the house on Hanover and Union, where Franklin arrived without warning, he received a warm welcome, the prodigal come home; but just as it was in the parable, his brother was a different story. The breach between them seemed to be irreparable.

When Franklin turned up at the printing shop in brand-new clothes, with his watch and a pocket full of English coins, James looked him up and down and then ignored him. It did not help when James's workmen plied Franklin with questions about Philadelphia, or when he stood them all a round of drinks. Sullen and very proud—another Franklin family trait—James took his brother's behavior as an insult. Time passed, and Abiah begged him to forgive her youngest son. James would not relent.

Franklin's visit to his hometown was brief and unsuccessful. It left him in no hurry to return to a place for which he had little affection, however much he tried in later life to pretend that this was not so. He would not see Boston again for another nine years. Josiah read Sir William's letter, and found it very odd: who had ever thought of setting up a boy in business, still three years short of adulthood? Impressed though he was by his son's success in Pennsylvania, he would not offer anything financial. Even when Captain Holmes stopped by, and told him what he knew about the governor, the answer was still no. The house on Hanover and Union still had a mortgage, Josiah had not yet repaid the money he borrowed to pay for James's printing press, and he had gone into debt again to help one of his sons-in-law. He wrote to Sir William thanking him politely, but refusing to help.

So Benjamin set off for Philadelphia, with his father's letter and a cargo of books. Early in May, he signed an IOU for three guineas in favor of a Boston bookseller, John Phillips. This was a lot of money to spend on books—in 1724, three guineas would have purchased five annual subscriptions to the *Courant*—and so it must be that Franklin was buying stock to sell from Keimer's shop. Phillips had a title on offer that would have been ideal: *Onania,* or "the heinous sin of self-pollution," an exposé of the evil effects of masturbation. The book had sold well in London. It was exactly the kind of thing that Keimer dealt in. Since the IOU would not fall due for repayment until the following January, they would have plenty of time to sell any copies they bought.[11]

At this moment, at the very outset of his business career, Franklin made a foolish error. Many decades later, it would still make him wince with regret. Once again, we find that the finest passages of Franklin's memoirs concern episodes of frailty—sometimes his own, sometimes other people's—and this one was even more painful because it involved his betrayal of a sibling.

The sloop that carried Franklin called in at Newport, Rhode Island. There amid the traders in rum and whale oil, his favorite brother, sixteen years his senior, followed the family craft of boiling soap and making candles. John Franklin was another ingenious artisan, who loved his copper vats and iron furnace and his imported English encyclopedias. A man with an eye for business—in the press, he promised to sell his wares "at the lowest prices for present money"—John was trying to develop a secret recipe for making "crown soap," a premium product that might make his fortune. He greeted Benjamin warmly, and then he introduced him to an acquaintance. And this led to the episode that caused Franklin so much distress.[12]

In affluent Newport, John was friendly with a silversmith, Samuel Vernon. A successful man in his forties, an elder of his church with a career in public service ahead of him, Vernon made bowls and tankards for clients that included Yale College. His business contacts extended as far as Pennsylvania, where Vernon had a debtor who owed him some £35 in local money. It was another large sum, about a year's earnings for a skilled

A tankard made by the Rhode Island silversmith and politician Samuel Vernon, who in 1723 entrusted Franklin with money Vernon was owed in Pennsylvania.

workman. But since Benjamin was John Franklin's brother, and John was a churchgoer too, Vernon had every reason to think that Benjamin could be trusted. The silversmith signed a document authorizing the young man to receive the money on his behalf.[13]

In England and the colonies alike, aspiring young men needed patrons; but they also needed to be seen as people of integrity, whose word was their bond. Their IOUs had to be honest, and when they acted as intermediaries their probity had to be unquestionable. How else could the economy function? In an America where hard cash was scarce, and paper money like Sir William's was new and unproven, people in business had to trust each other. Communications were slow. Long-distance debts would often go unpaid for months or years, as merchants waited for the harvest to come in, for trappers to return from the interior, or for ships to sail back from the West Indies or Great Britain. In trusting Franklin as he did, Samuel Vernon was taking a risk; but he was also setting the young man a test, to see if he was an honest broker who could meet his obligations. Despite his studies of virtue in Plutarch or the life of Socrates, Franklin failed the test first time around.

The problem began when the sloop arrived in New York. On the way down from Newport, Franklin had narrowly avoided two calamities, when the sloop scraped a rock at sea, and then when he caught the eye of two young women on board. Given what he knew about what went on by night on Boston Common, he should have seen that they were dangerous, but he was still all too naive. It was only when a Quaker lady on the boat warned him against them that he saw that he had to steer clear. They turned out to be strumpets and petty thieves, who had lifted a silver spoon from the captain's cabin. This had been a lucky escape, but when he reached Manhattan he could not avoid a hazard of another kind.

It was John Collins, fresh down from Boston, and on his breath he carried the odor of brandy. A prey not only to drink but also to gambling, he needed money, and thanks to Mr. Vernon the young Franklin had money to offer. Between them, John Collins and Governor Keith had the potential to end his career almost before it began.

IDLENESS AND INDUSTRY

Just as we remember Franklin as the master of the positive, so we also think of him as someone with a genius for sociability. The founder of clubs and societies, he was a fascinating companion whom people wanted to know: the only exceptions being the more pompous variety of British politicians. It was taken for granted that an ingenious person had to be affable. One had to be clever but also to wear one's intellect lightly, so as to be a person everybody hoped to run into at the coffeehouse. And not only that: an ingenious woman or man was also somebody with experience. He or she had learned to be discerning, knowing how to choose friends carefully.

That was the way Franklin was, but only after the age of twenty-five or so. In his youth and very early manhood, he was sociable but he knew nothing about discernment. His early friendships were mostly disastrous. It was inevitable, really. With his history of irreverence on *The New-England Courant,* his skeptical ideas, and with what the disapproving Josiah called his talent for "lampooning and libelling," Franklin appeared to be someone who could be persuaded to bend the rules. So it was with John Collins. Seduced by Franklin's tales of life amid the Quakers, he had quit his job at the Boston post office, and hoped to find a place as a clerk in Philadelphia.

During their years of friendship in Boston, Franklin had seen Collins as a paragon of virtue, industrious and sober. By the time they met again in New York he was penniless. Franklin had to pay his bill and his fare to Philadelphia, and when they reached the town things went from bad to worse. They were only together for three months before Collins left for Barbados in August, in search of a post as a tutor. These would be three of the longest months of Franklin's life.

While he went back to work for Samuel Keimer, Collins moved in with his friend at the Read house, where at the age of forty-seven John Read was gravely ill. He would die in September, bequeathing his mortgage debt to Sarah. Still drinking, and quarrelsome when he was in liquor, Collins with his taint of alcohol could not find a job. By now, Franklin had collected the sum owed to Samuel Vernon, and so Collins pestered him for loans. Of course Franklin should have said no, but he had more than a touch of vanity. Not one but two colonial governors had singled him out as a brilliant young man: the second was William Burnet, the governor of New York, who—while Franklin was passing through the town—had heard about his chest full of books from John Phillips and had given him a tour of his library. And so Franklin dipped into Vernon's money. In dribs and drabs he lent it to Collins, until it had all but disappeared.

In the meantime his conspiracy with Sir William continued, over more private dinners at the governor's mansion. Keith read Josiah's letter, politely disagreed with what he wrote, and made a very generous suggestion. He would lend Franklin the money to buy a printing press and whatever else he needed from England. Deeply grateful, Franklin compiled an inventory—the equipment would cost £100 in sterling, as much as James had spent on his apparatus—and the governor gave his approval. Better still, what if the young man went to London himself, to choose the lead type and everything else? Deeply flattered, Franklin said yes. It was agreed that he would sail for England later that year on the annual mail boat, the *London Hope.* He would carry a letter of credit from Sir William, promising to pay for everything the young man acquired.

What was going on? Franklin could not see what the governor was up to. On May 28—King George's birthday—while Franklin was in Boston, Keith and Colonel French had carried through their plan to make New Castle independent. Keimer was given the task of printing the city charter, issued in the name of His Majesty: something Sir William had no authority to do. And then in June at last James Logan reappeared from England on the *London Hope,* a ship so racked with fever that the master died soon after they landed. With him Logan carried the ultimatum from Hannah Penn, ordering Sir William to curtail the flow of paper money.

With Logan sure to be enraged by the events at New Castle, it was all the more essential for Keith to have allies in the press. For a while he could ignore the letter from Mrs. Penn, whose contents were private. But elections were due in the fall, and the assembly would meet in full session in January. Sooner or later Logan would reveal what Hannah Penn had written. Sir William would need the assembly's support, and then he would have to battle it out with Logan in the press, on the streets, and in the offices of ministers in London. And so Keith enlisted the help of his old Virginia friend Colonel Spotswood. By now the colonel had been fired from his post as lieutenant governor, with questions being asked about the quantities of land he had accumulated in the west. That summer Spotswood was off to England to defend himself; and since the colonel still had friends at court, Sir William wanted him to lobby on his behalf.[14]

Meanwhile James Logan gathered his own supporters. Of these, the most important was a lawyer, Andrew Hamilton. A Presbyterian, but also a freethinker, he certainly had Scottish roots but whether he was born in Scotland or in Ulster it is impossible to say. A man who never spoke about his past—it was rumored that he had come to the colonies as an indentured servant, or even as a felon—Hamilton was a brilliant advocate. He was also a bully. Another man who liked his drink, he had a manner so brusque that a judge in London once censured him for "scandal and impertinence." He too was in the game of real estate, amassing his own empire of American soil.[15]

Hamilton, Logan, Spotswood: these were powerful but dangerous men, whose names would recur time and again in Franklin's early career, long after Sir William Keith had vanished from the scene. Only by learning how to understand their tactics and their goals could he hope to prosper. When at last he did so, becoming especially close to Andrew Hamilton, Franklin could begin to make his own fortune; but that took time. As yet he was too young to understand their maneuvers.

But not too young to be contemplating marriage. As John Read succumbed to his final illness, Franklin and Deborah began to woo each other. With Mr. Read having died so deeply in debt, the Read family faced what might be a bleak future. Deborah had a brother, John, a carpenter like his father, but he was still only a boy: and so she had every reason to be responsive when their attractive lodger began to make advances. By the time Franklin was ready to sail for London, he had told her the secret of his intrigue with Sir William. Mrs. Read stopped them going too far, too quickly—she wanted to see Franklin set up in business as a printer, before they married—but by November they were more or less betrothed. Or as Franklin put it in his memoirs, as people put it at the time, he and Deborah had "interchanged some promises."

One obstacle had been removed: the appalling John Collins. He had continued to drink and to borrow money. He quarreled with Franklin, until their friendship reached its end with an ugly incident on the river. They had been out with some other friends in a rowboat, but on the way back Collins refused to take his turn with the oars. Exasperated with his friend, Franklin did the same. Collins swore at him and shaped up for a fight, stepping along the thwarts of the boat and lunging with his fists. Franklin ducked down, grabbed Collins under the thigh, and hurled him into the water. As Collins swam around the boat, still vowing not to lift an oar, Franklin and the others kept him at bay. Each time he came close, they pulled away. Only as night fell and Collins was nearly exhausted did they drag him on board. Soon afterward he vanished off to the West Indies, never to be heard from again. He left Franklin sick with worry about the money he owed to Mr. Vernon.

For consolation he could turn not only to Deborah but to other companions as well. Aquila Rose had made it the fashion for young men with literary tastes to ramble among the trees by the Schuylkill on a Sunday afternoon. So Franklin did the same with three new acquaintances, office clerks who shared his passion for books. Among them was a gifted young man named James Ralph, a few years older than Franklin, already married with a child but restless, frustrated, and eager to see London. His parentage and place of birth are unknown—while there is some evidence that Ralph came from the west of England, this is far from certain—but he was to replace John Collins as Franklin's closest friend. Their relationship would end almost as badly.

At the hands of most of Franklin's biographers, James Ralph has been treated still more unkindly than Deborah. While Mrs. Franklin has been sneered at for her looks, her poor spelling, or merely for being a woman, James Ralph has been brushed aside as nothing but an idle dreamer. Like Deborah, he deserves a better fate from posterity. Just as she had a life and a role beyond the making of her husband's breakfast, so Ralph was far more than merely a foil for Franklin's genius.

"The celebrated Mr James Ralph": so he was described in London after his death in 1762. Certainly he had his faults. In his youth he was feckless and unfaithful, a bigamist in fact, and he antagonized people who could ruin his career. But although Ralph came close to disaster, he recovered and eventually enjoyed a modest degree of fame as a fine historian and a shrewd writer about politics. Among his close friends he counted the greatest actor of the eighteenth century, David Garrick, and one of the greatest novelists, Henry Fielding. James Ralph would never have advanced that far if he had been no more than a wastrel.[16]

Although he could be pompous, Ralph had excellent manners. Somebody who knew him in later life recalled that in conversation Ralph was "agreeable, instructive, and entertaining." So he was in his youth as well: in Franklin's words, "I think I never knew a prettier talker." Besides their ingenuity, the two young men had other things in common. It seems that Ralph had been a Presbyterian, but under Franklin's influence he became a freethinker. And they both loved poetry. The difference was that Ralph intended to make it his career.[17]

Among their friends, they held a literary competition of a kind that Uncle Benjamin would have enjoyed. The old man had loved turning the Hebrew psalms into English verse. Now Franklin and his friends set themselves the same challenge, with James Ralph emerging as the winner.

He wrote with energy, with color, and with such a command of diction that his poem was met with a round of applause. And that was that: James Ralph decided he was born to be a poet, on a par with Dryden or Pope.

Franklin disagreed. Much as he loved poetry, and much as he admired his friend's sublimities, he took the same view as Josiah: you couldn't make a living in that way. He and James Ralph thrashed the matter out, until Ralph appeared to see sense. Married though Ralph was, with a child to provide for, it was agreed that he would cross the Atlantic with Franklin, but *not* to join the aspiring literati of the capital. Instead, Ralph hoped to make business contacts in England who would use him as their agent to sell their wares in Philadelphia: where, once established as a merchant, he could dedicate his leisure to his Muse. Again, Franklin believed what he was told: that James Ralph planned to remain in London only briefly. Again he allowed himself to be deceived.

At last, after months of waiting, October arrived and the *London Hope* was ready to sail, free from disease and with a new skipper. At the end of the month, with Franklin and Ralph on board, she dropped down the river to New Castle to pick up the mail. Besides the pelts and the deerskins gathered in by Logan, she was a rather empty ship by way of cargo. That year the tobacco crop failed in Virginia and Maryland, ruined by a tropical storm. Neither did she carry much bullion: in Philadelphia, the merchants still had scarcely a dollar to send to their English creditors, who were always hungry for Spanish silver. Her list of passengers was more impressive, and to Franklin they must have seemed like ideal company. In a month or so at sea, he could mingle as he pleased with men who might be as useful as Sir William Keith.

The list included the greedy Andrew Hamilton. Like Colonel Spotswood, who had left weeks earlier, he was bound for London: in Hamilton's case to advise Hannah Penn and to defend in the law courts his doubtful title to some real estate he coveted in Philadelpha. There were also two English ironmasters, off to the empire's capital to do business on behalf of a new forge and foundry in Maryland. For some reason, Franklin noted their names in his memoirs: Mr. Onion and Mr. Russell. It is not clear why they meant so much to him, but the reason may be this. Thomas Russell also came from the Reads' English hometown of Birmingham, where the Russells were in the iron trade. His partner, Stephen Onion, had his own roots nearby. Most likely, Franklin mentioned their names because steel and iron was a subject he enjoyed, and because he knew—how could he not, being married to Deborah?—how much that business owed to pioneers like these.[18]

And then there was a Quaker sailing on the *London Hope,* by the name of Thomas Denham. The son of a shoemaker in the English port of Bristol, he had known adversity and shame. In his youth he had suffered a fate like that of John Collins. He fell into bad company and ran up bad debts, until he had to sail to Pennsylvania. By the time Franklin met him on the boat, Denham had built a new livelihood importing wine and indentured servants, he was a friend of Andrew Hamilton, and he had raised the money to repay his creditors. A chastened man, wise by virtue of experience, Denham became Franklin's best source of counsel.[19]

His Voyage to London

So there we find Franklin and James Ralph, waiting on the ship at New Castle early in November 1724: but as Franklin tells us in his autobiography, something was wrong. Before leaving Philadelphia, Franklin had called at the governor's mansion—several times—to collect Sir William's letter of credit, and some others recommending him to people in London as a trustworthy fellow. Somehow the letters were never forthcoming. The governor would be at New Castle before the ship sailed, Franklin was told: and so indeed Keith was, but still no letters. Franklin went down to the governor's lodgings in the little town, to be told with the finest courtesy that the letters in his favor would be brought aboard the *London Hope* before she set sail.

Puzzled or even dismayed, but giving Sir William the benefit of the doubt, Franklin climbed back aboard. Just before the ship set out, Colonel French appeared with the mailbag. He greeted Franklin kindly. Deeply impressed, his fellow passengers invited Ralph and Franklin to share the largest cabin. Andrew Hamilton had gone ashore—in return for a handsome fee, he went back to Philadelphia to plead a case, on behalf of a ship arrested for smuggling—and so he would have to follow them to London on another vessel. But Denham and the ironmasters made the two young men very welcome. Assured by the captain that the pouch would be unsealed once they were in sight of England, Franklin put his anxieties aside, assuming that the letter of credit was inside.

Although Hamilton's stores kept them well fed, the voyage was long and miserable. The storms that had ravaged the tobacco crop went on until late in the year, crossed the Atlantic, and blew up a hurricane off the coast of Portugal. In such heavy weather they made slow progress. It was only on December 21 that the *London Hope* dropped anchor in the English Channel. Three days later, Franklin came ashore in the city where Josiah and his brothers had spent so many years: the London where they had listened to the preachers, read the word of God, and colored silk with arsenic and urine.[20]

A city with more than 600,000 inhabitants, vastly larger than any American town, it kept on growing and it kept on changing: and so London was now a different place from the one the Franklins of the past had known. The obvious temptations were still there, as they would be in any town—drink, and sex, and gambling—and so were the preachers: but the culture and politics of London had moved on yet again. Even James Franklin, who had been there only six years earlier, would have found that it had characteristics he would not recognize.

After the South Sea Bubble, for a while it had seemed that the Whigs were doomed, so deeply were they tarnished by the financial crash. But they refused to be defeated. Instead they found a new, more competent leader in the shape of Sir Robert Walpole. Obese and a lecher, a man devoid of high ideals, Sir Robert would never be anyone's hero, but he did have many talents and some virtues: including an aversion to war, and an aptitude for finance. He also commanded the support of George I. By the time Franklin arrived, Walpole had become in effect Great Britain's first prime minister. Cunning and resilient, he remained in power for the next twenty years.[21]

In London Sir Robert's influence was everywhere. To forestall any plots by the Jacobites, Walpole ran agents in every part of the city; and he kept an especially close eye on the corner of the capital where Franklin and Ralph rented a little apartment. They found their lodgings in a street called Little Britain, an obvious choice for two young men of letters. For more than a century, this neighborhood had been a home for bookstores, publishers, and printers. It was also politically suspect, lying within a city ward called Farringdon Without, a buzzing hive of radicals and Jacobites and Tories. As one of the area's booksellers put it at the time, he and his rivals were "taken for little better than a pack of knaves and atheists." The district Franklin chose could also be a brutal place, where dreams might be shattered and innocence corrupted.[22]

Chapter Ten

Little Britain

Sixty years earlier, when the Great Fire reduced so much of London to ashes, the blaze died down on the northern edge of the city just before it reached Little Britain. At one end of the street there stood the ancient church of St. Botolph. The flames licked up against the walls, and left them scorched, but the church, its steeple, and the area beyond it survived. In the 1720s the houses remained as they had been long ago. Built of wood and plaster, decked out with Tudor carvings of animals and birds, they rose to as many as five floors, shutting out the light from a labyrinth of courtyards and alleys.

At the heart of the maze, Franklin and Ralph took rooms in a tenement known as the Golden Fan, with behind it the graveyard of St. Botolph's. Until the eve of World War I, some of the oldest houses hereabouts were still intact. Photographs were taken that show us the streets as Franklin knew them. They had curious names, relics of the past: Cloth Fair, Duck Lane, and Pelican Court. The district was a blend of the sordid and the subtle, an assault on the senses and the intellect. From his reading, Franklin had an inkling of what he might discover; but nothing on a printed page could entirely prepare him for what he found.[1]

By 1724, London had no fewer than nineteen newspapers, and five of them were published from Little Britain. This street and Duck Lane were lined with bookstores, used books at one end, and new at the other. In the previous century, this had been "a perpetual emporium of learned authors," one book lover recalled, but now it was gradually losing its cachet. The better sort of booksellers had begun to leave, in search of more elegant premises beneath St. Paul's Cathedral, with its dome rising over the rooftops. They were keen to escape the squalor that surrounded Little Britain.[2]

A few minutes' walk away, the streets were foul with the stench of Smithfield, the cattle market—a "shameful place," in the words of Charles Dickens, who knew the area well, "all asmear with filth and fat and blood and foam." Between the holding pens and the Golden Fan there lay the sprawling premises of St. Bartholomew's Hospital. Each year six thousand of the maimed and sick and indigent passed through its doors. Next to the hospital there stood some old cloisters, ever more ruinous as each year went by.

Although their fate was sealed—the cloisters were knocked down in 1730, when the hospital began a great rebuilding—in the meantime they were rented out to shopkeepers, milliners especially. The cloisters had an evil reputation as the haunt of card-sharpers and whores. With inns and taverns on all sides, alcohol was everywhere, just as it was in America. The difference was that here they wrecked the brain or the liver with a spirit flavored with juniper, rather than with rum. In 1725, campaigners for temperance counted more than six thousand locations in London where gin was sold.[3]

When he set foot in Little Britain, Franklin entered the city of the artist William Hogarth. His painterly fables of ruin and sin bear a close resemblance to the stories of drink and failure that Franklin gives us in his memoirs. It was here, between Smithfield and Little Britain, that Hogarth began his observations of high life and low life, here that he first saw harlots, thieves, and apprentices, clergymen and hypocrites, and people degraded by gin. Born only nine years before Franklin, Hogarth spent his childhood in the area: until the fearful day when his father was slung into prison for debt.

Released from jail, Mr. Hogarth took William and the rest of the family back to Smithfield, where they lived in an old wooden house in Long Lane, close to the cloisters and the cattle pens. When Franklin arrived in London, the widow Hogarth was still there, a few hundred yards from the Golden Fan. She and the painter's sister were among the milliners who sold their wares from the stalls around the hospital.[4]

Because we mostly remember Franklin for the achievements of his later years, after the Boston Tea Party and Bunker Hill, it is all too easy to forget that he grew up in a very different era. He was already an adult long before the birth of the rest of America's founding fathers. Franklin came to maturity in the 1720s, in a world very different from the one

Engraved by William Hogarth in the 1720s, this shop card advertises the millinery business owned by his mother and sister in Smithfield, a short walk from Franklin's lodgings.

that belonged to Washington or Jefferson, men born to rural privilege whose take on life could never be quite the same as his. In his youth in London, Franklin's world was William Hogarth's world. They inhabited a city where the penalty for error was annihilation, on the streets, in the paupers' hospital, or in the debtors' prison.

Much later, when Franklin returned to England in 1757, the two men became directly acquainted, but Franklin had known Hogarth's work long before that. In 1739 he imported some of Hogarth's engravings for sale in his store in Philadelphia. The two men had a vast amount in common, not only in the circumstances of their lives but also in the themes that animated their work. Both were apprentices who never finished their indentures, but struck out on their own. Both Franklin and Hogarth were highly skeptical about orthodox Christian belief. Indeed they both became Freemasons, taking the masonic Craft as an alternative ethical creed. They read and admired the same books—the philosopher Shaftesbury, Daniel Defoe, and *The Spectator*—and came away with a fund of motifs and ideas that shaped the way they saw the world around them.

Hogarth and Franklin were people who reached the heights of success but never forgot just how easy it was to fail. Uncle Benjamin, the strumpets on the boat down from Newport, John Collins, James Ralph, and even Mr. Denham: these were characters who might have stepped out of one of Hogarth's narrative cycles. Among the stories Hogarth told in each of his series of paintings and engravings, the most relevant are those in his cycle *Industry and Idleness,* from 1747. Here William Hogarth shows us the parallel lives of two very different apprentices. One of them works and prays hard, goes to church, marries the boss's daughter, and rises to be London's lord mayor. The other apprentice runs away to sea, takes to a life of crime, and meets his death swinging on a noose at Tyburn. In telling this story and so many others, Hogarth gives us parables resembling those in Franklin's autobiography, where Franklin is so industrious, while John Collins plays the part of the idle youth who disappeared.

Readers have sometimes found Franklin insufferably smug, as he describes his brilliant career. And yet beneath the surface of Franklin's narrative there lies an undercurrent of anxiety, the same fear of ruin and of destitution that we find in Hogarth and later in Dickens. Perhaps it flows from Franklin's memory that he had made mistakes—dipping into Vernon's money, for one—and that he had escaped disaster only by the skin of his teeth. If he too had run away to be a sailor, as he yearned to do, Franklin's life might also have ended in catastrophe, like the idle apprentice or his brother Josiah, lost at sea. This was something Franklin always remembered: that although he had been industrious, he might so easily have done the other thing.

For all his achievements, Franklin never succumbed to complacency. Like Hogarth, in whose pictures the people who rise to the top of the pile are viewed ironically, shown up as hypocrites or mocked for their vanity, Franklin knew that what the world means by "success" is often just another kind of failure. If he wished to rise in the world, it was not because he wanted to be a bloated official like Hogarth's lord mayor. That was never Franklin's aim. Of course he aspired—like James Franklin with the *Courant*—to be "ingenious." But more than that, he intended to be an ingenious *gentleman,* with the leisure to practice his ingenuity for the good of society as well as his own enjoyment.

In the London of Hogarth, Franklin encountered incidents far more extreme than anything he might have witnessed in America. A crime wave had engulfed the capital; and just five weeks before Franklin arrived, its most notorious incident occurred within a half mile of his lodgings. Newgate Prison was the place where the warders had the keeping of a burglar, Jack Sheppard, who had been condemned to death. Three times Jack Sheppard broke out of his cell, taking refuge in the slums of Smithfield, until at last they hanged him like Hogarth's idle apprentice. Beneath the gallows Defoe stood by with his notebook, the diligent reporter waiting to take down Jack's final words. As the young Franklin came ashore in London, the press were running advertisements for ballads, books, and a musical that dramatized the Sheppard story.

It was also a city steeped in politics. That winter Sir Robert Walpole was tightening his grip on London by taking a new law through Parliament, the City Elections Act, intended to rig the ballots by striking thousands of voters off the rolls: a measure aimed at troublesome wards like Farringdon Without, where at election time the Tories could count on as many as one thousand supporters. In Little Britain and elsewhere, the act aroused a storm of protest that supplied the backdrop for everything Franklin saw as he found his feet in the metropolis. Almost everyone in London whom Franklin mentions in his memoirs had some kind of political allegiance or agenda, even if—at first meeting—their party ties were often far from obvious.[5]

He would spend eighteen months in the empire's capital before sailing home to Philadelphia in the middle of 1726. In his autobiography, Franklin gives this brief phase of his life more than ten printed pages of narrative, almost as much as he allocates to the entire decade after 1730. London served as his substitute for Harvard, giving him an education of a kind that college professors could not have supplied. Of course he saw plays and read books—Franklin tells us that in his autobiography—but what he remembered best of all from London was the people he met: some of whom opened up new vistas of imagination, while others revealed the nastier side of human nature. His schooling in the ways of the city began with the destruction of a dream.

An Illusion Lost

As the *London Hope* entered the English Channel, the skipper had kept his promise to Franklin. He opened the mailbag and showed the young man what he took to be the governor's letters, including—he presumed—Sir William's letter of credit in his favor. None of them had his name on the outside, but Franklin picked out six or seven that looked as though they came from Keith. Using his initiative, Franklin set out to deliver them, in the expectation that they included the letters he was promised. One of the envelopes came addressed to John Baskett, the king's official printer, with whom the governor had business dealings. Baskett owned the rights to English editions of laws made by the colonial assemblies. And so when the ship reached the city on Christmas Eve, Franklin made for Baskett's premises, in the shadow of St. Paul's Cathedral.

On the way, he stopped at a stationer's shop to drop off another of the letters. To Franklin's dismay, the owner had never heard of Governor Keith. But he did know the name of someone else: William Van Haes Dunk Riddlesden, alias William Cornwallis, crooked attorney, thief, and bigamist, wanted for trying to pass dud banknotes in France. In Maryland, where Riddlesden had left a trail of disaster behind him, that year the assembly had passed a special Riddlesden act, branding him "a person of matchless character in infamy." Franklin knew him as the fraudster who had cheated poor John Read of the little money he possessed.[6]

On the letter he was given, the stationer recognized Riddlesden's handwriting. "A complete rascal!" he exclaimed. He thrust the paper back in Franklin's hand, and turned away to serve a customer, leaving the young man aghast and—we must assume—deeply embarrassed. "The famous Mr Riddlesden," as newspaper readers knew him in London, was by now so notorious that when he was in Newgate his case was dealt with by Walpole's closest aides. Nobody, least of all Franklin, who was still two weeks' shy of his nineteenth birthday, would wish to be associated with such a villain.

And of course the episode raised a large question mark over Sir William Keith. How had Riddlesden's letter come to be in the mailbag? And where was the letter of credit that Sir William had promised, made out in Franklin's name? If he had gone on to see John Baskett, he would have discovered that Keith owed money to the printer, who was about to pursue the governor through the law courts of Pennsylvania. It was all such a mystery; and so the bewildered Franklin hurried off in search of advice from his new mentor, Thomas Denham, who had also just landed from the *London Hope.*

The Quaker merchant told his young friend the truth about Sir William, his unreliability, and his very shaky finances. Denham laughed at the notion that Franklin could obtain a letter of credit from a governor so deep in debt that he had no credit to give. They studied Riddlesden's letter—what happened to the other five or six is something Franklin does not tell us in his autobiography—and there they found something still more distressing. It seemed that Riddlesden and Governor Keith were working together, hatching a devious plot against Andrew Hamilton. It was all so very complicated, but Denham gave the young man some excellent advice. At this point, Hamilton was still in America waiting for the next ship to London, the *Samuel.* She would not set sail from New York until ten days after Christmas. But if and when Hamilton arrived, they would tell him everything: that was Denham's suggestion. It turned out to be very fruitful. In the meantime Franklin should find a job. He should learn the finer points of the printing trade of London, and then set up in business at home.[7]

Which Franklin agreed to do. But this left another question hanging in the air: what was to be done about James Ralph? While Franklin had some money, fifteen Spanish doubloons, Ralph was broke. Although he had a sister and some other relatives in London, they were poor and could not help him. To cap it all, Ralph suddenly revealed that his plans had changed again. Far from modeling himself on Mr. Denham, making business connections and then sailing home to his wife and child in Philadelphia, he planned to remain in London and become a poet: or perhaps an actor.

With a chutzpah that even Franklin could not surpass, James Ralph headed straight for the Theatre Royal in Drury Lane. There he applied for a place in His Majesty's Company of Comedians, led by the actor-manager Robert Wilks, a Dublin man. Ralph could not have chosen a worse moment or a more skeptical impresario. Wilks had been the promoter of the musical about Jack Sheppard, complete with a song from

Jack's paramour, Frisky Moll. But the show had been a fiasco, hissed off the stage on opening night. Wilks was a kindly old fellow but he could not be doing with amateurs, especially at a time like this. The Irishman told James Ralph that he had no future on the stage.[8]

So the poet thought of something else. In a fine location near St. Paul's there lived John Roberts, a theatrical publisher, whose list of plays included the Sheppard musical. Ralph went to see him with another idea: he would write a weekly paper, in the style of *The Spectator,* and Roberts would be its proprietor. It was not so hapless a notion as it might seem, because in time Ralph became an excellent critic of drama and painting. But again the answer was in the negative. Snubbed by John Roberts, he went down to the legal district, the Temple, in search of a vacancy for a copy clerk. Once more he asked in vain.

And so the feckless poet had to follow the example of John Collins, and borrow from Benjamin Franklin. Ralph "seemed quite to forget his wife and child," Franklin wrote, "and I by degrees my engagement with Miss Read, to whom I never wrote more than one letter, and that was to let her know I was not likely soon to return." This was one of the errors he would recall with grief in his autobiography; but, as Franklin also pointed out, how could he have found the cash to buy a ticket home? Their rent in Little Britain came to three shillings and sixpence a week, and he and Ralph loved to go to plays.

The cheapest seat at Drury Lane cost one shilling, and so—what with books to buy, appearances to be kept up, and Ralph incapable of earning a penny—Franklin's cash disappeared as swiftly as sand through the neck of an hourglass. From America, he had brought with him a small curiosity, a purse made from colonial asbestos, which could amuse an audience by failing to burn when thrown into a fire: but while it might be worth some money in London, it would not be very much. And all the while he was still in debt to the silversmith from Newport, Mr. Vernon. But Rhode Island was a long way off; and besides, Franklin came up trumps when he went looking for a job of his own.

Forty years earlier, his uncle Benjamin had worked with the very best London dyers of silk, adept in the latest techniques. Now Franklin could do something similar in the printing trade. It was a demanding business, requiring a rare combination of physical strength, a knowledge of words, a nimble hand, and an aptitude for focus on the job in front of you. Here in London he could develop these talents to the full.

A Regular Printer

Around the corner from the hospital, there stood the church where Hogarth was baptized. Somehow it escaped the wrath of Adolf Hitler, whose bombs laid waste the streets around it; and so the church still stands today, St. Bartholomew the Great, complete with the font and the Lady Chapel at its eastern end. It was here that Franklin found a job, with a master printer who used the Lady Chapel as his workshop.

Sixty feet long, with a stone floor and tall windows, it was ideal for printers who needed light to work by and a solid base for their equipment. Someone had built a wooden platform, so that the chapel had two floors, with the lower one occupied by a foundry where Thomas James cast lead type. On the upper level, there was a printing shop, owned by Samuel Palmer, Franklin's new boss. He had a link with Philadelphia—he had printed some material for a Quaker who had known Aquila Rose—and this may explain how Franklin found his way to Palmer's door.

In the 1730s, his career would end in bankruptcy, a fate that befell many printers in London, including Sir William Keith's creditor, John Baskett: the market was simply too competitive. It also required too much capital by way of machines, metal, and paper, and too many customers had, like Sir William, a habit of forgetting to pay their bills. But when Franklin knew him, Samuel Palmer was only thirty-three, and making his name as a fine exponent of his trade.[9]

At his death, Palmer left behind a manuscript, *The Practical Part of Printing*, which tells us the qualities he looked for in the people he hired. The choicest skills were those of a compositor, the job Franklin was given. The aristocrats of the workshop, they were highly paid, making about nineteen shillings a week, because their task was, wrote Mr Palmer, "laborious and difficult." The compositors had to decipher the author's handwriting, correct his English, and set his prose into type, five or six words at a time. They did so by plucking the lead characters—mostly one sixth of an inch across—out of two wooden cases: the upper case for capitals, and the lower one for smaller letters, punctuation, and spaces.

Using a precision tool, the composing stick, the compositor arranged and justified the text so that it would look clear and inviting. Then he slotted the body of type into the galley, a wooden tray that held columns of print. This had to be done as neatly and as firmly as possible. If not, then when the tray went down to the press, and the ink ball was applied, the ink would spread unevenly and the impression would be blurred.

Speed was essential, to meet deadlines and because the men were paid by their volume of output.

The wrist had to be supple, and the arms had to be strong—completed sets of type weighed thirty pounds each, and had to be handled carefully, never dropped or damaged—but it was consistency that counted the most in a compositor. "He ought to be very intent upon his business," Mr. Palmer wrote. "For if he suffers himself to be distracted, either by singing, chatting, or any other impertinences, I defy him, tho' he were the ablest workman, to make a correct composition." He took a dim view of men who ate as they worked and fouled up the galley with grease and crumbs.

"Regularity": that was Palmer's watchword. He must have seen it in Franklin, because he gave the young American a formidable assignment. Franklin was told to compose the text for a third edition of a book that was doing well and had to be perfect. The author, who had recently passed away, was a Cambridge graduate who had worked as a schoolmaster, inherited one fortune, married into another, and then devoted himself to learning. His name was William Wollaston, and his book was a work of metaphysics called *The Religion of Nature Delineated.*

The text was a daunting project, demanding all Franklin's powers of concentration. The book contained elaborate footnotes, with quotations from Hebrew and Greek as well as Latin. The type had to be set in such a way as to clarify the logical sequence of its ideas, with many sentences placed in italics, and it had to look elegant too: Mr. Palmer had a reputation to maintain. Not content with setting the book up to be printed, Franklin also engaged with what it said. There followed one of the most striking episodes of Franklin's remarkable young life.

In *The Religion of Nature Delineated,* Wollaston had produced a subtle, closely argued work of philosophical analysis. It was also very controversial. Although he wished to prove the existence of God—"one supreme and perfect Being," as Wollaston described him—the means by which he tried to do so were hardly very Christian. "The foundation of religion," he began, "lies in that difference between the acts of men which distinguishes them into good, evil, and indifferent." From that simple proposition his argument unfolded, by way of an investigation of the meaning of the words "truth" and "goodness," until the existence of a deity became self-evident.

It was all done with human logic alone, plus a little help from Sir Isaac Newton and the microscope, whose revelation of the secrets of nature had deeply impressed Mr. Wollaston: surely a cosmos so intricate must have a wise creator? But not once did he mention the name of Jesus. Original sin and the Holy Trinity were absent as well; Wollaston filled his footnotes with Jewish rabbis, not the Christian Fathers; and although he insisted we should all worship God, he would not lay down fixed rules about how to do so. "Every man knows best," wrote Wollaston, "how he may . . . perform this duty."[10]

In other words, he was a deist, open to the charge of subverting Christianity while pretending to defend it. In 1725, as *The Religion of Nature* became a best-seller, it led to a flurry of books from other authors, making the case for Wollaston or against him. Even Defoe the Calvinist entered the fray, with a pamphlet attacking the book for its failure to acknowledge the innate depravity of human beings. Benjamin Franklin joined in as well, but from a perspective very different from Defoe's.[11]

In the third week of February, at about the time Franklin was finishing work on Wollaston's book, Andrew Hamilton's ship reached England at last. As Denham had proposed, the young man tracked the lawyer down to tell him about the machinations of Keith and Riddlesden. The meeting had profound implications for Franklin's future. Hamilton thanked him, and a bond of friendship was sealed that would endure until Hamilton's death in 1741. It may also be that Franklin told Hamilton about his latest literary endeavor. Hamilton was yet another skeptic who would understand what Franklin was up to.

At only nineteen, and three thousand miles from home, Franklin wrote his own short essay taking issue with Wollaston. Using one of Palmer's presses, he printed off one hundred copies. Dedicated to James Ralph, it bore the title *A Dissertation on Liberty and Necessity, Pleasure and Pain.* For those who knew the writings of the deists, and especially those of Anthony Collins, the title alone would be a sure sign of what the essay contained. Although it was written in a form of code, its deeper meanings wrapped up in paradox, the message was not too hard to decipher. The *Dissertation* was a work of unmitigated atheism.

Franklin the Fatalist

"Truth will be truth," Franklin wrote, "tho' it sometimes prove mortifying and distasteful." With that revealing statement he brings the *Dissertation* to a close, but only after many words clearly meant to be shocking. More than fifty years later, when a friend inquired about the pamphlet,

Franklin did not wish to be reminded of this exercise in youthful bravado. He tried to disown the *Dissertation*, claiming that he soon had second thoughts about it. After giving away a few copies, he had burned the rest, in a fit of remorse for having written something that might have what he called "an ill tendency."[12]

Or so he told his friend in 1779. By that time Silence Dogood had long since vanished into obscurity. Nobody—except perhaps Franklin's sister Jane—remembered *The New-England Courant* or the name of Samuel Keimer. Franklin was in Paris, eager to avoid any hint of scandal that might jeopardize his diplomatic mission. And so he pretended that he had never really been a skeptic or an atheist, who took pleasure in being provocative.

It was a rather different story in 1725. No one—not even a youth of nineteen—could produce such a pamphlet without knowing precisely what he was doing. In his old age, when he briefly summarized its contents, Franklin said that he merely intended "to prove the doctrine of fate." This was an innocuous phrase in Paris in the 1770s, but not in the London of Walpole and George I. If you dealt in words like "fate" or "necessity," you were making a statement about yourself, and you were being political as well. You were aligning yourself with the most radical Whigs, men who could be stigmatized as agents of profanity.[13]

In 1723, the Tories had found a new tactic for opposing Sir Robert. Using the grand jury of Middlesex, which the Tories controlled, they tried to mount prosecutions of Whigs, accusing them of blasphemy. It was a clever way to get at Walpole by implying that the party he led was a friend to immorality. First the grand jury went after the authors of *Cato's Letters.* Then the Tories attacked a physician, Bernard Mandeville, who had friends at the highest level of Walpole's administration. Mandeville had written a scandalous book, *The Fable of the Bees,* which seemed to pour scorn on the most sacred notions of religion and morality.

Him the Tories accused of belief in something they called "absolute fate." In other words, the grand jury alleged that Mandeville had ventured beyond mere deism to become a more outrageous kind of thinker. He was a fatalist, or so the Tories claimed: somebody who regarded human beings as the pawns of blind necessity, impotent cogs in the mechanism of a universe governed by physical laws, with no need for a God to keep it in being. And so "fate" was a loaded word. If you called someone like Mandeville a fatalist, you were saying that he was an atheist as well as a Whig, a man bereft of faith and virtue and an enemy of Christianity:

and by writing the *Dissertation,* his own fatalistic treatise, Franklin placed himself in the same company.[14]

Behind the word "fate" there lurked the dangerous figure of Spinoza, the philosopher from seventeenth-century Amsterdam. Spinoza, it was said, had been the arch-fatalist, a man whose system of ideas left no room for free will, for morality, or for God. The defenders of religion always went out of their way to condemn Spinoza. And since he was a Jew and a Dutchman, this was easily done, in an England where xenophobia was a way of life. As it happens, Mandeville was Dutch as well. And so it was possible to brand *The Fable of the Bees* as a Spinozistic work of infamy and unbelief.

Among the writers who denounced Spinoza, there was one whose name will be familiar: the wealthy Mr. Wollaston. In an angry footnote, Wollaston chastised Spinoza for what he called his "impieties and contradictions." His system was nothing but "gross atheism"; because Spinoza had made out that if there really *were* a God, then—since God was everywhere, and all powerful—God must also contain "all the follies, madnesses, wickednesses that are in the world." Or in other words: God had made evil as well as good, and both were equal in God's eyes. A dreadful suggestion, and one that Wollaston beheld with horror.

But not so Benjamin Franklin. Just as Ralph plunged into the London of actors and writers, Franklin dived into the world of ideas with the same audacity. His pamphlet took the same side as Mandeville and Spinoza, setting out to prove the very notion that Wollaston found so offensive: that God (if he existed at all) had made vice as well as virtue, and found them equally acceptable.

The *Dissertation* had two parts, the first of which was pretty much the standard bill of fare from a skeptic. Section One, "Of Liberty and Necessity," did what had been done before, many times, by writers whose arguments Franklin had studied in America. You began by making God your hypothesis, a divinity all knowing and omnipotent. Then, and it was hardly difficult, you developed the idea of the Almighty in such a way as to make him the author of the grievous as well as the beneficial. "Pain, sickness, want, theft, murder etc"—Franklin makes a list—all of these evils could be laid at his door. By doing so, you made God out to be absurd and capricious. You also did away with the concept of free will.

If the cosmos really was a perfect system—"this great machine, the universe," as Franklin put it—then it had to be the system that Newton had described, working like a clock. Universal gravity and the laws of motion: if they were the source of order in the cosmos, they had to operate everywhere, among the planets but also on earth. In which case: there must be other laws as well, not quite those of Newton but somewhat similar, that governed the behavior of mankind. Permit the intervention of human free will—in Franklin's words, "an independent self-motion"—and you would disrupt the mechanism of the clock. Necessity and fate versus free will and liberty: Franklin came down on the side of fate, and so on the side of Spinoza.

It was a bleak way of looking at things, but neither new nor very profound. The original part of Franklin's *Dissertation* came in Section Two. Having disposed of God and free will, he moves on to demolish the traditional concept of the soul; which means that Franklin also does away with an afterlife. Here Franklin takes on a more formidable adversary: not Wollaston, but John Locke, whose work he had read so carefully.

A man who never ceased to be a Christian, Locke had taken the view that the soul is "an immaterial spirit, a substance that thinks and has a power of motion in a body, by will or thought." Franklin says something entirely different. *Thought* is not the quality that marks out life and consciousness from the inactive matter of the universe: instead, Franklin looks to *pain*—"the sensation of uneasiness"—as the thing that differentiates the living from the dead. According to the *Dissertation,* the human mind "must first be acted upon before it can react. In the beginning of infancy it is as if it were not; it is not conscious of its own existence, till it has received the first sensation of pain; then, not before, it begins to feel itself, is rous'd, and put into action. . . . Thus is the machine set in work; this is life. We are first mov'd by pain, and the whole succeeding course of our lives is but one continued series of action with a view to be freed from it." Pleasure was the goal of human life, in other words: by which he meant that everything that human beings do—eating, drinking, making love, good deeds and bad, idleness or industry—are merely efforts to stave off the uneasiness and pain that pursue them from their mother's breast.

In picturing existence in this way, Franklin stood alongside the most radical thinkers of the period. In the 1720s, a few clandestine writers in France were saying much the same thing. They too conceived of human beings as machines, with the mind and body serving merely as the site of fleeting impulses of pain and pleasure. Franklin cannot have known their work, because it was kept secret, and yet he reached conclusions similar to theirs. Like the French, he had a choice about which way to go next.

Having come this far, he could either confine himself to metaphysics, or he could take another path, the road of science—biology, or medicine, perhaps—as a way to develop his ideas about the mechanism of the body and the brain.[15]

In the *Dissertation,* Franklin stuck to technical philosophy, which was what he knew from Locke. Firstly he did away with ethics, by arguing that every thought and action—even when it seems to be altruistic—is just another exercise in what he calls "self-love." Then he discarded Locke's idea of the soul. According to Franklin, the soul is just "a faculty"—not unlike the skill of the compositor, as he plucks lead type from a tray—for gathering up impressions received by the brain. When the brain ceases to function, the soul must disappear as well. Heaven, hell, or immortality, or the resurrection of the body: none of these is feasible in Franklin's fatalistic scheme of things. Even if a human being came back to life, he or she could never be the person they had been first time around, because their recollections and their identity had vanished with the brain.

In the twenty-first century, when arguments like these are common currency, it is easy to be sneering about Franklin's *Dissertation.* The young man can be patronized, he can be called naive, and holes can be picked in his logic. But nothing can diminish the scale of his achievement. Franklin had first to become an excellent writer of English prose; then he had to read John Locke and much else besides, and understand what the writers said; he also had to master the difficult art of printing; and then he had to cross the Atlantic, survive in an alien city, talk his way into a job, read Wollaston, write the *Dissertation,* print it himself, and risk the consequences. And Franklin did all this before he left his teens.

This was ingenuity; and the pamphlet attracted the attention it deserved. Next door to Franklin's lodgings at the Golden Fan, there was a bookstore called the Green Dragon, owned by one John Wilcox. He had given Franklin the run of the place, allowing him to borrow what he wanted in return for a modest fee. Wilcox was also a publisher. Among his authors he counted a surgeon, John Lyons, who lived nearby at the Fortune of War in Bartholomew Close. A radical Whig, Lyons had written a book, *The Infallibility of Human Judgment,* hostile to the clergy and their doctrines, which briefly put him in jail. He read the *Dissertation* and sought out the young author to discuss his ideas. For Franklin, this would be another fruitful encounter, as Lyons took him into the heart of the avant-garde.

The Mysterious Mr. Lyons

He was one more of Franklin's eccentrics. In 1721, at the time of the epidemics in the Mediterranean, John Lyons devised a singular scheme for protecting the people of London. If—as he argued—smallpox and the plague were spread by what he called "malignant atoms," drifting in the atmosphere, then the best way to prevent infection was to purify the air. So he urged his fellow citizens to lay trails of gunpowder in the streets, to be ignited in a chain of small explosions that would burn away the pestilence. Individuals should arm themselves with miniature pistols, primed with a blank charge. They would pull the trigger when they felt in danger of catching the plague.[16]

It was a bold suggestion, if a rather noisy one; and it aroused the wrath of the authorities. In December of that year, as Lyons tried to publicize the scheme by writing a column for *Applebee's Weekly Journal* above the byline of "Pythagoras," he quoted some outspoken lines from his book about human judgment. Summoned before the officials who monitored the press, Lyons had to grovel and apologize. He escaped with a warning. After that, he continued to bring out new editions of *The Infallibility,* assuming that he had the approval of the government. Alas, in the spring of 1723, when the Tories were pursuing Mandeville, somebody complained about Lyons as well. And so Walpole's Whig administration felt obliged to act, if only to distance themselves from a writer so appalling.

Under arrest on a blasphemy charge, Lyons spent twelve weeks in Newgate Prison. There he was harassed by his fellow inmates, or so he claimed as he begged for his release, because he was a Whig while they were Tories. "Barbarous abuses, insults, and assaults I have met with from the enemies of the government," he wrote to Walpole's officials. But Mr. Lyons had some influential friends, who helped him post the money for his bail. In a fourth edition of his book, he thanked the man to whom he owed the most: the city's most famous physician, Dr. Richard Mead, a fellow of the Royal Society and a close friend of Sir Isaac Newton.

By making Lyons's acquaintance, Franklin met someone who could introduce him to some of London's finest intellects. It must be said that John Lyons led a double life. He was also a hack journalist, writing propaganda for Walpole and the Whigs, and as a reward he was given a job collecting excise duties. In the 1730s he acted as one of Walpole's paid informants, with the task of sniffing out any Jacobites who lingered in the capital. In all likelihood Franklin had no inkling of this side of Lyons's character. The Mr. Lyons he counted as a friend was the surgeon who took him down to Cornhill, ten minutes' walk away, where Dr. Mead dispensed his wisdom from a seat in Batson's coffeehouse.

We do not know if Franklin ever spoke to Dr. Mead. He must have known his name—Richard Mead had been mentioned in the *Courant,* during the smallpox controversy—but Franklin never refers to him in his memoirs. However, Lyons certainly introduced the young man to another friend of Mead's who was also close to Newton. At Batson's, Franklin met the scientist Henry Pemberton: only thirty-one years old but already a master of Newton's calculus and much else besides, he was another medical doctor and also a member of the Royal Society.

At this very moment, Pemberton was preparing the third edition of Sir Isaac's masterpiece, the *Principia Mathematica,* and so he and Newton were continually in touch. By all accounts Pemberton was an absent-minded but a friendly soul—"of a mild temper, and very free and easy in company," in the words of his earliest biographer—and he promised to take Franklin to see the great man. The meeting never occurred, much to Franklin's disappointment. Perhaps this was just as well. By now Sir Isaac was eighty-two, his health was poor, and he was famously impatient with lesser human beings. Even so, Franklin's exposure to Pemberton and the people around him was another turning point in his career.

Hitherto, although Franklin had a passing acquaintance with Newton's ideas, his interests had chiefly been literary and metaphysical. Of course in Boston he had met some physicians—how could he not, when the *Courant* was so obsessed with smallpox?—but they were very small fry by comparison with Mead or Pemberton. Early in 1724, Mead had produced a handsome edition of a textbook on the muscles of the human body, Cowper's *Myotomia,* for which Pemberton wrote the introduction. A bold attempt to use Newtonian physics to explain how muscles did their work, Pemberton's essay failed in what it set out to do. Even so it was immensely important for Franklin to mingle with people who were doing this kind of research.

If Franklin had never met John Lyons, he might have continued forever to dabble in metaphysics. He might have written more stuff like the first part of the *Dissertation:* clever but inconsequential, the spinning of words but not the making of fertile discoveries about the phenomena of nature. In the shape of Henry Pemberton, for the first time Franklin met the sort of experimental scientist that he would eventually become. The Franklins had always been highly skilled with tools and machines, with heat and with materials. So was Henry Pemberton. As his biographer put it, the amiable Mr. Pemberton "early discovered a talent for mechanics, readily performing any manual operation, as making of fire-works, and effecting other contrivances not unbecoming an active and ingenious youth."[17]

The same had been true of the Franklins, in the forge at Ecton and then dyeing silk. But what Pemberton also possessed—like Archdeacon Palmer—was a talent for theory. And although Franklin was never truly a mathematician, in the 1730s he *did* devote long hours to the reading of the latest scientific treatises from Europe. Put the two together, the mechanical skill of the artisan and the abstract ingenuity of the theoretician, and you had most of the ingredients for Franklin's achievements with electricity. Most, but not all: one more thing that Franklin had to have was Pennsylvania, with its ironworks, its civil liberties, and its open frontier.

From Batson's coffeehouse, it was only a few hundred yards to Cheapside and an alehouse called the Horns. Lyons took the young man to the tavern, where they sat down with their fellow Whig, Mr. Mandeville. Most likely, Franklin knew his work already. In the *Dissertation,* there are phrases that closely resemble lines from *The Fable of the Bees.* It appears that he rather liked Bernard Mandeville, who had a little coterie at the Horns, because Franklin describes him as "a most facetious entertaining companion." But that was all: it seems that Mandeville did not really meet his expectations. Franklin was about to encounter someone far more worth his while.

In the scientific pantheon of London, Newton reigned supreme. But on the second rung of fame there stood the founder of the British Museum. At the age of sixty-five, Sir Hans Sloane was also the secretary of the Royal Society, a man who had traveled in the New World and written a model of scientific travelogue, his *Voyage to the Islands,* with a superb account of the plants and animals of Jamaica. Somehow—at Batson's, probably—Franklin must have heard about Sloane's latest enterprise: a survey of the botany of the Carolinas. For the previous two years, the explorer Mark Catesby had been based in Charleston, gathering samples to be sent home to be studied by Sir Hans. So on June 2, Franklin picked up his pen and wrote to the scientist, offering Sloane his little purse made from asbestos, together with a slice of wood of a kind known to Americans as Salamander Cotton. "As you are noted to be a lover of curiosities," Franklin wrote—a phrase that was an apt description of himself—"I have inform'd you of these; and if you have any inclination to purchase them or see 'em, let me know your pleasure."

What happened next is not entirely clear. In his autobiography, Franklin claimed that it was Sloane who made the first move, and came to visit him at his lodgings at the Golden Fan, having heard of the purse. This is clearly false—the letter is proof of that—another reminder that Franklin's memoirs cannot always be taken at face value. But Franklin's purse is still in London today, preserved in Sloane's collection in the Natural History Museum. So they must have met and money must have been forthcoming. And this in itself was remarkable.

Sloane's papers survive in their entirety. They contain only one other example in the mid-1720s of somebody writing unintroduced to offer him a curiosity such as this. And so what Franklin did was daring and unusual. It was chutzpah again, but very productive: because Franklin would soon create his own brilliant journal of a voyage, almost certainly inspired by Sloane's descriptions of the Caribbean.

In the meantime, at their lodgings in Little Britain, he and Ralph had made a new acquaintance, whose arrival in their lives would give rise to some unpleasantness. "In our house there lodged a young woman, a milliner, who I think had a shop in the cloisters," Franklin wrote in his autobiography. "She had been genteelly bred, was sensible and lively, and of most pleasing conversation." In the sorry tale that ensued, we find Ralph and Franklin behaving like some of the obnoxious characters from London that Hogarth brought to life in his pictures.

The Milliner's Tale

Among the early works of William Hogarth, one of the most disturbing is his cycle of paintings *A Harlot's Progress,* completed in 1731. A wagon from the country pitches up in Cheapside, not far from the Horns, setting down a pretty young woman by the name of Moll Hackabout. Her pincushion and her scissors show that she is a seamstress or a milliner. From the moment she arrives, the city conspires to bring about her ruin. Moll Hackabout falls victim to a procuress, and wicked men exploit her, dragging her down into prostitution until she dies a painful death from syphilis.

The story caught the public's imagination, so that when Hogarth turned the paintings into printed engravings they sold immensely well.

As always with Hogarth, the pictures were full of ambiguity. They told a moral tale, and yet they also made it ironic; but at their simplest level these were works of intense realism, based on stories taken from the daily life that Hogarth observed. His mother and sister were among the milliners in Smithfield, and nearby in the cloisters at St. Bartholomew's they had a competitor, a young woman who also suffered at the hands of men: less tragically, perhaps, than Moll Hackabout, but even so her story was a sad one. Ralph and Franklin were the men who took advantage of her situation.[18]

The woman they abused was a milliner whom we know only as Mrs. T. This is what Franklin calls her in his memoirs. It seems, from a document that survives in London, that the milliner's true identity may have been Jenny Wilkins; but whatever her real name, Mrs. T was the young woman "sensible and lively . . . with pleasing conversation," who also roomed at the Golden Fan. Of an evening, she would read plays with James Ralph. Mrs. T fell for the poet, and they moved to new lodgings elsewhere, along with a child that Mrs. T had borne. It is not clear from Franklin's text whether Ralph was the father or if she had been in another relationship before. Even now Ralph failed to secure a paying job, and so he lived off the milliner's money until it ran short. At last he hit upon another of his plans: he would find a village school where he would be the master, teaching the three Rs by day and writing poetry by night.

James Ralph knew some members of the clergy, Presbyterian ministers who found him a post in a village in Berkshire, sixty miles west of the capital. There he taught ten or twelve boys, making no more than five shillings a week, a fraction of Franklin's earnings as a printer. As for his verse, like so many poets at the time Ralph aspired to write an English epic, a modern equivalent of Virgil or Homer. By mail he bombarded his friend with drafts of the poem, seeking his comments. Franklin pleaded with Ralph to desist, on the same old grounds—it was no way to make a living—but still the drafts kept coming. To add insult to irritation, Ralph had decided that when he became famous, he would not wish it to be known that he had plied a trade as menial as teaching school. And so in Berkshire he called himself "Mr. Franklin."

And then there was the matter of Mrs. T. On leaving the capital, Ralph had entrusted her to Franklin, but she had fallen on hard times. Because of Mrs. T's liaison with the poet, her business collapsed and her other friends fell away. Although Franklin had already lent so much money to Ralph, with little hope of repayment, he helped the milliner as well.

And then, like the horrid old lechers that Hogarth portrayed, he made a clumsy attempt to seduce her. Or, as Franklin puts it in his autobiography, in the euphemistic diction of the eighteenth century: "Being at this time under no religious restraints, and presuming on my importance to her, I attempted familiarities." Deeply offended, Mrs. T did what she should: the milliner pushed Franklin away.

It was only the latest and the most shameful episode of a sequence of errors that Franklin had committed. He makes a rueful list of his mistakes in his memoirs. Fifty years on, he still found their recollection painful. Running away from his apprenticeship with James and then spending Vernon's money, breaking off with Deborah Read, writing the *Dissertation,* and now this: it was not the path of goodness that Franklin had read about in books. Soon Ralph reappeared from Berkshire, still penniless. Outraged by Franklin's behavior, Mrs. T had written to her lover, telling him everything; and that was the end of Franklin's friendship with the poet. He told Franklin that he could whistle for his money.

Not once but twice—first John Collins, now James Ralph—the young Franklin had lost a friend to whom he had lent money. He had led them astray, or so he feared, with all his clever talk about philosophy. Under his influence, Ralph and Collins had become skeptics themselves, abandoning what they thought of as the obsolete conventions of morality. Ralph was certainly an avid reader of *The Fable of the Bees;* and the traces that he left in British archives suggest that he and Franklin both went with Lyons on his guided tour of the coffeehouses, meeting Mandeville and his scurrilous friends.

Was there a connection? Was it the case that skeptical ideas—or, worse still, downright atheism of the kind that Franklin had adopted—would always lead a youth astray? It was still rather early in Franklin's life for him to reach such a stark conclusion. Many freethinkers—Spinoza for one, and Anthony Collins for another—had been models of industry or public service. But the question went on hanging in the air. Franklin began to worry that *something* was wrong. He could never return to Josiah's form of piety—that was impossible, and he never did—but as a guide to life, he did need something better than the findings of his *Dissertation.*

Not that Franklin cared about the milliner. We will probably never know what became of Mrs. T, or Jenny Wilkins if so she really was. In 1726, she was still with James Ralph, but he had already abandoned a wife and child in America. In time Ralph deserted Mrs. T as well—that we can establish—and later still he became a bigamist by marrying again in

London. But for all Franklin's rhetoric of virtue and benevolence, Mrs. T did not matter enough to the sage of Philadelphia for him to record whatever destiny befell her. He might have found out, because when he came back to London in the 1750s he and James Ralph were reconciled. Ralph must have known where she was or how she died; but Franklin tells us nothing more about Mrs. T.[19]

His career was a subject he found more absorbing. To repay Samuel Vernon and then perhaps to start a business of his own, he would need some capital, and with Ralph no longer a burden perhaps at last he had a chance of doing so. In search of still higher wages, in the late autumn of 1725 he moved to a new employer, John Watts, a businessman far more successful than Samuel Palmer. Watts had his printing workshop a mile to the west of Little Britain in the newer, more fashionable district surrounding the garden square and the theater at Lincoln's Inn Fields. It was a long way from Smithfield to Holborn, as the neighborhood was known; and so Franklin looked for lodgings nearer at hand.

He chose to room on Duke Street, next to the square, at the same rent as he paid at the Golden Fan, but with a widow whose way of life would have horrified his family in New England. At times he had mixed in outrageous company; but in the eyes of a Bostonian, none could be worse than his new landlady. Her name was Elizabeth Holt, and she was a member of a minority viewed with fear and loathing by Sir Robert Walpole and his countrymen. The widow Holt belonged to the wicked Church of Rome. Beneath her roof the young American would enlarge his horizons yet again.

Chapter Eleven

The Papists of Duke Street

In the days when the Franklins were busy with their forge at Ecton, a developer had come to Lincoln's Inn Fields and seen that it had potential. He bought the land to the west, and soon more investors followed suit until, by the 1640s, the square was overlooked by two long terraces made up of houses very different from those of Little Britain. Built for the rich, they were miniature palaces, put up in the latest Palladian style, like a shaft of light from Paris or the Veneto suddenly revealed amid the fog of London. At the corner where the terraces met, one of the houses stood over an archway with a dark passage beneath it. The passage led to Duke Street, where Franklin came to dwell. Because the house above it was especially grand, it served as a home for envoys from Europe.[1]

Early in the 1720s the embassy of Sardinia moved in to occupy the house above the arch. They were Roman Catholics, of course. And so, behind the embassy and opposite Franklin's new home, they had a chapel to say mass. They also had a secret corridor where they could hide a priest or holy relics if a mob of Whigs threatened to attack. Because outsiders could attend the services, Duke Street became a focal point for Catholics, poor and rich; although by now a wealthy Catholic in London was almost as rare as a rattlesnake in Boston.

Protected by diplomatic immunity, the embassy chapels—this one, and those of Austria, Portugal, and so on—were the only places in the capital where Catholics could gather legally. This was an era when the arrogance of state deprived them of all their other civil liberties. In England they could not vote or hold public office. Catholic priests could be arrested at any time; and although few prosecutions actually occurred, the faith of Rome remained officially despised. In an effort to suppress the Jacobites, Walpole had imposed a tax on Catholics, hoping to raise £100,000 with a levy on Papists who would not swear allegiance to the king.

The Sardinian chapel offered them a rare space of freedom, drawing in a congregation as diverse as could be. They included laborers and seamen, Irish mostly, but also shopkeepers, actors, musicians, and singers. With Handel close at hand, writing his operas in Italian, the stage had become a nest of foreigners and Papists. Besides the many aliens who prayed at the chapel—the cooks, the hairdressers, and the dancing masters—there were printers from Farringdon Without, together with a few of the old Catholic gentry. Sightseers came as well, curious to hear the tinkling bells and the mass said in Latin. Among the worshippers they saw was Franklin's landlady, Elizabeth Holt. Talkative and funny, she was fond of telling anecdotes, and she was a martyr to the gout. It left Mrs. Holt very lame at the knees.[2]

In 1718, she had featured on a list of Papists who refused to swear the oath of loyalty. Three quarters of the names on the list were female. That was another feature of Catholicism in the capital: it was a faith that women kept alive. Since they were mostly widows and spinsters, the women on the list had to find an income, but Elizabeth Holt was a woman of enterprise. In the latter part of 1725 she and her daughter, Elizabeth Junior—"spinster of the same"—discovered a splendid way to make ends meet.[3]

At about the time she took Franklin as her lodger, Mrs. Holt placed a notice in the press, advertising her entry to the retail trade. The readers were told about an opening on Duke Street, where Mrs. Holt and her daughter were setting up in business. Their Italian warehouse would sell silk and satin, wine and olive oil, and capers and anchovies too—"weight no less than a pound, nor measure less than a pint"—and all to be offered "at the reasonablest rates."

Soon enough the two women widened their range of merchandise, to include so much else filled with the warmth of the Mediterranean. They sold violin strings from Rome, soap from Naples, Jesuit treacle—whatever that might be—and sausages from Bologna, not to mention aromatic oil from Tuscany. These were rarities in London, where the Holts had few rivals dealing in Parmesan and Chianti, and so they soon began to thrive. They did so well that in 1727 Mrs. Holt was able to move to the Strand, one of the finest retail pitches in the capital. To promote her new shop, she hired William Hogarth to design the cards she handed out to passersby.

By that time Franklin was at home again in America, and so he never shared her years of affluence. But of an evening, when he was working for John Watts, and eager to spend as little as possible, he would go to sit with Mrs. Holt in her room at the rear of the warehouse. They would dine modestly on anchovies, a little bread and butter, and a half pint of ale, while she told her stories about the days of yore, when her husband was alive and they mixed with what she called "people of distinction."

In choosing to lodge with Mrs. Holt, Franklin showed just how far he had come from the narrow New England of the Mathers. In the Bay Colony where he was born, so deeply ingrained was the hatred of Catholicism and the Irish that in 1732, when it was rumored that a priest was planning to visit Boston on St. Patrick's Day, the governor ordered the sheriff to scour the area for Papists, with a warrant to break down the door of any house that looked suspicious. Not for another fifty years could the mass be said publicly in the town.

Things were only a little better in London, and indeed the Sardinian chapel was destroyed in the infamous Gordon Riots of 1780; but Franklin had absorbed the different customs of the Quaker colony, where Catholics could worship more or less as they pleased. The Jesuits were free to visit from their mission on the eastern shore of Maryland; by the mid-1720s there was a Jesuit father ministering up and down the Delaware valley; and in 1734 they created their own church in Philadelphia. Even James Logan, who so detested Jacobites, helped the Penn family in London fight off attempts to curtail the freedoms Catholics enjoyed.[4]

Nonetheless their numbers were still very small. There were fewer than two hundred in Philadelphia even in the 1740s. It is unlikely that before he came to London Franklin had ever spoken to a Roman Catholic, let alone spent long evenings in their company. And so yet again his youthful visit to the empire's capital formed an essential part of his education.

Fresh from writing the *Dissertation,* with its derisory message about religious faith, there he was on Duke Street on splendid terms with a woman who prayed the rosary. He and Mrs. Holt got on so well—Franklin was an ideal lodger, sober and self-disciplined—that when he talked about taking cheaper rooms elsewhere, she cut two shillings off his weekly rent. Their friendship was bound to give him second thoughts about the insults heaped on "priestcraft" in the books he had read by John Toland and the like.

Another engraving by William Hogarth: ca. 1730, a printed card advertising the delicatessen owned by Mrs. Elizabeth Holt. She had been Franklin's landlady at her earlier premises on Duke Street in 1726.

Upstairs there lived another elderly woman whose faith and gentility the young man found still more impressive. The garret above the warehouse was occupied by "a maiden lady": Franklin's words. The daughter of Catholic gentry, in her youth she had entered one of the convents of

English nuns in exile in Belgium and France. Seventy years of age when Franklin knew her, she still lived like a member of an order. So that she could give away as much as possible, even though her income was small, the maiden lady made do with a diet of gruel.

Every day a priest would take her confession. He would step across the street to the bare little room where she was allowed to dwell rent free, because Mrs. Holt saw her presence as a blessing. Franklin was only permitted to enter the garret on one occasion: but that one visit left an indelible mark on his autobiography. "She was cheerful and polite, and convers'd pleasantly," he recalled. "The room was clean, but had no other furniture than a mattress, a table with a crucifix and book, a stool, which she gave me to sit on, and a picture over the chimney." The maiden lady explained that it was Saint Veronica, holding up the veil she had offered to Christ to wipe his brow on the way to crucifixion.[5]

In his memoirs, Franklin gives more space to Mrs. Holt and the maiden lady than he does to Cotton Mather or to any other Puritan minister from Boston. He also writes about the two women with affection and respect, which had not been the tone of *The New-England Courant.* As for the Calvinism of which Mather was a representative, Franklin scarcely writes about it at all: from which we can surely deduce that it meant very little to him. It is fair to say that these two ladies with their faith and generosity did at least as much as any Puritan in Massachusetts to shape the views about religion that Franklin held as an adult. In London he discovered that Catholics were not as dreadful as he had been led to believe; and so again his horizons grew wider.

Generosity and faith: those were not the virtues he would find in the printing shop of Mr. Watts. It was located a few hundred yards from Lincoln's Inn Fields, in a backstreet called Wild Court. A big and a bustling enterprise, it was full of rough and tumble, drink, and banter, exchanged between artisans working under high pressure. On two floors, John Watts had as many as fifty staff and a dozen presses. No printing works on such an industrial scale would exist in America until after independence; even at the peak of his career, Franklin would never employ more than a handful of journeymen.

This could hardly be otherwise. Before the Revolution the reading public in the colonies was simply too small—only one third the size of England's—and too widely dispersed to justify a printing business as extensive as John Watts's. Even so, Franklin's exposure to this sort of printing factory gave him a wealth of experience that he could redeploy in Pennsylvania. The technical skills he already had, for the most part. Although he refined them still further while he was with Watts and Palmer, what mattered more was that Franklin saw the different business models followed by the leading printers of the capital. In the 1730s and 1740s, the decades of *Poor Richard's Almanack,* he would take what he had learned, adapt it to American conditions, and produce his own formula for colonial success.

The Chapel and the Quaker

An excellent printer, John Watts could also show Franklin what it meant to be an entrepreneur. Instead of scrabbling around for small contracts, Watts had formed an alliance with London's finest literary publishers, the Tonson family, who worked with authors including Alexander Pope. Their list of books featured big, multivolume editions by eminent writers, with long print runs that needed a factory as large and as well equipped as Wild Court. Spotting a gap in the market, they and John Watts repackaged the books in question into a pocket-sized format, the duodecimo, intended to reach the widest audience. They used the Dutch typeface Elsevier, relatively new in London but ideal when the print had to be small but very readable.[6]

When Franklin first arrived at Watts's factory, his new colleagues were just finishing a sixteen-volume set of Addison's *Spectator,* which went on sale a few days after Mrs. Holt opened her delicatessen. It would be followed in 1726 by more of the same: more work for the Tonsons, reprints of Addison and Steele, also in duodecimo, small and elegant and perfect for the drawing room, the bedside table, or the coaching inn. As yet, it was not the kind of product an American printer could turn out, because the economics would not have made sense; but fifteen years later, a moment would come when Franklin could do something of the kind in Philadelphia.

For Watts's factory hands, including Franklin, books such as these meant hard, repetitive labor, done to meet tight deadlines. With so much capital employed—the presses, the ink, the paper, the type, and the premises—Watts had to move on swiftly from one big contract to the next. As for the quality, it had to be high, to satisfy the Tonsons and authors as demanding as Mr. Pope. In return, the printers could earn excellent wages from books turned out in such large numbers.

Franklin chose to work at the coalface, tending one of Watts's presses on the lower floor, rather than sitting quietly upstairs as a compositor. Too much sedentary stuff at Mr. Palmer's had made him long for exercise of the kind he was accustomed to in Philadelphia. Among the Londoners, he counted as an oddity. His accent, his size, and his muscles, they were all so unusual; but strangest of all to a cockney was his avoidance of strong drink. The rest of the pressmen were "great guzzlers of beer," Franklin recalled, and they had a boy from the alehouse who kept them supplied at the machines. Soon they took to calling Franklin "the Water American." It was a nickname that came to be tinged with respect, when they saw Franklin running up and down the staircase, carrying in each hand one of the wooden trays filled with lead type.

Working the press was a task less cerebral than the compositor's, but still very demanding. Seen today in a demonstration in a museum, the process of eighteenth-century printing looks simple and even sedate. If it has a quaint appearance, that is because what is absent is the commercial imperative. In the London Franklin knew, there was nothing relaxed about the printing trade. Because the pressmen were paid by the piece, they had to get the work done very rapidly, while still making no mistakes.

The pressmen were known as "horses," because the work was so hard and because they worked in pairs. Each press required two operators: the "puller," who did the heavy labor, and the "beater," who prepared the ink ball, a greasy wad of leather, and applied it to the rows of lead type, set in a frame on top of the marble slab that formed the bed of the press. As many as four times a minute, the puller would draw a wooden carriage, containing the paper, over the frame. As the carriage passed through the machine, he would heave on an iron bar, attached to a screw and a spindle that drove down a weighted wooden block that made the paper connect with the ink. Then they would withdraw the carriage, remove the paper and insert another sheet, and the process would begin again: all of which had to be done in fifteen seconds, without any slips or hiccups that might lead to blurs or smears or damage to the paper. They kept this up for sixty minutes at a time, until the beater and the puller took a break and swapped over.[7]

Again it was the speed and the consistency that counted. As the best technical manual put it, the men at the press, beater and puller alike, had to maintain "a constant and methodical posture and gesture in every action." If one of the two companions were weak or slapdash, or if he failed to turn up in the morning, the other one would suffer financially as their output fell away. Franklin saw how annoying it could be to have a heavy drinker as his partner, a man who would be prone to slack and break the rhythm.[8]

His companion drank six pints of beer a day, from breakfast until supper time. "A detestable custom," thought Franklin, who tried to use his science to convince his partner to stay away from alcohol. A pint of beer is no more than water and fermented grain, he pointed out. So why not follow the recommendations of Thomas Tryon, and simply eat a loaf of bread instead? Sound advice though this was, his partner went on drinking what Franklin called his "muddling liquor." On Saturday night, when the tally for the week was totted up, his companion had to give a quarter of his wages to pay for his beer.

"And thus these poor devils keep themselves always under," Franklin wrote in his autobiography. His dislike of drinking was never a matter of rigid principle; he had no religious objection to alcohol; and in time he came to relish his ale and his wine. What troubled Franklin was the money it absorbed, the risk that in drink people would do things they regretted, and the insidious way that liquor could destroy a life or a career. He would see this many times in Philadelphia.

Soon John Watts came to his rescue. Feeling that Franklin was wasted where he was, he sent the young man up to the composing room, where he promptly ran into another kind of problem with beer. In a printing works, the journeymen had to stick together, to negotiate the best rates per page from the master and to make sure that everybody pulled his weight. Because of all this, and because they took pride in their work, in every printing shop in London the journeymen had a labor union, the Chapel, with elaborate rules and customs, Chapel dues, and fines for anyone who stepped out of line.

Swearing, fighting, or untidiness, leaving a candle burning unattended, using another man's tools, or bringing a stranger into the works: all of these were forbidden. When rules were broken, the fines were paid into a fund, the Chapel Money, to be spent on beer at a weekly ritual known as the Chapel Drink, held on a Saturday night, when the oldest man—the "Father of the Chapel"—always took the first glass. And this was how Benjamin Franklin came to quarrel with his colleagues.[9]

His future lay in being an employer, a colonial John Watts. In London the printers had a maxim, "The Chapel cannot err," that did not sit well with the young Socrates, so keen to be his own master with his own set of rules. According to the Chapel regulations, every new arrival had to pay a fee called a *benvenue,* set at five shillings, to be put toward the drinking fund. When he joined the pressmen on the floor below, Franklin had already paid his *benvenue,* and he refused to do so a second time. Mr. Watts intervened on his behalf. This only made things worse, as the affair became a battle between capital and labor.

If a man refused to pay, standard procedure in London was for the Chapel to punish the offender by bending him over another marble slab and beating him eleven times on the buttocks with a wooden board. For some reason—perhaps the obvious one, that Franklin the boxer was a dangerous man to wrestle with—in his case the Chapel opted for a different tactic: a campaign of low-level sabotage. When Franklin's back was turned, they would swap around the type in his cases, transpose his paragraphs and pages, and "accidentally" break the galleys he had labored to create. All of this they blamed on a poltergeist, the Chapel Ghost who haunted any outsider who strayed into the composing room.

For a few weeks Franklin put up with this; then he surrendered, having learned that sometimes compromise made sense, especially for Americans in London. He paid the *benvenue* and set about to make himself more popular. With his satirical sense of humor, honed to perfection on the *Courant,* he kept his colleagues entertained. In time they came to trust him as well. Franklin was the man they and Mr. Watts could rely upon, quick on the job, never hungover, never late for work, and careful with his money and with theirs. When the compositors ran up too long a tab at the alehouse, they turned for help to the big colonial, who had the credit to keep them all in beer until payday. They even began to copy his eating habits. Some of them gave up their pint of beer at breakfast time, their cheese, and their bread, and made do with the Franklin diet of water gruel and pepper.

And so the months went by. Franklin might easily have settled into life in London as a printer of ingenuity, secure and highly paid, well thought of by Mr. Watts or by so many other bosses who would have been keen to hire him. But he chose not to do so. He was "grown tired" of the city, as he puts it in his autobiography. Once again ambition intervened, as it so often did with the Franklins, and sent the young man back to Philadelphia in the hope of making a fortune of his own.

He had kept in touch with his Quaker friend Mr. Denham, whose influence was decisive. In England, Denham had settled all his old debts with his creditors. He set about to develop a transatlantic business as a ship's chandler, importing rope and nails and so on to America with a view to fitting out ships in the Delaware. In the spring or early summer of 1726, he made Franklin an offer he could not refuse. With England, France, and Spain at peace, largely as a consequence of Walpole's wise diplomacy, the Atlantic trade had excellent prospects. Pennsylvania was going to thrive, by virtue of the rich resources of its hinterland; and Denham offered Franklin a chance to be part of the unfolding story.[10]

They would sail home, Mr. Denham suggested, taking with them a stock of goods from London, and open a store on the Philadelphia waterfront. Franklin would tend the store and keep the books. When the time was right he would go down to Jamaica or Barbados to market grain and flour to the slave plantations in exchange for sugar and molasses. In the meantime, Denham would pay Franklin a salary of £50 a year in the paper money issued by Sir William Keith: about half of what he made as a printer in London, but enough to tide him over. It was the kind of career that Robinson Crusoe had made for himself when he returned to England from his desert island, and Franklin saw the logic of the deal. He said yes.

In time, Franklin would come to see that a merchant's life was not for him: a wise decision, because although Denham's plan might have sounded attractive, in fact this sort of business—trading by sea in commodities—was inherently volatile and fraught with risk. Carried out at long distance, and subject to all kinds of hazards, it was a species of commerce that would always keep a man awake at night. It would never have given Franklin the peace and quiet and the leisure hours that he required for his science. Although the printing trade had perils of its own, it was still a better bet for Franklin; and during his time in London with Watts he had seen how well a printing business could be managed.

Among the printers of his own age that Franklin met in London, two were especially important. One was a very close friend, the other an acquaintance and then a business contact. The friend was John Wygate, "an ingenious young man," as Franklin describes him, twenty years old, a lover of books with some knowledge of French and Latin, whose life would end in yet another episode of ruin. The acquaintance was Charles Ackers, who would become a printer even more successful than Watts. His career and Franklin's would unfold in parallel, as on their different sides of the Atlantic they strove to become men of quality, printers but also public servants held in high esteem.[11]

SWIMMING WITH THE TIDE

A gentleman but only barely so, John Wygate's father had come up to London from a village near Bristol where he failed to make his mark. After settling close to Little Britain, he passed away, leaving his widow to seek openings for her children. She bought John an apprenticeship with a Tory printer who worked as a team with the fearless Jacobite, Nathaniel Mist. John Wygate never finished his indentures, but by 1726 he was employed alongside Franklin at Wild Court.[12]

Somehow Franklin conceived the notion that the Wygates had wealthy relations. This was not true; but his new friend certainly knew how to come across as a man of quality. One Sunday, with some gentlemen up from the country, Wygate and Franklin took a boat along the Thames to Chelsea, where Sir Hans Sloane's specimens from America could be seen in a botanical garden owned by the Society of Apothecaries.

Then as now, Chelsea was the place to go to cut a dash. The most elegant locale in the western approaches to London, the neighborhood sprang up around the Royal Hospital, erected by Charles II to house the aged veterans of war. Nearby some developers had created the chic little suburb of Cheyne Walk. Among its attractions was a coffeehouse, owned by James Salter, yet another of Franklin's eccentrics. "Don Saltero," as he came to be called, had been for many years the factotum of Sir Hans, from whom he had acquired a taste for curiosities. He also made a wicked bowl of punch.

On Mr. Salter's premises, the customers could gaze at his collection of exotica: mummified cats, an embryo in a bottle, a whip used by a nun to scourge herself (allegedly), a coronation sword, and much else, a mixture of the grisly and the picturesque. There were also bits and pieces from the colonies. Tomahawks, wampum, bows and arrows, and even another fragment of asbestos: just the kind of curiosities that Franklin loved to examine. So he and his friend joined the throng in Cheyne Walk.[13]

And then, on the way home in another boat, an idea occurred to John Wygate. He suggested that Franklin should jump into the Thames. Raised as he was by the Mill Pond in Boston, of course he was an excellent swimmer. Being Franklin, he had also studied the textbooks, learning the strokes recommended by a Frenchman who had written the best available. He had even taught Wygate and a friend how to swim. What better way to end the day but this—an exhibition of colonial aquatics? It would be almost as amusing as a petrified fetus.

So Franklin stripped off his clothes and dived in, displaying his accomplishments to the good people of London. Off he swam, ducking and diving, followed by applause, the Water American in his element. The Thames is a dangerous river at this point, tidal and the prey of powerful currents, so that today the Metropolitan Police issue strict warnings against this kind of escapade; and in 1726 the water was also filthy and foul-smelling, heavy with the drift of human sewage. But Franklin made it as far as Blackfriars, coming ashore on the mud beneath the dome of St. Paul's.

It was one way to become a celebrity. John Wygate was utterly thrilled. Seeing how ingenious his friend had proved to be, he came up with a new suggestion. Should they not cross the English Channel, and take their talents on a tour of Europe? They could pay their way as printers or as masters of the art of swimming. Franklin liked the idea. He thought about it for a while and referred the matter to the wise Mr. Denham: and then he said no.

He was set upon Philadelphia. A ship was due to leave that summer, the *Berkshire,* bound for the Delaware. Once again, it was time to be on the move. Franklin began to busy himself running errands for his new partner, and saying goodbye to his friends. Among those who had worked with him at Mr. Palmer's workshop at St. Bartholomew's was the young Charles Ackers, with whom he would keep in touch for many years to come. In the 1730s, when Franklin was publishing *The Pennsylvania Gazette,* Ackers was his principal contact in the press in the capital, the man to whom he could send his American newspaper in exchange for the latest journalism from London.

In the shape of Charles Ackers, Franklin beheld his mirror image. When they met, Ackers was about twenty-three, the son of a gardener, and just finishing his time as one of Palmer's apprentices. Like Franklin, he was capable of rare feats of technical skill. Ackers was one of the very few compositors in London who could set a book in Arabic. Indeed in 1726 he was the compositor for an Arabic translation of the New Testament, intended to assist with the conversion of the Muslims to Christianity.[14]

A year after that, Ackers had his own workshop, where he printed all the early published work of James Ralph. He went on to a prosperous career that made him a gentleman and a pillar of society, a justice of the peace for Middlesex with a town house and small country estate. Among his friends, Ackers counted people whom Franklin admired: not only a fellow printer, Samuel Richardson, who became the author of *Pamela*, but also William Caslon, the most famous English typefounder of the eighteenth century, renowned for the strength and precision of the letters he produced. By the 1740s, Caslon's lead type had become Franklin's favorite. Indeed he rarely used any other.

To survive in a market as competitive as London, a printer required a reliable flow of business from editions that would find a ready market. With his alliance with the Tonsons, John Watts had shown one way in which this could be done; but Charles Ackers was even more creative and adaptable. Besides printing a wide range of sermons, schoolbooks, and histories, plus a cookery book that sold extremely well, he became the printer and co-owner of a new monthly, *The London Magazine*, founded in 1732. One such periodical already existed, *The Gentleman's Magazine*, which had come into being early in 1731, offering a rich and varied diet of poetry, book reviews, political news and comment, and even scientific essays. Charles Ackers and his partners strove to do the same, promising "greater variety, and more in quantity, than any monthly book extant." In its heyday *The London Magazine* had a circulation of about eight thousand.[15]

Among its most avid readers was Benjamin Franklin, who often lifted material from both periodicals for reuse in *The Pennsylvania Gazette*. Indeed his early work on electricity owed its beginnings to detailed reports in *The Gentleman's Magazine* of experiments in Paris and Germany. In 1740, Franklin tried to launch his own equivalent, a venture that swiftly ended in failure. In the colonies, where the market was so much smaller, and the magazines imported from London already had a following, he could not make a monthly pay its way. But although their markets were so very different, Franklin and Ackers had goals and ambitions that were identical. Back home in Philadelphia, Franklin's career for the next two decades was a long attempt to achieve the kind of success that Charles Ackers achieved in England.

Both Ackers and Franklin began as highly skilled artisans, born the sons of tradesmen, but all the time they were striving to be accepted as something more. They wanted to be *gentlemen* printers. In other words, they saw their business careers as a means not just to make money, but also as a way to become respected figures in their community. For that to occur, they needed flagship publications whose high quality would establish their reputation as publishers with taste and ingenuity. They also required a product range so wide and so robust that eventually their business would almost run itself.

As we would say today, Franklin had to build a brand, a printing franchise so strong that one day he could leave it to somebody else to manage, giving him the leisure for civic virtue and for science. In America, Franklin had to be still more flexible than Ackers, and also more opportunistic. But eventually, by different means, they reached the same destination. America's gentleman printer: that was what Benjamin Franklin would become, before he turned to science and politics. But in 1726, he had yet to appreciate that this would be his future; and in fact he almost abandoned the colonies forever.

At the last moment, as the *Berkshire* was ready to sail, Franklin came close to changing his mind and turning his back on Thomas Denham. Word of Franklin's adventure in the Thames had spread around the city, reaching the ears of a Tory politician, Sir William Wyndham, who was making his name in Parliament as an opponent of Walpole and the Whigs. Somehow—presumably by way of John Wygate, and his Tory connections—he found the big American. Wyndham made Franklin another attractive offer: teach my sons to swim, and I will pay a handsome fee.

It occurred to Franklin that many other people might want the same tuition from a personal trainer. Why not stay in London and open a swimming school? An even more appealing proposition. But then he thought again: he had gone too far with Denham, with whom he had a deal. And so on the afternoon of July 21, the *Berkshire* slipped her moorings and left the river Thames for America, taking him with her and bringing to a close an extraordinary phase in the life of Benjamin Franklin.

He had seen many plays and read many books. By the time he left he had lost his virginity: Franklin hints at that in his autobiography. In his eighteen months in London, he had mixed with a demimonde of writers and intellectuals, and he had met Tories, Whigs, and scientists: "ingenious acquaintances," as he describes them. He had encountered the kind of eccentrics whom he so enjoyed, Papists and freethinkers alike, in far larger numbers than he could have found in the colonies and they had enlarged his knowledge of human nature. In the workshops run by Watts and Palmer he had also been through what amounted to a graduate school of the printing trade. Only one thing was missing: for all his frugal ways, Franklin had failed to save any money. To pay his fare on the *Berkshire,* Mr. Denham had to lend him £10 and he still had nothing to give back to Mr. Vernon in Rhode Island.

Long before he set foot in England, Franklin had already been ingenious. Now he was far more so: a brilliant youth who had been at the center of things, in the London of Walpole, Hogarth, and Sir Isaac Newton. For that there was a price to be paid, by way of the frustrations of maturity. After so enjoying the excitement of London, he had to return to a provincial town where perhaps no one would understand the talk he had heard in the coffeehouses.

He was still only twenty. For many years he was going to have to work very hard to make a living, for himself and for a wife and family, if such he came to have, with little likelihood that he would see London again and no guarantee that he would ever find the time and leisure to be a man of letters and ideas. Not until Franklin was more than forty could he pick up the trail of science that Sir Isaac had left for him to follow. In the meantime, he would require all the "regularity" that Samuel Palmer had prized so highly.

Part Four

The Weekly Grind

Chapter Twelve

Seaweed, Sickness, and the Junto

The voyage began as a jaunt, a bit of fun, as though Franklin were enjoying one last holiday before adult life closed in around him. As the ship lay at anchor off the coast of England, he took a bath by leaping into the sea and swimming around the hull, with porpoises basking in the distance. On the Isle of Wight, where they spent a week or so waiting for the wind, Franklin stepped ashore to visit the attractions. Carisbrooke Castle, already in ruins, covered in ivy and tumbling down: it was something that he had to see, and so up he went in the sunshine. Ever the student, he peered at the stones and listened to the guide, who kept an alehouse at the gate. The next day, he was the boy from Boston again, playing games like the old ones when he built his little wharf. When he and his friends were returning to the *Berkshire* in the dark, it was Franklin who waded into the mud, up to his waist, to borrow a boat to carry them over a creek: but without the owner's permission.

He was keeping a journal, his version of the log Sir Hans Sloane had compiled of his voyage to Jamaica. Once or twice in the *Courant,* Franklin had shown how well he could write descriptively, a skill he would require for the kind of science he would do later on. Here in his diary of life at sea he gives us everything we need, if we are to share his changing mood as the journey becomes an ordeal. They spent sixty days out of sight of land. It was not an especially long crossing; but long enough for their supplies to run short and for tempers to fray.[I]

"A contrary wind . . . puts us all out of good humour," he writes. "We grow sullen, silent, and reserved, and fret at each other on every little occasion." When a cardsharper is caught by his fellow passengers, they sentence him to pay two bottles of brandy. He refuses, and so they hoist him up on a rope and let him hang, "cursing and swearing," until he goes black in the face, cries "murder!" and they have to let him down. A ship comes by, sailing from Dublin with a cargo of indentured servants bound for New York. As the smell drifts over the water, Franklin shows that there are limits to the charity he learned from Mrs. Holt. He calls the Irish "a lousy stinking rabble," and pities anyone who has to travel with them.

Six hundred miles out from England, a "poor little bird" lands on the deck. Too weak to be fed, it disappears, falling victim to the cat. On a calm, hot day when the skipper has the steward flogged for using too much flour, Franklin strips for another swim in the sea, only to see a shark circling the *Berkshire* in "a slow majestic manner," surrounded by pilot fish, "the smallest not bigger than my little finger." Coming back from the West Indies, Sir Hans had seen the sailors catching dolphins with bait made to look like a flying fish. Franklin writes about the very same thing.

Best of all is his account of *Sargassum,* a kind of brown algae floating on the waves. On a branch of *Sargassum,* he found what he called "vegetable animals," tiny little fruit that resembled shellfish, attached to the weed on little stalks of gristle. Inspecting them closely, he saw that some of the fruit contained a soft jelly, like the flesh of an oyster, but others—the larger ones—were "visibly animated, opening their shells every moment, and thrusting out a set of unformed claws." Among them he found a miniature crab, "about as big as the head of a tenpenny nail." Since the crab was as yellow as the *Sargassum,* Franklin thought it might be "a native of the branch," growing out of the weed by a process of reproduction. He placed samples in a bottle filled with saltwater, to see if any more crabs appeared.

From his reading of Wollaston, Franklin was aware that one of the most tantalizing scientific questions of the age had to do with what was called "equivocal" generation. Could one species of organism—a flea, a worm, or perhaps a crab—emerge by chance, "spontaneously" or "equivocally," from another kind of creature, or from dead flesh? If so, then perhaps there existed no rigid distinction between animals and vegetables, or between fish and plants or the medium in which they lived. This theory worried men like Wollaston, who rejected it entirely because—like the ideas of Spinoza—it might lead in dangerous directions. If it were taken to its logical conclusion—as it was by French biologists, twenty years later—this kind of thinking might do away with God as a creator, and leave no room for the notion of a soul.[2]

As a young man aboard the *Berkshire,* Franklin was a long way from anything quite so sophisticated, but he certainly knew that this was the sort of question that scientists wanted to explore. His journal of the voyage is impressive for three things: his powers of observation; his skill with language; and his appreciation that odd phenomena like the *Sargassum* might one day supply a key to unlock the secrets of nature. With its echoes of Sloane and its allusions to biology, the journal shows how much he had learned in London. His meetings with Sir Hans and in the coffeehouses had started to give him a taste for empirical research. After flirting for so long with metaphysics, Franklin was beginning to leave it behind. He was gradually giving up abstract speculation in favor of natural science, a field where—in the 1740s—his talents could be far more productive.

At last, on October 9, after a few days when the wind stood fair behind them, blowing them in at a brisk seven knots, they saw a long spit of white sand and the tops of trees. The *Berkshire* was just where she ought to be, in sight of Cape Henlopen, at the very mouth of the Delaware. On the 11th, in fine autumn weather, Denham and Franklin landed in Philadelphia by night. On their arrival, they found that in their absence many things had changed: in politics, in publishing, and in the lives of their friends.

On Market Street, Miss Read had ceased to be a spinster. Her dead father had left the Reads in debt and with only a small income, so that Deborah had to find a husband. This she had done: but as we shall see in a moment, he was far from being an ideal companion. As for Sir William Keith, he had been dismissed at last, to give way to a new governor, Patrick Gordon. He was an elderly soldier from Scotland who had served without distinction in Marlborough's campaigns but appeared to the Penns to be a much safer pair of hands than Sir William to oversee their property. As always, there was talk of war with Spain, after a naval fracas said to have occurred in the West Indies; but as always, until the end of the next decade, the rumors turned out to be false.

Although maritime trade had dwindled a little, Pennsylvania was still doing well. The exports went out, mainly food to the Caribbean, and the imports still came in, especially people: the Irish of course, but also there were signs of a new wave of German migrants from the Rhineland. The iron trade was looking promising, with new projects for mines and furnaces in the hills above the Delaware and to the west in Chester County. But for Franklin, the most surprising thing of all would have been the success of his strange old employer: because Samuel Keimer had found a new way to make money.

After Franklin left his workshop, Keimer had moved to better premises and hired new staff. To the chagrin of his printing rival, Andrew Bradford, he had also begun to publish almanacs. It was a field in which the Bradfords had been active for forty years or more, in New York as well as Pennsylvania, selling calendars to farmers who required a diary for the year ahead. There they would find the times of dawn and sunset, the phases of the moon, the dates of sittings of the county courts, and even forecasts of the weather. There were blank pages too, where the farmer could jot down notes of his crops, the prices they fetched on market day, or the number of German laborers he acquired.

In the middle colonies, the leading almanac writer was a sea captain, Titan Leeds, who dabbled in astronomy and claimed to be a meteorologist. His work was published by Andrew Bradford. Each almanac featured a whimsical preface and quaint little poems, culled from English anthologies and intended to amuse the farmer in his evenings away from the plow. The Bradfords thought they had the market cornered; but then, at the end of 1725, Samuel Keimer burst upon the scene. To compete with Leeds, he published an almanac—"an Ephemeris," as he preferred to call it—authored by Jacob Taylor, a local poet who could also do some mathematics.[3]

The little book was quintessential Keimer. His almanacs came with extra features such as a Hebrew alphabet, riddles that the readers were asked to solve, and comical verses written by Keimer himself. The rhymes he composed were terribly tasteless, dealing in jokes about sex and diarrhea, and featuring the sort of misogynistic twaddle that was so pervasive at the time. To sell the almanac, he recruited a network of storekeepers from Boston down to Maryland, to each of whom he sent some copies. It was a shrewd thing to do, and it deeply annoyed Andrew Bradford: who was even more upset when Keimer coaxed away Titan Leeds with an offer of more money for his predictions of the rain and snow.

In Philadelphia, Samuel Keimer gave some of his almanacs to Deborah's mother to sell. And if Sarah Read needed the extra money, it may have been because of her daughter's appalling choice of husband. In the summer of 1725, in an Anglican wedding at Christ Church, Deborah had married one John Rogers, who made pots. Although he made them very nicely, the potter was "a worthless fellow," says Franklin in his memoirs, yet another wastrel who borrowed money that he could not repay. The marriage would not endure. Nor would Franklin's new relationship with Thomas Denham. On arrival home, Franklin had no idea that he would soon be driven back to work for Mr. Keimer; but such was the fate that he would suffer.

A Winter of Distemper

A few days after Franklin landed from the *Berkshire,* there was a flurry of excitement. In a vain attempt to stave off his dismissal, Governor Keith had turned for help to the press, with Keimer as his printer, engaging in a war of words with James Logan. When at last he was fired in the spring of 1726, by which time his debts were almost overwhelming, Sir William had only one card left to play. He stood for election to the General Assembly; and because he was still a popular man, the Keithites took all the seats in Philadelphia. In October, on the opening day of the session, to the sound of cannons from ships in the river, they paraded through the streets in triumph, with Sir William on horseback leading a company of artisans and tradesmen.

Franklin must have been there, somewhere in the crowd, to witness this typically British gesture of a kind that went back to Sir William's Tory days in the London of Queen Anne. The parade was impressive, but also rather futile. In Pennsylvania, the city and the countryside were at odds in politics, as bitterly divided as they are today. The rural counties controlled the legislature, and they were hostile to Sir William. The months and years that followed would see the slow death of the Keithite party, a process that would be complete by 1729. Gradually there came into being a new political order, led by Franklin's friend, the lawyer Andrew Hamilton. Beneath his spreading wings, Franklin would prosper in the next decade.

On arrival home, he and Denham set to work to build their business. An account book of Denham's survives, and it shows that he was very much the coming man, commercially astute and a trustworthy fellow. His shipowning clients were people of substance, merchants from England making regular voyages across the Atlantic. As for Denham's retail customers, they included the Quaker elite, with among them his friend Clement Plumstead, three times mayor of Philadelphia and a close ally of Andrew Hamilton. Meeting people such as this, and selling them candles, soap, and calico, Franklin made excellent contacts for the future, men and women whose confidence he would secure.[4]

He was in the mood to be sober and diligent. On board the *Berkshire,* Franklin had drawn up a personal creed, the first of several, a plan of conduct intended to ensure that he never went the way of Ralph or Collins. Although the plan owed nothing to religion—Franklin merely said that he wanted to live "like a rational creature," with no mention of God—it certainly smacked of remorse and a yearning to repent. "It is necessary," Franklin told himself, "for me to be extremely frugal for some time, till I have paid what I owe."

Since his only debts were to Denham and Vernon, neither of whom was clamoring to be repaid, perhaps he was being too hard on himself; or perhaps worse sins weighed on his conscience. In future, he promised, he would always be truthful and sincere, make no promises he did not mean to keep, and speak no ill of anyone. He would also work very hard: as if he had ever done anything else! As though he were Hogarth's good apprentice, Franklin took a vow "to apply myself industriously to whatever business I take in hand, and not divert my mind . . . by any foolish project of growing suddenly rich; for industry and patience are the surest means of plenty."

It was an odd little document, coming as it did from someone who—as far as we know—had never been prone to idleness or telling lies. Had there been other errors, besides those to which he admits in his autobiography? As it stands, the plan of conduct seems to hint at episodes of naughtiness that Franklin would never wish to disclose, even in a posthumous narrative. If so, it serves as another reminder that in his memoirs Franklin gives us only a fraction of himself. He tells us only what he thinks we ought to know. Indeed his account of his early life can sometimes resemble an eighteenth-century mansion where beyond the grand salon and the public rooms, there are many more intimate chambers kept firmly under lock and key.

A few months later, on his twenty-first birthday, Franklin wrote something equally strange: a brief, uninformative letter to his sister Jane in Boston. She was just fourteen, but soon to be married. Painfully polite, written in the style of Addison, the letter accompanied a gift of a spinning wheel: "which I hope you will accept as a small token of my sincere love and affection." He says precisely nothing about himself, his voyage home from London, or his other adventures. This is the only letter between Franklin and his family that survives from the 1720s. The rest of their correspondence has disappeared. Why that should be so, we cannot say, but we can harbor our suspicions: it may be that Franklin destroyed it all himself.

He wrote that letter to Jane in January 1727. The winter was unusually severe in Philadelphia: "snow on the ground, and the frost so violent," wrote another of Mr. Denham's clients, "that the ink freezes in the pen." With the cold came disease. A fever swept through the town, its most striking feature being a yellow tint to the skin, like an attack of jaundice, followed by weeks of fatigue. At the beginning of February, Franklin and Denham both fell ill. Franklin called it "a distemper," which he thought was pleurisy. Despite his strength he came close to death. His recovery was slow and dogged by feelings of depression; and when he was himself again, he would have sad news to hear from Boston.[5]

His uncle Benjamin was dead at the age of seventy-six. He had begun to fade away in the summer of 1725, fainting twice on Sabbath days. There was a year or so of failing health—dropsy and more fainting—until at last he died in the March of 1727, taken perhaps by the same disease that struck his nephew. Like his dying mother long ago at Ecton, the old man consoled himself with the psalms, making a list of verses that seemed to fit his case. "It is good for me that I have been afflicted": that was one. A notice appeared in the press, calling Benjamin Senior "a rare & exemplary Christian." With him there vanished rare memories of a distant age. No casual reader could have guessed that here was a man who had witnessed the Great Fire of London.[6]

Meanwhile Thomas Denham died his own lingering death. Not until the summer of 1728 did he pass away. Toward the end, he forgave the debt of £10 that Franklin owed him for the voyage, but while Denham lay ill the store had ceased to be viable, and Franklin had been left redundant. His seagoing brother-in-law, Robert Holmes, stopped by in Philadelphia and advised him to go back to being a printer. Wise counsel: not least because Keimer was hovering around, eager to hire the young man to run his press, so as to leave himself free to sell ink and sealing wax over the counter.

None of the merchants in the town wanted Franklin as a clerk. So at some point in the middle of 1727, reluctantly he went back to printing: not the fine craftsmanship that he had known in London, alongside men at the top of their trade, but Keimer's colonial workshop, still poorly equipped, where his colleagues were raw and poorly paid. They were the epitome of Pennsylvania: five restless men, from all corners of the British Isles, each one having come to Keimer by his own erratic path. It was up to Franklin to lick them into shape, but some of them would simply never learn the craft.

There was Hugh Meredith—already thirty, honest, well-read, but also a drinker—one of four sons of an Anglican farmer who had tagged along with the Quakers who left the Welsh hills for America. Out in Chester County the Merediths had found their niche, with a few hundred acres close to the new iron workings. They were comfortably off, with neighbors who included Mordecai Lincoln, the ancestor of Abraham; but for some reason Hugh preferred the town. There, to his father's dismay, he took to the alehouse. At Keimer's, he was supposed to work the press, while the books were to be bound by Stephen Potts. He was another farming man, but lazy.

Of course there had to be a wild Irishman, John by name. A bondservant, purchased by Keimer from a sea captain, he had four years left to run of his indentures. He was always looking for a chance to run away, which he soon did. They also had a dogsbody, David Harry, about eighteen years old and hired as an apprentice; but the cream of the bunch was George Webb, highly educated and picked by Keimer to be a compositor. He had a very curious tale to tell.

Still in his teens, Webb claimed to come from the English town of Gloucester, where at his grammar school he had shone as an actor and a poet. From there—or so he said—Webb had gone to Oxford University, where he spent a tedious year, before dumping his academic gown in a hedge and running away to London for a life on the stage. There he had suffered the same fate as James Ralph. Unable to find a place in the theater, he ran out of money, pawned what he had, and wandered the streets with an empty stomach, until he was recruited by a trafficker in laborers bound for America. Webb signed himself away as an indentured servant and duly arrived in Philadelphia, where he was bought by Samuel Keimer.

It was a remarkable story, repeated by Franklin in his memoirs with a touch of skepticism. He had little time for George Webb, who later betrayed him in business. Although the young Englishman was clever and charming, Franklin dismissed him as a good-for-nothing, idle and thoughtless. But the fact was that Webb really had gone to Oxford, Balliol College no less, and he was indeed the son of a landowner from Gloucestershire, Captain Obadiah Webb, who had a string of estates near Bristol. And far from being a hopeless scallywag, he published a book of his own poetry in 1731, made his way home to England via South Carolina, trained as a lawyer, and eventually came into his inheritance.[7]

Which was something Franklin never had, in financial terms. What he did have was a range of talents whose combination was unique in Philadelphia. For example, at St. Bartholomew's in London he had seen the type foundry run on the lower floor by Thomas James. And so at Keimer's workshop he was able to cut new letters and fashion a set of iron molds, relatively crude by British standards—molds of this kind were very hard to make—but still good enough to produce the characters they needed. Franklin also turned his hand to Hogarth's trade of engraving.

Soon the quality of their output improved by leaps and bounds. When Keimer brought out a book titled *A Collection of One Hundred Notable Things, Adapted for the Service and Delight of Young Persons,* it was evidently Franklin's handiwork. The title page was elegant, as beautifully set as a London book, with shapely italics, and the subject matter was utterly Franklinesque. The book was intended, so it said, for "the propagation of virtue and of knowledge in these parts." Inside, item No. 56 was an advertisement for his new printed typeface, saying that "by the help of some ingenious persons"—Franklin, in other words—Mr. Keimer had the use of "a mould, by which he can cast printing letters, of any form, shape, character, or size." The type would be ideal, they said, for printing paper money, in distinctive lettering "almost impossible to be counterfeited."

And so six months went by, with Franklin finding Keimer ever more irritating, with his bad manners and his deceitfulness. Franklin began to see that he was being used. Once he had trained up Meredith and the others, Keimer could do without him and his skills. And indeed, as time went on, Keimer became still more unpleasant, as though he wished to drive Franklin away.

It was at this frustrating moment, in the autumn of 1727, as though to keep alive his happy memories of London, that Franklin became the founder of his famous Junto. Meeting in a tavern on a Friday night, it was to be what he called "a club for mutual improvement," open only to friends he deemed to be ingenious. Every member would have to come up with "queries," meaning questions about science, morality, and politics, for the others to discuss. Every three months, each one would also have to write an essay and read it aloud, to be debated by his companions.

Wherein consists the happiness of a rational creature?—that was the sort of question they would pose; but they dealt in practicalities as well. Although metaphysics had their place at the Junto, Franklin also meant his club to be a school for what he called "mechanic arts," of the kind his family had always pursued. It was never Franklin's aim to be a narrow specialist. In the eighteenth century it was thought that a gentleman had a duty to be broad-minded—"variety," that should be his watchword—and no one was more various than Franklin. He wanted to put together the wisdom of Socrates, the science of Newton, the practical talents of craftsmen, and the eloquence of English writers whom he admired. He hoped to make people understand that science, engineering, philosophy, and wit were simply four sides of the same ingenious square.

Eventually—but not until the 1770s, when at last he lost patience with the British—Franklin would come to believe that this union of talents could only occur in a democratic republic, cut loose from the empire. Only in a free America would it be truly recognized that virtue, invention, and the arts depended on each other. This idea of Franklin's found its first embodiment in the Junto.

A Club for Ingenuity

Among the few papers that survive from Franklin's early manhood, one of the most revealing is a set of notes about the Junto. Jotted down by a fellow member, Nicholas Scull, a surveyor who kept the Indian Head, the tavern where they assembled, at first sight the notes are merely a list of their names and the money they owed for their drinks. It seems that to begin with the Junto had only ten members, though soon they went up to twelve. Four of them came from Keimer's workshop: Franklin himself, Meredith, Potts, and Webb. Among the rest the oldest was Scull, who was forty. The most eminent was a scrivener, Joseph Breintnall, from a Quaker family who had been close to Thomas Denham. The striking thing about the list is this: that Scull only called two of them "Mister." One of the two was Benjamin Franklin.[8]

Because the Junto was his idea, because he was so fine a craftsman, and because he was so clever with words, Franklin stood out as an obvious leader. Although he was one of the youngest, with no land to his name and with no family in Philadelphia, even so his fellow members looked up to him as *Mr.* Franklin: the title his grandfather and his uncle had acquired at Ecton, by means of their ingenuity, and the one Josiah had earned in Boston. Now it was Franklin's as well: not in the eyes of the authorities, perhaps, but in the opinion of the people who counted most to him. And seeing that he had no wealth and no lineage, that could only be because they saw Franklin as he was: someone very good at everything he did.

Since his boyhood by the Mill Pond, he had loved what Defoe had called "projects." The Junto was perhaps the most enjoyable, a gathering of professional men and artisans who almost without exception went on to leave their mark on Philadelphia. At the Junto, Franklin made the two dearest friends of his maturity, men about whom we know all too little. One was Robert Grace, the orphaned son of a planter from Barbados who had left him a portfolio of property in Philadelphia. Born in 1709, and raised in the town by his grandparents, the grandfather being a sea captain who also dealt in iron, Grace was to become an ironmaster himself. The other was a Quaker carpenter's son, William Coleman, who later served as town clerk. When he joined the Junto in the late 1720s, Coleman was a merchant's clerk and bookkeeper, and Franklin would remember him for having "the coolest, clearest head, the best heart, and the exactest morals of almost any man I ever met with." He was the other member referred to as "Mr." by Scull. But because they died quite young, both Grace and Coleman have been almost entirely forgotten.[9]

Even so, enough material survives to tell us what they were striving to achieve. In the Delaware valley, with Indian country still so close at hand, the Junto's members were immersed in the challenging affairs of a colony engaged in headlong expansion. In the year the club was founded, as many as 1,200 immigrants arrived from Germany, and by the early 1730s settlers from Pennsylvania had crossed the Susquehanna and were spilling to the south toward Virginia. In the next fifteen years, the population would double in the Quaker province.

For Coleman, Grace, and the other members of the Junto, all of this spelled opportunity. The opening up of the interior, the flying sparks of iron furnaces and forges, the ships sailing in and out of the river: to make the best of all this, they needed adult education of the kind the Junto could provide. Never meant to be merely a talking shop, the club addressed the practical needs of young men with work to do. Take William Parsons, for example, a Junto member whose career was very Pennsylvanian. Franklin remembered him as an agitated soul. Given how much he was trying to accomplish, this is understandable. Parsons is said to have been born in England in 1701 and brought over to America as a child. By the mid-1720s he was married to a German immigrant, devoutly Lutheran in her beliefs, and he was earning a living making and mending shoes for customers who included William Coleman: a menial trade from which he longed to escape.[10]

Somehow William Parsons made enough money to become a partner of Scull's in the Indian Head. He also acquired the skills of a scrivener; but his true love was mathematics and geometry. He dabbled in astrology, perhaps with a view to writing almanacs, but by 1730 he had found his calling as a surveyor of land. After a slow start, Parsons became the surveyor of choice for demanding clients, including not only James Logan and the Penns, but also German-speaking settlers staking out their farms around the new township of Reading, sixty miles inland. His field books survive, containing not only hundreds of surveys but also an exercise in which, by way of triangulation, he precisely measured the width of the Delaware.

It was just the kind of puzzle that Franklin also enjoyed. At the Junto, he and his friends could help each other by finding new clients, by learning how to write reports and letters, and even by perfecting their skills with algebra. Another member was Thomas Godfrey, a glazier who taught himself to be a fine mathematician. Awkward in company, Godfrey could be pedantic and tiresome; but he invented a new kind of quadrant, an instrument for fixing latitude on land and sea by observations of the sun and the stars. What better friend could William Parsons have?

And so at their Friday night sessions, well supplied with wine, the Junto cultivated their minds and each other. The meetings began with the reading of twenty-four "standing queries," as Franklin described them, a program of work ideally suited to the Pennsylvania of 1727. "Hath any citizen in your knowledge," it was asked, "failed in his business lately, and what have you heard of the cause? Have you lately heard of any citizen's thriving well, and by what cause?" And so the Junto queries went on.

Have we met good people, or bad ones, the healthy or the sick, what makes them as they are and what can be done to help them? What fascinating things have we seen or read about, in books to do with history, medicine, travel, or—of course—"mechanic arts"? Can the colonial laws be improved? Is freedom in danger, from what they called "any encroachment on the just liberties of the people"? There spoke Benjamin Franklin, the Whig; his club took little interest in party politics. "Do you think of anything at present, in which the Junto may be serviceable to mankind? To their country, to their friends, or to themselves?" It was as broad an agenda as anyone could wish for.

As well as being apolitical, the club was also entirely secular. As far as we know, nothing quite like the Junto had been seen before in America,

From 1703, the estate map of Ecton, Northamptonshire, the English home of the Franklin family. With the parish church and manor house at the center, and the River Nene flowing along the bottom, the map shows the medieval pattern of fields divided into strips, with somewhere among them the land held by the Franklins.

A twenty-first-century view from south to north across the Nene valley, with Ecton's Georgian manor house just visible among trees on the hillside toward the right. At bottom left, the stone farmhouse is a survival from the 1600s.

Close to the porch of St. Mary Magdalene, Ecton, the graves—marked with crosses against the headstones—of Thomas Franklin Jr. and his wife, Eleanor, Benjamin Franklin's uncle and aunt. Benjamin visited the graves in 1758.

An image of London as Franklin saw it in the 1720s, a wooden house from the seventeenth century in Bartholomew Close, Smithfield, where he worked as a printer for Samuel Palmer. The picture was taken in about 1870, before developers and German air raids swept away the buildings Franklin knew.

On arriving in London late in 1724, Franklin's friend James Ralph tried to get work from the bookseller John Roberts in Warwick Lane, in the shadow of St Paul's Cathedral. This photograph from 1875 shows the ancient coaching inn, the Oxford Arms, that stood in the street.

What Franklin saw out the windows of Palmer's printing shop at the church of St. Bartholomew the Great. Taken in 1908, the picture shows timber-framed houses from the 1600s—since demolished—facing the north side of the church.

In 1726, this was the Sardinian embassy in Lincoln's Inn Fields, London. The covered passageway—through which Franklin would have passed many times—led to Duke Street, where he lodged in Mrs. Holt's Italian warehouse opposite the embassy's Catholic Chapel. This picture was taken in 1882. All the buildings in the picture were pulled down in the early 1900s.

With barrels outside, Don Saltero's coffeehouse at 18 Cheyne Walk, Chelsea, visited by Franklin in 1726, from a watercolor of about 1800. The house is still standing, greatly altered.

Peter Cooper's panoramic painting of Philadelphia from the Delaware River in about 1720, making an interesting comparison with the nineteenth-century photographs of buildings from the era in Chapter Eight. *The Library Company of Philadelphia*

The milliner or seamstress Moll Hackabout arriving in London, a scene from William Hogarth's narrative cycle *The Harlot's Progress* (1731–2). As discussed in Chapter Ten, the subject matter of Hogarth's work from this period has close affinities with the themes of Franklin's autobiography.

Another Franklinesque scene, from Hogarth's cycle *Industry and Idleness,* with the two apprentices at their looms: one working hard, the other dozing. The two Bible texts beneath are very Franklinian: "The drunkard shall come to poverty" and "The hand of the diligent maketh rich."

Left: Franklin's friend and intellectual mentor, the Pennsylvania lawyer and agent for the Penn family, James Logan (1674–1751), painted about 1740 by Gustavus Hesselius. Right: Franklin's patron Andrew Hamilton (ca. 1676–1741), who dominated the politics of Pennsylvania in the 1730s. By Adolf Ulrick Wertmüller, 1808. *Courtesy of the Philadelphia History Museum at the Atwater Kent, the Historical Society of Pennsylvania Collection.*

The leading Freemason in Philadelphia, and also Pennsylvania's chief justice, William Allen (1704–80), painted from life in 1746 by Robert Feke. Although by the 1760s Allen and Franklin were political enemies, earlier they had been united in their opposition to Quaker pacifism during the wars with France and Spain.

The Scotsman Cadwallader Colden (1689–1776): medical doctor, official surveyor of New York, and scientist, who met Franklin in 1743 and helped put him on the path to his electrical experiments.

Left: Deborah Read Franklin, painted in about 1759—when she was about fifty-five—by Benjamin Wilson. Right: The earliest known portrait of Benjamin Franklin, painted by Robert Feke in about 1746, when Franklin was forty.

where the usual venues for debate were the elected assemblies or the chapel. And so the question arises: how did Franklin arrive at something so new to the colonies? Of course, when Franklin invented the Junto he drew upon his reading; but by now it had been so voracious that it is often hard to say exactly *which* of the books he studied had tilted him in a particular direction. One school of thought finds his inspiration for the club in Cotton Mather, who in the early 1700s had convened two discussion groups for "congenial gentlemen," with the aim of fostering civic and religious virtue in Boston. Possibly; but Franklin was not long home from London, a city full of clubs and societies, created in the pursuit of ingenuity, and above all the Royal Society, intended from its outset to be a vehicle for what its founders called "the improvement of peaceable arts." There were English models for the Junto more relevant than Mather's clubs, with their narrower focus on religion.[11]

Given that it met in a tavern at the end of the working week—because of Keimer's preference for keeping the Jewish Sabbath, he shut up shop at sunset on Fridays, not Saturdays—the club may really have begun as a more civilized version of the Chapel Drinks that Franklin knew in London. But if we need literary sources for what Franklin was trying to achieve, they can be found in John Locke, in *The Spectator*, and even perhaps in *Gulliver's Travels*. When Scull wrote a poem in praise of the sessions at the Indian Head, his proudest boast was that when they talked philosophy, they used "lofty language . . . such as fam'd Swift or Addison might own."[12]

In the opening essays of their masterpiece, Steele and Addison described their fictional society, the Spectator Club, devoted, as they put it, to "the advancement of the public weal": a phrase that described the Junto as well. As for Jonathan Swift, his most famous book went on sale in 1726 and rapidly made its way to America. In its pages we find the noble Houyhnhnms, the virtuous horses who pondered weighty questions while they munched their hay: and perhaps they were another model for the Junto. Of one thing there can be no doubt at all. For help in drafting the Junto's detailed rules, Franklin turned to Locke the philosopher.[13]

Each new member had to make an affirmation—not to swear an oath, which Quakers could not do—of his goodwill, his love of mankind and the truth, and his commitment to free speech. "Do you think any person ought to be harmed," they were asked, "for mere speculative opinions, or his external way of worship?" They were supposed to answer "no."

As the scholar Dorothy Grimm showed in 1956, Franklin took the text of the affirmation almost word for word from an essay by Locke, in which the philosopher laid down rules for a weekly society that met "for their improvement in useful knowledge."[14]

Three centuries on, we might choose to be cynical, dismissing the Junto as a clique of careerists who merely hoped to make friends, influence people, and grow rich. Of course there was an element of that; but as always with Franklin, there were also doubts and scruples and debates about what it meant to be successful. Just as Hogarth had asked questions in his paintings about the definition of virtue and success, in a new, commercial world where the Christian God so often seemed to be absent, so the Junto wondered what it meant to be good.

Certainly they wished to make money: how could they not, in such a dynamic colony? But their reading of Addison and the like told them that they should be gentlemen as well, tolerant, polite, and generous. Torn between these motives, they asked themselves: Should we be rich or should we be virtuous? And what did words such as virtue, gentility, wisdom, and prudence really signify? Did a life of commerce have to be filled with greed alone? Or was the pursuit of riches virtuous in itself, if it encouraged honesty and thrift, and provided the means for philanthropy? As they put it: "what general conduct of life is most suitable for men in such circumstances as most of the members of the Junto are? . . . Which is best: to make a friend of a wise and good man that is poor; or a rich man that is neither wise nor good? Which of the two is the greatest loss to a country, if they both die?"

These were pressing questions for young men who knew that if they were to survive in Pennsylvania, they would require powerful friends and patrons. From his differing experiences with Keith, Ralph, and Denham, Franklin also knew how difficult it was to find and to keep them. In the autumn of 1727, with the Junto only just off the ground, he met with a cruel reminder that he had yet to acquire the patron he needed. All he had was a boss, and a bad one.

OUT ON HIS OWN, AGAIN

A moment of crisis was bound to occur, when Franklin struck out on his own: he *had* to be independent. The moment came with a shout in the street and a melodrama in Mr. Keimer's workshop.

That fall they were printing the 1728 issue of Titan Leeds's almanac, enlarged by Samuel Keimer to include what he called "very remarkable and notable things, more than usual": chiefly a poem warning that excessive drinking led to sodomy and a report from the Royal Society explaining how to use pigeon dung to make a liquid fertilizer. Well before year end, copies of this edifying volume had to be shipped up to Massachusetts, where Keimer was now in competition with James Franklin. With the *Courant* now defunct, James had moved to Newport, where he entered the market for calendars with his new *Rhode Island Almanac,* also known as *Poor Robin's.* In Boston, John Franklin would sell it from his soap and candle store.

One day as Benjamin was hard at work, he heard a commotion down the street, outside the courthouse. Probably it was October 2, when the elections for the General Assembly were held, and Franklin put his head out of the window to see what was happening. From the sidewalk, Keimer saw him taking time off from his printing and instantly he lost his temper. The neighbors heard the vile words that Keimer threw at Franklin, making him out to be no better than a lazy chattel. Perhaps the bearded heretic was drunk—Franklin does not say so, but that is the way it sounds—and he stormed up into the workshop, where they had a fierce quarrel.

When Keimer gave him three months' notice to quit, Franklin did the inevitable. He walked out, pausing only to ask his colleague Hugh Meredith to mind his belongings. That evening, when the Welshman brought them round, he had more to offer than sympathy: he also had a business proposition. After persuading Franklin not to go back to Boston, he pointed out that Keimer, so careless, so rude, and so eccentric, had no real future in Philadelphia. Being heavily in debt, he was bound to fail sooner or later; at which point Franklin could take his place.

What if we set up in business together? That was Meredith's suggestion. His time as an apprentice with Keimer would be up the following spring. In the meanwhile, they could import from London the equipment they required. The money would come from his landowning father, Simon Meredith, who was in Philadelphia for the assembly: in that year's election, he won a seat for Chester County. The old man had a high opinion of Franklin, hoping that he could keep Hugh away from hard liquor.

Mr. Meredith liked the plan; so did Franklin; and a deal was rapidly agreed. The year's last ships for London were due to sail by the end of November, and one of them carried an inventory, drawn up by Franklin, setting out what they needed. With the new venture cloaked in secrecy, Meredith went back to Keimer while Franklin tried to find work with Andrew Bradford: who had nothing to offer. For a few days he was idle; and then Keimer sent an olive branch, offering to take him back, all bitterness forgotten, so that he could undertake a lucrative new assignment.

During the recession of 1722, New Jersey had also issued paper money, backed by mortgages granted by a land bank. By now the paper bills were worn out and ragged, passing as they did through many hands. In those distant days, New Jersey was seen as a paragon of fiscal prudence, and so its currency circulated widely and traded at a premium to notes issued elsewhere. Besides being faded and decrepit, the Jersey bills were also far too easy to forge.

So toward the end of 1727, the assemblymen of New Jersey decided to print £10,000 in new notes to be swapped with the old. Their usual printer was William Bradford in Manhattan, but they put the deal out to tender and Samuel Keimer made a bid, with Franklin as his selling point. With the skills he had acquired in London, Franklin could create a new, more elaborate bill that would be impossible to fake; and so they won the contract.

Off they went to Burlington early in 1728, where Franklin fit in at once. Having met so long ago with John Browne, the freethinking doctor at nearby Bordentown, he already had a link to the area; and now as he printed their new paper money, he gained a wider reputation in New Jersey as a young man of ingenuity. Where Keimer was difficult and crude, Franklin was refined and literary, but also very competent. In the three months he spent there, Franklin made a long list of new friends whose names he carefully recorded in his memoirs.

Allen, Pearson, Bustill, and Decow: none of whom were famous, so that today the list feels like an awkward interruption to the flow of Franklin's narrative, but if he thought the names had to be mentioned, then we must ask why this was so. Of course, they were a local elite—the officials who supervised the paper money—and so, by giving us their names, Franklin is telling us that he was moving up in the world. That had always been the Franklin goal, from Northamptonshire onward. In his memoirs, Franklin writes at length about Isaac Decow, who acted as surveyor general of the western section of New Jersey. Decow was "shrewd" and "sagacious," says Franklin, who likes the fact that Decow started his working life in a brickworks, wheeling a barrow of clay. He also admires the manner in which Decow came to be a surveyor: self-taught, like William Parsons or his uncle Thomas, land agent and surveyor at Ecton. In the shape of Isaac Decow, he saw the kind of person he wanted to be: someone who emerged from obscurity to command respect.

There was something else as well. During his period in Burlington, Franklin mingled with men whose lives revolved around real estate: not urban property, but rural land in what was still a frontier province, with empty space available for settlers from Europe. Although technically New Jersey was now a royal colony, governed from New York, the power in the province really lay with the men who owned its land, the Proprietors, as they were known; and the people with whom Franklin made friends were their local representatives.

Isaac Pearson, for instance: in western New Jersey, he was the Proprietors' clerk. Working with Samuel Bustill, in the late 1720s he secured Decow's appointment as the provincial surveyor, earning fees from every farmer who wanted to carve out his slice of soil. In New Jersey, each plot had to be registered with a map, and so Decow conducted many hundreds of surveys during his twenty-year career.[15]

For Franklin the printer, Decow and the others could be immensely valuable friends. In the 1730s, Bustill became the clerk to the governor's council, and John Allen and Decow took turns to serve as treasurer of western New Jersey, holding the colony's tax revenues. They would need not only new paper money, but also mortgage deeds, official forms, printed copies of laws and regulations, and much else which Franklin would supply. They could also be of use in a less tangible way, by helping with the evolution of his ideas about America.

Frontier expansion: that was the point. Throughout his career in politics, from the 1740s until his death, Franklin would always have a passion for the west. Franklin hoped one day to see the far away Ohio valley filled with former Europeans: preferably Anglo-Saxon, though if Englishmen were not available he was prepared to make do with the Irish or the Germans. Back in Boston, in the days of the *Courant*, western dreams of such a kind had never entered his mind. For James Franklin and the Couranteers, Indian affairs and the frontier might provide an opportunity for colorful tales and tasteless humor, but they did not command their serious attention. The Philadelphia Franklin was very different, with expansion to the west a fundamental element of his philosophy.

His passion for the frontier had its roots in the friendships he made in his twenties. In 1741 his fellow member of the Junto, William Parsons, became Decow's opposite number as the surveyor general of Pennsylvania. With friends and allies such as these, whose careers depended on the flow of immigrants and the opening up of new territory, it was bound to be the case that Franklin would also turn his eyes across the watershed, into the deep hinterland whose rivers drained down into the Mississippi.

In the meantime he had to break free from Samuel Keimer. In the spring of 1728, at last the London ships came back to Philadelphia, and with them the type and the printing press he needed. And so Franklin and Meredith left Keimer for good, took a lease on a house in Market Street, and sublet a part of it to the mathematical glazier Thomas Godfrey and his wife and children. In came the first printing client, a farmer with five shillings to spend on a small job; and so they on their way.

More work arrived from their Junto friends, with Joseph Breintnall the scrivener giving them their first big break. The son of a haberdasher who had been among William Penn's earliest settlers, Breintnall was their contact among the leaders of the Quaker community. For the past five years, the Quakers had been trying to publish an American edition of a history of their movement, seven hundred pages long, turning for help first to Bradford, and then to Keimer, only to be met with endless delays. Determined to get the job done, with Breintnall as the go-between they went to Franklin, asking him to print the final section of the book.[16]

It was a job well within his capabilities, just forty-four sheets, each one accounting for four pages of text, but with other work piling up much of it had to be done after-hours. The hard part was the compositing, which often kept Franklin up until eleven. With the tidy habits of a London printer, once each sheet of the Quaker book was printed off he insisted on replacing all the lead characters in the correct place in his racks of type before he went to bed, so that the following morning he could make a prompt start. Here again was the "regularity" that Samuel Palmer had looked for in his staff. One night, by accident Franklin broke one of his trays, scattering the little letters all over the floor. He put them all back together before turning in.

Like Hogarth's industrious apprentice, he became known for his diligence. Philadelphia was still a small city where reputations were swiftly lost and made by word of mouth. There was a Scottish surgeon, Patrick Baird, who inspected incoming ships for smallpox and plied his profession from an office next door to Nicholas Scull. Of an evening, Mr. Baird would go to a gentleman's club, where he heard people prophesy that with two other printers already in the town, Franklin and Meredith were doomed. He begged to disagree.[17]

"The industry of that Franklin," Baird told his friends, "is superior to anything I ever saw.... I see him at work when I go home from club, and he is at work again before his neighbors are out of bed." With a recommendation so glowing, the jobs were bound to keep coming in. By the late summer of 1728, even though the economy was faltering a little, Franklin felt confident enough to think, like his brother James before him, of launching his own newspaper. He intended to go head-to-head with Bradford's *American Weekly Mercury.*

It was a shoddy, provincial paper, Franklin thought, and one that he could easily defeat with his superior skills as a writer. True, there was talk yet again of war with Spain, which might wreck the West Indian trade on which the colony relied so heavily, but Franklin had little time for what he called "the croakers" who were always calling down the economic prospects for the region. The time seemed right for a battle with the Bradfords.

Six months or so earlier, his old bugbear Sir William Keith had at last been obliged to flee back to London, selling his land and his ironworks to pay down his borrowings. Franklin had passed him in the street, where the ex-governor tried not to look him in the eye. That year, the Keithites who remained had tried to fight on against Governor Gordon by staging a boycott of the assembly; a ploy that could only work for a time. Their cause was all but lost and instead Andrew Hamilton, Franklin's patron of choice, was moving center stage in the Delaware valley.

Down in New Castle, he had already supplanted Keith and Colonel French to become the power broker of the Lower Counties, which chose him as speaker of their elected assembly. Soon Hamilton would also be the boss of politics in Pennsylvania proper. That being so, the wind ought to be set fair for Franklin: assuming that he could master his turbulent feelings. By now Deborah Read was alone again, her spouse, John Rogers, having fled to the West Indies at the end of 1727 to escape his creditors. It was rumored that he had another wife in England, but no one could be certain, and so he and Deborah were still married in the eyes of the law.

With Mrs. Rogers spoken for in this way, Franklin had to look elsewhere. He had fallen into the habit of what he calls "intrigues with low women who fell in my way." In other words, he went for sex to women from the tavern or the street. Scared as he was of venereal disease—he makes that clear as well—and worried by the money all this cost, he knew that it could not go on.

That autumn he also suffered a setback in his career for which he blamed the Oxford man, George Webb. The young man had found somebody to buy him out of his indentures with Keimer, and so he came to Franklin in search of a job. Although Franklin had nothing to offer, foolishly he told Webb about his newspaper plan. Breaking a confidence, Webb passed this on to Keimer, who stole the idea. On October 1, with the elections due in two days' time and the town filled with folk from all over the province, Keimer put out a printed handbill advertising a weekly to be titled *The Pennsylvania Gazette, or Universal Instructor,* to start life in December. It would be sold up and down the coast from New Castle to New England by the same agents who stocked his almanac.

Lambasting Bradford's *Mercury,* which he dismissed as "nonsense in folio," Keimer promised "to please all and offend none," with what he called "a most useful paper of intelligence," filled with news but also with the arts and sciences, an A to Z of learning from Agriculture to Zoology. Not only would his new *Gazette* "far exceed all others that ever were in America," in Mr. Keimer's modest words; it would also present "the most compleat body of history and philosophy ever yet published since the creation." In fact, he merely intended to reprint pirated extracts from a British encyclopedia; but however absurd his publicity might be, Keimer might spoil Franklin's market. Eccentric he might be, but Keimer was also a sharp businessman. He offered free advertising space to anyone who bought a subscription.

Franklin had to postpone his own project until Keimer's paper folded. He also had his mind on subjects more sublime. Six weeks after Keimer's handbill appeared, Franklin wrote out a new personal creed, very different from the plan of conduct composed on the *Berkshire.* Where the plan had been terse and prosaic, his *Articles of Belief and Acts of Religion*—Franklin's title—were almost pure poetry, even though written in prose. A statement of principles but also a prayer book, meant for his own private use, they were only published long after his death.

Drawn up on November 20, 1728, dated and preserved among his papers, from which so much else went missing, the *Articles* are another extraordinary document. In his early days in Philadelphia, there were really two Franklins, the public and the private. The *Articles* show us how wide a gap there was between the two. In the eyes of people like Patrick Baird, he was Franklin the industrious. In private he was something else: the young man estranged from his parents and prone to lapses with women from the inn. Hidden away as well was the visionary Franklin. In the *Articles,* we meet the young man who read poems, dreamed of science, and pondered his place in Sir Isaac Newton's universe: an infinite cosmos that left him with mixed feelings of anxiety and awe.

Franklin the Poet

"I believe there is one Supreme most perfect Being, Author and Father of the Gods themselves," wrote Franklin in the *Articles,* as if he were an ancient philosopher and not a British subject in an empire still officially Christian. On the one hand, Franklin makes it plain that he is no longer an unbeliever. Atheism and infidelity, impiety and profaneness: these he rejects entirely, as he promises to shun all forms of vice and to live what he calls "a virtuous and holy life." But the God to whom he swears to be faithful is not his father's orthodox Jehovah.

Instead Franklin begins the *Articles* with a statement of heresy. Gazing up into the sky at night—"beyond our system of planets . . . into space that is every way infinite"—he imagines it filled with an endless multitude of suns other than our own. Above or behind all this astronomy, so orderly and so mathematical, as Newton had shown it to be, there must surely be a Creator, a being Supremely Perfect: but what can He possibly care about a species so puny as humanity? Confined on earth, "this little ball on which we move," we count for almost nothing. The Supreme Being cares not a jot whether we worship or praise him at all.

In his boyhood Franklin had read the philosopher Pascal. It may very well be that he was thinking here of the Frenchman's account of the terror he felt at the notion of infinite space; but his remedy was very different. Not for Franklin the solution of Pascal, the Catholic layman filled with guilt and fear, who wagered his eternal fate on a Gospel faith in Jesus. Deep inside, Franklin feels an urgent need to be devout, to worship *something;* and so he concocts a personal mythology, unbeholden to the Bible. Or rather he comes up with a *hypothesis:* Franklin's God will be a concept, and not a revelation.

"I conceive then," he writes, "that the Infinite has created many Beings or Gods, vastly superior to man, who can better conceive his perfections than we, and return him a more rational and glorious praise." Perhaps these Gods are immortal, or perhaps they exist only temporarily, to be superseded by others when they have served their purpose. Franklin cannot say for sure. He chooses to think that every planetary system, including our own, has a God of its own, good and wise and loving, and in *that* God, temporary or eternal, he intends to place his trust.

With that point established, his anxiety begins to fade and Franklin can move forward with enthusiasm. What he seeks is not a set of doctrines, but instead a source of inspiration and a program of action. Poetry is what he is after; and so he begins his personal liturgy with a long act of worship of the Being he calls his "Deity." At its heart is a hymn in praise of Creation, forty-eight lines taken from Milton's *Paradise Lost,* the epic that Addison had thought of as the most sublime of poems, second only to the *Iliad* of Homer.

"These are thy Glorious Works, Parent of Good!" With that pentameter from Milton, so alien in sound and rhythm to the sort of thing we write and read today, Franklin applauds the order of things. The planets, the stars, the seas and the rain, the endless varieties of birds and flowers and animals: these he finds in Milton's verse, praising their creator. And then, once elevated to the heights, he goes on to ask his God for help.

There follow long petitions to the Deity, in which Franklin asks for every virtue: love of country, love of freedom, loyalty, clemency, and fortitude, generosity, sincerity, and tenderness. As for the vices he hates, they include ambition, avarice, intemperance, and luxury, "craft and overreaching," perjury, calumny, detraction, and fraud. "That I may be just in all my dealings and temperate in my pleasures, full of candour and ingenuity, humanity and benevolence: Help me, O Father": so he writes.

At the end, he offers a prayer of thanksgiving: for peace and liberty, for "knowledge, and literature, and every useful art," and for "all thy innumerable benefits; for life and reason . . . for health and joy and every pleasant hour." For all of these, says Franklin, "my Good God, I thank thee." Along the way, he has parted company for good, or so it seems, with the cynicism he displayed in London in his *Dissertation* about fate. He has also set himself goals that are unattainable. Soon enough, in the early 1730s, he would have to climb down to earth and arrive at a more realistic creed.

We might ask why Franklin felt the need to write a piece as exalted as his *Articles of Belief,* at a moment when he was so busy with his printing business. His eagerness to distance himself from Keimer might be one explanation; or guilt about his sexual intrigues; or his problems with his family in Boston. Or it might have been something else entirely. In London, whose affairs he followed so closely, the literary world had moved on, in a direction that Franklin found entirely delightful. And so of course in his *Articles* he would wish to follow this new trend.

At just the time Denham and Franklin were leaving the capital, a great new poet had emerged in the shape of a Scotsman, James Thomson. His work was to be one of the lesser known loves of Franklin's life. In 1726, Thomson had produced a poem called *Winter,* the first installment of his masterpiece, *The Seasons,* with *Summer* and *Spring* following on in 1727 and 1728. As the eighteenth century unfolded, so *The Seasons* became immensely popular, with well-thumbed copies to be found in every coaching inn. No one admired the book more than did Benjamin Franklin. "Whatever Thomson writes, send me a dozen copies of," he once asked a friend in England. "That charming poet has brought more tears of pleasure into my eyes than all I ever read before."[18]

This is not the familiar Franklin of the *Autobiography,* so matter-of-fact and so pragmatic. The other, more private Franklin was the one who took pleasure in what Thomson had to offer: a new kind of religious poetry, not specifically Christian but always sublime. Writing in the blank verse of *Paradise Lost,* Thomson was a poet of nature and science, who strove to beautify the ideas of Sir Isaac Newton and to use them as a creed to which a modern person could pay homage. Like Franklin, James Thomson had steeped himself in the work of the deistical Lord Shaftesbury. Like Franklin, he believed in the infinity of space and the plurality of worlds. And like Franklin, he found the best proof of God—a benevolent creator—in the splendor of the world God had made.[19]

When Sir Isaac died in 1727, to be acclaimed in the press as "the boast and glory of the British nation," it was Thomson who wrote his poetic eulogy. By the year's end, this rhapsody in verse had gone into five editions, marking a new high tide of Newtonian literature in England. In his *Articles of Belief,* Franklin supplied an American equivalent: his personal combination of science, art, and religion, written in prose but as enthusiastic as the lines of Thomson. This was surely Franklin's aim in writing as he did, but he kept his *Articles* from the public eye, doubtless for the obvious reason: writing so lyrical would have left him open to derision.

Meanwhile an old friend was working in the same field. In London James Ralph exploded on the literary scene, with poems that he hoped might make his name. Influenced by Thomson, they also spoke of nature and sublimity, and they were intended to promote the ideas of Shaftesbury. As things turned out, Ralph's poetic career was disastrous, leaving him close to destitution. Throughout the early manhood of Benjamin Franklin, the fate of James Ralph would loom over him, as a warning of just how easy it was for an ingenious person to fail.

Chapter Thirteen

Citizen Franklin

Let us imagine that Franklin and James Ralph had both died at the age of forty. If so, then Franklin would be forgotten but his friend would always have a niche in history. Not as a success, but instead as a writer laid low by ridicule. Betrayed by his ambition, Ralph came to be known in London as "Jemmy Ninny Hammer" and his career collapsed beneath a torrent of abuse. He had made a terrible mistake: he backed the wrong side in a city where the arts were thoroughly political.

A new weekly paper had appeared, *The Craftsman,* Tory in its origins and beautifully written, with Alexander Pope thought to be among its contributors. With *The Craftsman* as their flagship, the Tories hoped to rally the opponents of the government in a chorus of indignation against the prime minister. On the stage Sir Robert Walpole had more enemies; and early in 1728, while *The Craftsman* continued to attack him tickets went on sale for *The Beggar's Opera,* the musical sensation of the age. The author was John Gay, a friend of Pope, and his songs and dialogue carried the same political message: Walpole and the Whigs, said Mr. Gay, were little better than a gang of thieves.

We know that Franklin read and admired *The Craftsman.* He followed the rest of the London press as well—this was his specialty, his knowledge of the empire's capital—and so he must have been aware of what happened to his friend. As *The Beggar's Opera* ran and ran, heaping satire on Sir Robert's head, it occurred to James Ralph that he might make his name by taking the opposite side, to become the poetic mouthpiece of the Whigs.

Since he and Franklin parted company, Ralph had become a published author, finding friends among the literati who hoped he might be a second James Thomson. He also won the backing of another newspaper that Franklin followed from afar, *The London Journal,* once an organ of the opposition but now a publication that Walpole secretly controlled. With their support, Ralph produced a stream of prose and poetry, printed by Franklin's old colleague Charles Ackers. He began with an exercise in Gothic horror, titled *The Tempest: or the Terrors of Death,* and after that there came a series of rambling efforts in Thomson's style. They met with acclaim from *The London Journal,* which said that they bore "the marks of genius." When Ralph wrote an ode in praise of George II, who had just come to the throne, the paper was even more effusive. They praised the poet to the skies and called him a finer writer than Addison.[1]

James Ralph was playing a dangerous game. Had he written these reviews himself? So it was suspected. He was also coming to be seen as a toady in the service of the government. And this Ralph proved to be, when he chose to pick a fight with the most distinguished writers of the period. Soon after *The Beggar's Opera* appeared, Pope brought out the first edition of his *Dunciad,* another masterpiece of Tory satire. Eager to please the men in power, Ralph produced a Whig reply—*Sawney: an Heroic Poem, Occasion'd by the Dunciad*—with which he more or less destroyed his own career.

It was a vicious piece, in which James Ralph plumbed the lower depths of unpleasantness. An invalid from childhood, Pope was severely disabled, tiny in stature and often confined to bed. And so in *Sawney* Mr. Ralph put these words into his mouth:

Nature curs'd me with a monster's form,
Shap'd like a bear, yet little as a worm.

Even then it was thought of as a wicked thing to heap contempt on the afflicted, but Ralph went further and described *The Dunciad* as a piece of "nonsense . . . execrably dull." As for Jonathan Swift, Ralph called him "a lewd-swearing priest," and he dismissed *Gulliver's Travels* as a "monstrous tale." Ralph rounded off the poem with an attack on *The Beggar's Opera,* which he labeled "wretched stuff," fit only for an audience of fools.

In the face of insolence so blatant, of course the Tories had to take their revenge. In the next edition of *The Dunciad,* Pope made cruel fun of Ralph's poetic style and added a footnote that nearly finished Ralph for good, calling him "a low writer . . . wholly illiterate." Worse was to come, when Mr. Pope's friends on *The Grub-Street Journal* slandered James Ralph as "a smock fac'd, self worshipping prig." Beneath so many insults, his writing career withered and died.[2]

William Hogarth's *The Distressed Poet* (1736). Although often thought to be a likeness of the impoverished writer Lewis Theobald, it would have served just as well as a portrait of James Ralph.

On the brink of ruin he was rescued by Henry Fielding. The author of *Tom Jones* was making his name as a playwright and theatrical manager, and he wanted Ralph as an assistant. For seven years they worked together until they were censored by Walpole and put out of business, a disaster that reduced James Ralph to penury again, so poor that he had to send out begging letters, some of which survive in manuscript in London: pathetic little items, full of humiliation. Although Ralph made a new career as a journalist, he never regained his standing as a poet.

Of all the many failures Franklin knew, Ralph has to rank as the most remarkable. He was also the closest to home: the one whose fate had the most to offer as a cautionary tale. Ralph had been his alter ego, the man who Franklin might have been if he had lingered on in London, among the skeptics in the coffeehouses. Even though later they met on friendly terms, in his memoirs Franklin showed little sympathy for Ralph. The path that Franklin had to tread was very different. In his years of labor at the printing press, Franklin had to stick to what he knew as "regularity": a talent that he had not seen in James Ralph's repertoire.[3]

At the beginning of 1729, as Ralph's career was heading for the rocks, Franklin had his own obstacles to surmount. First of all Keimer had to be crushed; and then he had to pick his way through the maze of politics in Pennsylvania, where Franklin had to be sure to be a winner. Nothing else would do for a printer so ambitious.

The Busy-Body

Franklin began by throwing in his lot with Andrew Bradford. The latter was still fighting the war of the almanacs against Samuel Keimer. And so he was very receptive when Franklin and his Junto friend Joseph Breintnall came forward with a series of columns for *The American Weekly Mercury*. Appearing over the byline of *The Busy-Body*, they were intended to make Mr. Keimer's new *Gazette* look foolish and inferior. The columns were composed as stylishly as possible, because—as Franklin knew from Boston—elegance in prose was a sign of gentility. They wanted to make it plain that this was a quality they possessed and the *Gazette* did not.

The shaggy Mr. Keimer had done something that left him exposed to scandal. As he printed his extracts from the encyclopedia, starting with the letter A, he soon came to "Abortion." Printing such a piece was not the way "to please all and offend none," as Keimer had promised he would do. Franklin seized his opportunity. He wrote two letters to the *Mercury*, purporting to come from Martha Careful and Celia Shortface, two ladies most upset by such material. While Miss Careful threatened to pull Keimer's beard, Miss Shortface took an oath to box his ears if there were any repetition.

And then on February 1 the *Busy-Body* series began. Seven years on from Silence Dogood, Franklin had become a still more expert writer in the manner of *The Spectator*. Cleansed of vulgarity, his diction was wide but always polite, his grammar was flawless, and his flowing syntax did what syntax should, always drawing the reader forward, making the columns immensely easy to read. Franklin quoted Alexander Pope and Latin poets too, Horace and Virgil; and although he intended to kill Mr. Keimer's *Gazette*, he did the job with wit, not acrimony.[4]

The best of the series was a lively sketch about a single woman with a shop. Was he thinking of Sarah Read, Mrs. Holt, or Mrs. T the milliner? Whatever his source, Franklin shows us a woman beset by awkward customers who run amok amid her wares. The columns were done with a light, entertaining touch, so as to disarm any critics. When Franklin called Keimer "a sowre philosopher" and labeled the *Gazette* a "book of crudities," his opponent could only look absurd by replying with clumsy insults. Keimer tried to make fun of Franklin's lack of money and the threadbare coat he wore, but Franklin dealt with this by creating a character called Cato. He is a poor but honest farmer who personifies the patriotic virtues of the Romans, transplanted to the colonies.

Poverty is not a sin, says Franklin. In the *Busy-Body* items, he chiefly intended to undermine Keimer's new venture: that was why Bradford wanted them for the *Mercury*. But apart from wrecking the sales of the *Gazette*, he had other things he wished to discuss. Politics, above all; in the shape of Cato, we can see Franklin sketching out a political philosophy of his own, with economics at its heart. By birth and education of course he was a Whig, committed to the Protestant succession and to "English Liberties." But by the late 1720s, the practical issues that arose in Pennsylvania were not the same as those that divided opinion in Great Britain.

In the Quaker province, they did not have a Walpole to protest against, and although there were élites and inequalities, they did not take the form of an English aristocracy. Religious freedom was already guaranteed; and there was no established Church of Pennsylvania with bishops to be mocked. The arguments that raged in England about Walpole's taxes and the heavy burden of the National Debt simply did not apply in Pennsylvania, where there were no armed forces and so the government spent very little. Although Franklin and his friends read *The Craftsman*, *The London Journal*, and so on, and often used the same language, it did not really fit their circumstances.

They had issues of their own to deal with, issues more specifically American. In Mr. Cato, a self-reliant man from the frontier, dressed "in the plainest country garb," but always kind and pious, humane and public spirited, Franklin is giving us a colonial farmer, not some crusty English Tory squire left over from the reign of Queen Anne. As his *Busy-Body* essays unfolded, so Franklin lost interest in his feud with Keimer. Instead, he began to touch on serious topics to do with the future of Pennsylvania.

The province had been built by farmers, Anglo-Saxon, white, and Protestant, people like Cato or the Merediths, each one freely settled on his homestead with his pigs, his orchards, and the Bible. But by 1729, Pennsylvania was also a land of speculators, whether their ambitions lay in the West Indian trade, in steel and iron, in westward expansion, or in all three. Could Cato really coexist with this kind of thing? Or to put it another way: could the patient, homespun virtues of the farmer or the artisan survive in a colony where so many people just wanted to get rich quickly? This was a question that troubled the Junto. The members had to decide what sort of Pennsylvanians they wished to be.

"The rational and almost certain methods of acquiring riches by industry and frugality are almost neglected or forgotten," Franklin wrote on March 27 in *Busy-Body* No. 8. "If the sands of Schuylkill were so much mixed with small grains of gold, that a man might in a day's time with care and application get together the value of a half a crown, I make no question but we should find several people employ'd there, that can with ease earn five shillings a day at their proper trades."

It was a question that William Hogarth dealt with and it would always remain a Franklin favorite: how should we try to get wealth? and how do we retain our virtue while we do so? No one was really panning for gold in the Schuylkill—Franklin was being metaphorical—but they *were* engaged in avid speculation, and that was what he was discussing. There are times when we might think that Franklin is too smug a moralist, but only when we forget that his writing always had a context. In this case, he was dealing with questions that exercised the minds of Pennsylvanians far beyond the confines of the Junto.

In March, the elected assembly was nearing the end of a session that would mark another turning point in the colony's history. They had two items on their agenda, each one intertwined with the other and with the economic dilemmas that the colony had to resolve. Immigration, first of all: how should they respond to the arrival by sea of so many newcomers, most of whom were Irish, including Catholics and felons? Alarmed by what they called these "crowds of foreigners . . . Papists and convicts," the assemblymen and the governor were at one in their desire for something to be done.[5]

The honest Catos of the Delaware did not wish to see their culture—or their wages—undermined by people whom even the most pious of Quakers dismissed as "idle trash" or "the scum of mankind." They needed a law, said Governor Gordon, "to prevent an English plantation being turned into a colony of aliens": their solution being a new tax imposed on the importers of every indentured servant or African slave who came ashore. But while it was very easy to be racist, it was rather harder to design policies that made economic sense.

In reality Pennsylvania needed more people: to work the forges and the furnaces, for instance, whose laborers were bondservants or slaves. The trade in human beings was one of the few branches of commerce that were thriving in the spring of 1729. Off Jamaica, Spanish ships from Havana were molesting British traders; and although Sir Robert Walpole was looking for a diplomatic means to keep the peace, an all-out war was still a possibility. And so that year the trade of Philadelphia was temporarily in the doldrums.

Hence arose the second item that the assembly was eager to debate. Although Sir William Keith was now a fading memory, his party still fought on with the same old battle cry: paper money. Since the session began in earnest in December, the Keithite members from the city had been pressing for a large new issue of currency as a way to revive the economy. If this was to occur, the relevant law would have to be passed by the end of the session in May. With time running out, and the governor dragging his heels, Benjamin Franklin plunged into the controversy. Hard on the heels of *Busy-Body* No. 8, he produced his first political pamphlet. Bearing the title *A Modest Enquiry into the Nature and Necessity of a Paper Currency*, it appeared on April 3.

There was nothing modest about the description he gives us of this episode. According to the Franklin of 1771, writing his memoirs, his essay was decisive, turning the tide in favor of the new paper bills. The essay, he wrote, was "well receiv'd by the common people in general; but the rich men dislik'd it; for it increas'd and strengthen'd the clamor for money; and they happening to have no writers among them that were able to answer it, their opposition slacken'd, and the point was carried by a majority in the house." There is just one problem with Franklin's account of what occurred: less than half of it is true.

Although his pamphlet was highly accomplished, Franklin did not win the day. New paper money was issued by the land bank, the Loan Office, but not in the way Franklin claims; and the real victor was his friend Andrew Hamilton. Even so, the episode amounted to another turning point in Franklin's career. The paper money affair proved to be the last stand of the Keithites, and its outcome was to make Mr. Hamilton invincible. The episode ushered in a new decade in which, in alliance with the Hamilton family, the young Franklin would indeed become a gentleman printer, affluent, relatively secure, and a force to be reckoned with in public life. He and the Hamiltons also came to share a common vision of what America should be.

Hamilton's Victory, and Franklin's Role

Since his return from London late in 1726, Andrew Hamilton had drawn ever closer not only to James Logan, but also to another broker of power, Jeremiah Langhorne. Depicted by their enemies as "the Triumvirate," they had several things in common with each other and with Franklin. In religious matters they were all freethinkers; they all worked immensely hard; and they had all fallen out with Sir William Keith and his followers.

Early in 1728 Logan suffered a dreadful accident, slipping on the ice outside his house in Philadelphia, which left him a cripple at fifty-four. And so although he lived on for more than two decades, still an agent of the Penns and still a leading figure in the colony, he played only a minor part in the paper money affair. But his allies Hamilton and Langhorne were energetic men still in the prime of life. At fifty-five Langhorne was the uncrowned king of Bucks County to the north of the city. There he held every major public office and he led their delegation to the General Assembly. In the autumn of 1728 he procured the election of Andrew Hamilton as one of the Bucks County members. Amid the signs of a recession, and with tempers running high in Philadelphia, both men fully accepted the need for some new paper money. So did Governor Gordon, who at this point was on excellent terms with Hamilton. Even the Penn family, who far preferred to receive their rents in sterling, were prepared to cut a deal to accommodate the public.[6]

Everyone knew that there had to be more liquidity, but the question was this: how *much* new money, and on what terms? On the last day of 1728—not in the spring of 1729, after his essay, as Franklin suggests—the assembly voted overwhelmingly to have some new paper currency; but the detailed legislation still had to be drawn up. If it were too large and the terms too generous, the measure might be vetoed by the government in England. If the issue were too small and the terms too strict, the assembly might not pass the law at all; and the Keithites might run riot.

Modern Americans will recognize what happened next: five months of horse-trading in their equivalent of Congress. Early in January the assembly voted for £50,000 in new currency to be secured by mortgages from the land bank, lent out to the borrowers at only 4 percent and for a term of sixteen years. Off went a committee packed with Keithites to write the legislation. Meanwhile Governor Gordon played for time, scratching his head over the complications and waiting until the end of March before he replied.

"I am fully persuaded," said Patrick Gordon, that there had to be more paper currency; but he could not consent to £50,000, and 4 percent interest was too low. The assembly made a lower bid, just £40,000, but left everything else in the bill unchanged. And that was how matters stood when Franklin entered the fray. One extra point is relevant. Six weeks earlier, Franklin and Meredith had made a pitch to the assembly to be chosen as their official printer, in place of Andrew Bradford, only to be turned down.

Thanks to fine scholarship by the Franklin biographer Leo Lemay, we now know that the *Modest Enquiry* was not his opening gambit. Earlier, when *Busy-Body* No. 8 appeared in the *Mercury* on March 27, it carried an appendix—almost certainly composed by Franklin—which took a more radical stance, calling for the new paper money law to be passed immediately, or otherwise there would be mayhem. "The whole country is at this instant filled with the greatest heat and animosity," the author wrote. He warned of "publick disturbances" if rich men tried to block a measure the people were eager to see. But those words appeared only in the *Mercury*'s first edition. "A gentleman" visited his office and called for the appendix to be removed. Under pressure from a powerful man, Bradford agreed.

As well he might: because this was a dangerous moment, with lawmakers complaining that they were being threatened in the streets. Rumors were rife, picked up by Logan, that protesters planned to storm the governor's mansion. Until now, Langhorne and Hamilton had stood on the sidelines, or so it appears: but with the situation looking ugly, Andrew Hamilton stepped forward to defuse the crisis. He persuaded the assembly to stand firm, passing a motion calling on Gordon to crush any riots that occurred.

With that the threat of violence died away. And then Franklin came out with his *Modest Enquiry*. Written in a hurry, said the author, even so it was an eloquent plea for paper money, with the interest rate to be set at no more than 4 percent. The arguments he advanced were not entirely original—there had been many such pamphlets before—and indeed in one long passage Franklin plagiarized an English treatise from the 1660s. But the *Modest Enquiry* made its points extremely well. Putting it in something close to modern terms, Franklin argued that a paper currency could be as reliable as gold if the colony that issued it had a robust, competitive economy.

Productivity: that was Franklin's point. If Pennsylvania was fertile and its produce in demand, if its people were hardworking and ready to turn their hands to trade as well as farming, then what did they have to fear? Some inflation would occur, but it would not be disastrous. Provided the economy was flexible and open—which meant that immigration would have to persist—the forces of the market would keep wages and prices from spiraling out of control. Demand for real estate was most unlikely to collapse, and so the value of their paper bills would be secure.

So long as the land bank lent prudently, the mortgages would always be repaid from the growing wealth of the province. In the meantime, the paper bills would keep the wheels of commerce turning; but there had to be enough of them available to do so. "Upon the whole it may be observed," wrote Franklin, "that it is the highest interest of a trading country . . . to make money plentiful." His arguments were excellent, but they were not decisive: it was Andrew Hamilton, not Franklin, who arranged a compromise that kept everyone content.

The day before the essay appeared, Governor Gordon had told the assembly that he would not authorize £40,000 of new notes. From that point forward the Keithites had to work with Hamilton to make a deal that the governor could accept. After another month of to and fro, at last the job was done; but the law that Gordon signed in May was not the one the Keithites had demanded. All they got in the end was £30,000 of new paper currency, issued for sixteen years but at 5 percent, and not the 4 percent that Franklin had preferred.

For Andrew Hamilton the episode had been a triumph, from which he had emerged as the person who could bring all the parties to the table. When the assembly met again in October 1729, they chose Hamilton as the speaker, the post he already held in New Castle, where the Lower Counties were at his beck and call. With the followers of Keith pushed to the sidelines, Hamilton remained the speaker of the Pennsylvania assembly for nine of the next ten years. The Triumvirate held all the winning cards.

Although James Logan's friendship with the Penns was weakening, even so they found him indispensable. Disabled though he was, for many years he sat as the chief justice of Pennsylvania with Jeremiah Langhorne as his deputy. When at last Logan stepped down, Langhorne took over. Meanwhile Andrew Hamilton served as the recorder of Philadelphia, meaning that he was the city's general counsel, a very useful post to hold. A hot-tempered man, still fond of his liquor, he could not keep himself from bad-mouthing Governor Gordon; and after they began to quarrel in 1732, Hamilton endured a rocky period when, in 1733–34, he briefly lost the speakership. Even so, with Langhorne at his side he regained his grip and the Triumvirate continued on its way. When Gordon died in 1736, the Penns chose Logan as the acting governor.

By then Thomas Penn, the co-proprietor, had come over from England to the colony to live, but he was less concerned with politics than he was with making money from his vast holdings of land. And so—until the late 1730s—while the Triumvirate sometimes had their differences with the Penns, the three men remained the real leaders of the colony. Not once did Franklin seek to question their hegemony. There was no reason why he should. His goals and values were the same as Logan's, Hamilton's, and Langhorne's.

Religious freedom, law and order, fiscal prudence: such were the Whig ideals of the Triumvirate. Franklin had no cause to disagree. Many years had yet to pass before, in the late 1740s, he had to enter politics himself in opposition to Thomas Penn and his supporters, who came to be known as the Proprietary Party. In the 1730s, Franklin had no reason to seek elected office: all he had to do was to cling to Speaker Hamilton. Franklin came to play the same kind of role as his uncle Thomas had performed in England. In Northamptonshire in the 1690s, Thomas had been a trusty servant of the local Whig grandees; and Franklin did something of the sort for Andrew Hamilton, acting as his ally in the press.

During the paper money affair, Franklin had shown how useful he could be. In his appendix to *Busy-Body* No. 8, he had appeared to side with the Keithites, which may be because he was still hoping to become the assembly's printer of choice. But the article was pulled, and when Franklin's *Modest Enquiry* appeared the following week it did Hamilton a favor. While his essay kept up the pressure on the governor, Frankln did so with reasoned argument, not a tirade of invective. As he negotiated with his fellow politicians, Hamilton could brandish the essay and use it to corral them into line. A piece of prose put together so well was something they could all admire.

We know for certain that Andrew Hamilton was very grateful. "I soon after obtained, through my friend Hamilton, the printing of the New Castle paper money," Franklin recalled; he already had a contract to print the mortgage deeds issued by the Pennsylvania Loan Office. By the autumn of 1729, with Hamilton as his patron he could begin to glimpse a bright future ahead. And all the more clearly, because Samuel Keimer had finally admitted defeat. Letting it be known that he was leaving Philadelphia, he put the *Gazette* up for sale with its paltry list of subscribers.

As Keimer prepared to ship out for a new life in Barbados, Franklin bought the newspaper for a song. On October 2 there came the relaunch, in which—like Charles Foster Kane, with his *New York Inquirer*—Franklin issued a declaration of principles. His paper would never be quite as exciting as Citizen Kane's; but by the end of that year it would be clear that Franklin knew an immense amount about the trade of journalism. The early issues of his *Gazette* drew on the best models he had seen in the eight years since his brother founded the *Courant.*

"To publish a good newspaper is not so easy an undertaking as many people imagine it to be," Franklin told his readers, assuring them that he would make *The Pennsylvania Gazette* "as agreeable and useful an entertainment as the nature of the thing will allow." As always in the eighteenth-century press, *variety* was the essential element, and so that was what he gave his readers: a miscellany of forthright political opinion, tales of crime and tragedy, drownings, fires, and gunshot wounds, jokes and puzzles, and serious news from Maine down to Jamaica. Franklin gave them London too, the city where he had learned so much.

On October 23 he listed the English papers he used as his sources. Franklin told his readers their politics, which—thanks to his period in Little Britain, that street so intensely political—he knew so very well: *The London Journal* and *The British Journal* (Walpolean Whig); *The Craftsman* (a blend of Whig and Tory, but above all anti-Walpole); and of course *Mist's Weekly Journal,* now renamed *Fog's* (which was still defiantly Tory). In America at the time, nobody could have understood these papers better than did Benjamin Franklin.

As for his own ideological slant, he made no secret of it: Franklin still believed in "English Liberties." In their defense, but rather ungratefully, Franklin took a swipe at William Burnet, the royal governor of New York who had shown him his library while he was traveling through the town so many years earlier. Burnet had been transferred to Massachusetts, where he feuded with the House of Representatives. Citing the Magna Carta they refused to commit to paying his salary, on the grounds that if they did so he would be free to act the tyrant.

Here was an issue—the governor's salary, and how it should be funded—that would remain a running sore in politics in Boston until the 1770s, the Tea Party, and the Revolution. In the late summer of 1729, Governor Burnet had brought the debate to a temporary halt by dying from a fever: only to be posthumously slandered by Franklin. A few weeks after his death *The Pennsylvania Gazette* published a stern editorial, calling Burnet a man of "arts and menaces . . . cunning and politicks," bent on the subversion of freedom. A radical Whig to his toes, Franklin praised the men of the Bay Colony for their stand against the governor. They had displayed, he wrote, "that ardent spirit of liberty . . . which has in every age distinguished BRITONS and ENGLISHMEN from all the rest of mankind."

In writing that, Franklin was merely giving voice to opinions that were widely shared in Philadelphia, where the editorial made him more friends. His circulation grew and grew, and so did his advertising revenue. The next step was obvious. Andrew Hamilton and his colleagues—"the leading men," as Franklin described them—were keen to have a printer so ingenious and so trustworthy. In the January of 1730 they gave him what he wanted, and made Franklin and Meredith the official printers for the Pennsylvania Assembly.

However, no amount of Whiggish talk of liberty would solve the economic questions that beset the colony. In his October declaration of principles, Franklin had touched on these again. From time to time, he would reprint items from the same encyclopedia that Keimer had been copying, but Franklin promised to do so only when they served a useful purpose. The articles he chose would be, as he put it, those that gave "such hints to the excellent geniuses of our country, as may contribute either to the improvement of our present manufactures, or toward the invention of new ones."

Not only was he picking up a theme from *A Modest Enquiry,* where he had urged his fellow colonists to raise and manufacture "hemp, silk, iron, and many other things." Franklin was also putting forth in America the language of "improvement" and of "ingenuity" that his family had known in the England of Cromwell and Charles II. In the Quaker province, these were words that influential people wanted to hear, including the Triumvirate: who had projects for improvements of their own.

PENNSYLVANIA'S TRUE INTEREST

In the early years of Franklin's Junto, his friend the surveyor Nicholas Scull would occasionally miss their debates. Working for the government, Scull would be away in Indian country. Sometimes he would travel a hundred miles or so to map out land and to visit Sassoonan, the leader of the Lenape, at his village above the Susquehanna River. These were sensitive missions. In the spring of 1728, native people and the European settlers had come to blows in incidents close to the new ironworks near Reading, and the lives of Lenape people had been lost.

That summer Sassoonan came down to Philadelphia for peace talks, held in public at the Quaker meeting house. Tensions were rising, and blood was being shed, because the ironmasters needed land and timber to feed their furnaces with charcoal. German settlers wanted land as well, and if they could they preferred to settle together on Tulpehocken Creek, where William Parsons was their surveyor. There were also looming questions about another region, the Forks of the Delaware, sixty miles north of the city. By fair means or foul, James Logan and the Penns were eager to take possession of the Forks from the Lenape who lived there.[7]

As the 1730s began, so the pace of encroachment on Indian land grew faster. At every stage the men around Franklin were deeply involved, and not only Scull and Parsons of the Junto. Andrew Hamilton had his eye turned further west toward the town of Lancaster, but his intentions were the same: he meant to see the colony grow swiftly into its hinterland. By 1731 he had outmaneuvered Logan to acquire the site of the town, which Hamilton and his son James sold in slices to German and Scots-Irish settlers. The town was strategically vital, because from here the Great Philadelphia Wagon Road led away into the wilderness toward the south. By the middle of the decade, the Irish and the Germans were pouring down the trail, traveling as far as North Carolina.[8]

Benjamin Franklin has been called "the consummate networker." Indeed he was; but the people with whom he networked most avidly were businessmen and public officials, not laborers or artisans. His friends were either members of an economic elite, or—like Joseph Breintnall, Scull, or Parsons—they were professionals who earned their fees from services they did for the same elite. Their commitment to good deeds might well be genuine, but sometimes it took second place to other, less high-minded goals: and especially the expansion of their province.[9]

A prime example was another of Franklin's associates, a rich young man named William Allen. A Presbyterian with roots in Ulster, he married Hamilton's daughter in 1734. Seven years earlier, at the tender age of twenty-three, William Allen had become one of James Logan's partners in a farsighted new venture. With Jeremiah Langhorne also among them but with Logan as their leader, the partners created the Durham Iron Company, building a forge and a furnace on top of rich deposits of ore at the northern end of Bucks County.

In his *Modest Enquiry*, Franklin had called for precisely this sort of enterprise. But Durham was only ten miles from the Forks of the Delaware, with its hunting grounds and streams and fields for maize still occupied by the Lenape; and so, in the years that followed, Logan and Allen made it their goal to wrest the Forks away from the native people. Their accomplices were the Junto members, Parsons and Scull, who mapped out the land they intended to acquire for the sake of its timber and its farming potential.[10]

In ventures like the ironworks at Durham, we can see a new economic model coming into being in America. In his *Modest Enquiry*, Franklin had urged his readers to ask themselves a question: *what is the true interest of Pennsylvania?* As the 1730s unwound, that question came to be answered in a new way; and Franklin and his Junto friends were among the people who made the new model viable and convincing.

Hitherto in Philadelphia the merchants who traded by sea had occupied the pinnacles of rank. Men of the ocean, Quakers or not, they cast their eyes across the Atlantic toward England, the West Indies, or to Portugal or Italy, to places where they could sell their grain and flour, trade in tobacco, slaves or indentured servants, and buy sugar, wine, olive oil, or British hardware and textiles. Of course this sort of seagoing enterprise would remain alive for many, many decades to come. Indeed in the early 1730s the Atlantic trade was gaining a new momentum, as the danger of war with the Spanish receded into the distance.

Late in 1729, Sir Robert Walpole and his envoys had struck a new deal with France and Spain, the Treaty of Seville, which kept the peace for another ten years. Protected by the *Pax Walpoleana*, the merchants of the Delaware could trade by sea in safety. Their shipping traffic grew by leaps and bounds, deepening the connections between Pennsylvania and the mother country. But essential though it was, maritime business of such a kind—based mostly on the trade in soft commodities—was *not* the economic future for what would become the United States.

By the end of the 1730s Andrew Hamilton and his allies would have a different vision of what might lie ahead for North America. A thrust into the wilderness in search not only of land but also of raw materials: that would be the aim. Coupled with that would be manufacturing, using the iron they made at places such as Durham, the copper they hoped to find, or the trees they felled. But all of this would require many more people to do the work of settlement. In 1739, when at last Hamilton decided to relinquish his role as speaker of the Pennsylvania assembly, he made an unusual gesture, giving a farewell speech, something that was not the custom. Rising to his feet, Andrew Hamilton put the case for progress, immigration, and the pushing back of the frontier.[11]

As he sang a hymn of praise to what he called "the excellency of our constitution," he spoke the familiar language of Whiggery, finding the secret of Pennsylvania's success in its commitment to what he called "civil and religious liberty." But when Hamilton sought to define the achievements of his colony, all of them were matters of material prosperity. He spoke of "the great progress this province has made . . . in improvements, wealth, trade, and navigation, and the extraordinary increases of people, who have been drawn hither from almost every country in Europe."

More voyagers to the west: this was what Andrew Hamilton hoped to see. Without more people, more improvements could not be accomplished, and so he urged his fellow Pennsylvanians to see the new arrivals as the sign of their success. But once ashore the people had to go somewhere; and that had to be into the interior, over the mountains, down to the Carolinas, or up the valley of the Susquehanna. And so Hamilton proclaimed his vision of the future: destiny made manifest along the Wagon Road.

His was a vision that Franklin would share but only with a few misgivings. A far more subtle person than the foulmouthed lawyer, Franklin certainly believed in westward expansion, but only if it came with virtue as well. He liked the notion of an ever-growing population; but Franklin did not think that wealth and trade were everything. The sensitive, private man who read Milton and *The Seasons* and composed the *Articles of Belief* could never conceive of "improvement" purely in material terms. For Benjamin Franklin, improvement had to be an inner quality as well. It had to be a means to be virtuous as well as to make money.

But virtue was not so easy to achieve. You do not get to be a genius by being tranquil or complacent or by never making mistakes: and Franklin had his share of those. He was never an uncomplicated human being, spared from inner conflict or from frailties. It does a disservice to his memory to pretend that he was. At some point in 1730—the precise date will never be established—Franklin ran up against the obstacle that he had feared he might encounter: his own emotions and their consequences.

As the year began, everything seemed to be going well. Keimer had been defeated, they had the printing contract from the assembly, and the Junto was great fun on a Friday night. Sadly, Hugh Meredith spent too much time at the alehouse, playing billiards or skittles or the like; but even so the firm of Franklin & Meredith was set upon the path to profit and success. There was just one small detail. Franklin had been at the women again; and one of them conceived a child. He never tells us the mother's name or anything about her, but she gave birth to a little boy who would be called William. It was just the kind of mishap that might have befallen James Ralph.

Chapter Fourteen

Years of Success

In the spring of 1730, the colonies appeared to be in fine shape and so did Benjamin Franklin. Far away in London, the government was pondering a concession, a law to permit the slave owners of South Carolina to ship their rice directly to eager buyers in Italy and Spain. Until now they had been obliged to send it by a costly detour through Great Britain. If Walpole gave the nod and the rice could flow freely, then Charleston, a port already thriving, would enjoy another spurt of growth. So might Philadelphia, whose ships would have many more cargoes. In the meantime, with so much paper money now in issue and with the economy again on the move, Franklin had his hands full of business.

Apart from *The Pennsylvania Gazette,* the paper bills, and the assembly's proceedings, he was doing printing jobs for his allies in New Jersey and for Nicholas Scull. He had become a deputy sheriff and so Mr. Scull needed bail bonds. With all this to do, Franklin worked very hard indeed. No more time for poetry: instead he was out with his wheelbarrow, carting back the paper he required to feed his hungry press. He never went fishing or shooting and he avoided the tavern. By now the Junto had moved its meeting place to a room in the home of Robert Grace.

Like anybody starting out on his own, Franklin had his share of disappointment and worry; but he was riding a wave of colonial prosperity, and so—given time and application—all of his problems were soluble. A letter arrived from Rhode Island, from the silversmith Samuel Vernon, asking about the money he had entrusted to Franklin six years earlier, money that Franklin still could not repay. He wrote back apologetically, promising to do his best, but in the meantime the Merediths had turned out to be a broken reed. Quite apart from Hugh's long sessions in the pub, his father suddenly revealed that, actually, he did not have the money to pay for the printing apparatus they had bought from London. Only half of the money had been put up in cash. The rest had been borrowed by Simon Meredith. Now the debt was falling due, and their creditor had filed a lawsuit. The case would come to court, and if it were lost the bailiffs would seize Franklin's equipment.

Just as he was falling into despair, two saviors arrived from the Junto. They came in the shape of his closest friends, William Coleman and Mr. Grace, who offered to put up the money to refinance the Franklin firm, but with one proviso. If they were to assume the debt, his tippling partner really had to go.

Not so fast, said Franklin—I have an agreement with Hugh, and I cannot break it—but when he discussed it with the Welshman, he found that his partner understood what needed to be done. A countryman by birth, Hugh Meredith had never really taken to the printing trade. All he wanted was a horse and saddle, so that he could ride down the Wagon Road to the Carolinas, where many other families from Wales intended to settle.

A new deal was done in July, dissolving the partnership. From that moment forth, Benjamin Franklin would be the boss. Earlier that year, he had already taken on two employees, one from Philadelphia—Joseph Rose, son of the poet Aquila—while the other was somebody he knew from London. Just around the corner from Little Britain, Thomas Whitmarsh had trained as a compositor in the workshop of a printer of sheet music: another demanding specialty. To America he carried with him the best London habits of diligence and regularity.

With their help, Franklin saw off the threat of competition from Mr. Keimer's former apprentice, David Harry. The son of another Welsh farmer with an ample plot of land and with friends in politics, he was as unprofessional as Hugh Meredith. Too showy and too sociable, Harry turned out to be another failure in business so that in the end he sold his equipment and followed Keimer to Barbados. That left Franklin with only one publishing rival: Andrew Bradford.

Although Franklin was inclined to sneer at Bradford, in fact he was a formidable foe, often quicker on the draw and also far less reliant on Andrew Hamilton, whom the *Mercury* attacked on many occasions. When it did so, Franklin had to leap to Hamilton's defense. Bradford also ran the city's post office, a position that enabled him to gather news and to distribute the *Mercury*. Franklin would spend much of the next ten years locked in professional combat with Bradford for the printing trade of Pennsylvania.[1]

In time, Franklin would supplant his rival as the postmaster: but not until 1737. Bradford had his own network—he was one of the investors in the Durham Iron Company—and he would not be defeated easily. Franklin had to play a very long game, but that was one of his best attributes: sheer persistency. In 1730 he was also building bridges back to his family in Boston, from whom he had become so distant. His sister Jane, who was now Mrs. Edward Mecom, suffered the loss of a child in May. In reply to the news, Franklin wrote to another of his sisters, Sarah Davenport, with a letter in which he was kind and charming, showing concern for all his many siblings, and mentioning each one by name.[2]

"At present I am much hurried in business but hope to make a short trip to Boston in the spring," he writes. But three more years were to pass before the trip took place, which is revealing in itself. Franklin harbored no compelling urge to revisit his old haunts. However tenderly he felt toward his family, he had little time for Massachusetts as a place or as a state of mind. Cotton Mather was dead—he passed away early in 1728—and not a trace of evidence survives to show that Franklin mourned his loss. By this moment in his career, Franklin had gone far beyond whatever Mr. Mather might once have offered. He was now committed to Pennsylvania, where the dynamics of history and ideas were so different from those of New England.

Be that as it may, his family in Boston had heard a rumor that he was about to marry. They felt entitled to know more. And although Franklin denied it, there was a grain of truth in the story. He had continued to share his house with his mathematical friend, Thomas Godfrey, whose wife had been trying to arrange a match between Franklin and the daughter of some relatives. The girl was "very deserving," Franklin says, their courtship proceeded, and her family offered every encouragement. All of this seems to have happened late in 1729 and in the first few months of 1730.

By the spring, the moment had come to talk about money. As a condition of the marriage going ahead, Franklin wanted £100 to clear away his remaining debts. This sort of gesture was a Franklin family tradition, dating back at least as far as his uncle John in Banbury, who had bided his time to marry until he found a wife with some wealth of her own.

In Benjamin's case the girl's parents refused, pleading poverty. Franklin advised them to mortgage their house at the Loan Office, which was now in business again and lending freely.

To which he received a deeply insulting reply. Mrs. Godfrey came back with the news that the family had gone to see the wily Andrew Bradford. A cunning adversary, he had informed them that printing was a wretched, unprofitable business and that Franklin would soon be bankrupt. And so he was barred from their house, and the girl was locked away. Of course, this might be a ploy—Franklin suspected as much—but when Mrs. Godfrey tried to keep the thing alive by hinting that the girl and her parents were still willing, he refused to have anything more to do with them.

Proud as well as miffy people, the Franklins did not care to be manipulated. Two years later he turned the episode into a sketch for the *Gazette,* writing as Anthony Afterwit, in which he called the girl's father an "old curmudgeon" and cast himself in the role of "an honest tradesman, who never meant harm to anybody." Although he remained a friend of Mr. Godfrey, an honored member of the Junto, Franklin and Mrs. Godfrey fell out. In April the Godfreys left his house and Franklin was on his own again. He found that everywhere the story was the same. There were wives to be had, but not ones with money. Their parents would not tolerate a printer, so bad a reputation had the trade acquired.

And so he cast his eye up Market Street toward his old flame. Abandoned by her spouse, Deborah was sad and solitary. For this, Franklin blamed himself: if only he had not forgotten her when he went to London, she might never have married the unreliable potter. Rogers was still a problem—until he was proven to be dead or a bigamist, he was still her lawful husband—but Deborah had something extra that made up for any inconvenience that he might cause.

The previous year, with her father's mortgage still outstanding, the Loan Office had repossessed the Read house. Mrs. Read had bought it back at auction—her ointment business was clearly doing well—and so in time Deborah and her siblings could expect to inherit the property. The house was small but it was tangible, worth nearly £400, an asset that might be leveraged to help the Franklin firm.

He was also very fond of Deborah, and she of him. In the summer of 1730 their courtship was resumed, and in September they became man and wife. Not legally—they could never marry while the fate of Mr. Rogers was unknown—but that did not seem to trouble anyone. A pillar of the congregation, Mrs. Franklin went on worshipping at Christ Church. It was a tolerant sort of place, where it seems that she was accepted as an Anglican without any quibbles about her marital status. The most distinguished member of the church was another woman cast aside by her husband: Lady Keith, left behind by Sir William when he sailed for England. In the circumstances of colonial life, where it was so easy for people to go missing, never to be traced, Deborah could expect her friends at Christ Church to be sympathetic.

If anyone had misbehaved, it was her new partner. At some date before the Franklins moved in together, Benjamin had become a father. And here we arrive at what might appear to be another mystery: a secret perhaps so shameful that Franklin kept it locked away in one of the sealed compartments of his life. Reluctantly or not, Deborah agreed to take in the child—when this happened, and how old William was when it did, we cannot say—and he was raised as her own. But beyond that we know almost nothing.

His Natural Son

Just as we might never know the fate of Mrs. T, so the full story of the birth of William Franklin will probably never come to light. Notoriously, in his memoirs Franklin passed over the episode in complete silence. But this does not mean that it was *always* a mystery, or that Franklin went out of his way to hide what he had done. As we shall see, the story was most likely very simple, a commonplace incident that would have raised few eyebrows at the time. For that very reason, the episode may tell us something revealing about the Philadelphia of Franklin's early life.

As we try to get grips with this murky affair, the best place to start is close to the end, in 1777 and 1778 when the British Army occupied the city. Every officer who held the king's commission would have seen it as his duty to sniff out any gossip that might damage the reputation of the traitor Franklin. But although they had plenty of time in which to do so, at parties or around the dinner table, nothing came to light. We know that the redcoats rifled through Franklin's papers. They came away none the wiser.

In England in 1779, an item about William's birth appeared in *The Morning Post,* a newspaper whose editor was secretly in the pay of the British government. Accusing Franklin of what he called "consummate hypocrisy," the writer claimed to know that William's mother was "an oyster wench." Franklin had left her to die of hunger and disease, or so he alleged: but he gave no further details. If the redcoats had unearthed anything concrete, the full story would have been all over London.[3]

From that, we can reach at least one firm conclusion: that by then, the wench in question had vanished long since, dead or gone far away. Did *The Morning Post* have a source? In all likelihood, the newspaper merely picked up old press clippings from the colonies and embellished the story, in British tabloid fashion, with an invented reference to oysters. In the 1750s and 1760s, when Franklin was fighting political battles with homegrown enemies in Pennsylvania, a few items had appeared in print in America seeking to smear his name. The most elaborate libel claimed that William's mother was a prostitute named Barbara. It was said the Franklins had taken her on as a servant, cruelly mistreated her, and then left Barbara to die a pauper's death. Could this really be true? If it were, the British would have left no stone unturned until they found someone who could confirm the story. And yet they failed to discover anything of the kind.

Was this because Franklin had taken the utmost care to cover his tracks? In the 1990s, Professor Carla J. Mulford made the suggestion that, in fact, William's mother was not a woman of the streets at all, but a lady of reputation. If so, then perhaps all the things Franklin said about his low intrigues were merely a smokescreen, intended to hide her identity forever. In the same vein, the Franklin biographer Leo Lemay argued that perhaps she was the wife of a friend, with whom he had an affair while the husband was away on business.

These are interesting ideas, but for two reasons we can probably leave them on one side. First, Philadelphia was still a small place. Even Franklin could not be ingenious enough to have the child delivered, spirited away, suckled by a wet nurse, and taken in by Deborah without the neighbors (or the cuckold) noticing that something was afoot. Pregnancies are not so easy to conceal. Second, we have some evidence from a family friend that points in a different direction.

It would appear that the British simply never persuaded the right people to talk. In 1777, the few old Junto members who were still alive in Philadelphia would have known the truth: but they were not the kind of people who would betray their old comrade. The most relevant was one of Franklin's closest friends and political allies, Hugh Roberts. A man by now in his seventies, he was ideally placed to have known who William's mother was. In the 1730s he owned a store selling tobacco and hardware on 2nd Street, a short walk from the house where Benjamin lived with Deborah. But Roberts was also a lifelong Quaker and a pacifist, who kept firmly neutral during the Revolutionary War, by which time he was devoted to the cause of freeing the African slaves. He had no reason to want to help the redcoats. Although he lived on until 1786, it seems that Roberts never told the British what he knew.[4]

However, in earlier times Hugh Roberts had been a garrulous fellow, happy to share his memories of the Junto. In 1758, when Franklin the scientist had recently sailed off to London to receive the acclaim of the Royal Society, Roberts attended a party to celebrate the news of his safe arrival. That evening he told a string of anecdotes—now sadly lost—about the young Franklin. Five years later, his son George wrote a private letter that appears to draw upon the stories he heard on this or a similar occasion.

He put pen to paper in 1763, when the speculation about William's mother was at its height. " 'Tis generally known here his birth is illegitimate and his mother is not in good circumstances," George Roberts wrote, "but the report of her begging bread in the streets of this city is without the least foundation in truth. I understand small provision is made by him for her, but her being none of the most agreeable women prevents particular notice being shown, or the father and son acknowledging any connection with her."[5]

I agree with another Franklin biographer, Walter Isaacson, that these words are the nearest we will get to the truth. There is nothing here that is unlikely. Indeed the story sounds all too familiar. Perhaps the most significant phrase is this: " 'Tis generally known." The conclusion to which we are driven has to be as follows. Hugh Roberts knew the facts because in the 1730s, when the affair was so recent, Franklin made no effort to conceal what had occurred. It would have been impossible to do so. Nor would anyone have expected him to try. On Market Street, so close to the waterfront where human beings black or white were put up for sale as a matter of routine, nobody would have found the incident surprising.

In the city of Andrew Hamilton, a freethinking place full of transients, it was taken for granted that young men would have affairs of the sort. Only later—when Franklin was an eminence, in politics and science—did he feel obliged to draw a veil over the episode. And by then, in the 1760s, perhaps the tone of public life in Philadelphia had changed as well, to become more pious or more hypocritical. He was also lucky to have friends like Hugh Roberts who knew how to keep what had become an embarrassing secret.

There is another thing of which we can be sure. In his young manhood, when he was still only twenty-five, the affair did Franklin no harm at all. On the contrary, his readiness to accept the little boy as his own may well have enhanced his reputation for honesty. In the twelve months after he and Deborah moved in together, Franklin enjoyed something close to an annus mirabilis. Happily married at last, he entered 1731 in what seems to have been a confident mood, ready to seize every chance that came to hand.

It would be an excellent year for him and for the Junto, a year in which he reached out beyond Mr. Hamilton to win the esteem of other men quite as influential. At the same time, his career in business entered a new chapter. By the end of 1731, Franklin had begun to create a publishing network that would take him far beyond the borders of his colony. Other men had tried to do this before; not only the Bradfords, but also Franklin's brother James and even Samuel Keimer, with his string of agents selling his almanacs from Maryland to Massachusetts. But Franklin would find a new, more ingenious way to spread his wings beyond Pennsylvania, at a moment that proved to be ideal.

He also arrived at a new philosophy. Since his teenage years in Boston, when he began to skip the chapel, he had been pondering deeply, thinking many thoughts about God, about metaphysics, and about the meaning of virtue. In 1731, at last Franklin completed the creation of his own personal, synthetic religion, in a form that would endure, with occasional shifts in tone and emphasis, until the day of his death. Best of all perhaps, it was a system of belief that he could own up to in public and share with other people.

The *Articles of Belief* that Franklin drew up in 1728 had been poetically satisfying, but they were too emotional. They contained elements—multiple worlds and multiple gods—that might sound too esoteric, or even bizarre. And so he kept the *Articles* a secret. His new creed would be rather vague, but that was all to the good: Franklin did not wish to be dogmatic. Although it could never truly be described as Christian, his system could not be called anti-Christian either. For all practical purposes, it was little different from the liberal Anglican views of the old "latitude man," Archbishop Tillotson. And it was a set of ideas that did not have to be concealed.

In a word: Franklin became a Freemason. His interpretation of what it meant to be a mason was very much his own, but that was part of the magic of Freemasonry. It was a form of belief that made perfect sense in the free and easy atmosphere of Pennsylvania. At one and the same time, a man could be a mason and also an Anglican, or a Presbyterian, or even a Roman Catholic, or he might choose to be a Quaker or to worship in no church at all. It was a creed for all seasons; and becoming a mason could also be rather good for one's career.

The Almighty Architect

In the middle years of the eighteenth century, there was nothing secret or subversive about the Freemasons of Philadelphia. The masons were the most respectable of people and they could be as visible as they chose. Indeed they were the rulers of the city, its landlords, and its most successful men of business. No one could imagine that among the oligarchs there might be a rebel in the making. Least of all Benjamin Franklin, who as yet had not the slightest inkling that he might one day be a revolutionary.

In the summer of 1755, on the feast day of their patron saint, John the Baptist, the Freemasons gathered in public at Christ Church, with Franklin among them, to hear a sermon from "their reverend brother," William Smith. An Anglican minister, he was also the provost of the town's new college. "My worthy brethren"—or so he described his fellow masons, sisters not being permitted to join—you belong to "a society of friends, linked in a strong bond of brotherly love, together with their other ties, for the advancement of humanity and good fellowship, rational religion, true liberty and useful knowledge." United they stood, as one in their allegiance to King George. The king was mentioned many, many times.[6]

Apart from his majesty, the Freemasons also acknowledged a rather higher deity. The God in whom they chose to believe went by the name of "the Almighty Architect." Alias "the Master Builder," he was an ecumenical divinity who smiled upon success, and there were few towns that had done as splendidly as this one. Or so they were told by William Smith. His oratory went down well. The masons gave a vote of thanks to Mr. Smith, and ordered that his sermon should be published.

Giving the decree was the merchant and land owner William Allen, grand master of the masons of the province, and also—since 1750—chief justice of Pennsylvania. Nearby was an Englishman, invited as a guest, their masonic friend John Penn, who was one of the co-owners of the colony. And at the very heart of the same elite we also find Benjamin Franklin. At the age of forty-nine, he was present at the meeting as William Allen's deputy. And when the sermon came to be printed, Franklin was the man who preserved it for posterity.

As we know today, in later life he would drift away from the complacency that was so obvious at civic functions such as this. As he grew older, Franklin would evolve to be more radical, and more egalitarian: an unusual destiny for someone who had been so successful. Over time, it seems that he gradually lost interest in the details of Freemasonry, with its meetings and its ceremonies. Perhaps he came to feel that it was rather phony; perhaps he did not care for the rhetoric about King George; or perhaps he just had other ways to spend his time.

But one thing he would never lose: his faith in the original ideals that Freemasons were supposed to embody. Franklin had been one of Philadelphia's first Freemasons, joining St. John's Lodge early in 1731. He ranked number nine in the list of members—the wealthy William Allen was number one—and soon the lodge came to overlap with the Junto. In its first decade, the lodge remained small and exclusive, with still only forty-six masons even in 1737, but among them were three other Junto members: Thomas Hopkinson, a recent arrival from England who joined the lodge in 1733; Joseph Breintnall, whose vintage was 1734; and a silversmith, Philip Syng Jr., who would later help Franklin with his experiments with electricity. Another early member was Andrew Hamilton's son James, who was Allen's brother-in-law.[7]

There can be no doubt that in those pioneering days Franklin was an enthusiastic Freemason. He helped to draft new bylaws for the lodge in 1732, and two years later he served as grand master. What did it mean to him? It may be—though this cannot be shown conclusively—that he had first encountered the movement in London. Even if he did not, by 1731 he would certainly have known that the members of the London lodges were often people of high rank and status.

They included not only stonemasons and architects, among whom the Craft apparently began, but also men of science; actors, who were especially keen masons; senior officials in Walpole's government; and members of the aristocracy. When Franklin arrived in the city in 1724, the grand master of England was the Duke of Richmond. His deputy was Martin Folkes, a physician who went on to become the president of the Royal Society. None of this was secret. The names of the leading

Freemasons and reports of their principal meetings were published in the London press, and although in theory their rituals were supposed to be private mysteries, in practice their details circulated freely.[8]

And so in becoming a mason Franklin knew that he was joining an international fraternity of distinguished people. Of course, one of his motives for doing so must have been ambition, plain and simple. However, evidence survives in plenty from the early 1730s to show that he was sincere in his belief in the principles of brotherhood that his lodge and others tried to uphold. Having witnessed the feuds of Whigs and Tories in England and Sir William Keith's efforts to bring the same tactics to Pennsylvania, at twenty-five Franklin was already disillusioned with "parties," in politics or in religion.

In the winter and spring of 1730–31, one of the London journals he followed—*The Craftsman*—ran a series of articles headed *Remarks on the History of England.* The writer traced the evils of the kingdom to what Jonathan Swift and others had called "the rage of party," dating from the 1670s when the Franklins had seen it at first hand. Whether or not he read those articles Franklin had been studying English history and he came to the same conclusion. In a little memorandum he sent to himself in May 1731, he called for an end to party strife, which he saw as nothing but a mask for self-interest and malice.[9]

"Few in public affairs act from a mere view of the good of their country," he wrote. "Fewer still in public affairs act with a view to the good of mankind." His solution? In his teens Franklin had known the work of Thomas Tryon, eccentric idealist, and now he proposed something that Tryon would have endorsed. He hoped to see the formation of "an united party of virtue," to consist of "the virtuous and good men of all nations into a regular body, to governed suitable good and wise rules." In other words: something like the Freemasons or the Junto, but expanded to encompass the globe.

While he waited for this brotherhood to appear, he did the best he could to cultivate his virtues. Because in his memoirs Franklin was often rather vague about chronology, it is hard to say precisely when he devised his famous "project of arriving at moral perfection." With its thirteen-week course of exercises, intended to instill thirteen kinds of virtue, from Temperance to Humility by way of Frugality, Industry, Chastity, and Cleanliness, the project has come in for its share of ridicule from modern writers. In places, as he describes the process, even the elderly Franklin makes gentle fun of his younger self, striving for excellence in morality by way of fearless self-examination: a form of striving, the old man pointed out, that might all too easily lead to what he called "a kind of foppery in morals." But if we place the project in its original setting—about 1731 or 1732, in his early years of married life and Freemasonry—there is nothing absurd or ridiculous about it.

Here was a young man who had seen what the *lack* of these virtues had done to the likes of Collins, Ralph, Governor Keith, and so many others. His affair with William Franklin's mother was fresh in his memory. While in the eyes of the world he had gotten away with it, his conscience was another matter. But now that he was married to Deborah, Franklin had every chance of being chaste; his industry was going well; and as for being humble, the sessions of the Junto and the masonic lodge were exercises in equality where no one lorded it over his fellows. He was also falling under the influence of James Logan, whose writings about morality in the 1720s consisted of similar lists of virtues—sobriety, industry, frugality, and so on—as he too, in a very Franklinian phrase, looked for what he called "ways to get wealth" that would also keep a man from doing evil.[10]

And so Franklin embarked on his course of ethical self-improvement, which—being Franklin—of course he had to put down on paper. "I made a little book in which I allotted a page for each of the virtues," he tells us. "I rul'd each page with red ink so as to have seven columns, one for each day of the week, marking each column with a letter for the day. I cross'd these columns with thirteen red lines, marking the beginning of each line with the first letter of one of the virtues, on which line and in its proper column I might mark by a little black spot every fault I found upon examination, to have been committed respecting that virtue upon that day . . . I was surpris'd to find myself so much fuller of faults than I had imagined, but I had the satisfaction of seeing them diminish." The little book traveled everywhere with Franklin: and ". . . tho' I never arrived at the perfection I had been so ambitious of obtaining, but fell far short of it, yet I was by the endeavour made a better and happier man than I otherwise should have been."

Where did religion come into Franklin's scheme? Although in private Franklin still clung to his *Articles of Belief,* they were too poetic for everyday use or for exposure to the public gaze. But by now—after ten years of reading the deists and Shaftesbury, Locke, Tillotson, and so much else—Franklin was ready to distill his conclusions into a few simple points. "Imitate Jesus and Socrates," he wrote, a maxim that neatly tied together practical ethics and sublime philosophy. The reference to Socrates tells us that Franklin believed in a divine creator, a God who was benevolent but not specifically Christian; he also believed in something he called "Providence," even though its workings were often hard to discern; and like Socrates, he thought the soul might be immortal. As for the best form of religious service, it consisted of doing good to other human beings, even at the cost of self-sacrifice: in other words, New Testament morality but without any excess baggage of theology.

He even conceived the idea of a new, ecumenical group, the Society of the Free and Easy, who would complete the thirteen-week course in virtue and then acknowledge this new creed as their own. Although this society never materialized, Franklin had the Junto and the masons to serve as an approximation. The Almighty Architect in which they believed was not so very different from the God of Socrates or Plato, a God of mathematics and reason, and Franklin could live with that. By about 1731 he had come to a resting place, intellectually speaking. Franklin had a system of beliefs that would serve its purpose: not only his, but also that of Pennsylvania, if only its people would listen. Here was a colony where great things were being born.

Ingenious Thoughts, Ingenious Books

Forty miles north of the falls at Trenton, a traveler who ventured up the Delaware would come around a wide bend in the river and see a high range of hills. Densely covered with trees, they fell steeply down toward the water's edge. Stepping ashore in the early 1730s our traveler would see men cutting timber; and if he climbed up the hills to the west, he would enter a valley filled with the sound of hammers and the smell of burning charcoal.

This was Durham, Pennsylvania, the site of the ironworks owned by James Logan, William Allen, and their partners. The fires of the forge and the furnace were lit on an eminence called Mine Hill. Just below the surface, there was a layer of red hematite, an iron ore mottled with veins of quartz. Today the little town is a place of beauty, green and fragrant, but the gaping black mouth of one of the tunnels of the mine can still be seen, to show that this is one of the most important sites in the early history of industry in North America.

It was a hard slog by wagon or by mule for supplies to get to a location so remote, or for the iron to get out again to reach the customer.

The Delaware ought to have made a far better highway; but there were too many stretches of shallow water strewn with rocks and boulders. One answer to the problem was this: to use long, flat-bottomed vessels, the famous Durham boats that carried George Washington's army across the river in 1776. Another solution was to go around the shallows with some kind of canal.

In 1731 a scheme for just such a canal was in the air. It gives us our first glimpse of Benjamin Franklin as an apostle of science and engineering as a means to make America wealthy. His Junto friend Thomas Godfrey knew a Presbyterian minister by the name of Joseph Morgan, a many-sided cleric with a touch of eccentricity. Morgan tended his flock at a chapel close to Trenton, but he also took a deep interest in matters scientific, and especially the works of Newton. Keen to open up the interior, Morgan conceived the idea of an artificial waterway, built into the bank of the Delaware, with dams to hold back the river and a system of locks to carry boats over any obstacles. Mr. Morgan wrote a paper describing the plan, and Godfrey gave it to James Logan, who had every reason to welcome a faster mode of transit for his iron. On May 1 Logan wrote a courteous letter back to Franklin with his comments.[II]

He called the young man "Friend B.F.": a form of address that speaks volumes about the esteem that Franklin had already won from the most powerful men in Pennsylvania. Logan thought it would be easier simply to remove the rocks, but he welcomed these signs of initiative from Franklin and his circle. "It would be well I believe to have the paper made public," James Logan wrote, "for 'tis a pity that such ingenious thoughts should be lost." And so Franklin did just that. He shared Morgan's paper with his friends, and then he ran it as a series in *The Pennsylvania Gazette* in the May and June of 1732.

Although it came to nothing, the scheme was a visionary foretaste of a later period, looking forward to the age of the Erie Canal. Which was exactly the kind of thing Joseph Morgan had in mind. With a view to challenging France for supremacy in the wilderness, in 1732 he sent the same material to the Royal Society in the hope of winning their support for this and another project. Morgan also proposed a new kind of military technology: a portable boat with which to explore the upper reaches of the Delaware and the Susquehanna, and to take troops and settlers as far as the Great Lakes.

And so, when he was only twenty-five, we see Franklin closely involved with men of science who hoped to put their ingenuity to work in the cause of western expansion. In James Logan's career as well as Morgan's, we find the same cluster of interests: Newtonian science, internal "improvements" such as mines and canals, the western frontier, and imperial defense. The last of these—defense—was gradually coming to be an obsession with Logan, and so in time it would be for Franklin as well.

Late in 1731, Logan's fur traders had brought word that in the Ohio country the Shawnee had hoisted the flag of France. Was this part of a cunning French scheme to encircle the British colonies with a chain of forts, and to bar their entry to the interior? Logan feared that it was. He was already trying to persuade the Penn family to create a frontier militia made up of Germans and the Scots-Irish. That winter, while Franklin was circulating Morgan's paper, Logan wrote a memorandum to Sir Robert Walpole, warning him that the empire was in danger.[12]

His paper reached Walpole's desk in 1732, only to be ignored. At this point, the *Pax Walpoleana* appeared to be secure, and so the government did not share Mr. Logan's anxieties. His memorandum was too far ahead of its time. It contained, for example, Logan's attempt to revive a frontier project first mooted in Virginia by Governor Spotswood, another man who loved iron and feared the French. Spotswood had wanted to see the British march over the hills and build their own forts on Lake Erie, in an alliance with the Iroquois. That would not happen for another thirty years; and Logan's other suggestion—to create a new colony of Germans in what is now West Virginia—was equally premature.

Even so, the Logan memorandum shows us what was on the minds of the leaders of the Quaker colony at the time when Franklin was emerging into public life. In matters of the intellect, Franklin's debts to James Logan were immense. At his country house at Stenton, five miles from the heart of Philadelphia, where the Iroquois would come to camp out on the lawn, Logan lived among his magnificent collection of books; and from there he maintained a lively correspondence with his friends in New York, in Ireland, and in England, who kept him in touch with the learning of the period. If the Franklin of the early 1730s needed a mentor, Logan was ideal. And at just this moment, when the young man was newly married, confident, and hitting his stride in business, Logan gave his support to one of Franklin's most successful and farsighted projects, the Library Company of Philadelphia.

In the Junto's early days, the members had pooled their books together to create a small collection kept in their meeting room at Robert Grace's house for all of them to use. The arrangement not working out—some of the books were lost or damaged—each member took his books home again. Then in the summer of 1731 Franklin suggested they create something more permanent. It was to be a lending library, paid for by subscriptions from the members. Each one would make an upfront payment of forty shillings to start the venture and then there would be an annual fee of ten shillings.

They formed a board of ten directors, including Franklin, Parsons, Grace, and Godfrey, and also the young Freemason, lawyer, and Junto member Thomas Hopkinson. He had come from London, where his family were real estate developers in the heart of the capital.* Hopkinson intended to spend some time in London the following year, and he would take with him a list of books they wished to have. They drew up articles of association, and had them signed and sealed. Franklin wanted everything watertight so that the company would endure.[13]

By November they had fifty subscribers and the venture was off the ground. Once the money was raised—Nicholas Scull was the treasurer—the next step for the Library Company was to choose the books they wished to acquire. And so in the spring of 1732, Thomas Godfrey and Benjamin Franklin made their way to Stenton to seek the wise counsel of James Logan. The list they compiled with the help of Mr. Logan can fairly be described as remarkable.

The most striking thing about the list of books is what it did *not* contain. No theology, no sermons—certainly nothing by Cotton Mather—no fiction, no drama, no metaphysics, and only the very best of poetry: the translations by Pope and Dryden of Homer and Virgil. Of course the Library Company wanted the complete works of Addison and Steele; perhaps because Franklin was tired of people borrowing his set of *The Spectator*. But most of all they wished to have modern history, geography, astronomy, and science. Textbooks of geometry, a teach-

* Born in 1709, Thomas Hopkinson is a neglected figure in Franklin biographies, but he had an exceptionally interesting background. His uncle and benefactor Matthew Hopkinson not only owned a portfolio of property in the newly built Soho and Piccadilly areas of the West End of London; he was also a founding director in 1717 of the Westminster Fire Office, one of the earliest British insurance companies. Thomas Hopkinson's presence in the Junto is significant for two reasons. First, it shows us that although the Junto began as a club mainly for artisans, it soon drew in gentlemen with a higher social status; and second, Hopkinson gave Franklin another channel through which to keep up with developments in London.

yourself guide to Newton's calculus, and a treatise on conic sections: that was the sort of thing. As far as philosophy went, the only author on their menu was Pierre Bayle, the notorious skeptic, whose name Franklin had known since his teenage years in Boston. Bayle's *Historical and Critical Dictionary* was now the favorite reading of enlightened people in London.

One item on the Library Company's list of books has an extra resonance, because it made such a special contribution to Franklin's scientific career. After consulting James Logan, Franklin and Godfrey and their friends chose to have something called *Gravesend's Nat. Philos. 2 vols.* To give him his title correctly, Professor Willem Jacob 's Gravesande taught science at Leiden University in Holland, where he was Europe's leading exponent of the work of Newton. He strove to apply Newton's ideas to every field of science, even those—such as heat and electricity—where Newton had run up against questions he felt unable to solve.

It was by reading 's Gravesande, in the hours he could snatch from the printing press and the *Gazette,* that Franklin prepared himself for his electrical discoveries. Writings such as these, recommended by Logan, would eventually give him his agenda for research; but only when he had the time, the money, and the moment of opportunity. Another thirteen years had yet to elapse before those conditions would be satisfied. While Hopkinson sailed off to London and came back with the books, Franklin had to ply his trade: and he did so splendidly.

Printing and *Poor Richard's Almanack*

While the Library Company was being formed, in Charleston the planters had obtained the concession they required. In future they would be allowed to ship their rice directly to southern Europe. South Carolina had also issued paper money; it had a popular, capable governor, Robert Johnson; and its frontier was steadily moving inland. The governor led the creation of new townships to be filled with the Germans, the Scots-Irish, and migrating Welshmen such as Hugh Meredith. Unhealthy though the climate was, with frequent epidemics, the colony entered a period of growth even more dynamic than Pennsylvania's.[14]

It was high time the colony had not only an official printer but also a newspaper. Franklin moved swiftly when in the summer of 1731 he heard that Governor Johnson was offering a bounty to a qualified printer who would move to Charleston and set up his workshop. Three men answered the call. One was Eleazer Phillips Jr., from Boston; the second was Franklin's old colleague, the Oxford man George Webb. The third was Franklin's London-trained journeyman, Thomas Whitmarsh, who had also become a Freemason at St. John's Lodge.

On September 13 he and Franklin signed up as partners in a six-year deal that would set Whitmarsh up in business in Charleston. As carefully drafted as the Library Company's constitution, their articles of agreement were more evidence of Franklin's new maturity and of the benefits of the Junto. It gave him the help and wise counsel of the likes of Joseph Breintnall and the lawyer, Thomas Hopkinson. The deal was this: Franklin would supply the printing press and as much as four hundredweight of lead type. He would also share the cost of the paper and ink and so on. In return Franklin would take one third of the profits. By the end of the month Whitmarsh had landed in Charleston, and in January 1732 he launched *The South-Carolina Gazette.*[15]

It was a risky venture for one very stark reason: the appalling death rate in the South. Phillips won the official printing contract, then succumbed to yellow fever in the summer of 1732. Webb disappeared back to England, and then Whitmarsh died in the fall of 1733. But if Franklin could find a successor, the government contract and the *Gazette* would be his. And here Franklin had another of those strokes of luck that were such a feature of his career. In September 1731 a Frenchman, Louis Timothée, had arrived in Philadelphia to open a language school.

In the Netherlands, where he spent his boyhood, Timothée had trained as a printer and so in 1732 Franklin took him on as a journeyman, specializing in printing in German. That summer they tried to establish a German newspaper, the *Philadelphische Zeitung,* only to let it expire after two issues when readers failed to materialize. When Whitmarsh died, Timothée changed his name to Lewis Timothy and took his place in Charleston. There he obtained the government contract and *The South-Carolina Gazette* reappeared in February 1734. He survived only another five years, whereupon his Dutch widow, Elizabeth, became the printer. This sometimes happened in London, where the rules of the Stationers' Company permitted a woman to take on her dead husband's trade. And indeed, although she called herself "a poor, afflicted widow," she proved to be more reliable than Mr. Timothy.

"He was a man of learning and honest," Franklin recalled in his memoirs, "but ignorant in matters of account," so that it was hard for Franklin to get his hands on the dividend to which he was entitled. Mrs. Timothy, on the other hand, possessed the estimable virtue of "regularity": Franklin's word, as it had been Samuel Palmer's. Although she had six children to raise she promptly sent his remittance every three months. When the Timothys' six-year deal expired in 1740, she bought Franklin out. But for many years to come the two *Gazettes,* in Pennsylvania and South Carolina, went on working together, swapping stories and columns, and she sold Franklin's books in Charleston. When she retired in 1748, her son Peter took over. And so the connection went on.

As the years passed, Franklin tried to take the same partnership model and apply it elsewhere. He started new printing ventures in New York, Connecticut, and even Antigua, and in 1749 among the German community in Pennsylvania. The results were mixed, because of the human factor. It was hard to find partners who were shrewd businesspeople as well as competent craftsmen. However, at the very least Franklin now had a network through which he could distribute what he printed.

And like his London counterpart Charles Ackers, Franklin built a product range wide and robust enough to keep the cash flowing predictably. One important point is this: that after the early stage when he relied on Grace and Coleman, it seems that Franklin never borrowed to finance his business. It might have been tempting to do so—for example, he might have bought the freehold of his premises on Market Street, and mortgaged it for paper money from the Loan Office—but he resisted the urge. He also had Deborah to help him keep his finances in order. Not only did she bear him a son, Francis Folger Franklin—"little Franky"—born in October 1732, to whom they were both devoted; she also played an essential role in the management of the firm. Deborah did the books and kept track of their debtors as well, never allowing the Franklin firm to run out of working capital. At about this time, Franklin finally repaid the money he owed to the silversmith Mr. Vernon in Newport, including the long arrears of interest.

As for the product: at the very end of 1732 Franklin entered the battle of the almanacs. Since 1729 he had been printing two almanacs—by his Junto friend Thomas Godfey, and by another astronomer, John Jerman—but the enterprising Andrew Bradford stole the contracts from under Franklin's nose. Instead of accepting defeat, Franklin decided to write one of his own. And so *Poor Richard's Almanack* was born.

Working at high speed, Franklin slung the first edition together in such a hurry that he transposed the two months of September and October, and had to reissue the almanac early in 1733. To begin with, *Poor Richard* was little different from its predecessors, with their calendars of forthcoming events—sessions of the county courts, Quaker meetings, and the birthdays of Britain's royal family—and their predictions of the weather. Like them he pillaged his material, little poems and proverbs and jokes and even the name "Poor Richard," from English collections from the previous century. His preface for the 1733 edition was built around a rather unoriginal hoax, a forecast of the death of his almanac rival, Titan Leeds. It was a device that Franklin borrowed from Swift, who twenty-five years earlier had done something similar in London.

As he worked under pressure, Franklin revived his old technique of inventing a fictitious author. Not Silence Dogood, with her faculty for double entendres, but Poor Richard, a henpecked husband as well as an astrologer. He and Mrs. Saunders—her name was Bridget—could be made to play out their domestic dramas in a soap opera unfolding in each year's edition. And in this first issue of his almanac, Franklin conjured up Poor Richard so vividly that he was there to stay.

"The plain truth of the matter is, I am excessive poor, and my wife, good woman, is I tell her excessive proud," Poor Richard tells us. "She cannot bear, she says, to sit spinning in her shift of tow while I do nothing but gaze at the stars; and had threatened more than once to burn all my books and rattling traps, as she calls my instruments, if I do not make some profitable use of them for the good of my family."

This was not the kind of thing that Franklin really wanted to be writing. As a Freemason, a friend of Logan, and a founder of the Library Company—that entity so high-minded in its taste—he would have preferred to be more erudite. But he had a market to serve. As the years went by, and the Quaker colony grew wealthier, so Franklin gradually refined the content of *Poor Richard,* so that by the 1740s he was filling it with extracts from the poets he treasured, James Thomson and Alexander Pope. But in the early days he stuck to the vernacular.

In *Poor Richard* Franklin gave his readers what they were used to and words that fitted their situation, proverbs familiar from the old country. "Scraps from the table of wisdom" was the phrase he used in the issue for 1739; and by "wisdom" he meant the traditional philosophy of farmers accustomed to worrying about a bad harvest that might wreck their lives. The Pennsylvania farmer could never be sure of what lay in store: cattle disease, smallpox, a hurricane, or a blizzard, or deception by a swindler from the town. And so it was best to be cautious, risk-averse, and sober. And that was the message of the almanac.

"When 'tis fair be sure to take your greatcoat with you," says Poor

Richard in 1734. "He that sells upon trust, loses many friends and also wants money," he writes in 1735. In 1736: "There's many witty men whose brains can't feed their bellies"; and then "There are three faithful friends: an old wife, an old dog, and ready money." Extravagance should be avoided; so should strong drink; and it was always best to be wary. "To whom thy secret thou dost tell, to him thy freedom thou dost sell," we are told by Poor Richard; and most of all we should be suspicious of a fancy exterior or shows of emotion. "Full of courtesy, full of craft," he says. "Onions can make even heirs and widows weep." The world that Poor Richard inhabits is a world fraught with risk and danger, where it is best not to expect too much, and where the most a human being can do is to be self-controlled and to carry on working. As he put it in 1735: "The thrifty maxim of the wary is to save all the money they can touch."

There speaks a settler by the Delaware, afraid that if the planters in Jamaica run short of credit from London he will be unable to sell his grain. But it would not do to think that what was printed by Franklin in the *Almanack* was actually his opinion. Poor Richard was an old curmudgeon, pessimistic and frustrated, a man who distrusted everyone around him. Although Franklin could sometimes sound like a cynic—having seen so much of human frailty and met his share of cheats and villains, he was bound to be occasionally—at heart he remained the Crusoe of the colonies, with an inner core of confident resilience. Poor Richard was just a guise he assumed as a way to sell the almanac to farmers. We can hear the authentic voice of Franklin not in the usual gloom of Poor Richard but in the most famous line from the series: "Early to bed and early to rise, makes a man healthy, wealthy and wise."[16]

Although this maxim was not entirely Franklin's creation but something he improved upon from an English original, the optimistic message was definitely his. Pennsylvania was growing fast, and health and wealth and wisdom were attainable, or so it seemed to Franklin; and although the money had yet to roll into his wallet, he had not lost his zeal for self-improvement. He had begun to study languages, teaching himself to read French, Italian, and Spanish, and then returning to the Latin he had begun to learn in his year at the grammar school in Boston. Meanwhile the city around him was improving too.

Although the streets were poorly paved, the sidewalks were slippery, and there were too many house fires, and too many drunks—all subjects that Franklin tackled in the *Gazette*—Philadelphia was on a roll. At the western end of the town, its affluence and its ambition found a symbol in an ambitious new project, the brainchild of Andrew Hamilton. As part of the paper money deal of 1729, it was decided to allocate some funds to the erection of a new State House. The assembly appointed a building committee. As such committees do, they spent three years squabbling about the cost and the architecture. At last they chose Speaker Hamilton's preferred design, which slowly evolved until in the 1750s they had the edifice we know today as Independence Hall.[17]

As the brickwork gradually rose toward the sky, so Franklin continued his ascent toward gentility. He was on a roll of his own: but not without the occasional mistake. Having become so close to Andrew Hamilton, he could not help but be drawn into political controversies. And when that occurred, Franklin was as capable as any other human being of making himself look foolish.

Chapter Fifteen

The Devil's Instrument

In the early years of his *Gazette,* Franklin had printed one of his most eloquent pieces of prose, his *Apology for Printers* of 1731. A witty but forthright defense of the freedom of the press, it set out his view that an editor had a right—almost a duty—to print all manner of opinions, provided they were free from mere spite or deliberate falsehood. "I shall not burn my press and melt my letters," he wrote, as he stood up for a profession whose task it was to serve the truth, even at the risk of upsetting the readership. Opinion was a fact of life, he pointed out. Human beings differed in their views as much as they did in their faces, and so the printer or the journalist was in the business of diversity.[1]

He was "educated in the belief," Franklin said, "that when men differ in opinion, both sides ought equally have the advantage of being heard by the public; and that when truth and error have fair play, the former is always an overmatch for the latter." These were fine words, written at a time when Franklin was being accused of offending public morals. It was a trivial matter, arising from a piece of schoolboy humor. Asked to print a poster to advertise the sailing of a ship for Barbados, either Franklin or the skipper had added a witticism at the bottom: "No sea-hens nor black gowns will be admitted on any terms."

A sea-hen was slang for a prostitute, while a black gown meant a minister. Pious folk took offense, threatening to boycott *The Pennsylvania Gazette* on account of what they took to be Franklin's contempt for religion and the clergy. He might simply have apologized and promised not to make the same kind of joke again, but that would have been a foolish thing to do, giving too many hostages to fortune. Instead he stood his ground, denying that he harbored any malice of the kind. "If all printers were determined not to print anything till they were sure it would offend nobody," Franklin wrote, "there would be very little printed."

Even at twenty-five, he was experienced enough with journalism to know that a fuss such as this soon blows over. Irritated readers who canceled their subscription to a newspaper soon found that they could not do without it. And so he replied with his refusal to be told what he could or could not publish. However, in the process Franklin made a promise that he did not always keep. He never printed anything, he claimed, that "might countenance vice, or promote immorality," or "do real injury to any person." The first half of this statement was true, since he mostly did his best to keep smutty stuff out of the *Gazette*, but not the second. From time to time, Franklin could be quite as partisan and vitriolic as any other journalist in the eighteenth century.

And especially on behalf of his patron. At election time in the fall of 1733, Bradford and the *Mercury* mounted a long, damaging campaign of insult and innuendo against Speaker Hamilton, calling him "an ambitious, selfish and designing man," and accusing him of using his influence over the electors and his fellow assemblymen to create "a monopoly of power." As these words were printed in September, Franklin was away on a business trip—this was when he gave Deborah a power of attorney over his affairs—during which he went back to Boston for the first time in ten years. He returned home to Philadelphia to find that Bradford's onslaught had hit home and Hamilton had lost the speakership.[2]

His ally Jeremiah Langhorne took his place, and Franklin held on to his post as the assembly's printer. Even so he had to rally to Hamilton's defense. In his absence, the *Gazette* had done the best it could, branding the *Mercury* "the unhappy birth of a sickly brain," but Franklin could do better. In November, he produced a rejoinder, titled "A Half-Hour's Conversation with a Friend," which amounted to an interview with Hamilton. Written with Franklin's usual flair, it dealt in mockery of Hamilton's opponents and ended with an appeal to the working people of Pennsylvania—"the bricklayer, the carpenter, the shipwright"—whom he portrayed as Andrew Hamilton's constituency.[3]

Hamilton survived, to come storming back as Speaker in the autumn of 1734, but Franklin was clearly now a party man, with his colors nailed to Hamilton's mast. He had all the more reason to cling to his patron because Hamilton was reaching the peak of his career. At the end of the year, Governor Gordon fell seriously ill, leaving him and Logan in almost complete control of the colony's affairs. Beyond its borders Mr. Hamilton was also a man to be reckoned with, the finest trial lawyer in the colonies, and he was about to achieve his finest victory, by securing the acquittal of John Peter Zenger, publisher of *The New-York Weekly Journal,* who had been charged with seditious libel. It was a landmark case, in which Hamilton stood up for the printer, the people, and their civil liberties against New York's royal governor. But although he must have seemed to be impregnable, the Speaker had some flaws in his armor, which Andrew Bradford did his best to expose.

Despite Franklin's efforts, the *Mercury* never surrendered in the war of words. For months Bradford kept up his anti-Hamilton campaign, far into 1734, and in subsequent years he came back again, hinting at corruption on the Speaker's part. No proof of that has come to light, but Hamilton had an Achilles' heel of another kind. Although he was a Presbyterian, everyone knew how unholy Andrew Hamilton could be; and so Bradford published a sly little poem, likening him to Spinoza, the infamous Dutch atheist, one of many items implying that Hamilton was an unbeliever.[4]

The stage was set for another battle with the pen, with Franklin once again on Hamilton's side. It took place in the spring of 1735, and this time it concerned religion: specifically, the Presbyterian Church. At that moment, Franklin had recently suffered a bereavement: the loss of the founder of *The New-England Courant.* In February, his brother James died in Newport at only thirty-eight, leaving his business to his widow, Anne. Brushing this aside, or so it seems, Franklin dived into a religious controversy in Philadelphia in which he did not hesitate to slander his opponents. We can call it the Hemphill affair, from the name of the Irish clergyman, Samuel Hemphill, whose dubious career enlisted Franklin's support.

Since his boyhood Franklin had liked to think of himself as a latter-day Socrates, defending the truth against authority and deceit. He was still only twenty-nine, and when Hemphill arrived in Pennsylvania, and found himself on trial for heresy, Franklin leaped to his defense. He saw the case as a clear-cut matter in which religious liberty was under attack, from what he called "ignorance . . . bigotry and superstition." Whig that he was, Franklin felt obliged to intervene, and all the more eagerly because Andrew Hamilton also supported the preacher.

"Let us endeavor," Franklin wrote as the affair was at its height, "to preserve and maintain Truth, commonsense, universal charity, and brotherly love in this our infant and growing nation." In fact his behavior was neither fraternal nor benevolent. Nor was the Hemphill affair the worthy cause Franklin took it to be. Far from being purely a matter of principle, it was really a clash of cultures, with its roots in an ethnic and economic divide between different sections of a colony now extraordinarily diverse. The case would teach Franklin a salutary lesson about the new America that was emerging around him.[5]

THE HEMPHILL AFFAIR

If the young Franklin were telling the Hemphill story as it seemed to him at the time, it would have looked like this. An educated man, thoughtful and progressive, Samuel Hemphill first set foot in Philadelphia in the fall of 1734, ready to preach an enlightened form of Christian doctrine. Seven months later he fell victim to a clerical conspiracy, in which he was done down by reactionaries who rejected his liberal ideas. They declared him a heretic, and kicked him out of the ministry: a wicked case of persecution by the powerful.

This was the simple view that Franklin put across as the events unfolded, but the truth was rather different. Far from being cut-and-dried, the Hemphill affair had many nuances and many complications. Religious disputes always do, especially when—as in this case—they come muddled up with politics. Let us begin at the beginning: first with Benjamin Franklin.

Coming as he did from a Presbyterian home, each year Franklin paid his fee to support the minister in Philadelphia. In the 1730s, the cleric in question was Jedediah Andrews, a Harvard man from the class of 1695, when the witch trials at Salem were a recent memory. Indeed he had been a protégé of Increase Mather, and technically Andrews was not a Presbyterian at all but a Congregationalist. At this period in America the two churches were practically identical.[6]

A friendly soul, Mr. Andrews would visit Franklin from time to time, urging him to come to Sunday service, which Franklin sometimes did—"once for five Sundays successively," he recalled—but with little pleasure. He soon stopped going to the chapel, preferring to use his own *Articles of Belief*, rather than listen to sermons that he found "very dry, and unedifying." The pastor tended to insist on the formalities of religion, rather than the moral teaching that Franklin wanted to hear.

Or so Franklin tells us in his memoirs: but there was another side to

Jedediah. True, his preaching style was soporific. According to a writer in the *Mercury*, he spoke "so dull and slowly that I fell asleep." But while he may have been boring, Mr. Andrews was never a bully. When colleagues tried to insist that everyone, clergy and laity alike, had to sign up to the Westminster Confession, a statement of orthodox Calvinist belief, Jedediah refused to cooperate. Not only was he tolerant of other people's opinions; he also presided over a rapidly expanding congregation.

Until about 1718, the town had only a few Presbyterians, but then Jedediah's church began to grow dynamically until at the end of the 1720s they had to extend the building. If this was partly a tribute to Mr. Andrews, it was chiefly a consequence of immigration as the Scots-Irish, who were mostly Presbyterians, came pouring in by sea from Ulster. In 1734, Andrews reached the age of sixty, and he felt that to care for such a large flock he really ought to have an assistant. He went to the local synod, whose elders included Andrew Hamilton, and they agreed. At which point another question arose: what *kind* of Presbyterian should the new man be?[7]

Just what sort of faith should he teach? Calvinist, or middle-of-the-road, or liberal? And furthermore: how should he be chosen? By popular vote, or by the elders, with the biggest say going to the wealthier members of the laity, who supplied the funds for the church? One of the problems was that the rich men, the lawyers and merchants, like Andrew Hamilton or William Allen—he was a Presbyterian too—were inclined to be deists and freethinkers, something that put them at odds with the rank and file in the pews.

In the British Isles, questions such as these had already given rise to the fiercest of quarrels in the Presbyterian Church. The deepest schism occurred in the middle of the 1720s in the north of Ireland, where the Hemphill case had its origins. On the liberal side, known as the "New Lights," there stood the merchants of Belfast and the wealthier owners of land in Ulster, people similar to Andrew Hamilton. Mr. Hemphill belonged to this faction in the church. But they were vastly outnumbered by their opponents, the "Old Light" ministers and their supporters, the tenant farmers of the Ulster hinterland. Clinging to Calvinism, the farmers saw only one means to salvation: rebirth in the Spirit, by way of a Gospel faith in Jesus. These were precisely the people—Scots-Irish Presbyterians, driven from their homes by poor harvests, high rents, and a chronic shortage of land—who were sailing westward to the Delaware.[8]

And so Ireland exported its religious conflicts to the colonies. In Pennsylvania, the diaspora from Ulster led to the creation of sectional divisions, as the Scots-Irish built enclaves in the interior; and this was partly the work of Franklin's friend James Logan. As he made grants of land, Logan channeled the new arrivals toward the fine soil near Lancaster: not to form some kind of ghetto, but because the area was strategically important, and because he wanted a buffer against the native tribes.[9]

By the early 1730s, the Scots-Irish had created a string of new townships between Lancaster and the port of entry at New Castle. As an Ulsterman himself, albeit a Quaker, Logan had his doubts about the settlers with their Calvinist ideas. In a complaining letter to Belfast, he called them "over zealous," "bigoted," and "tricky and contentious." Be that as it was, Logan needed them on the frontier, and they had come to stay. They built their own Presbyterian chapels; as their ministers, they chose Old Light preachers from Ireland; and soon they became a distinctive voice in the province.[10]

There was also another ingredient to be thrown into the mix. In the annals of religion in America, 1734 will always count as a date of high importance. A revival began, known to historians as the Great Awakening, which sprang into life at Northampton, Massachusetts, where Jonathan Edwards, a Calvinist through and through, was engaged in an arduous campaign of conversion. Not for him the flabby notions of liberals and deists. Instead Mr. Edwards looked for *emotion,* the weeping, the travails, and at last! the joys of a sinner lost and born again. Hundreds of souls were converted, and the movement began.

Northampton was a long way off; but something similar was happening far closer to Franklin. In New Jersey there lay the town of Freehold, where the minister came from a preaching family called the Tennents, who were Ulstermen, and there they led their own evangelical awakening. Like Jonathan Edwards, they were Calvinists, intent upon the saving of souls, but also striving to achieve what amounted to a second Reformation, this time in America, with the Presbyterian clergy as its leaders: but only those who shared their definition of their creed. Of all the family, the most energetic was young Gilbert Tennent, pastor at New Brunswick, who was also a member of the Philadelphia Synod. In the September of 1734, he urged the synod to apply a new and rigorous test to any minister they licensed to preach.

Did the preacher really know his calling? His task, according to Mr. Tennent, was to urge the sinners to repent, convincing them that they were "lost and miserable," until they felt the touch of the Spirit. If the preacher did not undertake that mission, he was no minister at all: or so said Gilbert Tennent. His message was uncompromising, but this much can be said for it. As the Great Awakening would show, it was a message that many tens of thousands of people dearly wanted to hear.

And especially the Scots-Irish. What they did not want was Samuel Hemphill. He shipped up in the Delaware that fall, to become the deputy pastor that Andrews required. In the winter of 1734 and 1735, Hemphill made a splash in Philadelphia with his New Light sermons, bringing people flocking to the meeting house: or so Franklin claims, since Franklin was one of his admirers. Mr. Andrews gives another side to the story. He makes it plain that Hemphill was foisted on him by the powerful, by which he can only mean Andrew Hamilton and William Allen. According to Andrews, the only people who wanted to hear Hemphill were "freethinkers, deists, and nothings," while what he calls "the best of people" began to stay away.[11]

What did Hemphill say about the Bible? Worth reading, he thought, but not entirely obligatory: because, or so he argued, Almighty God had given us "the light of nature," with which we could arrive at the truths of religion by ourselves. Those truths he and Franklin defined as "morality, virtue, and universal benevolence," words that had come into vogue with liberal thinkers in Scotland where Hemphill had attended the University of Glasgow.

Did Christians have to undergo a rebirth in the Spirit, of the kind the Tennents thought was indispensable? Definitely not, said Mr. Hemphill. All we need do, said he, is "to live and act according to our nature." He dismissed the idea that human beings are born in a condition of depravity. As far as Hemphill was concerned, the doctrine of original sin was nothing, or so he told his readers, but "a notion invented, a bugbear set up by priests . . . to fright and scare an unthinking populace out of their senses."

It was the kind of thing Franklin had encountered in the works of the deists, language he had used himself in Boston. Now he could hear it from a pulpit. But what Franklin did not see was this: that on the frontier, among the Scots-Irish, these ideas would be angrily rejected. A man of the street and the city, Franklin knew enough about agriculture to create Poor Richard, but he had no affinity with Irish farmers, and neither did Franklin understand their politics or their religion.

Before he left the shores of Donegal, Hemphill had made an enemy, an Old Light minister named Patrick Vance who heard him preach and decided that he was nothing but "a vile heretic." As Hemphill set sail, Vance wrote to his brother-in-law in Pennsylvania, warning him about the new arrival. In the letter, he called his New Light opponent "the devil's instrument," among many other epithets equally damning. The letter reached the eyes of Jedediah Andrews, who had already heard complaints from the frontier towns. If Hemphill had stayed put in Philadelphia, perhaps he might have survived; but he made the error of venturing forty miles to the west, to the little farming settlement of New London, where his sermons caused a stir among the settlers. Outraged, they contacted their friends in the city, where Mr. Andrews was already so unhappy with his new deputy.[12]

Armed with the letter from Vance, Andrews went to the synod and asked them to have Hemphill put on trial. Events moved fast. On April 7, 1735 Andrews filed his charges; ten days later, the trial began; and ten days after that, they suspended Hemphill from his ministry. He was never reinstated. This could scarcely be otherwise, because of the seven commissioners who conducted the trial, four were Old Light ministers from the colony's Scots-Irish interior. Gilbert Tennent testified, giving evidence that Hemphill had lied about his beliefs. In response, Franklin and Hemphill denounced the trial as a mockery or even worse, comparing it to "that hellish tribunal, the Spanish Inquisition." It was a fatuous remark, since the trial was nothing of the sort; because the Presbyterian Church had no prisons, no instruments of torture, and no status in law, and no means of redress other than those its members had freely given to their ministers.

The worst they could do was bar Hemphill from the pulpit. At this early stage of their history in America the Presbyterian clergy had no political clout, and their resources were slender. Among the most forceful critics of Hemphill was another Harvard man, somebody Franklin knew from Boston: Ebenezer Pemberton Jr., son of the late, methodical pastor at the Old South whose sermons he had heard as a boy. In New York, Pemberton Jr. eked out a meager living tending to a flock with fewer than a hundred members. If in the Hemphill affair anyone played the role of the brave underdog, it was Pemberton, who might risk the loss of his career by standing up against Franklin and his rich friends in politics: especially because, with the Zenger trial still under way, Andrew Hamilton was a hero in Manhattan.[13]

If anyone acted the part of the bully, it was Benjamin Franklin. In

May he fell ill, spending six or seven weeks fighting a severe attack of pleurisy. Before the trial began, the *Gazette* had taken Hemphill's side, printing a dialogue—almost certainly by Franklin—defending his views about the Christian faith. The prose was bright and witty; but once the trial was over, and when Franklin had risen from his sickbed, the sense of humor vanished and the Hemphillites began to savage their opponents. "I became his zealous partisan," Franklin recalled in his autobiography.

Between July and October 1735 he printed three tracts in defense of Mr. Hemphill, co-written by himself and by the preacher. By this time Andrew Hamilton had swept all before him in the courtroom, winning the Zenger case in August, a victory that also won him the freedom of New York and a salute of cannons. Now that Hamilton had reached the summit of his power and influence, his friend the young Franklin could write and publish more or less what he pleased; and indeed, with each pamphlet that appeared, his rhetoric on Hemphill's behalf became more coarse and more insulting. It reached its unpleasant climax at the end of October with a diatribe that dealt in misogyny and libel, sneering at Jedediah Andrews and his friends.

" 'Tis well known," said the pamphleteer, that "all the silly women of the congregation were . . . zealous abettors of Mr Andrews, who crept into their houses, and led them away captive to the Commission to say and swear whatever he had prepared for them." Earlier in the controversy, Franklin and Hemphill had already sneered at Andrews as a weak old man, filled with envy of his younger rival.[14]

The ministers refused to give in. Instead the Presbyterians fought back, with pamphlets of their own showing precisely how Franklin's friend had broken the rules of the faith. They pointed out that if anybody was a hypocrite, it was Hemphill. Not once but twice, first in Ireland and then in America, he had signed up to a statement of orthodox Calvinist belief, the Westminster Confession, dating from the 1640s, and having done so, he chose to disparage the creed it contained. And then, in January, the ministers fired their heaviest artillery and with it they blew Mr. Hemphill out of the Delaware. During the proceedings, he had been oddly reluctant to share his sermon notes. It had been rumored that he was a plagiarist, and now his guilt was proven. A pamphlet appeared in Philadelphia, printed by Andrew Bradford, who must have relished the opportunity to make Franklin look silly. Authored by one "Obadiah Jenkins," a nom de plume for Pemberton Jr., the pamphlet revealed that Hemphill had lifted his homilies, almost verbatim, from sermons published long ago in London, written by preachers who denied the sacred doctrine of the Holy Trinity.[15]

The game was up and Samuel Hemphill vanished forever. It does not seem that he possessed much of a vocation as a pastor because, try as one might, it has proved impossible to find his name in any document, ecclesiastical or otherwise, dated after 1736. One suspects that he sailed back to northern Ireland, where the records are often sparse, but there were Hemphills owning land near Londonderry.

As Franklin admits in his autobiography, he emerged from the Hemphill affair in a state of deep embarrassment. Among Hemphill's friends, the proof of plagiarism had caused "disgust," he writes; and indeed the affair came to represent one of the defining moments of Franklin's life. At this point, Franklin ceased to attend the Presbyterian Church. Although from time to time he went to Christ Church with Deborah—who was doubtless thanking goodness that she was an Episcopalian—he avoided any other kind of organized religion.

Never again would Franklin take sides in a public dispute about the details of theology. It was a minefield best left unexplored. As the years went by, he would often find himself at odds with the Presbyterian clergy in Pennsylvania, but for political reasons, not for the sake of differing notions about God or the nature of redemption. The Hemphill affair also taught him something about the place of religion in American life.

Prior to 1735, Franklin had never shown much patience with evangelical faith, grounded in the Bible, and indeed he behaved as if it were something that would one day disappear, probably in the not-too-distant future, as the ideas of Tillotson or the Freemasons steadily won over hearts and minds. As the Great Awakening unfolded, with the Hemphill affair as a curtain-raiser, Franklin began to see that this was most unlikely to occur. In America there would always be evangelical Christians, there would be revivals, and there would also be sectional differences, social, political, and economic, that would generate conflicts that took on a religious form as the pulpit, the pews, and the seminary became a theater of controversy. That was just the way America was. You could no more argue Bible Christianity away—or any other religion, come to that—than you could stop the Delaware River flowing down from the hills.

As Franklin approached the age of thirty, the Hemphill affair also began to free him from English models. Very far from entirely, of course: Franklin *always* loved London, and the values for which the best thinkers in London stood, whatever they might be, even when after the Boston Tea Party the English stopped liking him. But in the wake of the Hemphill affair a subtle change occurred in his thinking.

Time and again in his early life, Franklin had a modus operandi that came down to this: read London writers—or better still, sail away to the metropolis, as he did—and then apply their style and their ideas to the life of the colonies. Up to a point, this made sense; but not indefinitely. Sooner or later, Franklin had to cease to think that England—the country of Addison, Pope, and Tillotson—could be the measure of all things in America as well.

For his nourishment by way of ideas, Franklin had to look to other places too. France would have been the best choice; but as it happened he began with Glasgow. However plagiaristic Hemphill had been, the opinions he expressed mostly had their roots in Scotland. And so Franklin began to turn his gaze in that direction. By the 1730s, among the liberal Presbyterians the most influential thinker was Francis Hutcheson, professor of moral philosophy at Glasgow University, where Hemphill had studied. His ideas were similar to Hemphill's, and they came to be Franklin's as well. "The ingenious Mr Hutcheson"—as Franklin described him in 1749—served as one of the inspirations for the college that Franklin created in the town, which later developed into the University of Pennsylvania. With its wide and diverse curriculum, and its emphasis on the sciences as well as the arts, it would look very much like a Scottish university.[16]

After the Hemphill affair, Franklin also ceased to rely entirely on the London Whigs whose work he had been reading since his teens. In the pamphlets Franklin wrote with Hemphill, he had been influenced by the authors of *Cato's Letters,* when they attacked the bishops of the Church of England. And this did not really make sense. When the radical Whigs took on the Anglican Church, they were up against an immensely powerful organization protected by law and built into the fabric of English society. In the Quaker colony, nothing of the sort existed. And so the points the Whig writers made were largely irrelevant in Pennsylvania. Other issues were far more germane: paper money, the frontier, the best way to coexist with Maryland, Virginia, and New York, the odd situation with the Penn family, and of course the economy. Whigs in London, radical or Walpolean, had little to say about any of this. Above all—as Franklin was gradually coming to see—America had to build an infrastructure of ingenuity, so that the colonies could grow swiftly and sustainably.[17]

This was a subject to which Franklin would become devoted. Although Franklin never ceased to be a Whig, in his thirties and his early forties he did not feel obliged to make their obsessions with tyranny and so forth the center of his life: because, in this period so very long before the Stamp Act and the Boston Tea Party, for a white male in America from Franklin's social stratum there was rarely any tyranny to oppose. Science became a more fascinating subject, and it set his agenda in the next decade. In the meantime, Franklin endured something far worse than the embarrassment of the Hemphill affair. In 1736, he and Deborah suffered a true calamity, which came about by way of the scourge of the era: another epidemic of smallpox.

DEATH AND THE ASSEMBLY

It was a year of hard work and modest prosperity. *Poor Richard's Almanack* was making headway, its sales creeping up to overtake those of its rivals. The Franklin store was busy too. As well as books and newspapers, Deborah began to sell groceries, cloth, and haberdashery, while her husband toiled away in the workshop, regular as ever. At about this time, to feed his printing press Franklin was reaching out to new contacts, Dutch and German papermakers who had built their paper mills with water power on Wissahickon Creek to the northwest of Philadelphia.

A colonial printer might require at least 1,500 sheets each week, the paper had to be made with rags, and so—starting in 1734—Franklin had begun to run little notices in the *Gazette:* "Ready money for old rags may be had of the printer hereof." He and Deborah would collect the rags, two tons or more per annum, and ship them to the mill. At last, they no longer had to rely on paper imported expensively from England and bought through merchants such as William Allen.[18]

Like the ironworks at Durham and elsewhere, the paper mills were part of the beginnings of industry in Pennsylvania, and in 1736 their output was starting to soar as the colony grew wealthier. Besides the *Gazette* and the *Almanack*, Franklin printed at least eight books that year, including a German hymnbook and a long speech by James Logan. As time went by, Franklin and the sage of Stenton grew ever closer, bound together by mutual respect and by their shared commitment to the colony's expansion.

The previous December, Franklin had printed Mr. Logan's new translation of some Latin poetry, intended for schoolchildren. In April he sent a box of copies up to his sister-in-law, the widow Anne in Rhode Island, to be sold among the well-heeled citizens of Newport. And that same month, we find the first evidence that at last the Franklins could afford a little luxury. In their accounts, Deborah recorded the spending of five shillings on new shoes "for the maid."[19]

Until then their lives had been hard and austere, their table "plain and simple," as Franklin later recalled. In the *Gazette* he would advertise sales of tea, but he and Deborah could not afford to drink it themselves. It was too rare and too precious. But in the 1730s the British were ramping up their imports from China, bringing down the price of tea and making the leaves affordable to ordinary people. One morning at about this time, Franklin came down to breakfast to find something new. On the table he saw some china crockery—a little bowl—and a silver spoon: items of the kind that today we come across in small museums in colonial towns that have somehow escaped the juggernaut of progress.

For Deborah Franklin, these fragile articles, a spoon and a bowl, were deeply significant. She had to have a maid, but in her life she also needed some beauty. Coming as she did from Birmingham in England, that town so dynamic, she knew—the letters she received must have told her so—that her kin across the ocean possessed delightful objects such as these. So did other people in her street in Philadelphia. And so Deborah wanted to have the same lovely things, to remind her of her mother's country.

In his memoirs Franklin gives us his account of her desires. "She thought her husband deserved a silver spoon and china bowl as well as any of his neighbors," he says. Which may well be true; but Deborah also had a life of her own. Stranded in America, so far from her family, she needed to know that the hard work was worthwhile. Would her life ever be as satisfying as the one she might have had in England? The crockery and the spoon were a sign that one day the drudgery might turn out for the best, for her and for her son. Deborah could never join the Junto or the masons, which were only for men. Of an evening, when they met to ruminate about the secrets of the cosmos, she would have to stay at home, with at her side another small item as flimsy as a bowl of porcelain. Little Franky was only three years old: a dangerous age, all too exposed to the hazards of infection.

During the course of 1736, Deborah's husband went from strength to strength. Fortified by the Junto and by his alliance with Logan and with Hamilton, Franklin could not fail to be successful. In October the politicians had to appoint a new official to record their decisions. Once

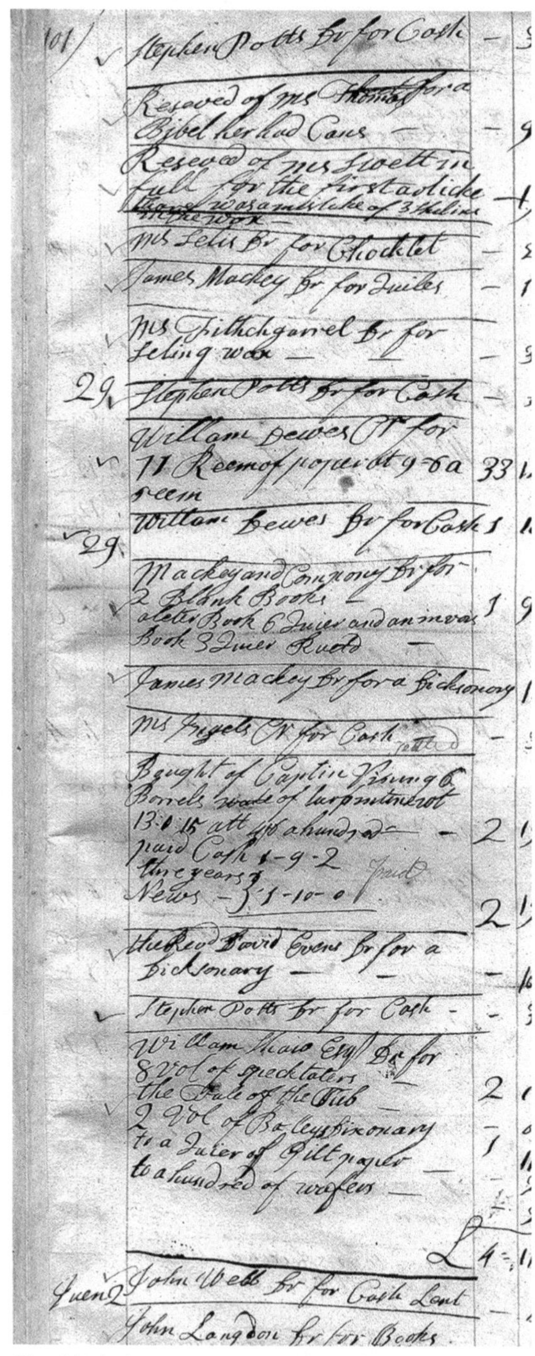

Stephen Potts Dr for Cash
Reseved of mrs Thomas for a Bibel her had Cans
Reseved of mrs Scott in full for the first adlicke [illegible]
mrs Lelis Dr for Chocklet
James Mackey Dr for Quiles
mrs Fithchgarrel Dr for seling wax
29 Stephen Potts Dr for Cash
Willam Dewes Cr for 11 Reem of poper at 9-6 a reem
Willam Dewes Dr for Cash
29 Mackey and Compony Dr for 2 Blank Books a letter Book 6 Quier and an invoas Book 3 Quier Ruled
James Mackey Dr for a Dicksonary
mrs [illegible] Cr for Cash
Bought of Captin [illegible] 6 Borrels [illegible] 13:0:15 att [illegible] a hundred paid Cash 1-9-2 three years News — 1-10-0
the Revd David Evens Dr for a Dicksonary
Stephen Potts Dr for Cash
William Shaw Esq Dr for 8 Vol of specktaters the Tale of the Tub 2 Vol of Baleys Dixonary to a Quier of Gilt paper to a hundred of wafers
£ 4
June 2 John Webb Dr for Cash Lent
John Langdon Dr for Books

A page from Franklin's shop accounts, May 29, 1738, in Deborah's handwriting with examples of her spelling—"chocklet" and "seling wax." The number of entries shows how busy the Franklins were. Also interesting are the books the customers bought, including Addison's *Spectator* and the *Historical and Critical Dictionary* by the French skeptic Pierre Bayle.

again, Andrew Hamilton was the Speaker; and so their choice fell upon his protégé. At a stipend of six shillings a day, Franklin became the clerk of the Pennsylania assembly. It was a post he would hold for fifteen years, until his son William took over in 1751.

In the meanwhile his other child was suffering. From the meager details that Franklin provides, all we know is that Franky was delicate. He suffered from "a flux," meaning some kind of gastric complaint that led to diarrhea. Because of that, his parents deferred the day when he should be inoculated. Two weeks after Franklin was made the assembly clerk, Franky celebrated his fourth birthday. A month after that, on November 21, the boy died of smallpox. They buried him in the graveyard at Christ Church, with above him a stone with the words: "The delight of all who knew him." Nearly forty years later, in a letter he wrote to his sister Jane Mecom, Franklin said that in all his life it was Franky "whom I have seldom since equalled in everything, and whom to this day I cannot think of without a sigh."

A few weeks after Franky's death, some unpleasant people went about saying that it was all his father's fault, for having him inoculated and thus giving him the disease. Which was the reverse of the case. In the last issue of the *Gazette* for 1736, Franklin printed a dignified rebuttal urging every couple to have their children vaccinated. His feelings as he wrote the piece can only be imagined. At a time when painting in America was in its own infancy, and they had little money, he and Deborah commissioned a portrait of their son, made after death, but as lifelike as the image could be done. Dressed up in red, against a green background of trees and hills, with his father's wide forehead and with his left arm flung out to his side in a gesture of happiness, little Franky can be seen: a child gone forever.[20]

Never again would Deborah bear a son. Seven years later she gave birth to a daughter, but the period in between must have been full of sadness. She kept on going to Christ Church while at this period it was being rebuilt to become what it remains today, with its tall east window, a peaceful place filled with sunlight. For her husband, the rest of the 1730s were also quiet years, with less by way of feuds or acrimony.

Every so often, he would have a burst of wildness—he was still young—and it would find an outlet by way of his pen. Seven weeks after Franky died, Franklin wrote one of his funniest columns for the *Gazette*. In *The Drinker's Dictionary,* he gives us a long alphabet of intoxication. He lists all the words he knew for drunkenness, running into hundreds, from "addled" to "wet" by way of boozy, fuzzled, hammered, oiled, pungey, stewed, and soaked, and perhaps the best of the lot: "he's had a thump over the head with Samson's jawbone." In modern England many of the terms on the list are still current with the same meaning, serving as a reminder that Franklin knew London, and he knew the waterfront, and he never wanted to lose touch with the way the sailors spoke. Or it might be that for a while after Franky's death he took more solace from alcohol than he cared to admit in his memoirs.[21]

Which would be understandable. Briefly he also came to be caught up in a dismal affair, a prank that went terribly wrong, when some scallywags in Philadelphia played a cruel trick on a young apprentice, Daniel Rees. The boy hoped to become a Freemason. And so in the spring of 1737 the comedians pretended to give him the oath of membership, embroidered with obscenities. They showed the oath to Franklin, who thought it was hilarious. But the joke turned sour when they tried to make Rees undergo a fake ceremony of initiation. Carried out in a dark cellar, it involved a flaming bowl of brandy, and two days later Daniel Rees died of his burns.

While all this was going on, Franklin was still at war with the wily Andrew Bradford. The Rees affair became a cause célèbre that the latter could exploit to Franklin's detriment. When the case came to trial early in 1738, with Franklin as a witness for the prosecution, the *Mercury* made out that although Franklin had never set foot in the cellar, he had been something close to an accessory to murder. These were "false and malicious insinuations," Franklin wrote: but in the *Gazette* he had to print a long statement of self-defense.[22]

When news of all this arrived in Boston, his parents were appalled, and especially his mother. And so once again he had to try to mend a breach with Josiah and Abiah, composing a letter of apology. Their letter to him has not survived, but from what Franklin wrote it is painfully clear that Abiah was aghast at what she heard about the freethinking ways of Freemasonry. Benjamin assured her that they were "a very harmless sort of people," but he did not pretend to be orthodox himself.[23]

"I think vital religion has always suffered," he wrote, "when orthodoxy is more regarded than virtue. And the scripture assures me that at the last day, we shall not be examined what we thought, but what we did; and our recommendation will not be that we said, Lord, Lord, but that we did good to our fellow creatures." To reinforce his case he cited the Gospel according to Matthew, but he might also have mentioned his role in a new project. Two weeks after Franky died, he had helped to create the Union Fire Company, a body of people pledged to douse any blaze that broke out on Market Street. Like the Junto, the Library Company, and the masons, it was virtue in action, a civic entity that would endure.

And so would Franklin and Deborah. In the autumn of 1737, while the Rees affair was still in the news, at last his rival Andrew Bradford lost control of the town's post office. Bradford had fallen out with America's postmaster general, Governor Spotswood, long ago the ally of Sir William Keith. Every six months Spotswood had to file reports with his masters in London and send over the cash that was owing to King George. But Bradford was slow about accounting; and so Spotswood fired him and handed the role to Franklin. Here was another coup, bringing with it a new stream of income at a time when Pennsylvania was expanding yet again, by way of a push deep into the interior.

Franklin began his career as postmaster on October 5. Just two weeks earlier his patrons and friends Logan, Hamilton, and Allen had achieved their ambition: the seizure of the Forks of the Delaware. Reviving an ancient title deed, dating back to the 1680s, they claimed that William Penn had acquired from the Lenape people an area to the north of the ironworks at Durham. In the document, it was defined by the distance a man could walk in a day and a half. At Stenton in August they met the leaders of the Lenape and insisted that the walk should take place without delay.

Knowing that Logan had built a firm alliance with the Iroquois, who far outnumbered them, the Lenape had little choice but to agree. The walk began on September 19; Edward Marshall, a frontier settler and athlete, kept on going for nearly seventy miles; and by the evening of the 20th he had encompassed a tract of land that amounted to more than 700,000 acres. The Junto member William Parsons had been the surveyor who supplied him with a map. At once the Penn family took possession and began to sell the land, with the largest piece going to William Allen, who created a new settlement which he called Allentown.

Not a word appeared in *The Pennsylvania Gazette* about the Walking Purchase, as the incident came to be known. We cannot say what Franklin thought about it, but here was the shadowy side of the projects for virtue and improvement of which he and the Junto were so fond. It was an act of fraud, and among the Lenape it left the bitterest of memories. Nineteen years later they took their revenge. In 1756 they raided Marshall's homestead in New Jersey, where they murdered and scalped his wife, his daughter, and his son.

Chapter Sixteen

War and Mr. Whitefield

For Franklin there had to come a moment when the quiet years after Franky's death drew to a close, to be replaced by a new era of uncertainty. It arrived in the fall of 1739, when Andrew Hamilton stepped down as speaker of the assembly. As he slid away into retirement, so a changing of the guard began, and Franklin's allies in the Triumvirate began to lose their grip on the province. A new speaker emerged, John Kinsey, leading an alliance of Quakers and Germans that won a sweeping victory at the election in October. For the next decade, Mr. Kinsey—a master of the hustings—occupied the chair of the assembly.

Although Franklin kept his post as the assembly clerk, they were never close. He and Kinsey had nothing in common. The new speaker was not a Freemason, and his name rarely appears in Franklin's shop accounts. He took no interest in the Library Company or Franklin's other civic good deeds. Heavy drinking, lavish parties, and corruption were more in Mr. Kinsey's line. He was a pacifist, a Quaker, a broker of deals but also a hypocrite. When he died of a stroke in 1750, it was revealed that while Kinsey was chief justice of Pennsylvania he had stolen vast sums of public money.[1]

With Hamilton gone and Kinsey in the ascendant, Franklin had to pick his away across a less familiar landscape, still with many friends but without the Triumvirate behind him. His business faced new challenges as well. For years he had been sailing steadily forward with a wind of economic growth behind him, but at last the economy began to falter. As 1739 began, he and Deborah had felt bold enough to move house, four doors down Market Street, to a larger property rented from his

Junto friend Robert Grace. In February, they fell victim to a thief, "a tall, thin Irishman," and the list of stolen goods that Franklin printed in the *Gazette* showed that their days of austerity were over. The list included a coat lined with silk, four fine sheets, a ruffled shirt, new shoes, and a new beaver hat. But as the year drew to a close, the horizon grew darker amid rumors of a shooting war in the West Indies.

After so many false alarms, this time the stories were true. On October 23, George II declared war on Spain, a move that spelled the beginning of the end of the *Pax Walpoleana* that had endured since Franklin's boyhood. For many years, the Spanish from Cuba had been seizing British ships for trading illegally with Mexico and Panama, testing to the full Sir Robert's powers of diplomacy. At last a moment came when Walpole could do no more. In London his opponents were eager to fight, and the press was howling for blood. The War of Jenkins' Ear began, taking its name from an English skipper part of whose ear had been sliced off by a coast guard from Havana.[2]

Although the king's proclamation would not reach Philadelphia until the spring of 1740, the effects had already been felt months before. "Trading is dead," wrote a Quaker merchant, as he saw the return of what he called "troublesome times," the worst since the South Sea Bubble and its aftermath. Business fell away and money grew scarce again, as Spanish privateers took to sea. For the Franklins this must have been a worrying time, because they had been among the beneficiaries of peace, immigration, and transatlantic trade. As the reading public grew by leaps and bounds, so had Franklin's sales and his advertising revenue, as he ran items posted by sea captains, ironmasters, and the purveyors of slaves.[3]

Would the Franklins be sabotaged by the war and the slump it might cause? So long as the Spanish were Britain's only enemy, and the fighting was confined to the Caribbean, the military threat to Pennsylvania was only indirect. Ships would be lost, but galleons of Spain were unlikely to come sailing up the Delaware. However, anyone who followed European politics—and Franklin most certainly did—would know of the *pacte de famille*, the alliance between the French and Spanish branches of the Bourbon dynasty.*

If the Bourbon pact were invoked by the Spanish, then the War of Jenkins' Ear might escalate into something more alarming. All that was

* *The Pennsylvania Gazette* often devoted much of its front page to diplomatic news from Europe.

required was a crisis in Europe, and by the early 1740s such a crisis was imminent. The fate of Austria held the key to international politics. The Habsburgs in Vienna were Britain's closest allies; but they had long-standing differences with Madrid and Paris. Until now, with Walpole as prime minister, the British and the French had watched each other warily but still kept the peace. If a point of crisis arrived, and worst of all if Austria came under attack, then a general war in Europe would be the result, pitting the British and the Austrians against the might of France as well as Spain.[4]

And if that were to happen, the people of the Quaker province would find themselves close to the front line. For many years, James Logan had been warning that one day this was bound to occur. The French up in Canada, with their allies among the Indian tribes: he had always viewed them as a looming threat. Hence the effort he devoted to strategies intended to protect the frontier.

For those with eyes as sharp as Logan's, the winter of 1739 and 1740 marked a turning point in the history of America. For Benjamin Franklin, the next ten years would present fresh challenges but also new opportunities, as he came to share not only Logan's anxieties about colonial security, but also his preoccupation with biology and physics. In time, Franklin would make contact with like-minded people in New York, equally worried about a French advance down the Hudson valley but also devoted to science. These fertile interactions, between New York and Philadelphia, but with input from London as well, would eventually lead to Franklin's work with electricity.

At the end of 1739 his work with sparks and batteries still lay a long time in the future. For now he had more pressing matters on his mind. Late at night on November 2, as the Royal Navy were on their way to war, Philadelphia welcomed a new arrival. Dressed in clerical black, he was a young evangelist from England. In time he became the finest exhibit in Franklin's museum of eccentric human nature.

Waking Up America

Into the town rode an Anglican minister, George Whitefield, weary from sixty miles in the saddle. After sailing into the Delaware a few days earlier, he was about to begin a preaching tour of the colonies. In the space of the next fifteen months, Whitefield took the Great Awakening, which until that time had been a sporadic affair of Christian revivals in little towns connected only by the letters that passed between the clergymen involved, and turned it into a national movement. In doing so he stamped his mark on North America. Quite how deep and lasting that impression would turn out to be is a question that historians still debate. But we can be sure of this: Whitefield had a powerful effect on Franklin. For one thing, the preacher helped him achieve perhaps the greatest commercial success of his career.

Whitefield was twenty-four, slender but extremely fit. He had piercing blue eyes, one with a squint left behind by measles in his childhood; and as he called on sinners to repent and come to Jesus, those eyes would often overflow with tears. He looked so young that Londoners called him "the boy parson." Youthful he might be, but Whitefield, cofounder of the Methodists, was perhaps the finest English preacher of the eighteenth century, vying for that title with John Wesley: his friend, his rival, and in time his adversary.[5]

You might love or hate George Whitefield, and indeed he divided Franklin's circle of friends, some of whom loathed the preacher as a charlatan. What you could not do was ignore the young man or the questions he posed so vehemently. "The churches will not contain the multitudes that throng to hear him," wrote Wesley's brother Charles, during Whitefield's first preaching campaign in London. There he made his name as a superb fund-raiser, bringing in money for charity schools in England and for missions and later an orphanage in the new colony in Georgia. In his school days in a cathedral city where his parents ran a coaching inn, Whitefield had adored the theater. His preaching style was always dramatic, as though he were performing a soliloquy from *Hamlet*. In later life the strain of doing so became so severe that after he preached he would vomit uncontrollably.[6]

His listeners were just as passionate. As he wept, so would they, and then they would faint, tremble and fall, and at last proclaim that he had rescued them from Satan. Despite his success—or rather because of it—Whitefield also made a host of enemies. They included the Bishop of London, who wrote a pastoral letter in the summer of 1739 telling his flock that the young man was deluded. Barred from the pulpits of the city, Whitefield took to the open air, holding prayer meetings in the fields and drawing in vast crowds of artisans, milliners, and merchants.[7]

As he strove to break down what he called "the partition wall of bigotry," Whitefield tried to go everywhere to preach. His brother was a sea captain, a privateer who captured at least one Spanish ship, and

An English print from 1739 mocking the preacher George Whitefield. Titled *Enthusiasm Displayed*, it portrays him at an outdoor meeting in London surrounded by admiring female figures labeled Hypocrisy, Deceit, and Folly.

he helped organize the expedition to America. There Whitefield styled himself "an amphibious itinerant," as he hurried up and down the coast, on horseback or by boat, from Savannah to New Hampshire and back. Venturing deep inland as well, he met Quakers, Germans, Matherites, and merchants, and also the African slaves.[8]

On the face of it, he and Franklin had nothing in common. Eventually, they became personal friends, but only in 1745, when Whitefield was toning down his rhetoric. To begin with, their relationship was cordial but no more, as Franklin trod carefully in dealing with a man whose views about religion were the opposite of his. Like a frigate arriving fully armed for war, Whitefield made himself the ally of the Calvinists, with among them the Tennents, who had been so hostile to Franklin during the Hemphill affair.

For Whitefield, like the Tennents, to be a Christian meant to undergo rebirth in the Spirit. This could only come about when a sinner admitted his or her depravity. And so he found his closest soul mates among the Presbyterian Scots-Irish, who shared the same beliefs, a creed that Franklin rejected entirely. Gilbert Tennent led Whitefield out toward the frontier and then up through New Jersey to New York. There he was given a hero's welcome by Mr. Pemberton Jr., who four years earlier had helped to end Hemphill's career. And so, at least in theory, Franklin should have kept his distance from the young evangelist.

However, by this time Franklin was nearly thirty-four. He had learned from past mistakes, including those he made in the Hemphill case. Cautiously, Franklin the journalist took his time to express an editorial opinion about the preacher. Long before Whitefield set foot in Philadelphia, the colonial press had been following his activities, picking up stories from London. *The Pennsylvania Gazette* had been among the papers that did so. As yet, however, Americans could not be sure what Whitefield meant to do when he came among them. And so in the early weeks of Whitefield's mission, the *Gazette* kept its coverage to a minimum, allowing Andrew Bradford and the *Mercury* to make the running with the story.[9]

At first it seemed that Whitefield meant to shun controversy. At Christ Church the Anglican minister, Archibald Cummings, greeted him politely; so did the colony's co-proprietor, Thomas Penn; and everything was light and sweetness. Five days into his visit, Whitefield preached from the steps of the courthouse to a crowd he estimated at six thousand. While his figures are open to doubt—if we add up the numbers he gave for his audience on each occasion when he spoke in Philadelphia, they come to many times the town's population—there can be no doubt that people flocked to hear Whitefield as eagerly as they had done in England.

"The multitudes of all sects and denominations that attended his sermons were enormous," Franklin recalled. At first he stood among the throng rather skeptically, but soon he could see that Whitefield was extraordinary. The preacher's delivery, for one thing: it was so loud and so clear that it carried for nearly two blocks down Market Street. Franklin measured the distance by pacing backward toward the waterfront, listening as he went. As the years went by and Franklin heard Whitefield speak many times, he came to admire the way the preacher kept on polishing his sermons, until "every accent, every emphasis, every modulation was . . . perfectly well turn'd and well plac'd."

His skill at extracting money from his audience: that was remarkable too. On one occasion when Franklin had a pocket full of gold and silver coins, none of which he meant to donate, he found Whitefield's oratory so compelling that he left them all in the plate for the orphanage in Georgia. One other thing struck Franklin very forcibly: that when Whitefield told his listeners that they were wicked sinners—"half beasts and half devils"—the crowd only loved him all the more.

To the Franklin of the 1720s, a skeptic and for a while an atheist, this would have seemed absurd. But now that he was in his early middle age, Franklin had come to recognize that there were more things in heaven and earth than were dreamed of in his earlier philosophy. At one time, it had seemed to Franklin that the colonies were evolving into a thoroughly secular society: that is what he must have thought, to make him behave as he did during the Hemphill affair. Now it was clear that he had been mistaken. Time and again, as the centuries went by, Christian revivals would take place in America, with profound implications for politics as well as for religion. Why this should be so is a question too deep for a Franklin biographer to fathom. The relevant point is this. In the face of the excitement that Whitefield aroused, Franklin had to recognize that in his America, evangelical faith was a permanent feature of the landscape. Like it or not, Franklin would have to come to terms with it.

How should he react to Whitefield? In the *Gazette,* Franklin began by maintaining a strict neutrality. In the early weeks he did not flatter Whitefield with glowing accounts of his adventures. Nor did he seek to slander the man by reprinting the fiercest attacks on Methodism from the London press. Instead, as the Delaware froze over and the town fell quiet for the winter, Franklin simply tried to make some money from the Calvinist revival. He did so with the help of Whitefield's friend and business manager, William Seward.[10]

In London, Seward had made a small fortune working for the South Sea Company and dealing in bonds and commodities. The rest of the time he also raised funds for the charity schools. Converted to the cause of Methodism, Seward became a literary agent, arranging the publication of Mr. Whitefield's journals of his travels. In England the *Journals* had sold very well, and so it made sense to look for an American edition. Soon after their arrival in Philadelphia, Seward met both printers in the town, but Franklin came up with the better offer. In November they signed the contract: seven volumes already published in London, and also the ones that Whitefield would write in the colonies.

The timing was perfect. So was the product. At this time of year, with work just finished on the new issue of *Poor Richard,* Franklin always had some spare capacity. And by now—thanks to the almanacs—he had created a network of agents through which he could push the *Journals* out to the largest audience. Being so religious, Boston was likely to take the lion's share; but Franklin also had his sister-in-law in Rhode Island, the Timothys down in Charleston, and keepers of country stores all the way up the Delaware, in southern New Jersey, and in Maryland. In New York, he could rely for distribution on Hamilton's friend, Mr. Zenger. In fact he could probably sell as many books as he could print.

Having worked in London in a printing factory, Franklin had the skills to handle a very long run of a book meant to be a best-seller. In 1726, when he was employed by John Watts, Franklin had been part of a team who dealt in mass production. In the Watts workshop, the most lucrative moneymaker had been the pocket editions, done in the small format of duodecimo, to be sold at attractive prices to a wide market eager to read the finest writers of the age. For the Whitefield *Journals*, Franklin would use the same format in a way that had not been viable in America before.

At last the reading public had reached the necessary size, and—thanks to Mr. Whitefield—Franklin had a series of books that might be as popular as those of Defoe or Addison. The preacher was causing a sensation, and his books were bound to sell. The little volumes, only five inches tall, were advertised in the *Gazette* in November. Within days, Franklin took advance orders for two hundred sets. The readers would not be disappointed.

George Whitefield had a flair for writing. Breaking new ground in literature, his *Journals* were a hybrid of autobiography, travelogue, and Christian piety. Composed in plain but sprightly English, they also supplied some barbed social commentary from a young man willing to be controversial. Often they read like a novel. That was another secret of Whitefield's success: his readers were keen to have new forms of narrative. In London, Samuel Richardson was writing his best-seller, *Pamela*, to appear in the fall of 1740. James Ralph's old friend Henry Fielding was soon to follow suit with *Joseph Andrews*. These were novels that Franklin would come to know and love, dealing as they did with themes akin to those of his memoirs. In Whitefield's *Journals*, he would find something similar: a picaresque account of a young man's adventures, the only things absent being erotica and violence. At this early stage, although later he changed his mind, Whitefield opposed the War of Jenkins' Ear.

That winter Bradford filled the *Mercury* with coverage of the Awakening. Some of it was excellent. For example, in December the *Mercury* printed something new, a personal profile of the preacher, of the sort that every journalist has to write today; in the eighteenth century so far, such a thing was very rare. As Whitefield began to make enemies, especially in Boston, where the Puritan clergy—Harvard people—saw him as a dangerous man, who divided families and congregations, so Bradford kept his readers fully informed. In the meantime Franklin kept on churning out the books. They would turn a far better profit than a few extra copies sold of the *Mercury*.[11]

At last, by the end of May, the *Journals* were ready for their readers. Nothing like this had been seen in America hitherto. Off they went from Market Street, the boxes of books, up and down the coast and deep into the hinterland. But not before Mr. Whitefield had given rise to some unpleasantness. After his trip to Manhattan, the preacher had traveled to the Carolinas and to Savannah. In rice and tobacco country, he saw the slave economy up close. Whitefield was horrified. In time his views about Africans would prove to be as ambivalent as his feelings about the military. But to begin with, the preacher was ready to be outspoken: not only about slavery, but also about his superiors in England.

A Rash Young Man

In April 1740, Whitefield came hurtling back from Charleston, entering Philadelphia with Seward on the evening of Monday the 14th. Earlier that day, the citizens had heard the royal proclamation: the British and their colonies were now at war with Spain. "The people express'd their joy in loud huzzas," wrote the *Gazette*, in a gleeful item welcoming the chance to loot the Spanish towns in the Caribbean. As Whitefield arrived the liquor was still flowing, and a bonfire was burning on the highest spot in the city. The following morning, while Whitefield prepared to preach again, he ran into Mr. Cummings. Never again would he be welcome in the pulpit at Christ Church. The rector told him that quite plainly.[12]

Along with the news of war, there had come stories from London making it clear that Whitefield was finished as an Episcopalian. Before he left for America, he had formed an alliance in Scotland with rigorous men from the Old Light wing of the Presbyterian community. The closer he drew to Calvinists such as these, the more distant he became from most of his colleagues in the Anglican Church. In 1739, as he fought back against Bishop Gibson, he had scandalized his brethren by insulting the memory of Archbishop Tillotson, saying that the grand old latitude man knew "no more of Christianity than Mohammed." He repeated the charge in an open letter published in South Carolina.

While Whitefield was on his way north, Franklin printed the same letter in the *Gazette*. Mr. Cummings was furious; and all the more so because, he told the preacher, the press were refusing to carry items putting the case for authority and tradition. It was said that Mr. Seward had both printers in his wealthy pocket. That afternoon Whitefield found a balcony from which to speak. Again he denounced John Tillotson, his creed of good works, and his liberal species of Christianity. The prelate was worse than a deist, said Mr. Whitefield. He likened the late archbishop to "Goliath of the Philistines," and cast himself in the role of David.

Two days later, the *Gazette* came out again and Franklin tossed gunpowder on the flames. While Whitefield hurried to and fro, preaching six times in three days, the *Gazette* ran another of his open letters: this time a polemic against slavery, addressed to the planters of the South. Just seven months earlier, there had been a slave revolt near Charleston. The Stono Rebellion had ended in a massacre of the rebels, their heads cut off and mounted on the mile posts by the highway. As he rode by, Whitefield must have seen the skulls; and in his letter he makes it clear that he knew all about the insurrection and its aftermath.[13]

"God has a quarrel with you," he told the planters, "for your cruelty to the poor Negroes." He listed the sins of the white man—"cruel task masters"—and against them he invoked the retribution of Jehovah. To Africans and whites alike, he vowed to preach the Gospel, but the planters were the ones who had most to fear. Smallpox and fever, the threat of murder by the slaves, and now the danger of invasion by the Spanish, such were the vessels of the wrath of God: "and unless you all repent," said Mr. Whitefield, "you must all expect to perish."

In the whole of Franklin's long career, he published no other words as forceful. It cannot be said that in 1740 he agreed with George Whitefield, because for many years to come Franklin continued to advertise the sale of slaves, and he owned slaves himself: at least one in 1745 and at least two in 1750.* He also printed many notices offering rewards for runaways. In Charleston, his partner Lewis Timothy had been just the kind of vicious man Whitefield had condemned; and Franklin knew that this was so. In 1735 Timothy had bought a slave and shaved off his hair as

* Indeed, an item from Franklin's shop accounts suggests that Franklin might have acquired his first slave as early as 1735. An entry from that year, dated December 16, refers to Franklin buying a pair of shoes for a "negro boy." Not until the 1990s, when Professor David Waldstreicher examined the accounts at the American Philosophical Society, did this detail come to the attention of historians.

a punishment. When the young man ran away and was caught, Timothy clapped an iron frame over his head. When the slave escaped again, *The South Carolina Gazette* published the details as part of his description.[14]

Franklin must have read this item. Even so their partnership went on. Not until the early 1750s can we find Franklin voicing doubts about slavery, and even then his qualms were purely economic. The pious words about benevolence spoken at the meetings of the Junto were, to this extent, tarnished with hypocrisy. If Whitefield could see the wickedness of what occurred in the Carolinas, then Franklin should have done so too. Even in Boston in the 1710s, Josiah's friend Judge Sewall had felt deeply unhappy about slavery; and by the end of the 1730s it was already becoming the custom in Pennsylvania for principled Quakers to liberate their slaves. And yet it is only in 1772 that we come across Franklin opposing slavery on humanitarian grounds. In the 1740s he turned a blind eye to the terrible things that Whitefield saw. Whitefield had been to the South. He came away appalled. Franklin did not go there at all.

During this phase of his career, Franklin had his mind on other things: including making money. The Whitefield story was simply too good to miss. With the boxes of the *Journals* almost ready to be shipped, Franklin felt he could be controversial. On Sunday, April 20, with Whitefield sitting in a pew at Christ Church, where Deborah could be found as well, they heard Mr. Cummings explode with his own tirade.

Outraged by what he read in the *Gazette,* he called the boy parson "a rash young man." At first he had thought George Whitefield was well-meaning; but now Cummings recognized that the preacher was full of "wild, distracted notions," someone who dealt in "rude language" and "low scurrility." It was just the kind of thing that Whitefield wanted to hear: the sort of condemnation he received from the clerical establishment in England. His followers had crowded into Christ Church. Afterward they told him what they thought of Mr. Cummings.[15]

In the weeks that followed, Whitefield circled around again through New Jersey. He preached many times, with Gilbert Tennent at his side, before making another foray to New York and then another tour of rural Pennsylvania. Nobody rode so swiftly, worked so hard, or talked so much. Meanwhile in Philadelphia, his friend Mr. Seward had opened another battlefront against the ungodly. And here at last Franklin found himself in a little difficulty. After having been so cautious during the winter, in the spring he came to be caught up in a quarrel, and one that was more than just another Philadelphia story.

Down south, Mr. Whitefield and William Seward had been shocked by something else besides the treatment of the slaves. Dancing: that was it. Everywhere below Annapolis, the planters and the merchants loved to dance and sing, to play music, or stage amateur theatricals, vices that Whitefield had come to despise. In between epidemics, how else could the planters maintain their morale? Surely it was healthier than merely drinking rum: but not so in the eyes of Mr. Seward and his friend.

By this time Philadelphia had an assembly room, maintained by Robert Bolton, a dancing master. On Tuesday nights he held a ball and concert party, attended by some of the town's most eminent people, men and women who were Franklin's neighbors and clients. It was quite disgraceful, thought William Seward. He decided that the music and the dancing had to stop. Somehow he obtained the key to the ballroom. Although it was April, with the social season near its end, and only one last party left to come, Mr. Seward locked the door.

This was too much to bear. The concert party broke the door down, and for many weeks the strife continued, with Seward and the dancers trading insults on the streets and in the columns of the press. The quarrel became all the harder to resolve when Whitefield converted the Boltons, who renounced their sinful ways. Since Mrs. Bolton and Deborah were friends, the affair was all the more embarrassing for Franklin, who had a foot in both camps.

By now, with the *Journals* soon to appear, he was so close to Whitefield and Seward that he really had to take their part. On the other hand, the concert party included someone he did not wish to offend: Richard Peters, aged about thirty-six, a director of the Library Company, and a trusted servant of the Penns. He was an Anglican clergyman, but it seems that he had a little problem with bigamy; and so, having married a wife too many, Peters left the church to become an official of the province.

Mr. Peters was also one of Franklin's most important customers. He would put in big orders for paper, pens, and books, by the same authors that Franklin admired—Addison, and Shaftesbury, and Tillotson—and most of all he bought parchment for making out official documents. An influential man, Peters was a contact Franklin did not wish to lose, but for a while they came close to a permanent rift. Early in May, Peters was in Franklin's shop with some political friends from the assembly, when in walked William Seward. The two men abhorred each other, and there was a verbal fracas. Peters and his friends "boiled with rage," wrote Seward in his diary. Although nobody threw a punch it seems that this was only narrowly avoided.

Even after Whitefield and Seward left the town—Whitefield for Savannah, and Seward for the mother country—the anger refused to die down, continuing until the end of May. Later that year, Seward met his death in England after being struck on the head by a stone while he was trying to preach. In Philadelphia he left behind a legacy of bitterness, and a new source of controversy between Franklin and his rival, Andrew Bradford, who fought out the concert party quarrel in their publications.

In the *Gazette*, a writer in the guise of "Obadiah Plainman"—who must have been Franklin—took the side of Seward, accusing his opponents of "impertinent babble," who dealt in what he called "the merriest gibberish." Down the street at the *Mercury*, under an equally silly nom de plume, "Tom Truman" pointed the finger at Franklin. By aligning himself with Whitefield, said the *Mercury*, Franklin had shown that he was a hypocrite, "a false fellow of two faces . . . the author of much mischief."[16]

Goodness knows what their readers made of this. Up to a point, these tawdry exchanges were merely another episode in the long feud between the two printers: a vendetta that would only end when Bradford passed away. But trivial though the affair might seem, Franklin's business ties with Seward put his standing in the town in danger. Not only in Philadelphia, but even more so in New England, Whitefield was a man who created enmity, with his extremes of language and his open contempt for anyone—especially the learned—who preferred either a quieter, less intense species of religion, or no religion at all. And that description would apply to most of Franklin's oldest friends and his partners in his civic projects.

Mr. Whitefield's revival failed to excite the members of the Junto. In Franklin's shop accounts, we find that only two of them—Robert Grace, and a carpenter, William Maugridge—signed up in advance for copies of the *Journals*. Did James Logan buy a set? This is most improbable. Neither his name, nor those of Andrew Hamilton or William Allen, appear in the list of subscribers. As for the Library Company, on May 5, at the height of the concert party feud, it held its annual meeting to choose its directors. Franklin's support fell away, and he was nearly voted off the board.

Had he upset his fellow members, by siding with Seward and the preacher? It seems highly likely that he had. In 1746, when the Library Company compiled a catalogue of the books it had bought in the previous five years, it contained not a single item by Whitefield, or indeed by any other preacher from the Great Awakening. While they devoured the works of skeptics, such as Bayle or Voltaire, they never owned a page of Whitefield's *Journals*. In the eyes of the Library Company, always defiantly secular, the Awakening was something to be ignored.

Three centuries on, it serves no useful purpose to take sides in controversies like these. The important thing is this. Far from being trivial, the dance hall affair and the rifts that Whitefield caused were a symptom of a wider malaise, as the Quaker colony became in the 1740s a more polarized, acrimonious society. New sources of conflict had emerged, which a politician like Speaker John Kinsey could mediate but not resolve. The war, the economic downturn, religious strife, bitter and sectarian, and ethnic rivalries as well, not to mention the old, familiar struggle between the town of Philadelphia and the farmers inland, the burden of taxes each one should share, and the rents the Penn family required in return for grants of land: there were so many subjects on which people could disagree.

As newspaper editor and public servant, Franklin was always in the thick of it. At his desk in the assembly, at the Junto, or with the proofs of the *Gazette*, he would hear every rumor, know many secrets, and try to make a profit while also seeking to keep his moral compass. His was not an easy path to tread. And so this period served as another important phase in Franklin's education as a statesman. It was all the more essential for his future because—for the first time in Franklin's life—the hostilities with Spain raised a question that would recur throughout his later career.

How—if at all—should Americans prepare for battle? In the summer of 1740, a few Scottish merchants began to arm a privateer, a sloop called the *George*, to sail out to take the war to the Spanish. The Quakers could not do so, for reasons of belief. With Kinsey at their head they refused to form a militia or to levy taxes for cannons to guard the Delaware. By now the Penns had found a new governor, George Thomas, a planter from Antigua, duty bound to serve the king and also disposed to protect the British West Indies. He called for volunteers, for a regiment to join an expedition against the Spanish bases in Cuba or on the coast of South America.

These volunteers were to be the first American marines. In May, as the dance hall feud dragged on, the *Gazette* and the *Mercury* printed the governor's appeal for men in German and English, with James Hamilton—

Andrew's son—as one of the recruiting agents for Philadelphia. For their commanding officer, the marines were to have Franklin's ally, Colonel Spotswood, who had chosen him to be the town's postmaster. The Scottish privateers were also people Franklin knew well. Like his wife they were Episcopalians, kneeling every Sunday in the pews at Christ Church.

It was a costly war, without much justice and with no real victor. It would divide Pennsylvania more deeply than any issue had done before. On one side, committed to peace and piety, and to low taxation, there stood John Kinsey and his allies, Quaker and German, with the rural counties behind them. On the other, in favor of King George, privateering, and a militia, there were the Philadelphia men: the governor and his officials, but also James Hamilton, William Allen, and their ally, Benjamin Franklin. However, in the second half of 1740 the war was still in its infancy. The divisions in the colony had yet to crystallize entirely.

Instead, Franklin had to fight another kind of campaign: one last, annoying round in his bout with Andrew Bradford. After that, there would be more of Whitefield, stirring up the province again; and then at last, after so many years of delay, Franklin began to find his true vocation as a scientist.

VILLAINY AND LIBEL

In England meanwhile, his old printing colleague Charles Ackers had gone from strength to strength. The monthly he co-owned, *The London Magazine,* had come to be a feature of the parlors of the affluent. Since its authors were up against Samuel Johnson in *The Gentleman's Magazine,* they were never quite the best; but they did well enough to make Mr. Ackers a profit. By 1740, the moment had arrived for Franklin to try to produce his colonial equivalent.

That summer, as the privateer *George* set out to pillage the Spaniards, Franklin held some talks about a monthly with a lawyer, John Webbe, an Irishman who hoped to be an editor. After the success of Whitefield's *Journals,* Franklin was in search of something new. To assist him he took on an extra member of staff: his nephew James, aged about eleven, son of the founder of *The New-England Courant,* just leaving school in Rhode Island where Franklin had helped to pay for his education. The plans were laid for a monthly magazine with a target circulation of one thousand, conceived—as Franklin put it—"in imitation of those in England." Alas, the scheme collapsed when he and Webbe fell out about the formula for sharing the profits.

A grievous loss for literature: so Mr. Webbe went down the street, and did a deal with Andrew Bradford. In November 1740, the *Mercury* advertised their new periodical, to be called *The American Magazine.* Encroaching on Franklin's territory, it would supply "a Monthly View of the Political State of the British Colonies." It was just the sort of thing that Franklin, who knew the London press so well, regarded as his rightful territory. Determined not to be outdone, the following week he issued a scornful rejoinder, printed in the columns of the *Gazette,* telling his readers that in January he would launch a monthly of his own, *The General Magazine and Historical Chronicle.* In the process, Franklin also accused John Webbe of stealing the idea.

Now Franklin had been here before, at the time of the almanac wars, *The Busy-Body,* and his feud with Keimer. This time, however, in successive issues of the *Mercury* Webbe unleashed a stream of invective more horrid than anything Franklin had yet endured. He found himself accused of lies, and ignorance, "scandalous insinuations," and "sneaking villainy." Most dangerously of all, John Webbe alleged that he had been guilty of misconduct in his office as the town's postmaster.

According to Webbe, Franklin had unlawfully barred the mailmen from carrying the *Mercury* free of charge, a privilege newspapers were supposed to enjoy. For a few weeks Franklin kept his temper; but at last, in the middle of December, he printed his own version of events. As Franklin pointed out, by imposing sanctions on the *Mercury* he was merely following the orders of Colonel Spotswood, who was trying to compel Bradford to pay the overdue money he owed to the king. The diatribe from Webbe was all the more vexing because, at his home in Annapolis, Spotswood had recently passed away.

Spotswood's death left the American regiment bound for the Caribbean without a seasoned commander. It also meant the loss of a man Franklin admired, a visionary who—since the days of Queen Anne—had been beating the drum for colonial expansion. Old pillars of stability were disappearing, not only Colonel Spotswood, but also Andrew Hamilton, who was fading fast: he would die in 1741. As Franklin's patrons vanished from the scene, the *Mercury* attacked him all the more aggressively. Seven days before Christmas, Webbe made one final onslaught, filling most of that week's issue, claiming that Franklin had "a violent inclination to defame." This time Franklin refused to rise to the bait. He waited until the new year, and then ran just a few little articles making fun of Webb's Irish brogue.

As for the new monthly magazines, both of them flopped for lack of readers. This was a pity because the six issues that Franklin produced of his *General Magazine and Historical Chronicle* did indeed contain some excellent material, almost as diverse and entertaining as those of its older rivals in London. Instead of reprinting English articles, Franklin trawled up and down the eastern seaboard, and as far as Barbados, to find American poetry and prose that was as witty as it was informative.

There were dispatches from the Caribbean war, patriotic verses but also skits and satires, more essays about paper money, a scheme for a factory in Boston, and instructions for making molds for casting bullets. Political news as well, and of course religion: all the many aspects of colonial life found their way into Franklin's short-lived magazine. And by including many articles about George Whitefield, both for and against, Franklin could clear himself from the charge that the two men had become too close. This was all the easier because at last the preacher's mission to America had drawn to a temporary close.

Early in 1741, George Whitefield left Savannah, where he had founded his orphanage, to travel home to England where John Wesley was developing the Methodist movement. What mark had Whitefield left in Pennsylvania? He had certainly helped to keep Franklin in business. Besides the *Journals,* he printed another forty books and pamphlets inspired in some way by the Great Awakening. Other than that, Whitefield's legacy was mixed and also very difficult to assess.

In the summer of 1740, the *Gazette* had given its verdict in a story that must have been written by Franklin, because—nearly fifty years later—he quoted it in précis in his memoirs. "The alteration in the face of religion here is altogether surprizing," wrote the author. "Never did the people show so great a willingness to attend sermons, nor the preachers' greater zeal . . . religion is become the subject of most conversations. No books are in request but those of piety and devotion; and instead of idle songs and ballads, the people are everywhere entertaining themselves with psalms, hymns and spiritual songs. All which, under God, is owing to the successful labor of the reverend Mr. Whitefield."[17]

Much of this was true, no doubt. From comments in business letters written by Quakers—people who had no cause to exaggerate the preacher's success—we can see that, indeed, many people found George

Whitefield deeply moving. For a while he set the tone of life in Philadelphia. In politics, however, the voters kept on reelecting Speaker Kinsey, who appears to have shunned the Awakening. Neither he nor the Penn family or their officials wished to bring about a godly renewal of the sort that Whitefield hoped to achieve. Even if they had, the preacher was a man of faith and charisma but not an organizer. He could not create the institutions he needed to carry on his work. On the contrary: as his most visible memento, Whitefield gave Philadelphia a building that stood empty for many years.

At the time when Franklin's story appeared in the *Gazette,* Whitefield's friends were raising money to build a new meeting house, the largest in the city. It was ready by November. Whitefield had briefly returned, in search of donations for his orphanage, and to preach a few times before he left for England. But then the building fell quiet. From time to time, Gilbert Tennent would turn up to fill the seats, but other than that the hall lay vacant. Money was owing to the owners of the land; the debts piled up; and the trustees could not agree about what to do. For nearly a decade the wrangling went on. At last, with a combination of diplomacy and sound finance, Franklin resolved the situation. The building became the home for his brainchild, the new Philadelphia Academy, the town's first university: a place where the students would study the work of Archbishop Tillotson, the Anglican dignitary whom Whitefield so despised.

Time and again with his heated language, Whitefield merely set people at each other's throats. By the midsummer of 1741, the Presbyterian Church in Pennsylvania and New Jersey had split down the middle. The schism lasted for nearly twenty years, with Gilbert Tennent and Whitefield's allies on one side, and more conservative pastors on the other. Seeing that schisms of the kind had already taken place in Scotland and in Ulster, this was probably unavoidable; but it was Whitefield's campaign that brought the trouble to a head. All this rhetoric, and weeping, and the boasts about his audience: was it really helpful? Could faith of such a kind be sustained for a lifetime, once the moments of passion had faded away?

Only rarely did Whitefield finish what he started. Although in his youth he attacked the evils of slavery, as he grew older he lost interest in the subject. Indeed, at his mission in Georgia he owned slaves himself. Later, in the 1760s, when Whitefield was still preaching in London—he died in 1770—the anti-slavery movement began to gain ground in the city. Whitefield might have led the campaign: but as he strove to be respectable, somehow he forgot about the Africans, and so the movement had to do without him. As for the future of Methodism, in Great Britain it belonged not to Whitefield but to the Wesleys, people more subtle and more scrupulous, who displayed the talent for organization that Whitefield so very plainly lacked.[18]

What lasting impact did he have on Franklin? In his autobiography, the latter makes it clear that Whitefield's teaching had no influence on his beliefs. "We had no religious connection," Franklin wrote. The most we can say is this. In George Whitefield, Franklin saw a gifted but a troubled man—in later years the vomiting was evidence of that—of the kind he always found fascinating. There can be no doubt that he admired Whitefield for his energy, his dedication, his voice, and his skill as an orator. Franklin also recognized that Whitefield, for all his arrogance, spoke to the genuine needs of people hungry for some form of spirituality. Although Franklin did not feel that religion—which, in his century in America, was almost bound to mean some form of Christianity—had to be codified into a specific set of doctrines, the yearning for faith was something Franklin came to value as a force that might help to build and to preserve a republic.

Having been through the Hemphill affair, and then been a witness to the Great Awakening, the middle-aged and elderly Franklin took a pragmatic view of the benefits of religion. As a lover of poetry, a Freemason, and a follower of Tillotson, he preferred to keep his distance from rigid dogma. Indeed, this may explain why it is that in the twenty-first century Franklin scholars find it so hard to define his creed. While Franklin believed in something he called God, he kept his faith deliberately vague. It was ethical and poetic, a generalized belief in benevolence and beauty: but it could not be said to be specifically Christian.

However, Franklin also knew that this would never satisfy all of his fellow Americans. If they wished to subscribe to Christian doctrine, and revivals such as Whitefield's, he would not stand in their path. It was wiser to accept their faith and, if need be, try to channel it away from bigotry, in the hope that faith would also make for justice and for virtue. And so in 1787, when the convention met in Philadelphia to make the Constitution, it was Franklin who proposed that they begin each day's session with a prayer "imploring the assistance of Heaven." Christian he might not be: but Franklin had evolved since the scandalous days of *The New-England Courant.*[19]

Fascinating though it was, Whitefield's American tour amounted to nothing more than a passing episode in Franklin's life. It did not produce the new departure he required. As he approached the age of thirty-five, Franklin was going around in circles, doing very well as a printer but not yet achieving the feats of creativity of which he was capable. If he were to do so, Franklin would need to find a higher calling that would lift him out of feuds and anger, small-town stuff and futile journalistic prose, however witty, the grinding out of endless words without a practical result.

Or rather he needed *two* callings. In the second half of his life, he would have two vocations—politics and science—and gradually the moment approached when he could fulfill them. For the time being the politics would have to wait, as the war with Spain settled into a stalemate that also left the Quaker colony in a state of deadlock. In the spring of 1741, the American Regiment went into action under British officers, making an assault on the Spanish base at Cartagena on the coast of what is now Colombia. Poorly planned and led chaotically, the attack was a bloody fiasco. After failing there, the British force moved on to Guantánamo Bay, where their losses from fever—the infamous "Yellow Jack"—were almost as severe. In March, on the eve of Cartagena, the American Regiment was two thousand strong. By the time they left Cuba in December, fewer than three hundred were fit to bear a musket.[20]

So the war dragged on and on, blighting the economy but posing—as yet—no direct military threat to Pennsylvania. The Quaker party still refused to raise a militia or to fortify the Delaware, and there was nothing the governor could do to persuade them otherwise. Politics ground to a halt for a while, while beneath the surface the divisions grew deeper. In the meantime, however, at last Franklin found a practical use for the science he had studied in the books at the Library Company.

The winter of 1740 and 1741 was said to be the worst of the eighteenth century so far. Ice sealed up the Delaware, the cattle died of cold and hunger, and the price of bread and firewood soared. "The poor have suffered much," wrote a Quaker merchant in January. Not until the end of March did the snow start to melt. With times so hard, Franklin was thinking about a practical way to keep his neighbors warm if the next year's winter proved to be equally severe.[21]

Further back than any living Franklin could remember, his family's finest powers of ingenuity had lain not with words but with things: iron in the forge, and skill with a hammer, a vat of dye, or a copper full of molten wax for candles. In the course of 1741, Franklin rediscovered this heritage of craftsmanship and added the scientific theory he had acquired from the best European authors. He was going to build an iron fireplace: an emblem of the new, ingenious America that was gradually coming into being.

The Wagon, the Rifle, and the Fireplace

In those early days of Pennsylvania, the colony gave birth to three famous inventions. Two of them were highly successful, new products that would help to transform the continent. The first was the Conestoga wagon: long, narrow but sturdy, covered with canvas, and built to carry loads down a rocky trail or across a river, or to feature in films by John Ford. We can be sure that wagons of the sort had emerged by 1717. In that year the name appears in the papers of James Logan, who had settled the portion of Lancaster County around Conestoga Creek, where the wagons were created. The second was a gun: the Pennsylvania rifle, with the distinctive long barrel that made it a weapon ideal for hunting, the firearm of choice for Hawkeye and Daniel Boone.

The third invention was the Franklin fireplace, made from cast iron and first manufactured in 1741. Intended to be economical with fuel, for a while it sold well until some flaws in its design became apparent. It had to be modified before it could evolve into the Franklin stove that made its name in the next century. But despite its defects, the original Franklin fireplace richly deserves its place in history alongside the rifle and the wagon. If we step back from the detail and view these items as part of the broader sweep of events, they take on a new significance. All three were part of the same phenomenon: the birth of engineering in the colonies, and with engineering there came science.[22]

By the late 1730s, in places like the valley of the Schuylkill, small clusters of technology had come into being to serve the practical needs of people in the wilderness. The paper mills at Wissahickon were a fine example, but what they required most of all was iron: all three of the Delaware region's notable inventions were made with that or with steel. Even the wooden Conestoga wagon relied for its strength and its flexibility on the bolts and braces with which it was fitted. And by now the iron industry of Maryland and Pennsylvania could provide local craftsmen with almost everything they required. In Parliament in London in 1737, a Birmingham ironmaster, another friend of Logan, testified about the quality of the iron and steel these two colonies produced: it was good enough, said Joseph Farmer, to make the firing mechanism for the British army's muskets. He urged the House of Commons to remove the taxes the British imposed on imports of American iron: because if this were done the Americans would swiftly overtake the Russians and the Swedes to become the mother country's principal suppliers of metal.[23]

Farmer's arguments fell on deaf ears at Westminster. Unable to satisfy all the vested interests who argued the case for and against free trade between Great Britain and the colonies, Parliament chose to do nothing, leaving the import duties in place. And so in the years before the Revolution the colonies shipped only modest quantities of their iron to Great Britain. Instead, the metal remained at home in America to satisfy the ever-increasing demand from a growing population for tools, construction materials, and kitchenware, and to make parts for the ships the colonists built. But while steel and iron were fine things for the Quaker colony to have, even more important were the people: the migrants flowing into Pennsylvania from the British Isles, Switzerland, and Germany, bringing with them their different traditions of artisan skills. Precisely because the colony had grown to be so diverse, Pennsylvania became an environment ideal for innovation. Borrowing from each other's heritage, craftsmen from many parts of Europe mingled in the Delaware region, swapping ideas until they had the solutions they needed to their problems of manufacture and design.

If we examine the origins not only of the Pennsylvania rifle but also of the Franklin fireplace, we find that both products arose from this process of cultural exchange. By the 1740s at the latest, the long rifle had emerged as a new, distinctive kind of firearm, probably invented by a Swiss German blacksmith, a Mennonite—in other words, a Baptist refugee—who lived not far from Lancaster in a tract of land that Andrew Hamilton had opened up for settlement. A fusion of English and German designs, the gun derived from the short Swiss hunting rifle of the seventeenth century, and so it had a flintlock and an octagonal barrel. If the barrel was extended to the length of an English fowling piece, as it was in Pennsylvania, the rifle could hit a target at twice the range of a conventional musket. In the case of the fireplace, the same kind of intermingling of cultures occurred. Franklin took a German model, borrowed some features of the design, and then adapted it to appeal to English-speaking customers. With the appliance of some science, Franklin created what he hoped would be the ideal heating engine.[24]

When they arrived in America, the Germans had brought with them

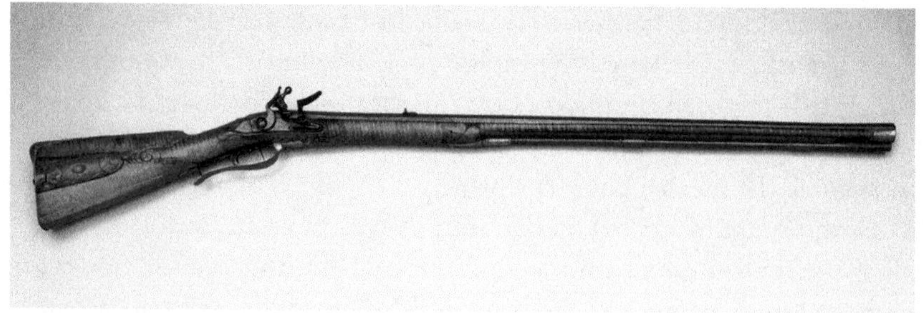

An early example of a Pennsylvania rifle, dating from about 1740. This gun belonged to Edward Marshall, the frontier settler who, during the notorious Walking Purchase of land from the Lenape Indians in 1737, covered seventy miles on foot in thirty-six hours. *From the collection of the Mercer Museum of the Bucks County Historical Society*

their traditional iron stoves, built to cope with winters far colder than those in England. "The German stove is like a box, one side wanting," wrote Franklin. " 'Tis composed of five iron plates screwed together; and fixed so that you may put the fuel into it from another room, or from the outside of the house." Because they were Lutherans or Mennonites, the German immigrants wished to do more with their stoves than merely heat a room. The stove plates were cast with images of Bible stories, each one intended to teach a holy lesson.

Hundreds of the plates survive in the Mercer Museum at Doylestown, not far from Philadelphia; and because they have a date and a maker's mark they can be used to chart the prehistory of Franklin's fireplace. At first, the Germans relied in America on the stove plates they had carried across the Atlantic. As yet, the English iron foundries in Pennsylvania only made simple cast iron firebacks for the open hearths the English had always preferred. But then—in the 1720s—the Germans began to order new plates when the old ones were damaged or they had a house to build. At first it seems that they bought only single plates, but soon enough the English ironmasters started to make complete five-sided stoves on German lines. In 1738, the tide of immigration reached a peak, when in that one year alone more than three thousand Germans arrived in the Delaware. With such a large market to cater to, by 1740 all the leading ironworks in Pennsylvania were selling German stoves.[25]

At the heart of the trade stood a Baptist elder, William Branson, whom Franklin had known for fifteen years, since the days when Branson had been one of Thomas Denham's customers at his waterfront store. By the end of the 1730s, Branson had risen to become not only the larg-

Examples of the cultural traditions that gave birth to the Franklin fireplace: on the left, an iron fireback made at the Durham ironworks for Franklin's mentor, James Logan, and preserved at Stenton, his country house; and on the right, a German stove plate made in the Delaware region in the same period with a design showing David and Goliath.

est ironmaster in the colony but also a pillar of society in Philadelphia, where he was an ardent devotee of Whitefield. He also shared Franklin's zeal for civic projects. Besides his workshop on Market Street, Branson owned the forge and furnace deep in the woods at Coventry in Chester County, with a crew of indentured servants who turned out iron bars and slabs and shipped them down to Philadelphia. In 1738, Franklin went to Branson and bought two stoves and some imported English steel: perhaps for his new home on the same street but more likely to be used in some kind of scientific experiment. By this time, the properties of iron had come to fascinate Franklin and his closest friends.[26]

A few years earlier, his landlord Robert Grace had sailed to Europe for a long trip to study the latest techniques for smelting iron and for testing rocks for minerals. Safely home again in Pennsylvania, in 1740 Grace married into one of the colony's oldest ironmaking dynasties, by taking as his wife a widow, Rebecca Nutt. She was, as Franklin put it in the *Gazette,* "an agreeable young lady, with a fortune of £10,000": Franklin was never the most romantic of men. As her dowry, the new Mrs. Grace supplied a half share in another Chester County ironworks, the Warwick Furnace, where Robert Grace became the manager. It was here, a few miles from Branson's enterprise, that the Franklin fireplace was assembled.[27]

In the fall of 1741, Franklin drew up a detailed set of designs, built a model, and gave it to Robert Grace. His men made the molds for casting the eight iron plates from which the fireplace was screwed together. In December, as the winter set in with a vengeance, the *Gazette* ran its first advertisement for "the new invented iron fireplaces," in large and small sizes available from Franklin's store. By February he had sold all his stock and he was waiting for a new delivery from Warwick, where Grace had high hopes for the future, with plans to turn out each year at least four tons of iron plates for Franklin's pride and joy.

The Breath of God

"Iron is always sweet," wrote Franklin, "and every way taken is wholesome and friendly to the human body—except in weapons." These words appear in one of his most important texts, published in the fall of 1744, a brilliant little essay describing his fireplace.* As a master of technical prose, lucid and logical, detailed but never pedantic, Franklin has rarely been surpassed. Here we find his talent for this kind of writing on show for the first time in his career. With a copy of the essay and a bricklayer to help him, any modern blacksmith could install a replica of Franklin's invention, so precise are his instructions. The essay also shows us how deeply Franklin had immersed himself in the work of the finest physicists in Europe.[28]

The German stoves were clean and effective, thought Franklin, with the smoke, soot, and ash all kept out of the room, but they lacked the glowing hearth that the English loved to see. And although the stoves were an efficient source of heat, the atmosphere inside the room was often stale and stuffy, as the people inside were obliged, as Franklin put it, "to breathe the same unchang'd air continually, mix'd with . . . the perspiration from one another's bodies." This was less of a problem with open fires of the English kind, but they had flaws of their own. They were dirty and unsafe. All too often they set chimneys and houses ablaze, and they wasted fuel by sending too much heat straight up the flue.

As coastal Pennsylvania began to fill with people, and firewood grew scarce—as it had in 1741—this last defect in an English fire became all

* *An Account of the New Invented Pennsylvanian Fire-Places.*

the more irksome. And so, with the help of science culled from his reading, Franklin tried to solve all these problems simultaneously, by exploiting the properties of hot iron and hot air. Iron, he knew, was slow to warm up, but once it did so it retained its temperature far longer than other substances, and it sent out heat in all directions. Better still, iron did so *cleanly,* with no fumes, no smell, and no detritus. As for the properties of air, Franklin could find them described in his textbooks, written by Sir Isaac Newton's disciples.

Air, the books told him, was an "elastic fluid," consisting of tiny particles. When heat was applied to a body of air, these little globes expanded in diameter, so that the air became "rarified" or "distended." If the number of particles remained the same, but the space they occupied grew larger, then the *weight* of the air must fall: and so, in a kitchen or a parlor, hot air will always tend to rise toward the ceiling. Or as Franklin put it in his fireplace essay: "Air rarified and distended by heat, is specifically lighter than it was before, and will rise in other air . . . till it either comes to air of equal weight, or is by cold reduc'd to its former density."

So iron made a splendid radiator, while—with a little ingenuity, and some skillful engineering—currents of air could be made to flow around a room. In 1709, one Nicolas Gauger, a Frenchman, had brought out a book titled *The Mechanics of Fire*—which Franklin had read—describing how he used these principles to build his own new fireplace. Its iron frame contained hidden cavities, filled with hot air, with slits at the top to allow it to escape. Franklin took the same idea and developed it into a far more ambitious device.

At the center of his fireplace, above the hearth where the fuel was set alight to warm the iron frame, there stood the essential component: the "air box." A vertical compartment, it contained a system of internal ledges creating what Franklin called "winding passages," to maximize the surface area of metal and therefore the heat it would conduct. At the bottom of the air box, there was a hole that communicated with a long tube or channel sealed into the brickwork beneath the floor of the room.

From outside the house, a continuous stream of fresh, cold air flowed through the channel and entered the air box. As it was warmed by the hot iron, so it spiraled upward through the winding passages until it entered the room through an opening at the top. This feature of the fireplace required precision casting by the iron founder. The plates would have to fit tightly together to stop the hot air leaking out through the joints.

Meanwhile the smoke from the fire rose over the air box, and passed down behind it, to be fed into another, separate channel sealed beneath the brickwork. The smoke flowed along this second channel, and then rose up a funnel set into the wall behind the fireplace. From there it disappeared into the chimney, which was shut off from the room by an iron lid that could be opened for the chimney to be swept.

Perhaps the only surviving example of an original Franklin fireplace from the 1740s, albeit damaged and missing a key component, the air box. The fireplace was found in 1911 by the architect and historian Henry Chapman Mercer in a farmhouse in Montgomery County, Pennsylvania. *From the collection of the Mercer Museum of the Bucks County Historical Society*

It was a heating system that seemed to have everything: a cheerful fire in the hearth, iron as a radiator, and a stream of warm but fresh, clean air to heat each corner of the room and clear away the fug from human beings. None of the heat would vanish up the chimney. Alas, the early models of the fireplace failed to go according to plan—it was hard to get the outer air into the air box, unless the fire in the grate was very hot indeed, and the smoke tended to back up into the room—but it was the *concept* that counted.[29]

Franklin was thinking like a physicist. From the treatises in the Library Company collection, he had taught himself the language of science and gradually mastered its subtleties. "Rarified air," for example: that was a phrase Sir Isaac had used in the 1680s in his masterpiece, the *Principia.* Although it seems that Franklin never studied the book in detail, he knew its contents from later works by the Dutchmen 's Gravesande and Herman Boerhaave and their London translator, John Theophilus Desaguliers, all three of whom he deeply admired. Followers of Newton, they had tried to extend Sir Isaac's theories to encompass the phenomena of heatas well as those of motion, gravity, and light.

Perhaps as early as 1732, inspired by an experiment by Boerhaave, Franklin had begun to think about the puzzles of heat. On a patch of snow, he placed pieces of cloth, colored black and white, and red and blue and yellow. It was a procedure that came naturally to Franklin, coming as he did from a family of dyers. As the sun shone down, he saw that the snow melted at different speeds beneath the different shreds of fabric. The white cloth kept the sun at bay, so that the snow beneath it did not melt. Meanwhile the darker shades absorbed the solar heat and passed it on, turning the snow into slush. It was a crude exercise, and the concepts at Franklin's disposal were too vague to tell him what it meant. In 1737, his Junto friend Joseph Breintnall repeated the experiment, with the same results, and also came away unable to explain them.[30]

One solution might be this: that heat and light were really something else, a substance—or perhaps a *fluid*—which the Dutch Newtonians called *Fire.* "The intimate nature of Fire is unknown," wrote 's Gravesande, "but wherever we find Heat and Light, we say that there is what we call Fire." Somehow this mysterious fluid, infinitely subtle and elastic, and moving at immensely high speed, could penetrate solid bodies. As it did so, it produced effects that varied according to the density of the tiny particles of which those bodies were composed. From the language of Franklin's essay, it is clear that when he built the fireplace he was thinking about heat and light in just such a way.[31]

Odd though these ideas might seem today, they served a fruitful purpose: they also set people thinking about electricity. Three decades earlier at the Royal Society, with Sir Isaac Newton in the chair, it had been seen that if a glass sphere was spun around at high speed with a pad of leather pressed against it, flashes of light could be produced inside the glass. Newton's assistant, Francis Hauksbee, showed that the glass would attract or repel filaments of brass or copper. Later, other scientists discovered that if the glass was rubbed for long enough, and an iron rod or a finger were placed nearby, a spark could be made to jump across the gap between them.

In the mid-1730s, chiefly in London and Paris, experiments such as this were repeated, refined, and taken much further. By attaching the iron rod to a long line of thread, the effects of electricity could be transmitted for a distance of more than two miles, with sparks appearing at the end of the line. What did this mean? As yet, no one could say; but there was a hypothesis that became ever more attractive.

As early as 1712, Newton had begun to speculate about something he called "an electric spirit," "exceedingly active," which permeated every particle of matter, gluing the atoms together. Not only that: having seen Hauksbee's experiments, Newton wondered if perhaps this "very subtle potent active elastic spirit" might also account for the behavior of light—its emission, reflection, and refraction—to which he had devoted many years of research.[32]

In the decade after Newton's death, the questions he had posed continued to fascinate his followers. Light and heat, the baffling sparks and flashes produced by Hauksbee and other researchers, Newton's "electric spirit," and the mysterious substance the Dutch knew as "Fire": somehow they were all connected. If the connections could be understood, then the deepest secrets of the cosmos would be laid bare. Or so it appeared to the era's most brilliant minds, including in the colonies Franklin's friend and mentor James Logan.

Via his Quaker friends in England, Logan kept abreast of the latest research. In 1737 he completed the writing of a treatise of his own, in which he hoped to create a synthesis of moral philosophy and the most advanced scientific learning. Never published in his lifetime—not until the twenty-first century, in fact—the book bore the very eighteenth-century title *Of the Duties of Man as may be deduced from Nature.* Parts of it he shared with Franklin, seeking his comments on the chapter that strove to define moral virtue. In passing, Logan also touched on electricity.

In the past, he wrote, its curious effects had been regarded as merely "a trifling appearance in nature." But when he studied Hauksbee's findings and the experiments of the 1730s, Logan began to wonder if perhaps the study of electricity held the key to what he called "more just and extensive notions . . . of the world we live in." Steeped in the work of Newton, he knew that late in life Sir Isaac had been moving in the same direction. Even so, it was still a bold statement for Logan to make.[33]

His comments were all the more significant because he was writing on the edge of the wilderness, in a colony still thought of in England as little more than a source of pork and grain and a destination for felons or indentured laborers. But the fact was that by now—with its iron foundries, its craftsmen, and its Library Company—the colony had the makings of a scientific culture, with James Logan as its guiding light. Infirm or even crippled though he was, Logan could still write and think with the utmost clarity, and the questions that exercised his brain—and Franklin's—were the same as those that baffled scientists in Europe. With his fireplace, his reading, and his fascination with heat, Franklin was already working in parallel with the best minds in Paris and London.

A case in point was a French aristocrat whose background could not have been more different. She was a woman of ingenuity—Émilie, Marquise du Châtelet—who took as her lover the philosopher Voltaire. In that same year of 1737, as Logan was finishing his magnum opus, the marquise and Voltaire retreated for the summer to her château by the Marne, there to enjoy intimate moments and to ponder the mysteries of physics. Like Franklin, they read the Dutch Newtonians. At a blacksmith's forge, she and Voltaire heated rods of iron. Like Franklin they tried to understand the properties of "Fire." By the end of the year, Madame du Châtelet had written a dissertation on the subject, to be published in 1739.[34]

With eloquence and poetry, the marquise expressed ideas identical to Logan's. It seemed that behind the phenomena of heat and light, there lay what she called a "universal agent" that kept the cosmos in motion. It was, she wrote, "the breath of life that God has spread throughout his handiwork." Madame du Châtelet knew the best electricians in Paris, and in their work she saw what she called "new miracles of nature." She longed for the day when an "ingenious philosopher" would find the path that led to the center of the maze.

Part Five

THE DAWN OF AMERICAN SCIENCE

Chapter Seventeen

A Change of Life

At the end of 1742, as Franklin approached the age of thirty-seven, his neighbors beheld a sound, successful man who made the best of every opportunity. He had just created another printing partnership—this time it was in New York with a former employee, James Parker—and Franklin had even published a novel. The first to be printed in America, it was a pirated edition of Volume I of Samuel Richardson's *Pamela.* Readers must have found this rather frustrating, because they had to wait two more years for Franklin to give them the end of the story. But he had been very busy.

Although the economy was in the doldrums as the war continued and the West Indian trade fell away, Franklin had found a wealthy new client to keep him occupied. He had become the printer of choice for Count Nicolaus Ludwig von Zinzendorf und Pottendorf, a missionary from the German fatherland. The count was known for short as "Brother Ludwig." A Moravian Christian, and a friend of John Wesley, he conceived the bold idea of unifying all the German sects in Pennsylvania: a notion that failed to appeal to the Amish, the Mennonites, the Dunkers, and the Schwenkfelders, to name but four of the denominations. Also taking umbrage were the Lutherans. From Germany they imported their own evangelist to do battle with Brother Ludwig.[1]

Once again Franklin found that he could make a profit from religious strife. In 1742 the count asked him to print no fewer than sixteen books and pamphlets in German. With so much work on hand, Franklin became more deeply involved in the making of paper as well. In the fall of that year, he formed a new alliance in the South, helping a printer from Williamsburg build a mill in Virginia, using rags that Franklin sent from Philadelphia.

And then, in November, at last his old enemy passed away. The death of Andrew Bradford at the age of fifty-six left Franklin in full command of the printing and publishing trade in the Delaware valley. Indeed with his network of partners along the coast, he was now the dominant force in printing in America as a whole. Even so Franklin could not feel secure. Far from it: like almost every businessman in the eighteenth century, especially in the colonies, he knew that his success was precarious. So was his status in society.

It was an age when the high road to distinction lay by way of real estate. And here Franklin had yet to make a permanent mark. He had acquired two properties—a three-acre field, perhaps for young William to graze his pony, and a vacant building plot in Philadephia—but these were tiny transactions compared to the vast deals done by the Pennsylvania Hamiltons or by William Allen. By the middle of the 1740s, Franklin would be comfortably off, but even by the American standards of the period he would never be truly rich. Cautious by nature, and jealous of his reputation, he did not smuggle Spanish rum or molasses. Nor did he speculate in tobacco, Carolina rice, or slaves or stolen Indian territory or contracts for the British military. Although Franklin was solid, he was not yet a guaranteed survivor.[2]

Following a path that resembled that of his old London colleague Charles Ackers, Franklin had created a mixed portfolio of businesses, grounded in the printer's art. *Poor Richard*, the *Gazette*, the German tracts, paper money, and his postmastership: put them all together with the ventures in Charleston and New York and his clerkship of the Pennsylvania assembly, and Franklin had done very well. But had he done enough? He had made some brilliant maneuvers. Perhaps the shrewdest was his alliance with the new papermakers of Wissahickon, which was essential for his success in printing. Even so Franklin could not be sure that he and Deborah would enjoy a comfortable old age.

For the time being their marriage was sound, but what passion there was had faded away. At about this time Franklin composed a poetic tribute to Deborah. It was a ballad apparently written to mark their twelfth wedding anniversary, in which he called her "my plain country Joan." She was "the joy of my life," he wrote, "a companion delightful and dear," tender and supportive, a good housekeeper and a welcoming hostess to his friends. She "could not be a better wife, might be a worse." In short, she was "lovely old Joan." Besides romantic ardor, something else was missing, and that was motherhood. Since Franky's death, Deborah had been childless. For an entrepreneur in the eighteenth century this was a catastrophe in waiting. Of course they had William, but one son was rarely enough; and in any case, the boy did not aspire to be a printer, any more than the teenage Franklin had wanted to boil fat to make soap and candles. But without a successor, Franklin could never retire to devote himself to public service: and his accomplishments would die with him.[3]

That very fate had overtaken his clever uncle Thomas in England, whose death without a son had doomed the Ecton Franklins to extinction. In colonial America, the problem was all the more acute. With no banks and no bond market, there was no one to sell Franklin an annuity to serve as a pension, or a life insurance policy to protect his widow if he died young. Although in London the first life insurance companies were being formed, to help professional men in Franklin's position, nothing of the sort existed in the colonies.

He and Deborah needed somebody with the talent and drive to take on the family business when the moment came. If it could not be a son or another kinsman it would have to be a former hired hand. But although journeymen came and went on Market Street, they lacked the wide range of skills that Franklin had acquired, and which he would need from a partner. Only one man in Philadelphia might have fitted the bill: a clever Welsh immigrant, Lewis Evans. A former Quaker but now an Episcopalian, he became a Franklin family friend, with Deborah serving as godmother to his daughter when she was baptized at Christ Church. Evans made a living as a merchant, scrivener, and draftsman. He did jobs for Franklin; he shared Franklin's fascination with iron; and from his home he sold the iron fireplaces. But for all his talents—he was, said a friend, an "ingenious engineer"—Evans had a difficult temperament. He was "a queer fellow," said another. Besides, he was too old to be Franklin's successor. Evans was already in his forties.[4]

So everything still depended on Franklin's and Deborah's hard work and their physical health. But this could never be taken for granted, in colonial towns so often swept by epidemics. Three of Franklin's sisters had failed to see the age of forty-five. His brother James had died at thirty-eight. Nor could Franklin be certain of keeping his assembly clerkship, and the government printing contracts that went with it. By 1742 the glory days of the Triumvirate were a distant memory.

In October, Jeremiah Langhorne followed Andrew Hamilton to the grave. That left only James Logan still alive, sixty-eight years old and too frail to shape the political future. Now the General Assembly danced to a different tune. Led by John Kinsey, the Quaker party were still firmly in control, still against a militia and still refusing to vote any but the bare minimum of money for the use of Governor Thomas. At the election that fall, there was a riot when sailors came up from the docks—"beating and abusing a great number of people," said one eyewitness—and tried to bar the Quakers and the Germans from voting. The people of the town fought back, chasing the sailors back to their ships, and the poll went ahead. Once again it was a triumph for the Kinsey ticket.[5]

It was widely rumored—with some justice—that William Allen organized the riot, in collusion with the mayor, Andrew Hamilton's old partner Clement Plumstead. If so, it was a sign of just how desperate they had become. While the Quaker-German coalition remained intact, Allen and his supporters were doomed to impotence. So was the governor, with whom they were loosely aligned. As for Franklin, again his loyalties were divided. Never a pacifist, he supported the war, he wanted to see a militia, and he and William Allen were old friends. Nor did Franklin have much time for Speaker Kinsey. When the latter passed away eight years later, the *Gazette* ran only the briefest of obituaries. On the other hand, Franklin was dismayed by the riot—the sailors, said his report of the incident in the *Gazette*, were "strangers," with "no right to intermeddle"—and at the assembly he had to work with the ruling party.

And so Franklin found himself in a sort of no-man's-land: fascinated by politics, about which he had written and read so much, but unable to play an active role himself. It may be that he also suffered from the occupational disease of journalists in middle life. A mood of frustration overtakes them, as they tire of chronicling other people's adventures and feel their own lack of lasting achievement. It seems that sometimes he was deeply bored. At his desk in the State House, during sessions of the assembly, Franklin would doodle with numbers, creating mathematical puzzles for himself to solve.

His problems would have been less acute if he had been nothing more than a writer like James Ralph. But for Franklin, writing could never be an end in itself. If he had wished, he might have become a colonial version of Samuel Richardson. But an American answer to *Pamela* would not have done justice to Franklin's other talents. Writing could not be the *serious* vocation he required. Despite Franklin's love of satire, his hoaxes, and his affability, at heart he was always profoundly serious. He was also intensely ambitious. In fact he was so serious and so ambitious that he felt obliged to hide these attributes behind a cloak of levity. What Franklin needed was a new career. It had to be one that made full use of *all* his faculties: not merely his skill with language, but also his mechanical genius, with tools and apparatus, and his powers of logical analysis.

Early in 1743, a calamity occurred that gives us Franklin at his best but also shows us how far he had yet to travel. Two hundred yards from his printing shop, down by the wharf where he landed twenty years before, there stood a wooden shed where a retired sea captain, Mr. Clymer, sold a variety of nautical tackle. It was wintertime, the season for fires, caused by warming pans or candles carelessly left burning. At two in the morning of January 5, with a cold breeze blowing down the Delaware, suddenly the word went up that the shed was ablaze.[6]

Among the neighbors was a saddler who belonged to Franklin's Union Fire Company. So out they turned, with their buckets, hooks, and chains. For three hours, as the wind blew the flames toward Market Street, Franklin and his comrades fought to control the fire. It was only halted by the stout party wall of a merchant's new home. Even so, eight houses had been destroyed, a bakery, a tavern, and the saddlery. Franklin had lost two of his fire buckets. He placed a notice in the *Gazette* in the hope that they might be returned.

The worst fire the town had witnessed for many years, the incident had its silver lining. In the days that followed, Philadelphians hurried to copy Franklin's example and form new fire companies of their own: something that served as a vindication of Franklin's zeal for neighborly virtue. But even now, he and his friends had to turn to the British for help. Five weeks before Clymer's shed caught fire, the Union Company had voted to order the best apparatus they could find. And of course it had to come from London.

They ordered England's finest, an engine that could shoot water one hundred feet in the air. It came from a workshop in Smithfield that Franklin must have seen in 1725, when he sat at his printing bench at Mr. Palmer's only a few minutes' walk away. As yet, no American engineer could build a machine of such sophistication. Although the Union Fire Company broke new ground in America, it was still a London idea transplanted to the colonies; so that Franklin had yet to show that he was more than an imitator of English models.[7]

This was about to change. Seventeen forty-three would prove to be a watershed year for Franklin. It was his climacteric, when at last he began to fulfill his vocation as a scientist. It was also a year that brought some happiness for Deborah. By the spring, the Franklins knew that Mrs. Franklin was pregnant again, with a child conceived at about Christmastime. He left so few personal papers from this period that we cannot say precisely how Franklin felt about the news; but in May, after a gap of ten years, the expectant father went to see his family in Boston. This is surely evidence that he was delighted about it.

Much as he disliked that irritating town, his journey back to Massachusetts would prove to be decisive for his future. In New England he made new acquaintances with people of learning who threw open new windows in Franklin's life. Step by step, between 1743 and 1746, Franklin resolved his dilemmas and began to achieve the originality he craved. These were also years when the pace of political life in the colonies began to accelerate, as three decades of peace between Britain and France came to a close.

Amid the clamor of war, Franklin's circle of friends grew ever larger. In these critical years, he and like-minded people from New York and New England began to collaborate with a degree of urgency rarely witnessed in the colonies. In the birth of science in America, patriotism and military zeal walked hand in hand with botany, physics, and the study of terrain. The colonists most committed to philosophy, including Franklin and his new acquaintances, were also among the most eager to fight the French, and to use their expertise to secure the interior. It was against this background, in the spring of 1743, that Franklin produced one of his boldest ideas: his scheme for an American Philosophical Society. He meant it to be a club for what he called "virtuosi or ingenious men": a scientific version of the Junto writ large.

Indians, Philosophers, and Maps

Soon after the waterfront fire, the *Gazette* ran a tale of bloodshed in the wilderness, a clash between the Iroquois and settlers in Virginia. Appearing on January 27, it was a story of a kind that Franklin rarely covered at length. It seems that his readers cared more about the price of corn in Jamaica, a fiery sermon in Boston, or the death of a European king than they did about Indian affairs. Even the Walking Purchase had gone unrecorded in his columns. But in the early weeks of 1743, any news of a skirmish with the Iroquois was worth an inch or so. They were supposed to be allies of the British, who at this moment in their history in America needed all the friends they could find.

Franklin called the incident "this unhappy action." The first reports of the affair had arrived a few days earlier, from a frontiersman, Thomas McKee, who kept a store on an island in the Susquehanna. Governor Thomas summoned him to Philadelphia for a session of his cabinet, the Provincial Council. The previous fall, said McKee, a band of Iroquois had come down the river, on their way to settle a feud with some enemies in the Carolina Piedmont. The Iroquois called on a judge at Lancaster, who gave them a pass to take them as far as Maryland. Beyond the line, they could expect to be treated as hostiles.[8]

On they went until they entered a tract of land, sixty miles west of Charlottesville, recently settled by the Scots-Irish. Cold and hungry, the Iroquois killed and ate some of the settlers' hogs, and then they ran into a troop of Ulstermen on horseback. Seven days before Christmas they fought a battle that left ten settlers dead and four of the Iroquois. The Indians escaped to the north, pausing at McKee's to tell him their side of the story.

Whoever was to blame, the incident came as a cruel surprise to George Thomas and his colleagues. For the next nine months it filled their agenda as they scrambled to find a way to keep the peace. Their problem was obvious. For the past fifteen years, since Logan struck his first deal with the Iroquois, the colony's alliance with them had held firm. It was only with Iroquois consent that Logan and his friends could trample over the rights of the Lenape and make the Walking Purchase. To the southwest, the same alliance had allowed Pennsylvania to grow into the interior. By the early 1740s, Irish and German farmers had followed Logan's traders across the Susquehanna, to create the township of York, ninety miles from the sea. From there, the Conestoga wagons were rattling down the southern trail toward the Shenandoah.

If the Iroquois went to war with the Virginians, and Virginia called for help from its neighbors, the treaties would be broken. And if that were so, far more would lie at stake than the fate of a few homesteads in the wilderness. On the contrary: the gloomiest of Mr. Logan's prophecies might be fulfilled. Hitherto, Logan had been a lonely Cassandra, with his talk of a global war between Britain and France and the effect it might have in America, if the French and their Indian friends swept down the Hudson valley to invade the colonies. In 1732, Walpole's officials had ignored the memo about defense that Logan sent over to England; but now, after the debacle at Cartagena, Sir Robert had fallen from power. His system of diplomacy had collapsed as well. A terminal rift between London and Versailles seemed to be inevitable: the outcome that Logan had feared for so long.[9]

The fate of Austria had always been the thing to watch. By the summer of 1742 the young queen in Vienna, Maria Theresa, was facing an attack from a coalition of her enemies, with France at its head. In response the British sent an army to Flanders, from which it could enter the War of the Austrian Succession on her side. If and when the redcoats crossed the Rhine, they were sure to collide with the French. As 1743 began, this was widely expected in America, not least by Franklin. In the year's first issue of the *Gazette,* he printed some somber lines of poetry—"On the Present Troubles in Europe"—warning of the horrors that would flow from what he called "infernal discord."

Hence the mood of alarm when McKee arrived with his story. Thirty years later, when he wrote his memoirs, Franklin said that in the early 1740s he had two regrets about the state of the colony. The colony had, he wrote, "no provision for defence, nor for a complete education of youth." At the time of the skirmish in Virginia, Franklin was trying to correct the lack of schooling with a project for an academy in Philadelphia. He was also beginning to fret about the danger of war: not a distant war in the West Indies, but a war at home against the Indians as well as the French.

Until the autumn of 1742, and despite the American losses in the West Indies, Franklin had been a detached observer of the fighting. To be sure, he printed the exploits of the town's privateers, especially those of a Scotsman, John Sibbald, who worshipped with Deborah at Christ Church and captured Spanish ships at sea.* He and Sibbald became personal friends. But the war on land, such as it was, did not capture Franklin's imagination. In the new edition of *Poor Richard,* printed in November, he made fun of the latest little battle between the British and the Spaniards in Florida. The almanac featured a sarcastic little poem, ending with the words: "Say, Children, is not this your Play, Bo-peep?"[10]

But then, as the War of Jenkins' Ear threatened to become a war with France as well, this kind of joke ceased to be amusing. Out west the Shawnee were already pawns of the French, seduced by gifts of guns

* In 1757 Captain Sibbald was one of the witnesses of Franklin's will.

and liquor: or so it was believed. If the Iroquois succumbed as well, and abandoned the alliance with the British, America would lie at the mercy of King Louis XV. As the weeks went by, Governor Thomas hurried to and fro, looking for people to help him defend his province. To win some support from the assembly he gave the corrupt John Kinsey the post of chief justice. In return the assembly voted the governor some money from the taxes.

Mr. Thomas also looked for help from members of Franklin's circle. The first man to answer the call was his best bookstore customer, the Anglican cleric Richard Peters. In February, the Provincial Council chose Peters for the post of secretary that James Logan had held for so long. This was why Franklin had to postpone his scheme for an academy. Franklin had seen Peters, he later recalled, as "a fit person to superintend such an institution"; but Peters, who needed a better-paid job, preferred his new role with the government.

In his turn, Peters enlisted the support of a Junto member, William Parsons, the surveyor. Beyond the Susquehanna, rumors were rife of an Indian plot to kill every white fur trader in the region. Peters and Parsons were already due to go out to Lancaster County on some business for the Penn family. With panic setting in among the settlers, the two men were told to calm them down, and to assure them that the Iroquois treaties were secure.

And so, one by one, Franklin's allies in Philadelphia were recruited into public service, as the colony's future seemed to be in peril. With his printing business and the assembly still taking up so much of his time, Franklin could do little directly to help, but in the spring he found another way to be of use. On May 14, as the governor entered talks with the Iroquois, Franklin published his manifesto for a new scientific club. It would be his gift to the patriotic cause: a society of clever people, working together to promote the well-being of what he called "the British plantations in America."

To begin with, it was somebody else's idea. It came from one of Franklin's many friends, John Bartram, a truly extraordinary person: a farmer, an explorer, and a self-taught expert on America's botany and animal life. Seven years older than Franklin, born of Quaker stock but by now a freethinker, Bartram lived in a gray stone house, complete with Grecian columns on the porch, that he had built himself. It still stands today, with its scientific garden on a bluff above the Schuylkill and a distant view of the office towers in downtown Philadelphia. From there

Mr. Bartram made long forays into the wilderness, collecting specimens for clients in England. He was "a most wonderful genius," said the best of them, Peter Collinson, a Quaker friend of James Logan. A successful merchant in textiles, Collinson had helped to arrange the first shipments of books from London for the Library Company.

In 1737, after a field trip to Chesapeake Bay, gathering seeds and pinecones, Bartram wrote to Collinson to tell him about his pet project: an "academy or society" of "most ingenious and curious men," who would pursue research in America into the arts and sciences. A member of London's Royal Society, Collinson liked the idea of an American equivalent but he had his doubts about its feasibility. He did not think such a thing could be achieved during what he called "the infancy of your colony."

And so at first John Bartram's concept came to nothing. However, he was already acquainted not only with Robert Grace, who met Collinson while he was in England studying metallurgy, but also with Franklin. When Franklin saw scientific items in the press, he would pass them on to Mr. Bartram. As the years went by, the two men became close collaborators. In 1742, when Bartram needed money to fund his travels in the interior, the *Gazette* ran a notice asking for donations to support him. The following year, the Library Company gave Bartram free membership: devoted as he was to natural history, he never had much money to spare and he could not afford the subscription.[11]

As their friendship matured, he and Franklin put together the scheme for an American Philosophical Society. In the spring of 1743, the time seemed right for such a project. By now the colonies—and especially Pennsylvania—had outgrown their childhood. Contrary to what Mr. Collinson had said, they had developed to a point at which the pursuit of science was feasible. The State House in Philadelphia, the making of furniture, clocks, and silverware, the Franklin fireplace, the rifle, and the fine country houses that gentlemen were building near the town: all of them were evidence of a new creativity in the Delaware region where the economy, insecure though it was, appeared to be ready for a new adventure of ingenuity.

"The first drudgery of settling new colonies," Franklin wrote in his manifesto, "is now pretty well over and there are many in every province in circumstances that set them at ease . . . to cultivate the finer arts, and improve the common stock of knowledge." To "men of speculation," as he put it, "many hints must from time to time arise, many observations occur, which if well-examined, pursued and improved, might produce discoveries to the advantage of some or all of the British plantations, or to the benefit of mankind in general." Far from being purely academic, his society would aim to satisfy practical needs as well to delight the intellect. "*Useful* knowledge": that was his goal. He and his colleagues would seek to cultivate what he called "all new arts, trades and manufactures," of a kind that would "increase the power of man over matter, and multiply the conveniences or pleasures of life."[12]

Mines, minerals, quarries, and new mechanical inventions: these were dear to the hearts of Franklin, Logan, and the ironmasters. And so they featured high on his list of the sciences they would investigate. Chemistry, botany, and new techniques for farming: Franklin mentioned them as well. Long ago in Northamptonshire, his uncle Thomas had belonged to a similar cult of ingenuity, with some of the same preoccupations. With a war with France so close at hand, Franklin and Bartram also had to think about defense. On Franklin's scientific menu, there was an item that could not have been more relevant at this anxious time in Pennsylvania's evolution.

His new society would, he wrote, produce "surveys, maps and charts" of the coast and the interior, charting "the course and junction of rivers and great roads, and the situation of lakes and mountains." It was something that John Bartram saw as his next priority. Two months after Franklin printed the manifesto, Bartram lit out again for the territory, on an expedition to map the wilderness that lay between the Delaware and the Bourbon enemy in Canada.[13]

His mission arose from the negotiations with the Iroquois. As Governor Thomas tried to preserve the old alliance, he relied on Conrad Weiser, a German and a brilliant linguist, who had helped to smooth the way for the Walking Purchase. In the spring and summer of 1743, Weiser journeyed back and forth unceasingly in the hope of making peace between the native people and the Virginians. On June 7, the Provincial Council in Philadelphia decided to send him on a hazardous journey to the village of Onondaga, 250 miles to the north, which served as the Iroquois capital. Few settlers from the Delaware had ever ventured this far up-country. So Weiser took with him two companions, chosen for their eye for terrain and their skill as surveyors.

One was John Bartram: an obvious choice. The other was Franklin's neighbor and friend, the ingenious engineer Lewis Evans. He carried a quadrant for taking readings of latitude. Their role was to study the soil, the timber, and the mountains, and to plot the course of the rivers whose sources lay to the south of the Great Lakes. A task the British had shirked for far too long, this had now become imperative.[14]

For twenty years or so, James Logan and a few counterparts in New York had complained that the French had the only detailed maps of a region that, if it came to war, might hold the key to North America. Although every British colony had a surveyor general, their role was to mark out grants of land, calculate the rents due to King George or to the Penns or the other colonial proprietors, and to settle disputes about the boundaries of each province. They had little time for exploration. John Bartram had done what he could, making sketch maps in northern Pennsylvania and the Hudson valley, but he was the first to admit their failings.

His maps were "clumsily done," Bartram wrote, "as in ye travails hitherto I have laboured under ye great inconveniency of being always in a hurry." They had to do better, and here was the opportunity. With the words of Franklin's manifesto fresh in his mind, Bartram set off for Onondaga with Evans at his side, pausing on the way to visit William Parsons at his farm near Allentown.[15]

Making noonday sightings of the sun, they traveled as far as Lake Ontario, where in the heat of July Bartram and Evans took a swim. While they did so Conrad Weiser plied the Iroquois with gifts, looking for another treaty to heal their quarrel with Virginia and to open the Ohio country to white settlers. Their expedition had also been a practical example of just the kind of research Franklin's new society was supposed to undertake. In the meantime, Franklin had made an overland journey of his own, snatching a few weeks away from his workshop while the assembly was in recess. He was off to New England, there to be met with a mixed reception.

To Boston, Again

Soon after printing the manifesto, Franklin set out for Massachusetts. He reached Boston no later than May 25. On that date his name was listed among the Freemasons who attended the St. John's Lodge. From the masons, Franklin could expect a convivial welcome. His family were another matter. To be sure, he had been reconciled with his parents, who were now very old—Josiah was almost eighty-six, and Abiah was seventy-five—and he was on excellent terms with his brother John, the tallow chandler, who sold Franklin's products from his store. The rest of his kin were more difficult.

At the Blue Ball Franklin met his brother-in-law, Edward Mecom, the husband of Jane. He was always deeply in debt. Often the worse for ale, and too poor to rent a home of his own, Mecom had been left with no option but to come to live with his relations. The wooden house at Hanover and Union had to accommodate the Franklins, the Mecoms, and their seven children. Jane gave birth to the youngest, a little Josiah, only eight weeks before Franklin arrived.

Among his many sisters, Jane was always Franklin's favorite. The proof of that is plain to see from the letters that passed between them. But at some point during this visit, they fell out with each other, and the rift took at least two months to heal. It was more than merely a family row, of the kind that might erupt in an overcrowded dwelling filled with noisy children and an irritating husband. It seems that Jane scolded her brother for being a heretic. She appears to have said as much in a letter—now lost—that she sent him after he returned to Philadelphia. As Franklin put it when he replied, in an attempt to call a truce, "you express yourself as if you thought I was against the worshipping of God."[16]

This had often been said about Benjamin Franklin; but in Boston in the spring of 1743, Jane Mecom had every reason to be annoyed with her brother. From what little we know about her beliefs, it seems that Jane had become another follower of George Whitefield. As well she might. Her life had been hard and her husband feckless. Three years earlier Whitefield had preached at her church; and now she stood up for his doctrine that only by born-again faith in Jesus Christ could a sinner win redemption.

As far as she could tell, Franklin held to the woolly notion that good works alone could engineer salvation. Jane must also have known about the Hemphill affair. And so she accused her brother of impiety. Jane was bound to feel all the more dismay at his freethinking views because Whitefield and his followers were under attack from all sides. That very week, the Boston newspapers were running stories about yet another controversy that the preacher had aroused.

The previous year, in the Scottish town of Cambuslang, Whitefield had preached to vast crowds, but his techniques had alarmed even his closest allies in the Presbyterian Church. He quarreled with his Calvinist friends, who found his theology too vague and himself too conceited. Worst of all, they feared that the conversions he claimed to bring about were hallucinations created by the devil. In the months that followed, Whitefield came under fire in Scotland in sermons and pamphlets of which the most strident bore the title "Fraud and Falsehood Detected." The controversy at Cambuslang spilled over to America, where it filled the front page of *The Boston Gazette* on May 24. The following day, as Franklin met his fellow Freemasons, another meeting took place a few streets away: the annual convention of the clergymen of Massachusetts. By a narrow margin they voted to condemn the excesses of the Great Awakening.[17]

As so often in the past, Mr. Whitefield was the cause of strife and angry words. It was said that he was on his way back to America, where Jane Mecom was one of many Christians who felt a duty to take sides, even if this meant a feud with her brother. With some courtesy and a little time, Franklin found a way to smooth things over. "There are some things in your New England doctrines and worship which I do not agree with, but I do not condemn them, or desire to shake your belief," he wrote to Jane later that summer, before signing off as her "affectionate brother." Even so the incident serves as a reminder that Franklin could never have lived happily in Massachusetts. Only in the Quaker colony did he have the space and the freedom he required.[18]

He spent only a few weeks in Boston, selling books and almanacs, before heading south again by way of Rhode Island, where in Newport he could visit another good customer, Anne Franklin, the widow of his brother James. However, his time spent in his hometown had been long enough for Franklin to rediscover at least one aspect of New England that he found attractive.

If Jane was his dearest sister, the brother he liked best was John. At fifty-three he was quietly prosperous. Although his spelling was as bad as Deborah's—for John Franklin, the Eighth Commandment was "Thou shalt not steel"—he was also a keen student of Boston's history. And so John upheld a town tradition by joining its militia, the Artillery Company. On June 7 they held their annual parade with Franklin looking on. He went with them when they sailed out to Castle William, the British fort in the harbor, to exercise the cannons. A militia was just what Philadelphia did not possess. The Quaker colony had yet to create a citizen army, such as Boston's, made up of "tradesmen and shopkeepers," as Franklin described the part-time soldiers with their guns. Later they served as a model for a force he helped to create to defend the Delaware against the French.

While he was visiting his family, Franklin had also been able to deepen his knowledge of science. As luck would have it, his comrades among the

Freemasons had another visitor, a man of ingenuity from London. Time and again, Franklin had crossed paths with unusual people with a flair for showmanship, whose company he enjoyed because they extended his horizons, leading him on to be all the more creative. Whitefield, for all his flaws, had been just such a person. So was the new friend that Franklin made in Boston.

The Electric Boy and Doctor Rhubarb

In April the first London ships of the year had reached the harbors of New England, with their usual cargoes of calico, tea, and Irish bonded laborers, hoping for a chance to skip overboard and vanish into the streets. They also carried the latest political news. A year after Walpole fell from power, his opponents were still baying for his impeachment. All the time war with France drew nearer.

On board one of the ships was a man in his forties, dressed in black, who wore a wig that made him resemble an army chaplain. His eyes were gray; his complexion was fair, but pitted by smallpox; and he spoke in a Scottish accent. A bankrupt and a fugitive, he had left angry creditors in London, where a bailiff posted his description in the press. In Britain, the Scotsman went by the name of Archibald Spens, physician, man-midwife, and lecturer in science. In America he altered his identity to Spencer and swiftly found friends. A Freemason, he made contact with his brethren at St. John's, and on May 11 1743, they enrolled him in their ranks.[19]

When biographers write about Franklin, sometimes they dismiss Dr. Spencer as nothing more than an entertainer or a quack. This is unfair. He certainly had his critics in America, to whom he was known as "an ostentatious pedant," or even as "Doctor Rhubarb," for his habit of pontificating at the dinner table. But although he was down on his luck, Archibald Spencer was a clever man who wore his learning with a touch of wit and style. Coming from humble origins, he had acquired his medical degree with the help of some eminent members of the Royal Society. He had also made his mark in London.

In Spencer's words, taken from his advertising copy, he was "well known to the nobility and gentry" for his "easy manner of teaching philosophy." Since 1736 it had kept him in business in the empire's capital. There he gave his lectures in what he called his "experimental room," moving it from one site to another until he finished up above a grocer's shop in Soho, his last address before he fled to America. If he failed financially, the reason was probably this: he had a more illustrious rival, John Theophilus Desaguliers, whose books were among Franklin's favorites. Above a coffeehouse in Covent Garden, Desaguliers kept his own experimental studio where he too gave lectures. The English papers ran their advertisements side by side.[20]

In his London heyday, Spencer would give talks to twenty people at a time, telling them about the human eye, the circulation of the blood, and much else. With a microscope, Spencer revealed the antics of the tiniest of creatures dancing on the head of a needle. With a prism he repeated Newton's experiments with light, conjuring up a rainbow in a darkened room. With an orrery, a mechanical model of the planets, he explained the workings of the solar system. In the closing talk of the series Dr. Spencer would display what he called—with the same excitement as Madame du Châtelet—"the wonderful effects of Fire."

Asking for silence, he would take a young boy and suspend him by cords from the ceiling. The doctor picked up a long glass tube and gave it a hearty massage with his hand or with a cloth. To the surface of the tube he applied little shreds of brass which would jump back and forth, now attracted, now repelled. He would rub the tube again, and hold it up against the boy. After a pregnant pause, Spencer would invite a member of the audience to approach the youth and stretch out a finger. From the boy's hands, sparks would appear and flash across the gap.

While in Boston, most likely at the lodge—in London, Freemasons often heard a scientific lecture from one of their number—Franklin saw Spencer perform his trick with electricity.* And although Franklin felt that the doctor's technique was clumsy, he came away "surprised and pleased," as he recalled in his memoirs. The two men kept in touch as Spencer made his way up and down the seaboard giving his lectures. Eventually, when the doctor retired to become a country parson in Maryland, with a little brick church on a hill above the tobacco fields, Franklin bought his apparatus.[21]

At the time he first met Spencer his own electrical experiments were still a few years away, but their encounter set Franklin on the path that led toward them. From his reading of Desaguliers and the Dutch textbooks,

* In his autobiography Franklin says that he first saw Spencer's displays of electricity in 1746. As the Harvard historian of science I. Bernard Cohen showed in the 1940s, this was a lapse of memory by Franklin: their first meeting was definitely in 1743.

The "electrical boy" experiment, first performed in Paris in the 1730s, in an illustration from the *Essai sur l'électricité des ccorps* (1750) by the Abbé Jean-Antoine Nollet.

and probably also from his conversations with James Logan, he already knew that the finest minds in Europe were fascinated by "Fire," electricity, and the connections between them. Spencer could give him something else: firsthand exposure not only to the latest practical techniques for making electricity visible, but also to the most advanced thinking on the subject.

What Franklin had seen was more than just a parlor game. Among the electricians of the 1730s the finest was a Frenchman, Charles Du Fay, who electrified all kinds of things—rocks, crystals, wood, animals, and human beings—and the trick with a boy had first been performed as a serious experiment in his atelier in Paris, intended to show that electricity lay dormant everywhere in nature. He was the scientist who had sent a current four thousand yards along a wire to make a spark flash at the other end. But Du Fay had died young, struck down by smallpox in 1739, leaving a puzzling legacy of unanswered questions.[22]

It was from Du Fay that his friend Madame du Châtelet had learned about electricity; and that was how she had come to share Newton's belief that here the deepest secrets of nature could be found. But there was a problem. Electric boys were fun to watch, but taken as a whole the effects that Du Fay created seemed to be too weak, too fleeting, and too trivial to bear a heavy weight of scientific theory. In an attempt to show how powerful electricity could be, Du Fay tried to make a flame strong enough to ignite a trail of gunpowder, only to fail every time. Nor could he find a way to store the electricity he created. His dangling boys and his electric crystals swiftly lost the charges he had made them carry.

In England his counterparts repeated his experiments, only to find that the outcomes were confusing or even contradictory. In 1742, shortly before Spencer left London, his rival Desaguliers had completed a series of electrical trials at the Royal Society, which had won him the society's gold medal. But when he wrote up his results, Desaguliers had to admit that he could not explain how they came about. All he could say was that electricity seemed to be a kind of fluid, or vapor, or "effluvium," which could be released by friction, so that it filled the atmosphere around an electrified object.

And that was how matters rested when Spencer set foot in Boston. In Europe the electricians were at a dead end, lost amid vague theories and ambiguous findings. When Desaguliers died early in 1744, there was no one in London to carry on his research. For the next two years the Royal Society lost interest in the subject. In time, this situation would create a perfect opportunity for Franklin: because, when at last British scientists did return to electricity, prompted to do so by exciting discoveries in continental Europe, he was as well prepared as they to make the next advances in the field.

In the intervening period, Franklin cemented a series of new friendships on both sides of the Atlantic, building perhaps the most important of the many networks he brought into being. This one gave him swift, unfettered access to the latest scientific intelligence from London, Paris, Holland, and Berlin. Dr. Spencer was one of its members, and so were Bartram and Collinson. But the person to whom Franklin owed most was another man he encountered on his travels in New England in 1743.

Their meeting occurred by chance, somewhere on the highway and probably in Connecticut. Free at last from the miffy stuff with his family, on the way home from Boston at the end of June Franklin ran into Cadwallader Colden, the surveyor general of New York. Their interests were all but identical, and they were both old friends of Logan. So the two men hit it off at once. Scottish by birth, Colden was fifty-four, a physician and another keen student of Newton. Frustrated by what he saw as the backward state of science in the colonies, he was delighted to hear of Franklin's scheme for a philosophical society. Later that year they began to exchange a series of letters. They were to give Franklin the stimulus he required to devote himself to scientific research.

When Franklin came to write his autobiography, he chose not to refer to Mr. Colden. It was an understandable omission. By the time Colden died in 1776 the two men were politically estranged and Colden was one of the most hated people in the colonies. In old age he was a die-hard Loyalist, gloomy and cantankerous. As the Revolution approached, he served as lieutenant governor of New York, filling his letters to London with tirades against sedition. However, by failing to mention his old comrade Franklin did him a disservice. Colden made an essential contribution to the birth of science in America. By leaving him out of the story, Franklin produced a misleading account of what took place.[23]

In his memoirs Franklin made it all sound rather casual, almost as if he picked up a glass tube one day and began to rub it merely out of curiosity. In fact, in matters of science Colden and Franklin were the least casual of human beings. They read very hard and thought very deeply. They also shared a common vision of what colonial science might be. As time went by, they discovered that their minds worked in different ways—Franklin, always so methodical, had a far more rigorous approach—but they both knew what they wanted from science. Not a pastime, but a *profession:* and this was something new in America. What had gone before was not enough.

As far back as the 1630s, the colonies had been a home to people fascinated by science, beginning with Puritans in Boston who saw mathematics as an avenue to the mind of God. Later on at Harvard, students were taught Newton's theories and in 1728 the college appointed a professor of natural philosophy. Beyond its walls, the press ran scientific stories—even Samuel Keimer did that—and there were many keen researchers who hoped to make new discoveries. Almost as soon as it came into being in the 1660s, the Royal Society had begun to publish reports from correspondents in America. The most famous was Cotton Mather, a man in love with astronomy and medicine, who became one of the society's fellows. By the 1730s, up and down the seaboard there were pastors, lawyers, and physicians gazing at the stars, taking notes on meteorology, collecting specimens, and doing small experiments. But in all of this two elements had been lacking.[24]

One of them was urgency, and the other was originality. With his concept of a philosophical society, Franklin was calling—as a matter of necessity—for what amounted to a national scientific endeavor. It had to be unified and disciplined, with the aim of raising the American game to new heights of achievement. No one had said this before. Colden shared his sense of urgency, but also something else: he wanted to see colonial scientists produce a body of original work fit to stand up to scrutiny from the most brilliant minds in Europe. In the course of his exchanges with Cadwallader Colden, Franklin would begin to see what form his originality might take.

Chapter Eighteen

Colden, Franklin, and the Two Frontiers

They could not have chosen a better time to meet. On his farm in the Hudson valley, seventy miles upriver from the Bronx, Colden often felt like a castaway in the wilderness. He was yearning for new friends who shared his passion for science. Seven months before he met Franklin, he poured out his frustration in a long letter to Peter Collinson, with whom he had just begun to correspond. "The encouragement to a mere scholar is very small in any part of North America," Colden wrote. "We are very poor in knowledge and very needy of assistance."[1]

Hence his excitement when Franklin told him about his manifesto. Nearly twenty years earlier Colden had suggested something of the kind, "a voluntary society for the advancing of knowledge" to be based in Boston, but the scheme had never come to fruition. After their meeting in the summer of 1743, Colden wrote to Franklin with a message of support for his more ambitious version of the same idea. "I long very much to hear what you have done," he wrote. Soon he was describing his new acquaintance as "a printer the most ingenious in his way . . . of any in America."

That autumn Franklin replied with a charming letter—"I cannot but be fond of engaging in a correspondence so advantageous," he wrote—and their friendship was sealed. It came to extend beyond philosophy and science and into politics, because Colden, like Franklin, was a man of many parts. They shared the same concerns about the military threat from France. In the defense of America the two men would find another unifying purpose.[2]

When Colden called himself "a mere scholar," he was being rather modest. Long ago, as a trainee doctor in the London of Queen Anne, he had studied Newton's treatise on optics and met Edmund Halley, the astronomer who gave his name to a comet. Moving to America, he tried and failed to make a medical career in Philadelphia. But he met James Logan, who for a while regarded Colden as perhaps the cleverest person in the colonies. In New York in the 1720s he became a trusted aide of Governor Burnet, carrying out enormous surveys of the Hudson and the Mohawk. In the process Colden became an expert on the Iroquois, people who filled him with a mixture of admiration and alarm.

He and Franklin had many things in common. Both had been raised as Presbyterians; indeed Colden was a minister's son, from a Scottish country parish near the English border, but both men had long since abandoned any Calvinist beliefs. Instead Mr. Colden had come to adopt the liberal creed of Francis Hutcheson, the Glasgow philosopher, that Franklin also found so appealing. Like Franklin the mason, Colden believed in what he called "that general benevolence of mankind, which is the true principle of virtue." Like Franklin he loved to read *Paradise Lost,* and especially Milton's account of the Garden of Eden.[3]

There Colden found—as Franklin did—a poetic kind of faith which, when combined with scientific knowledge, could be used to replace old Bible doctrines. If they wished to find God, he wrote, people should begin with what Milton had described: in Colden's words, "the infinite variety and beauty of the works of the creator." And so he studied botany as well, making collections of the flora of New York. This was how he came to swap letters with Collinson, the London Quaker, who gave him an introduction to John Bartram. While on a field trip to the Catskills in 1742, the explorer had stayed at Colden's farm by the Hudson.

At this point in his life, Colden was not yet an embittered old Tory. On the contrary, he was a Whig like Franklin, and Bartram found him "ye most facetious agreeable gentleman I ever met with." He was brimming with ideas and eager to share them. Like Franklin with his fireplace, he saw himself as a promoter of "useful knowledge," an inventor or an engineer. And so Colden designed a new, improved version of the portable quadrant, to help surveyors such as himself, and he sent the details off to London in search of an expert opinion from instrument makers. Colden also devised a new method of printing, using metal plates rather than movable characters, writing it up in a paper that he sent to Franklin.[4]

On a bluff above the Schuylkill River four miles from downtown Philadelphia, the house and garden of Franklin's friend John Bartram, the farmer and botanist, begun in 1728 and then gradually added to until his death in 1777.

Once again Franklin had to use his powers of diplomacy. Colden's invention had no future—the method had been tried before, wrote a London printer, and it was "expensive and inconvenient"—but Franklin did not wish to offend his new friend. He replied to Colden in November, always his busiest period with the new *Poor Richard* in production, but the fall of 1743 was all the more hurried because his summer trip to Boston had left him behind with his work. Even so Franklin was very polite. He was "much pleased" with the invention, he wrote. "I shall consider it very attentively . . . and in a post or two send you some observations." It seems that Franklin never got around to doing so.[5]

Soon afterward word arrived from England that Mr. Colden's quadrant was equally impractical. Clever and hardworking though he was, Colden had a tendency to stray out of his depth. On his farm, he was living close to the Indian frontier but he also saw himself as a man at the very boundary of knowledge. He saw it as his duty to try to push back both frontiers, the territorial and the scientific, but in doing so he was often far too ambitious. And yet—in a way—this was his most valuable contribution. In the 1740s, science in America stood in need of overreachers, people who were ready to be bold and take the risk of wasting time or looking foolish. The important thing about Cadwallader Colden was this: because he was so daring he made other people think, including Benjamin Franklin.

When they met, Colden was surveying the boundary line of New York and Connecticut, but in his leisure hours he was working on perhaps his most audacious project. Or rather his most foolhardy. Having read so much of Newton's physics, Colden believed—as Sir Isaac had himself—that scientists stood on the shore of a vast ocean of knowledge, awaiting new voyages of exploration. And so Colden decided to plunge in headfirst. What had been Newton's two most important discoveries? Universal gravitation and the calculus. As yet, nobody had explained why they had the power that they possessed. In the Hudson valley, Colden meant to be the man who did so.

Exactly what *was* gravity? Colden thought he knew. And how could it be that a science as abstract as mathematics could predict the workings of the universe? In other words: what grounding could be found for Newton's equations in the realities of nature? To supply the answer to these questions, Colden began to write two treatises. One was to be titled *An Explication of the First Causes of Action in Matter, and of the Cause of Gravitation*. The other was an essay on the calculus, which Colden still referred to as "fluxions," using Sir Isaac's terminology.

He had not the slightest chance of success. As James Logan pointed out when he saw the manuscripts, Colden made some glaring errors in his mathematics, suggesting that he never grasped the calculus at all. However, the hours he devoted to the project proved to be worthwhile, albeit indirectly, because Colden's speculations became a talking point for like-minded people from Boston down to Virginia. As his ideas passed to and fro, his network of contacts grew larger, to encompass people that Franklin hoped to recruit for his American Philosophical Society. And so the study of physics gathered a new momentum in the colonies, helped along by Dr. Spencer's lectures and also, as things turned out, by the war with France that was just about to begin.

To help him refine his thinking, Colden had another new friend, a young Scottish soldier named Captain John Rutherfurd. A man in his early thirties, Rutherfurd had already served as a member of Parliament in London, but like so many members of the Scottish landed gentry he was deeply in debt. Desperate to find a salary, Rutherfurd obtained a commission in the British Army. The only command he could find was in New York. In 1742, he had arrived at Albany to lead the garrison: four companies of fusiliers, ill-equipped and understrength. And there, in the long winter evenings, the captain pored over Mr. Colden's ideas.[6]

An educated fellow, Rutherfurd counted among his relations some of the luminaries of the Scottish Enlightenment. He too had studied the authors—the Dutchmen Boerhaave and 's Gravesande—whose books had meant so much to Franklin. Colden admired them too; and so he and the captain discussed the deepest secrets of nature. "The search of truths has something in it so soothing," wrote Rutherfurd, "that I dare say you'll never repent your labor you bestow in it." They worried away at the questions that the Dutch had posed about the phenomenon of "Fire." What was it? What was heat? What was light? What was electricity? Were they all the same? Did they emanate from the sun, as a stream of particles? Or were they intrinsic to every piece of matter in the earth and in the planets? Rutherfurd stood up for Newton, while Colden saw defects in Sir Isaac's theories.[7]

Back and forth the letters went, with the captain reading drafts of Mr. Colden's *Explication.* Rutherfurd also went down to Philadelphia, where he met John Bartram, just before he left for Onondaga. There the captain mingled with the Scottish merchants of the town. His brother, William Rutherfurd, had recently arrived to join the firm of one James Mackey, an importer of British hardware, whom Franklin knew well. Mackey had served for eleven years first as the doorkeeper and then as the sergeant at arms of the General Assembly where Franklin was the clerk.[8]

And so, by the end of 1743, there had come into existence a new network of people, spanning the Atlantic and united by bonds of friendship, by ties of commerce, and by a zeal for science. In New York there were Rutherfurd and Colden, who also had correspondents in Boston; in Philadelphia, there were Bartram, James Logan, and Franklin; and by way of him the network spread out to embrace the Library Company and the other members of the Junto.

Over in London there was Peter Collinson, who played an essential role as an intermediary. As far back as 1737, Collinson had read to the Royal Society a long letter from Joseph Breintnall of the Junto about the zoology of rattlesnakes. It was only the first of many letters from Breintnall, Bartram, and Colden, describing earthquakes, meteors, wasp's nests, plagues of locusts, and much else that Collinson took to his colleagues.

Although they aroused little interest, Collinson had at least created a channel of communication between the leading scientists in London and the most ingenious minds in the colonies.[9]

All of this took place at a time when, as Franklin had put it in the *Gazette,* the affairs of Europe were descending into an era of "infernal discord." In his early manhood, the peaceful conditions in the Atlantic had helped to create the environment in which he could flourish, as he grew his business in a stable and relatively prosperous economy. This era of equilibrium was now at an end. But—paradoxically—Franklin was about to become the beneficiary of war. While the flow of trade and news would be disrupted, many ships would still get through; and the war had the effect of deepening the ties of friendship between the people who belonged to Franklin's circle of allies.

Almost to a man—even John Bartram, despite his Quaker origins—they were as strongly committed to colonial security as they were to science. And this gave them all the more reason to communicate with each other. For many years, Cadwallader Colden had shared Logan's fears that the colonies would be surrounded by the French. In 1738, Colden had sent his own long memo to London, very similar to Logan's six years earlier, in which he warned the government about the weakness of New York's perimeter.[10]

From Canada the French were reaching out to the Iroquois, seeking to prise them free from British influence. Worse still, they had built a base in the upper reaches of the Hudson, the fortress known later as Crown Point, from which they could launch an invasion of New York. By 1743 this was more than a theoretical risk. The French fort lay only a hundred miles from Albany, where Rutherfurd had fewer than five hundred men. In January he gave Colden his assessment of the situation. "In a week's time, they can plunder Boston," he wrote. In the letters they exchanged, military thoughts of such a kind could be found side by side with their debates about Newtonian physics.[11]

In Philadelphia, for the moment the situation seemed less alarming: because Weiser had returned in diplomatic triumph from his mission to the Iroquois. Making peace between them and the Virginians, he also prepared a new treaty between the Six Nations and Pennsylvania, due to be signed at Lancaster the following year. Meanwhile William Allen was fitting out a new privateer, the *Wilmington,* to put to sea to attack the Spanish. In the *Gazette,* Franklin printed more reports from her captain, his friend John Sibbald, about his adventures in the Caribbean. Indeed the reports were so vivid that at about this time William Franklin, at only thirteen or fourteen years old, sneaked out of the family home to join a privateer and his father had to go aboard to fetch him back. "No-one imagined that it was hard usage at home that made him do this," Franklin wrote to Jane Mecom. "Everyone that knows me thinks I am too indulgent a parent, as well as master."[12]

Other than that all was quiet; but the calm was deceptive. Late in June, while Franklin was returning from Boston, at last the shooting war began in Germany. At Dettingen, near Frankfurt, although hostilities had not yet been officially declared the British and the French went into battle, the French were defeated, and with that the die was cast. The peaceful world of Franklin's youth had disappeared.

Franklin Moves On

It must have seemed to Franklin in 1743 that his life was just one Scotsman after another. He reached Philadelphia at the end of June. Deborah was now very pregnant—she would give birth in September to their daughter Sarah, or Sally—but Franklin also found waiting for him a message from a Scot named William Strahan. An Edinburgh man, he had built a thriving business as a printer in London. Although Mr. Strahan was only twenty-eight, he was already the printer of choice for the Methodists, running off a stream of tracts and journals by Whitefield, William Seward, and John Wesley. Somehow—perhaps by way of Seward—Strahan had heard of Franklin's high reputation. He had also met James Read, a cousin of Deborah's, who had been in England on business. Strahan wrote to Read, who showed his letter to Franklin. It contained a business proposition that Franklin found highly attractive.[13]

Now that he had three printing houses—his own, and his partnerships in Charleston and New York—Franklin hoped to establish a fourth, but that he could not do until he found the right person. It was the same old colonial problem, a shortage of skilled labor, but Strahan could offer a solution. His letter referred to a fellow Scot, David Hall, eight years younger than Franklin and a trained compositor. Hall had worked for Franklin's old London employer, John Watts, and then for William Strahan, but he was keen to set up in business by himself.

The young man had a problem of his own—like the young Franklin, he lacked the capital with which to buy equipment—but he was willing to sail to America. Strahan suggested that Franklin might like to take him on. On July 10 Franklin replied, offering Hall the chance to manage a new printing house if he turned out to be "a proper person." Even if he did not make the grade, he would guarantee a year's paid work for Hall and meet the cost of his passage back to England. It was one of the best letters Franklin ever sent: not for its style—though as always with him, it was impeccably written—but because David Hall was exactly the person his business required.

Since Strahan had a wide range of products, including medical textbooks, which were challenging things to set into type, Hall came equipped with skills as advanced as Franklin's. He was, as Franklin later described him, "obliging, discreet, industrious, but honest." In short, he had the makings of an ideal partner in the firm. Franklin's reply also marked the beginning of a beautiful friendship between him and Mr. Strahan, a gentleman printer of his own kind, who became his literary eyes and ears in London. In his early career, Strahan's most notable success was the printing of Henry Fielding's first novel, *Joseph Andrews,* which in time supplanted *Robinson Crusoe* to become Franklin's favorite work of fiction. Their relationship, which deepened still further when Franklin went to live in London, endured until Strahan's death in 1785, gravely tested though it was by the revolutionary crisis.

Franklin had a gift for friendship. Sometimes he also had the devil's own luck. Not until March of 1744 did David Hall set sail from London on the *Mercury,* reaching Philadelphia on or about June 20, sick with jaundice but alive. This was an achievement in itself, because the Atlantic was now more dangerous than it had been at any time since the Royal Navy swept Blackbeard and his fellow pirates from the ocean. Nine days or so before the *Mercury* arrived, Governor Thomas made the long-awaited proclamation: Great Britain and France were officially at war.

On June 11, with an honor guard of seamen—"a parcel of roaring sailors," wrote an eyewitness—George Thomas led the town's elite in a procession through the streets. It was said that as many as four thousand people gathered to hear the beating drums and to watch him climb the courthouse steps. Richard Peters read the declaration, and then the governor spoke a few words. Every able-bodied man in Pennsylvania should pick up a musket, powder, and ball: "for depend upon it," said Mr. Thomas, "this province shall not be lost through any neglect or oversight of mine."[14]

If only the elected politicians would listen and respond in kind; but as Governor Thomas knew full well, Speaker Kinsey and his Quaker party would never vote the money for a militia or for the armaments it needed. The previous October, when the assembly convened for its autumn session, Thomas had made a request for military supplies only to be met with a rude rebuff. The one thing the governor could do was this: in the name of the king, he could issue letters of marque to yet more privateers like Captain Sibbald. This had to be done because, to protect the seaborne traffic of the Delaware, the best means of defense was attack.[15]

The British fleet could not do the job alone, stretched thinly as it was, guarding the English Channel and keeping watch on the enemy in the West Indies and the Mediterranean. The Royal Navy had few ships to spare for convoy duties. Spanish privateers were still at large, and now they were joined by French ships from Saint-Malo in Brittany, which made deep forays into colonial waters. The French enjoyed a happy time when they could strike at American vessels as freely as they chose. Because their sailing times were predictable—before and after the tobacco harvest—the ships that plied between Great Britain and the Chesapeake made a splendid target. In Pennsylvania the price of shipping and insurance soared; and when early in July a cargo of gunpowder arrived, every barrel soon found a buyer.

That summer eight privateers put out to sea from Philadelphia. Here at last was Franklin's chance to join the fray, albeit from the safety of his store on Market Street. In June, the account books kept by Deborah began to feature a stream of new entries for sums of £5 or so at a time. In each case the formula was more or less identical: "Cr. William Allen by his bill against schooner *Wilmington*." The meaning was easy to decipher. Mr. Allen, Franklin's fellow mason, was the owner of the town's most successful privateer, skippered by John Sibbald, and Franklin was helping to equip the vessel. In payment he took IOUs from William Allen, to be redeemed from the proceeds of the *Wilmington*'s raids against the enemy.

As the months went by, and the naval war intensified, so dispatches from the privateers came to fill the pages of *The Pennsylvania Gazette*. All his life Franklin had been fascinated by the sea, and as a boy he had read about the exploits of Sir Francis Drake. Now he became a stay-at-home war correspondent, fed with his stories by John Sibbald and the other privateering captains. He printed so many that one wonders why he did not rename his paper *The Weekly Privateer*. Indeed the subject became so all-absorbing that when Franklin's Junto friend Thomas Godfrey set the newspaper's readers a mathematical puzzle, it concerned the time it would take a swift privateer to catch a slower-moving target ship.[16]

Because most of her merchants were Quakers, Philadelphia lagged far behind Rhode Island and New York in the number of privateers the town commissioned. And yet, in the four years of war against the French, Franklin ran far more stories about privateering than any other American editor. There were hundreds in fact, especially at the peak of the campaign in 1744–45, when stories of the kind in the *Gazette* outnumbered those in the press in Boston and New York by a factor of two or three to one. Franklin loved the war, or at least this side of it, and his patriotic fervor led to something new. He began to print pictures on the page. When the *Gazette* ran notices calling for "gentlemen sailors" to join the *Wilmington* and the other privateers, each one carried an illustration of the ship.

Here was another component of Franklin's change of life. He found the war exciting. And why not? While the Quaker merchants of the town worried about the disruption it caused to peaceful commerce, Franklin found that as the war went on the pace of his own career accelerated. In business, he now had David Hall to help him.

In the first twelve months after Hall's arrival, the two men trod rather warily around each other, each one suspicious of the other man's intentions. Franklin gradually came to feel that Hall could be relied upon, but Hall remained uneasy. He complained to Strahan, who wrote back urging Hall to trust his employer.

"He seems to me by his manner of writing to have a very good heart," said Strahan, "as well as to be a man of honour and good sense." Soon enough the atmosphere improved, and instead of sending Hall to start a printing venture in the West Indies—that was his initial intention—Franklin made him the foreman of his workshop. Here was the man who might be his successor, taking the business forward while Franklin devoted himself to public affairs and to science.[17]

He was making progress in that direction too. In April 1744, while Hall was still at sea, Dr. Spencer came down to Philadelphia to give his lectures, advertised in the *Gazette,* and they helped to build support for Franklin's scientific club. James Logan was a little skeptical about it, but John Bartram remained an enthusiast. As he wrote to Colden, "our Philosophick Society increaseth very finely," even though, as he explained, "I am full as much hurried in business as our friend Benjamin." At about the same time Franklin went up to Manhattan, where he collected a letter from Colden, and when he replied he also had splendid news about the club.[18]

They had their first roster of members: from Philadelphia, Thomas Hopkinson as president, Bartram as the botanist, William Parsons as the geographer, and also two physicians, Thomas and Phineas Bond. There were nine in all, with Franklin as the secretary, but the best news he had to tell concerned the members he recruited from New Jersey and New York. If his club was to function as Franklin intended, it had to be truly American and so it could not remain confined to a single province. It also had to feature people of distinction: not for reasons of snobbery, but because that was the best way for it to make its mark, and because—to be blunt—Franklin needed people who had money, time, and influence.

Among his new recruits, the member from New York was the most impressive: yet another Scot, James Alexander, a powerful and wealthy man of fifty-three. In his leisure hours he studied astronomy and he was another of Colden's closest friends. By profession Alexander was a lawyer, perhaps the finest in the city. Seven years earlier, he had been the attorney who briefed Andrew Hamilton in the landmark case of John Peter Zenger, the printer accused of seditious libel. In reaching out to people of this caliber, Franklin was being highly ambitious. He was also transmitting a message about the wider aims he hoped to fulfill.

In New York, Mr. Colden was surveyor general; Parsons held that office in Pennsylvania; and Alexander had the same title in New Jersey, where he amassed his own portfolio of soil. Moving to and fro across the Hudson River, he acted as the agent for New Jersey's principal landlords, the people for whom Franklin had been doing printing work for nearly twenty years. Not content with Mr. Alexander, Franklin also sought out New Jersey's chief justice, Robert Hunter Morris, another man who spanned both sides of the river: he came from one of the wealthiest families in New York.[19]

Nearly three centuries on, lists of names such as these might make for tedious reading, but the pattern they reveal is the point to grasp. Like Franklin's old mentor Speaker Hamilton, the people he recruited for his philosophical society shared his commitment to colonial expansion. They were also high officials, advisers to the governor in each colony. In New York, both Colden and James Alexander sat on the governor's council, while down in Philadelphia William Parsons reported directly to the Penns and to Governor Thomas.

None of these people had been voted into office. On the contrary, in all three colonies often they found themselves at loggerheads with the elected assemblies: Colden most of all. He loathed the New York assembly, whose members included men who traded illegally with the French in Montreal. In their turn, they detested Cadwallader Colden. And so, at this critical stage of Franklin's life, he found his best allies among the elite, people like Logan and James Alexander, men of property whose loyalties lay chiefly with the Crown in England.[20]

Today we mostly think of Franklin as he was in his heyday in the 1770s and 1780s, a democrat with a small "d," helping to make new, republican constitutions for the United States and also for Pennsylvania. Some writers argue that Franklin had always been a champion of the common people, and that his Junto began as a "leathern apron club" for artisans. In fact, no contemporary record has been found in which Franklin or his fellow members used that phrase to describe it. Although most of the founding members were employed as printers by Samuel Keimer, its proceedings show that the Junto was really a society for people who aspired to be gentlemen.

One of the most remarkable things about Franklin was that as he grew older he became more radical and more democratic, a friend of populists and revolutionaries such as Thomas Paine. In the 1740s, this sort of radicalism did not feature in Franklin's program. At that time, the promotion of democracy would have been irrelevant to his concerns. At heart he was always an old-fashioned Whig like his uncle Benjamin, with values harking back to London in the 1680s, where "English Liberties" was the Whig battle cry. Indeed Franklin never ceased to believe in English liberties—taxation by consent, trial by jury, and so on—but in 1744 these freedoms were not in danger from King George. As for the Penns, the colony's proprietors, they certainly behaved like grasping landlords, but as yet they did not seek to undermine Pennsylvania's constitution. It was only much later that Franklin became the consistent opponent in politics of the family's leader, Thomas Penn.

In the 1740s, the powerful ruler Franklin had to fear was not an English king or landed plutocrat but a Frenchman, Louis XV at Versailles. He was the enemy, while George II was a friend who did not try to curtail the freedoms the Quaker colony enjoyed. Since democracy was not in danger from a homegrown enemy, Franklin had no cause to be its strident advocate. Indeed he had mixed feelings about a system of government that could not be relied upon to produce sound leadership. While democracy might be a worthy concept, in practice it gave birth in Pennsylvania to a machine politician, the embezzling Speaker Kinsey. And anyway, at this phase of his life what Franklin really cared about was ingenuity. America had to be improved, and it also had to be defended militarily—in the 1740s *those* were his priorities—and Franklin made common cause with people who shared the same agenda.

Which actually meant the powerful, unelected likes of Cadwallader Colden or James Alexander, whose genteel support Franklin had to win if he were to make a go of his American Philosophical Society. In its first incarnation the society turned out to be a disappointment. It fizzled out in 1745, when its other members failed to sustain the momentum that Franklin and Bartram had given it. It was only in 1767 that the society came to life again, revived to become a fixture of the American scene. Even so the early days were highly productive. Franklin's efforts to create it had the effect of speeding up the circulation of ideas.

After drawing in New Jersey and New York, he wanted to broaden his society by bringing in people of science from the South. Soon a qualified candidate arrived. In 1741–42 there had been epidemics of yellow jack in Virginia and New York, spread no doubt by veterans returning from the Caribbean war. The death toll had led John Mitchell, a physician from a harbor town on the lower Rappahannock, to investigate the disease. Visiting Philadelphia in September 1744, he spent a day with Bartram and Franklin, showing them his essays about yellow fever, which Franklin gave to Lewis Evans to copy out. Franklin shared them with Colden.[21]

And so Franklin's network became ever wider. That autumn, he took another step forward by publishing his pamphlet about the fireplace. Like the Conestoga wagon and the Pennsylvania rifle, it was tangible proof of the virtues of "improvement." To reproduce the technical drawings, he had to hire an engraver up in Boston—he and Bartram badly needed a Hogarth of their own in Philadelphia—but the job was done, with the money to print the pamphlet coming from Robert Grace. James Alexander thought the little book was excellent, its author "a man of sense and of a good style," and Colden agreed. In December 1744 he sent a copy to Leiden, the home of the Dutch Newtonians, the very people whose books Franklin had been reading for so long. Calling Franklin "a very ingenious man," Colden urged the scientific Dutchmen to study the pamphlet closely, if only as a means "to keep you warm at your studies."[22]

Before the essay about the fireplace appeared, Colden had primarily seen Franklin as a printer—albeit the best in the colonies—and as a go-between. That fall he had sent Franklin a draft of his two essays, on the nature of matter and on Newton's "fluxions," asking him to pass them on to James Logan. Franklin took the essays up to Stenton, where Logan spotted the mistakes in Colden's algebra. As for Colden's piece on "the different species of matter," Logan could make neither head nor tail of it.

But what Colden could now see, after reading the fireplace pamphlet, was that Franklin was a highly talented scientist in his own right. As the snow began to fall on the Hudson, he received a message from Franklin informing him about the errors Logan found in his mathematics. It was another diplomatic letter—no one could be as courteous as Franklin—in which he assured Mr. Colden that doubtless the mistakes were merely slips of the pen. Taken aback though he was, Colden replied to Franklin in terms that showed that his respect for Franklin was increasing all the time.[23]

As Colden lost a little of his faith in his work on Newton's calculus, so he came to place more emphasis on his other treatise, the one that dealt with gravity. In a moving letter, written by a man eager for scientific recognition after laboring so long in the wilderness, Colden begged Franklin to give it his full attention. "I know none besides Mr Logan, Mr Alexander and yourself in this part of the world," Colden wrote, "to whose judgment I can refer any thing of this kind." High praise indeed. In the next two years Franklin repaid the compliment as Colden would have wished, by studying his letters closely and always replying at length. But the problem was this: Colden had simply too *many* notions, none of which he mastered completely.[24]

Confined to his farm that winter, he revived another old obsession, dating back some twenty-five years. It was an analysis of what he called "animal economy." Like Henry Pemberton, the Newtonian whom Franklin had known in London, Colden hoped to show that Newton's physics could explain the inner workings of the human body. Here was another hugely ambitious project, undertaken by Colden at a time when he was busy with another bold scheme. He was also drawing up plans for a fort at Oswego on the shore of Lake Ontario: something he and Captain Rutherfurd believed was essential as a bulwark against the French.

Trying always to do too much, Mr. Colden achieved far too little. He was a catalyst, giving Franklin food for thought, but a moment had to come when Franklin left behind the sort of unfocused speculation to which Cadwallader Colden was all too prone. That moment was close at hand. In Europe people of science were yet again preoccupied with electricity. Four years after the death of Du Fay, a series of new experiments had been carried out in Germany, and early in 1745, the spectacular details appeared in the London press. Although they had elements of theater, the results the Germans produced with electricity breathed new life into the subject. By way of Peter Collinson and the British papers, the excitement was conveyed to the colonies; where Franklin, the avid reader, would soon see its significance.

The German Spark

In the middle of the eighteenth century, there existed a gradient of power in Europe. At the summit stood the French, because their population and their army were the largest, and their intellectuals the most illustrious. England occupied the next step down, with her much smaller army but her powerful navy, her robust finances, and her trading empire. Then came Austria and Spain, while everyone else—including the Dutch, whose economy had fallen into stagnation—lay somewhere far below. Away to the west, the colonies in America were barely visible at all. The slope of power was also a gradient of ingenuity, where the ranking was rather different, with the Dutch still holding their own. Even so, the leadership in science belonged to Paris and to London.

The nations and cities that lagged behind were eager to catch up, and none more so than the military state of Prussia. And so Franklin had a counterpart in Berlin, a man as keen as he was to improve his country and to climb the hill of knowledge. Six years Franklin's junior, King Frederick of Prussia held sway over a chain of provinces from the Rhine to the Baltic that, like Pennsylvania, were rich in grain. Unlike the Quaker colonists, he had his army too, which Frederick unleashed against the Austrians. In 1740 he annexed the Habsburg province of Silesia, a lawless incident of theft by force of arms that helped to bring about the wider war between Great Britain and France. What Prussia did not possess was industry, technology, or prestige in the world of learning.

And so, in the year when his troops plundered the Silesians, Frederick the Great revived the Berlin Academy of Sciences, which had become entirely moribund, offering salaries and honors to the eminent philosophers he hoped to recruit. "I wish my capital to become the temple of great men," he wrote to his friend Voltaire. With his improved academy, the Prussian king meant to reach or to surpass, as soon as he could, the level of knowledge that existed in London and Paris. Though conceived on a much grander scale, it was a project with aims identical to those of Franklin's new society in Philadelphia. Here were two visionaries, who felt adrift on the periphery of culture and did not wish to remain so.[25]

To the south of Prussia lay the kingdom of Saxony, which had fine universities at Wittenberg and Halle but also saw itself as a nation with unrealized potential. Here the visionary was a politician, Ernst Christoph, Graf von Manteuffel. As his country's envoy in Berlin he had shared ideas with Frederick over endless cups of coffee. The count created a club of his own that even more closely resembled Franklin's, calling it the Societas Aletho-Philorum, the society for the lovers of truth. All he and the Prussians required was an interlude of peace in which to concentrate on the pursuit of wisdom. In 1741 and 1742, Frederick defeated the Austrian army, a treaty was signed, and in the two years that followed, Germany became the electrical heart of Europe.

At Halle and Wittenberg, Manteuffel urged the professors into action. Rather than making new theories, the Germans strove for technical advances that could enhance the power of electricity. In London in the early 1700s, Newton's assistant Francis Hauksbee had used a whirling globe of glass to produce his flashing lights and dancing threads of brass. However, in their later work in the 1730s in London and Paris the electricians had preferred to make do with a glass tube rubbed by hand. At Wittenberg in 1743, Georg Matthias Bose returned to the earlier British technique, building a new electrical machine using a glass sphere attached to a system of pulleys and a wheel that could be turned at high speed. The word "conductor" had already come into use, coined by Desaguliers. Bose's "prime conductor" consisted of a long iron rod or gun barrel, suspended by silken threads and brought up close to the sphere.[26]

Making a host of technical improvements—for example, by reducing the quantity of potash used in making the glass, or by oiling its surface—the Germans found that they could amplify the effects Du Fay had produced. Bose charged up a dinner table, so that when the guests sat down, sparks flashed from the cutlery and gave them a hefty shock. He sat a man in a seat and created an electric halo around his head, calling the experiment "the chair of beatification." One of his colleagues electrified a lady's whalebone corset so that it could send forth "flashes of pure lightning."

Most dramatic of all was the event that took place at the Berlin Academy in January 1744. With Frederick looking on, the scientists filled a tank with a mixture of alcohol and sulfuric acid and brought the prime conductor to bear. They accomplished what Du Fay had failed to do: the liquid exploded in a ball of flame. Eager to spread the word, Manteuffel arranged electrical shows for the princes and nobility of the German states, including Hanover, where George II spent his summer vacation. There "the ladies of quality did yet more," it was reported. "They procured machines, tried the experiments themselves, and electricity took the place of quadrille."[27]

From a German point of view, electricity made an ideal subject for research: a field where the British and the French had struck a dead end, giving their competitors across the Rhine the opportunity they needed to take the lead in physics. As yet, Herr Bose and his colleagues did not have a theory to make sense of their findings, but they could at least confirm that thinkers such as Madame du Châtelet had been looking for the secret of "Fire" in the correct location. It did indeed appear that light, heat, electricity, and magnetism were—in some strange way—all variations on a common theme. The effects of electricity were startling and powerful enough to make it what the marquise thought it was: the path to the center of the labyrinth of nature.

Perhaps there was some fundamental force, or indeed some fundamental form of *matter,* the underlying stuff of the universe, of which heat, light, and electricity were all manifestations. But if this was so, how did it square with the system left behind by Sir Isaac Newton? Mostly, he had seemed to think of matter as something passive and inert, doing nothing by itself without the action of some external force. Or at least that was *one* way to read what Newton had written; in fact, in his later work, the subtle Sir Isaac had been far less categorical. Be that as it may, when Manteuffel and his friends thought about the new phenomenon of electricity, it did not seem to them that "matter" was inert. On the contrary, it seemed to be dynamic, full of something like the vigor of a living creature.

It was all very confusing. It was also very exhilarating. And all the more so, when the sister science of biology produced what seemed to be another refutation of Newton. In the summer of 1743, Manteuffel exchanged a series of animated letters with the eminence of German philosophy, Christian Wolff. Their letters dealt with two subjects: not only the new electrical displays, but also the bizarre behavior of the polyp, a tiny aquatic creature, living in ponds, which looked like a plant but squirmed and crawled about like an insect or an animal.[28]

First identified three years earlier by a Swiss scientist, Abraham Trembley, the polyp was as strange as electric fire. Cut a polyp in half, and it would not die. Instead it would regenerate, to produce two wriggling creatures where only one had existed before. For Wolff and for Manteuffel, the polyp seemed to be the lively proof that Newton had been wrong about the properties of "matter." Leaping to more than a few conclusions, Professor Wolff began to revive the concept of "spontaneous generation," to the effect that life could emerge unbidden from a primal soup of mud and water. Nearly twenty years earlier, on his voyage home from London, Franklin had pondered the same kind of notion when he peered at the mysterious *Sargassum.**

Suddenly it seemed that science was ready to escape from Newton's shadow, with a host of new things to be seen and new theories to be proposed. In 1743 and 1744, these two sets of results—the German work with electricity, and Trembley's investigation of the polyp—came together to produce the sense of excitement that Peter Collinson transmitted on to America. Since the death of Desaguliers, in London the Royal Society had been through a rather dormant phase. After learning of these new discoveries, the membership sprang back into motion.

Hearing about the polyp, they scoured the countryside in the outskirts of London, where they found some patriotic English polypi in residence in a pond in Hackney. In November 1743 they gave Mr. Trembley their highest award, the Copley Medal; and eighteen months later, when full reports came in from Germany about the electrical shows, the Royal Society were equally receptive. On March 14, 1745, they listened to a long account of the German experiments, including Professor Bose's "chair of beatification." In its April issue, *The Gentleman's Magazine* published the story in full.[29]

On March 30, Collinson wrote an ecstatic letter to New York telling Cadwallader Colden of what he had seen and heard. "The surprising phenomena of the polypus entertained the curious for a year or two past," he wrote. "But now the virtuosi . . . are taken up in electrical experiments." Collinson too had been among a group of gentlemen who saw a spark of electricity detonate a charge of gunpowder. In the new discoveries he found what he called "an inexhaustible fund of enquiry . . . of very great moment no doubt to the system of the universe." If only Sir Isaac were still alive, said Collinson: "Had these great discoveries happened in that great man's time, his illuminated mind would have applied them to wonderful purposes." It would fall to Franklin to be the new genius they required.

* Franklin ran a story about the polyp in *The Pennsylvania Gazette* on March 31, 1743.

In the meantime there was still a war to be fought. In the summer of 1744, Frederick the Great had sent his army to attack the Austrians in Bohemia, with Saxony also drawn into the fighting. In alliance with France he was about to win more victories. The following year, the Americans would teach the French a painful lesson of the same military kind; but for Franklin, it began with melancholy news that he had been expecting to arrive.

Chapter Nineteen

A Calling Found

Sir Robert Walpole was a dying man, and his last years were blighted with the agony of kidney stones. He shared at least that measure of equality with Josiah Franklin, who suffered from the same complaint. Franklin wrote to his parents, suggesting drugs, promising to speak to Bartram about herbal remedies, and also advising a mixture of honey and molasses. It might help Josiah's urine flow more freely with less gravel. Meanwhile Jane Mecom nursed him with devotion. "Dear sister," wrote Franklin, "I love you tenderly for your care of our father in his sickness."[1]

On January 16, 1745, Josiah passed away at the age of eighty-seven. He had been sixty-one years in America, his life mostly quiet and his habits sober and industrious. Again—as with his brother Benjamin—when his obituary appeared in the Boston press, praising Josiah as a man who had always displayed "the strictest piety and virtue," from its brief and stylized contents no one could have guessed that here was an Englishman, one of the earliest Whigs, who remembered the distant London of Titus Oates and the Popish Plot. And yet the conflicts of that era remained unresolved. The Jacobites were still at large, with a new leader, Charles Edward Stuart, grandson of the old King James of the 1680s. In March, Walpole died as well; and as the statesman breathed his last, with his diplomacy in ruins, it was feared that the Jacobites were poised to swoop on England, carried to the beaches by an invasion fleet from France.

Which was close to the truth; although when the Jacobite invasion came later that year, it was routed through the Scottish Highlands, and the French army were noticeably absent. At Versailles the officials were never really sure about the Jacobites, and still less about the young Prince

Charles. In Massachusetts, it seemed to be time to come to England's aid by opening another front in the war. Up in Nova Scotia—or more precisely on Cape Breton Island—the French had their fortified naval base at Louisbourg. If it could be taken, not only would the French privateers lose a depot for supplies. The way might also be made clear for a British and American assault on Canada.

And so in Boston the governor, William Shirley, drew up a plan to strike at Louisbourg. It was something he had been discussing for years with his friend Peter Warren, a naval officer from Britain whose squadron of ships were based in the Bay Colony. Early in 1745 Commodore Warren and his little fleet were off in the West Indies, guarding the sugar islands. But if they broke away and made a dash for the north, and if New England raised an army of its own, perhaps they might catch Louisbourg by surprise.[2]

Never before had a British colony conceived a plan so daring; and no one was more eager than Franklin to see it succeed. At his desk in the State House in Philadelphia, he seethed with anger as he listened late in February while the assembly debated the question of the hour: should Pennsylvania join the expedition to Cape Breton? As the assembly clerk, Franklin was supposed to keep the minutes and be neutral. However, among his papers there survives a fragmentary document—meant it seems for his eyes only—that records his feelings about the affair.

He was furious with Governor Thomas, for calling on the members to help in the attack on Louisbourg, while knowing all the time that Speaker Kinsey and the Quaker-led majority would refuse his request. Franklin was only a little less angry with the Quakers. In the summer just gone, a French privateer from Cape Breton had taken four ships from Philadelphia at the mouth of the Delaware: but the Quakers were content to turn the other cheek. "In short the governor and the assembly have been only acting a farce," he wrote, "playing tricks to amuse the world."[3]

What could Franklin do? For one thing he had the power of the press; but to use it to best effect he needed news. On March 24 the militia set sail from Portsmouth, New Hampshire, blessed on their way to war with a homily by George Whitefield, who had somehow forgotten the teachings of the Sermon on the Mount. The preacher had reappeared in America, where he sought to widen his appeal by adding a dose of patriotic fervor. Eager for more information, Franklin sent a letter to his brother John. "Our people are extremely impatient to hear of your success at Cape Breton," he wrote. "My shop is filled with thirty inquiries at the coming in of every post." His only fear was this: that America's lack of trained engineers might doom the assault to failure.[4]

There it was again, the thing that had so often troubled Franklin: the shortage of craftsmen in the colonies. On this occasion his anxieties were misplaced. In April Warren's ships hurried north from Antigua, making rendezvous with the volunteer marines from New England. On May Day they landed five miles from the fortress, three thousand strong, dragging their cannon on sledges. While Warren kept French warships at bay, the siege of Louisbourg began. It lasted seven hard-fought weeks, with the Americans bringing their batteries ever closer to the walls. On June 17, seeing that their defenses were about to be breached, the French had no choice: the garrison surrendered.

Greeted with exultation in Britain and America alike, the fall of Louisbourg had many consequences. For the first time in colonial history, news from the western side of the Atlantic became the principal talking point in London; and so in future, Walpole's successors would have to pay more heed to the dispatches they received, and think more deeply about their American strategy. Wiping out the stain of the disasters at Cartagena and Guantánamo Bay, the victory led to a surge of confidence in Boston and the other towns along the seaboard.

It even helped heal some of the wounds left by the Great Awakening. In the summer of 1745, Whitefield and his opponents in the clergy could unite in rejoicing at the defeat of the Papists. For some time Whitefield had been toning down his sermons, making them less divisive, and in January he had come close to issuing an apology to his opponents among the Harvard ministers in New England. Even so, it was only *after* Louisbourg that he and Franklin became personal friends as opposed to business contacts. For Franklin the Cape Breton campaign had also been a professional triumph.

When Franklin's journalism is discussed, his talents are usually seen to lie in the quality of his prose: Silence Dogood, *The Busy-Body, The Way to Wealth,* and the hoaxes and satires he went on writing until the 1770s. But nothing beats news in a newspaper. Working at long distance, but with his wide array of contacts to help him—privateers, merchants, and politicians—Franklin broke fresh ground in his coverage of Louisbourg. It was detailed, it was sustained, combining hard news with analysis, and it was fast.

On May 23, for example, while the Americans were still in the trenches, he ran a column in *The Pennsylvania Gazette* explaining the significance of

Louisbourg, putting it in its context, economic and military, and setting out the origins of Franco-British rivalry. On June 6 he did still better, with vivid eyewitness accounts of the landings and the first nine days of fighting onshore. In the same issue, Franklin printed a gem of the newsman's art: a detailed plan of Louisbourg and its defenses, with each point carefully numbered and explained in notes beneath the map.

Franklin apologized for the quality—"rough as it is, for want of good engravers here"—but no one in America had printed the like before. And when Louisbourg fell, the news reaching Boston on July 8, it took only ten more days for Franklin to get a full report—from three different sources, two officers and an army chaplain—into the *Gazette.* It filled the front page and spilled over onto the second. Below it he ran more news from the *Wilmington* privateer.

After twenty-five years in the business, more or less, Franklin had nothing left to learn about editing a newspaper. A journalist on top of his trade, he was in a cheerful, even ebullient mood that year, despite his father's death and his irritation with Governor Thomas and the Quakers. The success of his fireplace pamphlet, his philosophical society, his ever widening circle of friends, his little daughter, and even young William, who was mostly shaping up well: Franklin had many reasons to be happy. David Hall was turning out to be a treasure. This must have helped to make the Louisbourg coverage go so splendidly for the *Gazette.*

In the middle of February, Franklin had written a lively letter to William Strahan that takes us into his buoyant frame of mind. Praising David Hall to the skies, Franklin was eager to hear all the latest news and to see the latest books from London. "Let me have everything, good or bad, that makes a noise and has a run," he wrote to Strahan. "For I have friends here of different tastes to oblige with the sight of them." In particular he asked for poetry by Alexander Pope and by his beloved James Thomson. Although Pope had passed away the previous year, Thomson was still in full flood. He had recently brought out a new, enlarged edition of *The Seasons.*[5]

"I wish it were in my power to return him any part of the joy he has given me," said Franklin. Over the years, as he revised *The Seasons,* so Thomson had included more and more allusions to the latest scientific theories: about biology, astronomy, the phenomena of light and heat, and—a favorite Thomson subject, as it was for Franklin—the origins of thunder and lightning. Binding poetry and physics ever more closely together, Thomson was the poet laureate of British science. With his writings he fed the mood of intellectual excitement in London. An eloquent spokesman for patriotism as well, especially when displayed by the Royal Navy, James Thomson also wrote the words for "Rule Britannia." In every way he appealed to Franklin—scientist and patriot—whose work in both domains Thomson helped to inspire.[6]

Animal Spirits

At some point in 1745, Cadwallader Colden sent Franklin his essay about what he called the "animal economy." It was a curious piece, in which the Scotsman tried to argue that the human body works its miracles partly by way of Newton's laws of motion, and partly thanks to something chemical that he called "fermentation." Somehow or other, deep in the capillaries or in the liver, this strange process occurred. As a result, said Mr. Colden, "the animal juices gain their greatest perfection, and produce the fluids called animal spirits."[7]

The essay was very odd indeed; but in the summer Franklin carefully read what Colden had to say. It was very hot in Philadelphia, plagued by mosquitoes—Franklin complained to Colden about them—but he persevered with "animal economy." Franklin even tried to build a model, fashioned out of glass tubes and siphons, to test the truth of Colden's strange theories. Thrilled by the victory at Louisbourg, Franklin felt he could do anything.

At the American Philosophical Society, his comrades were failing to do their bit: they preferred the coffeehouse to chemistry. But Franklin persisted. He told Colden of some plans to launch a new scientific magazine. He would have so much material: Colden on animal spirits and "fluxions" and "the different species of matter," Mitchell on yellow fever, and himself on whatever "matters of invention" he might choose. And in this same mood of euphoria, Franklin put pen to paper with something in very bad taste.

On June 25, while the siege of Louisbourg was still under way, Franklin wrote a crude, misogynistic piece about the bodies of women. Not made the least bit public until 1885—and even then only in a limited edition, which very few people saw—his article was titled "Old Mistresses Apologue." Those who wish to read the witty sketch in full can find it in the Yale edition of Franklin's papers, freely available online.

The gist of it is this: if a young man feels in need and does not wish to marry, he should seek his pleasure with an old woman. Why? Because she will be discreet and undemanding. While her face, neck, and arms will be wrinkled, in bed her other parts can still perform their function: even in the dark, which will be required because she is so ugly. The best of it will be that an old woman will be "so grateful!!" So we are told in the "Apologue."

In idle moments or in drink, a man might think or say such things: but why should Franklin write them down, seeing that they were never to be published? And why should he date the article so precisely? And at such a time, when he was so busy with the war and *The Pennsylvania Gazette*? Another odd thing is this: the "Apologue" survives in two manuscripts. One is in Franklin's handwriting and the other is a copy by somebody else with Franklin's revisions. In other words: he was proud of it and he meant the piece for private circulation among his friends.

You may make of this what you will. Twenty years earlier *The New-England Courant* had dealt in the same kind of stuff, but why should Franklin do so at the age of thirty-nine? Given its timing, simultaneous with Louisbourg, when he was feeling so fired up for the war, most likely Franklin wrote the "Apologue" in a mood of masculine bravado, to be shared for a laugh with his new friend David Hall. And then—one suspects—Franklin kept the sketch as something to be read out for amusement over a bottle of wine or a few at clubby meetings of the Junto or the masons, to which women were not admitted. But whatever the circumstances, the lesson of the "Apologue" is surely this. It was high time for Franklin to get on with something more serious.

The war against the French, for example: a war in which so many of his acquaintances were involved. In the letter he sent to William Strahan in February, Franklin had asked after his old friend from the London of the 1720s, John Wygate, whose career had been checkered. After setting up as a printer on his own, Wygate had suffered the fate of so many others in the same trade. He became a bankrupt. When his mother died in 1737, leaving him a modest legacy, Wygate had put himself back on his feet, done some more printing, and then found a new career at sea. He took a job as a clerk on a warship, the *Furnace*, bound for the Canadian Arctic in search of the Northwest Passage.

This Franklin knew from accounts of the expedition written by its leader, Christopher Middleton, that Strahan had sent to Philadelphia. He also knew that the voyage had ended in failure; that John Wygate had become a witness against Middleton in an unseemly inquiry that followed; and that his old friend had gone to sea again, as the purser of a naval sloop, the *Hind*. William Strahan had told him so. What Franklin could not know was that HMS *Hind* had put out to the West Indies. She arrived in Antigua in March, just as Warren was about to speed away to Canada.[8]

At the time John Wygate and the *Hind* were busy patrolling in the Caribbean, taking two French ships off Curaçao; and indeed in one way or another, in 1745 almost every one of Franklin's friends, new or old, from England, the Junto, or his philosophical society, were caught up in the conflict with the Spanish and the French. Pursers or privateers or makers of maps, people of letters like Richard Peters, soldiers like Captain Rutherfurd or strategic thinkers like Cadwallader Colden: each one had his role to play.

In the second half of the year, Franklin did his own patriotic duty by bringing to a climax his coverage of privateering. Every issue of the *Gazette* contained fresh news of the naval war, whose tide was starting to turn. While in Flanders the British had suffered a reverse at the battle of Fontenoy, soon to be followed in August by the Jacobite landing in Scotland, the war in the Atlantic became a matter of attrition that the Bourbons could not win. Deprived of Louisbourg, and up against the British navy and the mercantile marine of Britain and America combined, the French and the Spanish gradually conceded defeat.

In the closing weeks of 1745, Franklin felt that he was winning too. Across the ocean, the Jacobite Prince Charles had marched with his small, ragged army from Scotland into England; but after the victory at Louisbourg, Franklin did not feel unduly worried. He and his landlord, Mr. Grace, signed a new lease, to run for fourteen years, on the premises on Market Street where Franklin had his home, his printing works, and his shop. Nobody in business does that unless he or she feels confident about the future. And in 1746—as Franklin approached the age of forty-one—at last he would make that future take the form of a vocation rather than a trade.[9]

Grand Enterprises

Up in New York the frontier war went on, a matter of scalping raids by the French and their Indian allies against the fringes of the colony. In the autumn of 1745 the French had come down the Hudson and plundered the small British post at Saratoga: a modest reprisal for the loss of Cape Breton. At Albany Major Rutherfurd—he had been promoted—waited for reinforcements. New orders had arrived from England calling for an invasion of Canada, to be achieved by marching up the Hudson and taking the French fort at Crown Point while the British sent a fleet and an army into the St. Lawrence. And so in the new year he and Cadwallader Colden and James Alexander did what they could to gather the troops this would require.

They were now trusted advisers of the royal governor of New York, George Clinton. Before any such invasion could be mounted, they would need not only more soldiers but also a firm alliance with the Iroquois, whose language Colden spoke. To that end he went upriver to Albany in the middle of 1746 with Clinton, there to hold talks with the tribes. Meanwhile Clinton and his fellow governors in the other colonies called for volunteers for a new American army to be concentrated in the Hudson valley. Franklin would do the very most he could to help his friends: he sent his only son.

Young William Franklin, who had been so keen to be a privateer, decided to be a soldier instead. At sixteen he was old enough to be a combatant. Even after Louisbourg, and even though the Jacobites were not yet defeated, the Quakers of Pennsylvania still refused to take steps to help defend the colonies. Something had to be done; and so in June Governor Thomas called for four companies of volunteers to march to the north. They left for Albany in September, with William Franklin serving as an ensign in the German company led by Captain Diemer, a surgeon and physician.[10]

This time the boy went with his father's blessing. Franklin was still feeling highly confident, and the fine flow of news that year made him all the more so. The summer of 1746 was filled with disease in New York and Philadelphia—smallpox again—but in April he and Deborah had taken the precaution of having little Sally inoculated. She did not succumb. And then word arrived from Scotland about the defeat of Charles Edward Stuart at the battle of Culloden. Spelling the end of the Jacobites, it made Great Britain safe for the Protestant cause to which the Franklins had always adhered.[11]

As William set off for New York with his fellow soldiers, Franklin wrote to Strahan again. Mr. and Mrs. Strahan had sent a gift for Sally, for which she would thank them when she reached an age to do so. "I congratulate you on the defeat of Jacobitism," Franklin added, "and the restoration of peace and good order." Franklin wrote those words on September 25. Four weeks earlier George Whitefield had appeared at his meeting house in Philadelphia, so often vacant but now filled to overflowing, to crow over the defeat of the Highland clans. The preacher described Culloden as "the bloody and deserved slaughter of some thousands of the rebels." In the twenty-first century, there are still some American pastors who regard Mr. Whitefield as the very model of a Christian minister.[12]

But while the Jacobites were finished, the king of France was not. In October Franklin heard some troubling news from Albany. With a view to helping in the talks with the tribes the expert negotiator Conrad Weiser had been up the Hudson, met Colden, Major Rutherfurd, and Governor Clinton, and then come back to Philadelphia. Although in August a deal had been struck with the Iroquois, who listened to a long speech from Colden and then agreed to take up the hatchet against the French, the situation had deteriorated. There was little hope of launching a British offensive that year.

"Our grand enterprise against Canada," as the major called it, would have to be postponed, but as the troops gathered in Albany, smallpox spread about the billets and the town. Supplies were short; the British had failed to send their fleet and their expeditionary force; and down in Manhattan, the New York assemblymen were almost as reluctant as their counterparts in the Quaker colony to pay for a long campaign.[13]

And so the Franklins would have to endure a long and anxious interval before William could return from the front. In the meantime the ideas continued to flow back and forth. Committed though he was to the war effort, Cadwallader Colden also found time for philosophy. In the spring of 1746 his treatise—*Of the First Causes of Action in Matter, and Gravitation*—had appeared in print in New York, published by Franklin's partner James Parker. It was prefaced by a letter of dedication to James Alexander, in which Colden gave his modest appraisal of its significance. His findings would, he wrote, open up "a prospect of great improvement in all the useful sciences in human life." Eager to have it reviewed by his peers, he exchanged more letters with Franklin and his other friends on both sides of the Atlantic.

"Pray God these wars may soon cease for they are destructive to learning," Colden wrote to his Dutch acquaintances in Leiden; but despite the fighting, the impetus of science could not be deflected. In the spring the press in London began to publish stories about a new development in the quest for the secrets of electricity. Between them the Germans and the Dutch invented a device, which came to be called the Leiden jar, with the power to deliver electric shocks far more dangerous than any felt before. While the jar might be lethal, it might also help to answer the riddle set by Émilie du Châtelet for her contemporaries. In the right hands—those of the "ingenious philosopher" whose advent she had foretold—the jar would reveal new epiphanies of nature.[14]

The Leiden Jar

For the Prussians, 1745 had been a year of triumph in battle, ending in defeat for Austria and Saxony and a victory parade in Berlin. A few weeks earlier, word had arrived in the city of another bold stroke of Prussian ingenuity. In the eastern province of Pomerania, there lived Ewald Jürgen von Kleist, scion of a Junker family and dean of a Lutheran cathedral. In November, he wrote to the Berlin Academy about an electrical discovery.

Taking a small glass vial of the kind used by apothecaries, with a little mercury or some alcohol in the bottom, he had dangled into the vial a nail or a thick piece of wire so that it touched the liquid. First the dean charged up a prime conductor, and used it to electrify the nail. To his amazement, he found that if he or an onlooker touched the nail with one hand while holding the vial with the other, they received a powerful shock. Kleist refined his technique until he could knock a boy of nine to the ground.[15]

Word of his achievement swiftly arrived in Paris and the Netherlands, where scientists pondered this new enigma. The odd thing was this: that the little glass container appeared to *magnify* the effects of electricity, producing forces far stronger than those seen hitherto. Because Kleist wrote badly, his descriptions being hazy and confusing, his readers had to struggle to repeat his results. In January 1746—to their delight but also to their horror—as they did so the Dutch at Leiden hit upon their famous jar.

'S Gravesande had died four years earlier; and so it fell to his successor at the university, Professor van Musschenbroek, to describe its potency. As he was working with a glass bottle in place of the vial, he received a visitor, a lawyer who decided to try the same thing at home. As he was holding the bottle in one hand, with the other he drew a spark from the prime conductor, and he suffered a massive shock. He hurried back to Musschenbroek, who bravely repeated the experiment and described it in a letter to his fellow scientists in Paris.

To generate his electricity, he used one of the whirling glass spheres of the kind that the Germans had made popular. And then, as Musschenbroek reported, "having suspended an iron cannon horizontally upon silken cords, with one end near the electrical globe, he fastened to the other end a wire, which descended into a bottle half full of water; then holding up the bottle with his right hand, while the cannon was electrifying, he put forth a finger of his left hand toward the piece, in order as usual to draw off a spark; and was struck such a violent blow that he thought his life was at an end."

A demonstration of the Leiden jar, with on the right the electrostatic generator, again from the Abbé Nollet's 1750 essay on electricity.

His account of the Leiden jar soon made its way to London, where the newspapers printed Musschenbroek's letter in the final week of March. Eight weeks later the story reached America, where *The Boston Post-Boy* printed the same thing on May 19. In Paris meanwhile, the French were eager to produce for themselves what the Dutch professor called "a commotion . . . like a clap of thunder." By now it had also been discovered that the effects were all the more dramatic if they coated the outside of the jar with a membrane of lead or tinfoil.

At the Louvre the French king had a scientist in residence, the Abbé Jean-Antoine Nollet. In April he gave an electrical display in a grand gallery at Versailles, where he arranged in a line no fewer than 180 members of the court, holding each other by the hand. With Louis XV as a spectator, the abbé sent an "electrical commotion" along the human chain. A few weeks later and despite the war at sea, news of the show appeared in the press in London, where the Royal Society intended not to be outdone.[16]

They had their own Nollet, Dr. William Watson. As he began to work with the Leiden jar, so in England the craze for electricity intensified. Eight books on the subject appeared in London in 1746, including Watson's first attempt to produce a systematic theory to account for its effects. Like the Dutch Newtonians, he thought of electricity as an elastic species of matter, identical with the phenomenon to which they gave the name of "Fire." Over in Paris the abbé agreed. He wrote his own treatise to explain the workings of the Leiden jar. Nollet saw them as the product of what he called "electric matter . . . a very subtle fluid," distributed throughout the universe, including the human body, and working its effects by way of something he called "double repercussion." In other words, like Dr. Watson the abbé tried to picture electricity as though it were mechanical: a system of particles, bouncing off each other like pool balls, and causing explosions of the kind that occurred with the jar.[17]

It was an interesting theory, but it was premature. Although Watson and the abbé were scientists far more competent than Cadwallader Colden, in this instance they shared his tendency to leap ahead too hastily. If the Leiden jar were ever to be fully understood, what was needed was something else. The necessary thing was this: observation first, theory second, and then more observation to test and to refine the theory. If electricians were to move forward, they had to make a rigorous appraisal of the data—in other words, of the behavior not only of the jar, but also of the techniques used by the experimenter—carried out in such a way as to isolate those features of the procedure and the apparatus that made the shocks appear.

If this kind of exercise sounds austere and demanding, that is because it was. It was with this kind of work that Franklin would make his contribution to physics. For experimental research, he had all the necessary qualities. As a player of chess, he was used to being cool and disciplined. As a writer and a thinker, he was methodical. As a printer, Franklin was a patient man, with the habits of "regularity" that had won him well-paid work in the London of the 1720s. He was also the offspring of a family of craftsmen, blacksmiths and dyers, men who could work with the wrist and the hand as well as with the mind. And he had studied the literature, the textbooks from London and the items in the press. Franklin also had the scientific benefit of his long friendship with James Logan.

As yet—we are talking about the spring and summer of 1746—Franklin did not have enough information about the Leiden jar to begin any electrical work of his own. He probably saw the item in *The Boston Post-Boy,* but it was brief and sketchy. Nor did he have the apparatus. The making of glass jars and tubes was not quite yet an American activity. For the time being, items such as this had to come from England, though Franklin would soon do his best to get his fellow colonists into the business of blowing glass. He was also still a little in awe of Cadwallader Colden, whose influence in matters scientific was something Franklin had to overcome.

His Electrical Moment

In June, a parcel of books arrived in Philadelphia from New York, copies of Mr. Colden's treatise in which he hoped to solve the mysteries of gravity and matter. Franklin shared the book with the Junto, with James Logan and with many others: lawyers, officials, and what he called "merchants and ingenious men." They found it a very hard read. In the middle of October Franklin wrote to Colden again, telling them what had transpired. "All I can learn of their sentiments concerning it is, that they say they cannot understand it," he said. With his usual diplomacy he tried to break the news gently.

"People do not seem to suppose that you write unintelligibly," Franklin wrote, "but charge all to the abstruseness of the subject, and their own want of capacity." Franklin was being very generous, because Colden's book really was nonsense. At its heart there lay the idea that "matter" existed in three varieties: "resisting matter," which did nothing, but remained inert; "moving matter"—light and heat, for example—which had the power of motion; and "elastic matter," which communicated motion by way of something he called "momentaneous vibration." From the interaction of all three, Cadwallader Colden proposed to explain the inner secrets of Sir Isaac Newton's cosmos.[18]

As they puzzled over Colden's strange theories, Franklin and his friends found themselves debating another book on a similar subject. It was a gift from yet one more Scot, Archibald Home, a government official in New Jersey whom Franklin had recruited for the American Philosophical Society. A lover of literature and a talented poet, Home had presented the Library Company with a work of philosophy from Edinburgh, written by one Andrew Baxter and published in 1737. It purported to prove the immortality of souls and the existence of God by way of some dubious reflections on Newtonian physics.[19]

Armed with Baxter's *Enquiry,* to give the book an abbreviated title, some of Franklin's friends tried to produce their own account of the fundamentals of the universe. At this point—in the autumn of 1746—it seems that at last Franklin lost his cool. One evening, when his friends were singing the praises of Andrew Baxter, Franklin made it clear that he thought the book was absurd. Asked to justify himself, Franklin wrote a pungent little essay pointing out the flaws in Baxter's arguments.

Deeply irritated by Baxter's style and by what he had to say—and even more so by the way his feeble book was admired in Philadelphia—Franklin tore the book to pieces. The *Enquiry* was vague, convoluted, and full of non sequiturs. With a heavy dose of sarcasm, Franklin exposed them for what they were: egregious errors by an author addicted to metaphysics. In London twenty years earlier, Franklin had tried his hand at just such a thing, when he wrote and published his *Dissertation on Liberty and Necessity.* He had decided that it was an exercise in futility.

It was market day in Philadelphia, and the street outside was filled with noise. This made him feel all the more frustrated. Franklin had always had to *work* for his living. With only his few leisure hours available for study, he was always being distracted from the pursuit of learning that he knew was rightfully his. It was profoundly annoying to be asked to defer to an author so ridiculous.

"The din of the market increases upon me," Franklin wrote. As he ripped Baxter's book to shreds, he also made it clear that he rejected entirely the kind of speculation for which Baxter stood. Metaphysics had to go, said Franklin. "The great uncertainty I have found in that science; the wide contradictions and endless disputes it affords; and the horrible errors I led myself into when a young man, by drawing a chain of plain consequences as I thought them, from true principles"—he meant the *Dissertation,* and his period in London with James Ralph—"have given me a disgust to what I was once extremely fond of."

The moment had arrived for Franklin to pick up the threads of experimental science that Newton had left dangling behind him. If not now, when? He may not have known this proverb from the Jewish rabbis, but it was what he must have been thinking. For twenty-five years, since he was a boy in Boston reading John Locke, Franklin had been training his intellect, studying the best things he could find, and thinking hard about what he read. His body was strong, and his mind was clear. He had also acquired a vast store of knowledge.

Franklin was forty; he had built a thriving business, and found a likely successor in David Hall; and he had a son old enough to be off at the war. In short, he was a gentleman. And that is how Franklin is depicted in the first authentic image we have of him, the portrait in oils that hangs in the art museum at Harvard. Commissioned by his brother John, and probably painted in 1746 by the artist Robert Feke, it shows us a prosperous Franklin, solid and secure, with white starched linen and a long brown wig. The Franklin it portrays is also a man who, by the usual standards of his era, was more than two thirds of the way through his life. He could not allow the field of inquiry to belong to the likes of Baxter or even to Colden. Instead Franklin had to stake his own claim to scientific originality, and as soon as possible; or it might be too late.

Although he already knew that electricity was one of the two pressing questions of the era—the other one being the polyp, which also invited new theories about the nature of "matter"—no evidence survives from before the autumn of 1746 to indicate that Franklin saw it as his specialty. On the contrary: from his diplomatic letter to Colden, written on October 16, it is plain that he did not, since he made no mention of electrical science. Before the year was out, it would become Franklin's obsession.

First he had to finish the next year's edition of *Poor Richard.* As clerk of the Pennsylvania assembly, Franklin also had to spend a few days taking the minutes of the autumn session. On the 17th the assembly adjourned, not to reconvene until January. That gave him time for another business trip to Boston, Rhode Island, and New York. On October 21 he settled up accounts with his mother-in-law, Mrs. Read, who was still hard at work selling books and almanacs on his behalf. Then Franklin set out for the north, where he was about to find what he required: a vastly better piece of scientific prose, written in Paris by two men who shared his preference for the empirical.

Before he left Philadelphia another gift had arrived, this time from Peter Collinson in London. In the spring of each year, he would assemble a consignment of letters, books, and specimens for his American friends, but this time he also included a piece of apparatus. In April, when Collinson made up a trunk of books for the Library Company, addressed to its secretary, Franklin's old Junto friend Joseph Breintnall, he put a glass tube in the trunk. At the Royal Society, Collinson had seen the electrical displays by Dr. Watson, and so he sent the Philadelphians what they needed to begin experiments of their own.

With the war still raging at sea, Collinson took the precaution of dividing his parcels between two ships, the *Carolina* and the *Friendship.* In May and early June they made rendezvous in the English Channel with the warships that were to take them out in convoy. The wait was long, the voyages dangerous, but both ships made a safe arrival in Philadelphia: the *Carolina* on September 25, and the *Friendship* three weeks later, on the very day when Franklin composed his critique of Andrew Baxter. One or other of these ships carried Mr. Collinson's glass tube.[20]

Busy as he was with so many other things, it seems that Franklin had no time to look at the books or the tube before he left for Boston in late October or early November. We know all too little about what Franklin did in Boston or whom he saw; but—as so often with Franklin—his timing was superb. Boston was the place of publication of a monthly journal, *The American Magazine,* whose October issue was on sale in the town by November 10. It contained an article about electricity, written with the same combination of detail and clarity that Franklin had achieved in his essay on the fireplace.[21]

The article came from France. In Paris, the experiments made by Nollet the previous year had been witnessed by a young medical doctor, the abbé's friend Louis-Guillaume Le Monnier. Building his own Leiden jar, he undertook a series of trials in the royal botanical garden and the grounds of the Tuileries Palace. As he began to write them up in a paper, he shared his work with another friend, this time an Englishman: a Catholic priest in exile by the name of John Turberville Needham. A man enchanted by science, equally at home with the polyp and the sparks of electricity, Father Needham made a précis of Le Monnier's results and sent them to the Royal Society in London early in July 1746. At the end of that month, the précis appeared in *The Gentleman's Magazine.*[22]

Over it went to the colonies, avoiding the French privateers, to be reprinted verbatim in Boston in the October *American Magazine.* "The electrifying glass is an oblong spheroid, its diameter from pole to pole sixteen or seventeen inches": so Father Needham began. His article went on for two pages of small print. A manual for the electrician, it described to perfection all the things involved: the electrostatic generator, with two men to turn the wheel; the prime conductor; the Leiden jar; and of course the astonishing results that Le Monnier had produced. "At the grand convent of the Carthusians, the whole community formed a line," it was reported. "And when the two extremities met in contact with the electrified phial, the whole company at the same instant gave a sudden spring, and all equally felt the shock."

We can be sure that Franklin saw the piece because he held the contract to distribute *The American Magazine* in Pennsylvania. Throughout his career, Franklin had loved to encounter curiosities, whether they took human form, if they came on the printed page, or if they arrived by way of nature: an odd kind of seaweed, a chunk of asbestos, or a shock that could electrify Carthusians. Here again was ingenuity. Furthermore, it was the very *latest* ingenuity. Franklin was reading the article from Paris at almost the same time as it was being discussed in London, where the Royal Society heard the paper read on October 23.[23]

Back he went to Philadelphia, reaching the town no later than December 29, when he took part in a meeting of the Union Fire Company. Six days after that, Franklin wrote to William Strahan with his first letter of 1747, complaining that the British had failed to send a fleet to protect the colonies from a French attempt to recapture Louisbourg. While the French had been defeated it was only, he said, by the hand of God. Meanwhile his friend John Bartram was grumbling about the war in a letter to England. Prevented from traveling by the risk of encountering what he called "ye French Indians," John Bartram wrote about what he called "these troublesome times . . . a great hindrance to any curious inquiries."

But even as Bartram wrote those words in December, Franklin was about to prove him wrong, by beginning in earnest his scientific career. After so many harsh winters, this one was so mild that ships could still come and go in the Delaware. As the ice remained at bay, Franklin was still in an optimistic mood. At some point—we will never know the date exactly—Franklin found the glass tube sent by Collinson and he set to work with a passion to do his own experiments with electricity. In the fall he had been exasperated, and quite rightly so, as he watched his neighbors lose their way in a fog of metaphysics. Now—as he turned forty-one—Franklin discovered his vocation, empirical and ingenious, rubbing up the tube to generate the forces that the Europeans had unleashed.[24]

He enlisted three friends: from the Junto, Thomas Hopkinson and Philip Syng, the silversmith, and also a Baptist preacher, Ebenezer Kinnersley. With their help Franklin began to repeat the European results with electricity, beginning with the old Hauksbee trick of making a ball spin for hours around an electrified body. As his confidence grew, he wrote to a friend he had made in New Haven urging him to press ahead with plans for a glassworks in Connecticut where Americans could make apparatus of their own. By the time a cold snap set in in the middle of

February, Franklin had made so much progress that he was ready to share the results with the demanding Mr. Logan.

On February 22, Bartram rode up through the frost to Logan's house at Stenton, to tell their mentor what Franklin was up to with electricity. Fragile though he was, and now seventy-two years old, James Logan could still rejoice to see Americans carrying on the work of Newton. What Bartram told him—tales of spinning balls, sparks and fire, attraction and repulsion—filled him with enthusiasm. Logan knew about the trials with the Leiden jar in Paris, since Collinson had sent him the same paper that Franklin had read. He felt sure that his protégé, the ingenious printer, was already doing even better. Bartram left, and next day Logan sent Franklin a letter full of warmth and admiration, urging him to come out to Stenton to give a demonstration.[25]

"Your experiments exceed them all," he wrote. And there we leave them both, James Logan to his books and his memories, and Franklin to his science: a calling found at last.

Epilogue

An Uneasy Spirit

He is a dangerous man and I should be glad he inhabited any other country. . . . However, as he is a sort of tribune of the people, he must be treated with regard.

—Description of Benjamin Franklin by Thomas Penn, Proprietor of Pennsylvania, 1748[1]

So many of his friends disappeared before their time. While Benjamin Franklin had four decades still ahead of him, so that he would survive beyond the storming of the Bastille and to see George Washington as president, the people to whom he was closest had begun to fall away even before his work with electricity began. The saddest case was that of Joseph Breintnall, who never received the glass tube and the trunk of books from London. In March of 1746 his body washed up on the Jersey shore of the Delaware, apparently a suicide. By then John Wygate had passed away as well, in the fever hospital on Antigua, his death recorded with a line in the log of his ship and a little item in the English press.

The next of Franklin's friends to die, in 1751, were James Logan and Thomas Hopkinson, the latter at the age of only forty-two. Six years later it was the turn of William Parsons; and then John Rutherfurd fell in action against the French at Ticonderoga. Robert Grace was gone by the end of 1766 and William Coleman died in 1768, as did the English benefactor Peter Collinson. Six years after that Deborah Franklin died too. They laid her to rest in the Christ Church cemetery while her husband, hated by the British, was preparing to sail home from England to join the Revolution.

All the time Franklin went from strength to strength. While his siblings had died away so that by 1767 only he and Jane Mecom remained, Franklin kept forging ahead, a prophet of a kind, with the vigor and longevity that prophets are supposed to command. Never ceasing to make new friends, neither could he stop writing: so many letters and private memoranda, but also satirical sketches, political pamphlets, and scientific papers. Until his own death in 1790, Franklin retained his love of curiosities, especially when they were eccentric human beings. When people turned up at his door with crackpot schemes, unpublished books they wanted him to read, or simply to touch the hem of his garment, he was mostly inclined to give them an audience.

After all: there had been so *many* chance encounters in Franklin's life that had proved to be worthwhile. Who could say what gifts of ingenuity a stranger might possess? This was one of Franklin's most attractive features, and one of his most valuable assets: his passion for "variety," that quality of being that the eighteenth century prized so highly. He always wanted to find something new, and better still to do new things. The finest example of this was his work with electricity, the scientific core around which Franklin built the second half of his life.[2]

Like a stone tossed into the Schuylkill, Franklin's electrical experiments sent an ever-widening circle of vibrations through the life of his time. The details of his work are not the subject of this book. Like every author I have to stop somewhere; but the gist of his achievement was this. By 1749, Franklin had developed a new theory of electricity far simpler and more accurate than anything his predecessors had suggested, so that for most practical, everyday requirements his ideas are still quite sufficient.

With his little team of collaborators, Franklin examined the mysteries of the Leiden jar. With patience and precision, he identified the effect of each element of the procedure: the glass, the liquid in the bottle, the wire dangling into it, the metal jacket on the outside, and their interaction with the prime conductor and the electrician. The craftsman Philip Syng created an electrical machine, a better version of the ones that Hauksbee and the Germans had developed, with a glass sphere made to spin around like a lathe. With that, Franklin and his team had the powerful generator they required. They devised a set of eleven experiments whose results, when taken together, gave Franklin his new concept of electricity.

It was a fluid, or so he believed, subtle and elastic and distributed everywhere in nature. This was something like Newton's idea of an electric spirit, but Franklin added an essential refinement. His electrical fluid could pass from one body to another because, as he put it, "common matter is as a kind of sponge" that soaks up electricity. But one thing never changed: the overall quantity of the electric fluid. When electricians performed their displays, they merely collected the fluid and altered its distribution: between, for example, a dangling boy and the finger of a spectator. Add or subtract some electrical fluid from a body, and you would create an imbalance, a plus or a minus, or rather a *positive* or a *negative* charge.

And here was the secret of the Leiden jar. Franklin found it in the difference between the positive charge on the outside of the bottle, and the negative charge on the inside. To restore the equilibrium, all you had to do was hold the jar and touch the wire, creating a circuit that equalized the charges. You would give yourself a painful shock, but also help to prove what came to be known as Franklin's "one fluid" theory of electricity. It was an elegant theory, far simpler than the Abbé Nollet's "double repercussion," and it served its purpose.

Of course Franklin's work was only a beginning. No one had any inkling that there might be particles called electrons that performed the role of Franklin's fluid. A hundred years had yet to pass until, in Scotland in the 1860s, James Clerk Maxwell transformed electrical science into an edifice built entirely from mathematics, opening the way for the physics of the twentieth century. Maxwell's great system of equations lay far beyond the scope of Franklin's work. Even so, the American sage had been a scientific revolutionary. Before him, the scientists who studied electricity had tended to depart too swiftly into the realm of speculation, with the result of muddle and confusion. Like Newton, Franklin made things clear.

Other people had suggested that lightning might be a form of electricity, but Franklin was the person who explained why this was so and designed an experiment to prove it. Of all his many writings, the finest was surely this one: Franklin's essay, composed in 1749, in which he described the electrification of clouds, rising off the sea in hot weather and then discharging their energy by way of thunderstorms. Armed with the essay, his counterparts in France took what Franklin said and made it happen in Paris and the countryside nearby.

In the spring and summer of 1752, they put up metal poles to wait for stormy weather, and with them they drew sparks from the sky. In doing so they confirmed what Franklin had predicted. They showed that he was also correct about something else: that a metal rod, erected next to a building, could protect it from destruction. At that moment the French physicists—not all of them, but most—fell in love with Franklin and he with them. In time, like so many enlightened Americans in centuries to come, he would make Paris his city of choice.

In America meanwhile, Franklin found many other things to do. Fired up with confidence, knowing what he was achieving with electricity, in 1747 he burst into politics in Pennsylvania, no longer an observer, but now a protagonist. Franklin set himself another goal: the defense of his colony. Tired of obstruction by the Quaker politicians, and alarmed by the threat of raids against the towns along the Delaware by French privateers, he organized a militia and wrote a fiery pamphlet—*Plain Truth*—to justify its creation. Up in New York, his friend Cadwallader Colden drew upon the pamphlet as he urged the citizens to make their own efforts against the king of France.[3]

Not everyone cared for what Franklin was up to. In the words of Thomas Penn, the owner of his colony, Franklin was "a very uneasy spirit." Which was true. The evidence was plain to see in Franklin's hyperactivity. Even when in Paris in his seventies he lingered over breakfast, he was reading, thinking, making plans, and putting them into practice. As we grow older, many of us prefer to live in our memories, and to rest on whatever meager laurels we possess; but Franklin did not. He always wanted to do something *more,* including the creation of America's republic.

For every biographer of Franklin, there is a central question that demands an answer. Long after so many of his friends and his family were dead, his career and his ideas continued to develop, so that he evolved into a radical whose views about politics became less conservative the older he grew. Franklin even came to advocate the abolition of slavery, a project that in his youth he would have found unthinkable. So the question is this: What was the source of Franklin's energy? Why was he so restless and so driven?

It seems to me that the answer is as follows. Although he did not disclose it to the full in his memoirs, Franklin knew that in England his family had been far more than simple country folk. Lifting themselves up from Ecton, where they had met people of science, the Franklins had gone on to be Londoners as well, where they acquired the knowledge and the adventurous attitudes that came with life in a metropolis. Their skills were high, with the hands as well as with the intellect. It was only because of accidents of death and infertility, and because they owned too little land, that the Franklins did not become a successful dynasty in the mother country.

They were also very mobile people, living in many different places, and this was important too. Never tied to one location, the Franklins had to be flexible, ready to cut themselves loose from their roots when the need arose. They knew that while roots have their benefits, mostly they have to be severed if life and ideas are to move on. Another thing the Franklins knew was this: that however ingenious they might be, they were still social inferiors in England. So they were again in Boston on their first arrival, where their problem was even worse: because Josiah had lost his hard-won status as a dyer of silk and a citizen of London.

Boston could not satisfy all their needs; but when he set foot in Philadelphia, the runaway Benjamin Franklin found a far more friendly environment. It was a town where he could fulfill the aspirations that his family had developed in their native land. With its ironmasters, its merchants, its literary people, and its open frontier, the Quaker province offered him the terrain on which he could deploy his talents. As time went by, Franklin took the many things that Pennsylvania offered—the freedom of the Quakers, the skills of the Germans, the learning of James Logan, and the patronage of Andrew Hamilton—and from these elements he created his future. Blending them together with the ideas he acquired in London and from books, and also with his heritage of craftsmanship, Franklin became a master of the printing trade and journalism: and then a scientific genius. He also achieved the social rank and esteem that his family had always striven to acquire.

Close behind him all the time there lay the specters of failure and premature death. Smallpox, yellow fever, drink, and syphilis, and debt: there were so many risks a young man had to run. Franklin saw them everywhere. Having known the dangerous London of Hogarth, having met so many people whose lives disintegrated, and having mourned so many early deaths, Franklin was all the more a driven man. In the years of his maturity, he knew that in his youth ruin, disgrace, or the graveyard might have been his destiny too. Hence the need to fill each day with the quest for knowledge and achievement. Twenty-four hours: the only space a human being has in which to be ingenious.

Acknowledgments

For an author, the publication of a book should be a happy moment, but in the case of *Young Benjamin Franklin* it comes with sadness as well. I was not far advanced in the research and the writing when in the late summer of 2015, I received the news of the death of the renowned Carol Brown Janeway—linguist, raconteur, and devotee of Schubert—my editor at Knopf. It was Carol who commissioned not only *Young Benjamin Franklin* but also my two previous books. Her colleague Andrew Miller became my new editor, gracefully shepherding me through the editorial process, but Carol's passing left us mourning the loss of someone whose like will not be seen again. A Scot by birth, with an Edinburgh accent untamed by her forty-five years in Manhattan, Carol would have been delighted to see Franklin's cultural debts to her country explored in the closing sections of this book.

Once again, I have to thank above all my patient, wise, and perceptive wife, Sue, without whom none of my books could have been written. My thanks also go to my tireless and unflappable agent, Bill Hamilton, and his colleagues at A. M. Heath; my oldest New York friends, Steven Margulis, M.D., and Sherida Paulsen, former chair of the city's Landmark Commission, and their sons, Isaac and Noah Margulis; and the staffs of all the many libraries and archive collections referred to in the notes. In particular, I wish to mention the Cambridge University Library with its superb resources in American history and the history of science; Jim Green at the Library Company of Philadelphia; Karie Diethorn, chief curator at Independence National Historic Park, Philadelphia; Hugh Alexander at the National Archives at Kew, England; Kimberly Toney Pelkey at the American Antiquarian Society in Worcester, Massachusetts; Carenza Black at the Northamptonshire Archives; Maia Sheridan of the St. Andrews University Library in Scotland; and the teams at the Historical Society of Pennsylvania, the Mercer Museum not far away in Doylestown, and the Winterthur Museum and Library in Delaware.

Because I try to spend as much time as possible on location, so to speak, I also need temporary landlords, people to unlock English parish churches, and guides to colonial sites in the United States. My peerless genealogical friend Sandra Hewlett helped me track down the locations of ironworks in Pennsylvania; but I am also grateful to Laura Keim, the ingenious curator of James Logan's house at Stenton, and her partner, the architectural historian Stephen Hague; Walter Ferme and Mike Eruzione in Boston; Michael Zuzu in Philadelphia; Joy Bond and Linda Richards, the churchwardens at St. Mary Magdalene, Ecton; Tim Allebone, churchwarden of St. Peter and St. Paul, Easton Maudit, Northamptonshire; and the Reverend Alistair So and his Episcopalian congregation at All Hallows, South River, Maryland, especially Bridget Blake and Joan Placido, who accompanied me in my quest for traces left by Alistair's distant predecessor, the electrical Dr. Archibald Spencer. I came to love Philadelphia during my many weeks of work there, and so I offer my thanks to a host of anonymous citizens who helped me enter into the life of the town—people in bus lines or at Whole Foods Market, the attendants at the Philadelphia Museum of Art, and the Avis car rental staff at the airport—and also to a chance acquaintance from the world of politics, Frank Rizzo Jr., son of one of Philadelphia's more controversial mayors.

I also owe a special debt of gratitude to three distinguished Franklin scholars—Jonathan Dull, Robert P. Frankel Jr., and David Waldstreicher—for reading the text in close to its final form, offering valuable suggestions, and saving me from errors, and to Gordon S. Wood. At Knopf, besides Andrew Miller, I wish to thank the wonderful Zakiya Harris, Kim Thornton Ingenito, and Victoria Pearson, and their production and design colleagues Kelly Blair, Michael Collica, and Roméo Enriquez.

The dedicatee of this book, Henry Chapman Mercer—architect, scholar, and collector—possessed the very qualities of variety and ingenuity that Benjamin Franklin admired. In a twenty-first century when people seem to think that strident opinion counts for everything, H. C. Mercer's museum of patient American craftsmanship serves as a reminder that there is more to life than angry words.

Notes

Abbreviations

AAS: American Antiquarian Society, Worcester, MA

APS: American Philosophical Society, Philadelphia

AWM: American Weekly Mercury, Philadelphia

BFP 1-42: Leonard W. Labaree, William B. Willcox, Claude A. Lopez, Barbara B. Oberg, Ellen R. Cohn, et al., eds., *The Papers of Benjamin Franklin* (Yale edition, New Haven, 1959–2017), primarily: Vol. 1 (1706–1734), Vol. 2 (1735–1744), and Vol. 3 (1745–1750).

BFSA (1717): Benjamin Franklin Senior, *A Short Account of the Family of Thomas Franklin of Ecton in Northampton Shire, June 21st 1717,* printed in Nian-Sheng Huang, "Franklin's Father Josiah: Life of a Boston Tallow Chandler, 1657–1745," in *Transactions of the American Philosophical Society,* New Series, Vol. 90, No. 3 (2000).

BFSCPB 1&2: Commonplace Book of Benjamin Franklin Sr., ca. 1725, two manuscript volumes at the American Antiquarian Society, Worcester, MA, Mss. Octavo Vols. F

BL: British Library, London

CCP 1, 2, and 3: The Letters and Papers of Cadwallader Colden, Vol. 1 (1711–1729), Vol. 2 (1730–1742), and Vol. 3 (1743–1747) (New-York Historical Society, 1917–1920).

CJB: Edmund and Dorothy Smith Berkeley, *The Correspondence of John Bartram, 1734–1777* (Gainesville, FL, 1992).

HSP: Historical Society of Pennsylvania

Lemay 1,2, and 3: J. A. Leo Lemay, *The Life of Benjamin Franklin* (Philadelphia, 2006–9), Vol. 1, *Journalist, 1706–1730;* Vol. 2, *Printer and Publisher, 1730–1747;* Vol. 3, *Soldier, Scientist and Politician, 1748–1757.*

LLP 2 and 3: Craig W. Horle et al., eds., *Lawmaking and Legislators in Pennsylvania: A Biographical Dictionary,* Vol. 2 (1710–56) (Philadelphia, 1997); and Vol. 3 (1757–75) (Philadelphia, 2005).

LMA: London Metropolitan Archives

MHS: Massachusetts Historical Society

NAK: National Archives, Kew, England

Northants RO: Northamptonshire Record Office, Northampton, England
ODNB: Oxford Dictionary of National Biography
PCC: Prerogative Court of Canterbury
PG: Pennsylvania Gazette, Philadelphia
PMHB: Pennsylvania Magazine of History and Biography
RoySoc: Archives of the Royal Society, London, England
WMQ: William and Mary Quarterly

Prologue: The Enigmatic Seer

1. Rodin: Quoted in C. H. Hart and E. Biddle, *Memoirs of the Life and Works of J. A. Houdon* (Philadelphia, 1911), pp. 108–9.
2. Franklin's appearance and his "handsome leg": Emmanuel de Croy-Solre, Duc de Croy, *Journal inédit, 1718–1784* (Paris, 1907), Vol. 5, p. 295; and Charles Coleman Sellers, *Benjamin Franklin in Portraiture* (New Haven, 1962), pp. 2–4. For an account of his gravitas, see Mercy Otis Warren's description of Franklin's "dignity of deportment" when she met him in Massachusetts in October 1775, in *Papers of John Adams,* Vol. 3 (May 1775–January 1776), (Cambridge, MA, 1979), p. 279. Calling him "this venerable person," Ms. Warren says she was "pleased to observe the affability and politeness of the gentleman, happily united with the virtues of the patriot." However, the finest descriptions of Franklin as he was in Paris can be found in Stacy Schiff's *A Great Improvisation: Franklin, France, and the Birth of America* (New York, 2005), especially on pp. 36–53.
3. Edmund S. Morgan, *Benjamin Franklin* (New Haven, 2002), p. 44.
4. The Houdon bust: Jack Hinton, Melissa Meigham, and Andrew Lins, *Encountering Genius: Houdon's Portraits of Benjamin Franklin* (Philadelphia, 2011), pp. 17–18 and 30–37.
5. Rodin on Franklin: See note 1 above. Franklin's self-control: Jonathan R. Dull, "Franklin Furioso, 1775–1790," in David Waldstreicher, ed., *A Companion to Benjamin Franklin* (Oxford, 2011), pp. 65 and 78–79; or for a different perspective, Jerry Weinberger, *Benjamin Franklin Unmasked* (Lawrence, KS, 2005), pp. 222–23 and 314–17.

Chapter One: His Ingenious Kin

1. Survey of Houghton Magna, ca. 1604, in Tresham Papers, BL Add. Ms. 39,829, fol. 68. For a beautifully written account of the Nene valley in the early modern period: John Morton, *The Natural History of Northamptonshire* (London, 1712), pp. 19–24.
2. The family memoir by Benjamin Franklin Sr., dated June 21, 1717, and referred to below as *BFSA (1717),* is reprinted in Nian-Sheng Huang, "Franklin's Father Josiah: Life of a Boston Tallow Chandler, 1657–1745," in *Transactions of the American Philosophical Society,* New Series, 90, no. 3 (2000): 106–13. The original document is in the Beinecke Library at Yale University. Among the errors it contains is a statement by Benjamin Senior that Henry Franklin was his great-grandfather and that he was an attorney. Archival material relating to Houghton Magna makes it clear that the Henry Frank-

lin in question was actually Benjamin Senior's grandfather, and that he was certainly not a lawyer. Wherever possible I have tried to authenticate details in *BFSA (1717)* by checking them against contemporary records. One thing that cannot be verified is Benjamin Franklin's statement that his family had lived at Ecton for three hundred years, because the parish register only begins in 1559.

3. Henry Franklin and Michael Jones at Houghton Magna: Chancery lawsuit (1605–6), *Baude et al. v. Tyndall, Franklin and Jones,* at NAK C2/JasI/B18/20. The Franklin and Jones families, Henry's marriage, and his social status as a husbandman: Ecton Parish Register, transcript at Northants RO, Ecton 114P/202. In English villages in 1600 or so, laboring men with no land at all or only a very small holding ranked at the bottom of the social scale; skilled craftsmen or husbandmen like the Franklins, occupying about twenty to thirty acres, came next above them; one step higher stood yeoman farmers, with (say) thirty to fifty acres of land; and above them were large yeoman farmers and members of the gentry. To be securely classed as gentlefolk a family needed at least five hundred acres. See Keith Wrightson and David Levine, *Poverty and Piety in an English Village: Terling, 1525–1700* (Oxford, 1995), pp. 31–36. It is impossible to say precisely how much land Henry Franklin occupied at Ecton. In his autobiography, Benjamin Franklin tells us that the family owned "about 30 acres," which checks out well against the surviving records from the village: see note 17 on the size of the family holding in the 1640s. However, Franklin was referring only to the freehold property they owned outright; husbandmen often rented extra land as leasehold tenants, and indeed Henry's son Thomas Franklin Sr. did just that.
4. Tresham family: Mary E. Finch, *The Wealth of Five Northamptonshire Families, 1540–1640* (Oxford, 1956), Chapter 4, with references to Houghton Magna on pp. 73–76; and *ODNB* entries for Sir Thomas Tresham and his son Lewis.
5. Baude to Sir Thomas Tresham, July 19, 1605, in BL Add. Ms. 39,829, fol. 188; and the Chancery lawsuit of 1605–6. Also: report of the depopulation commission for Northamptonshire, August 1607, at NAK, C205/5/5, with Houghton Magna on Membrane Four, with the statement that "this town of Houghton is dispossessed of two hundred persons or thereabouts." More details can be found in a 1608 Star Chamber prosecution of Ferdinando Baude (or Bawde, an alternative spelling): *Attorney-General v. Baude et al.,* at NAK, STAC8/8/12.
6. Josiah's letter, with anecdotes about the family: May 26, 1739, *BFP 3,* pp. 229–32. Henry Franklin's imprisonment: I have found no contemporary record, but it would be surprising if one remained. It seems to me most likely that Baude and his allies pressed charges against Henry Franklin for trespass or criminal libel. If so, his trial would have occurred at the Northampton Assizes, but assize records rarely survive from this period. Baude's Chancery lawsuit against Jones and Franklin must have been dropped, since the Chancery records show that it never came before the judges in London.
7. Baude and the mob: NAK, STAC8/8/12. Enclosure and the Midland Rising: Joan Thirsk, ed., *The Agrarian History of England and Wales* (1500–1640), (Cambridge, UK, 1967), Vol. 4, pp. 232–36.

8. "Improvement": Paul Slack, *The Invention of Improvement: Information and Material Progress in Seventeenth Century England* (Oxford, 2015), especially pp. 4–8, 50–52 (referring to the Midland Rising), and Chapter 7.
9. Chancery lawsuit (1622), *Wade v. Jones and Franklin,* NAK, C3/388/45; Northamptonshire assessments for Ship Money, 1628, at NAK, E179/157/414; and Joan Wake, ed., *Quarter Sessions Records of the County of Northampton* (Northampton, 1924), pp. 78–79. When the American writer A. B. Tourtellot was researching his book *Benjamin Franklin: The Shaping of Genius* (New York, 1977), dealing with Franklin's early life and origins, he drew upon some unpublished notes about Henry Franklin's period at Ecton after 1620 compiled by P. I. King, the county archivist at the Northamptonshire Record Office. King's notes seem to have been lost, and so I had to start again from the beginning.
10. Benjamin Franklin to Deborah Read Franklin, September 6, 1758, *BFP 8,* pp. 133–38.
11. Landscape and history of Ecton: At Northants RO, Thomas Holmes's map of Ecton in 1703, Map 2115, and the Sotheby (Ecton) Papers, especially *Useful Memorandums Relating To My Estates* (1743) in Box 1071. Also: Glenn Foard, "Ecton: Its Lost Village and Landscape Park," in *Northamptonshire Past and Present* (Northampton, 1993–94), pp. 335–53; and David Hall, *The Open Fields of Northamptonshire* (Northampton, 1995), pp. 113–17. There is an old and unreliable village history by John Cole, *The History and Antiquities of Ecton* (Scarborough, 1825). More useful is the brief section on Ecton in L. F. Salzman, ed., *A History of the County of Northampton* (Victoria County History, London, 1937), Vol. 4, pp. 122–27. For a description of Ecton by Benjamin Franklin Sr., see his poem "On Ecton 1702" in his commonplace book: see note 10 to Chapter 2. Rector's income at Ecton: £250 per annum, in H. I. Longden, *Northants and Rutland Clergy from 1500* (Northampton, 1938–52), Vol. 1, p. 33. National average: Christopher Hill, *Economic Problems of the Church* (Oxford, 1956), pp. 108–13. By 1690, the value of the rectory had increased to £300 a year: see note 16 to Chapter 2. Further evidence of the village's prosperity can be found in the records of the Parliamentary election of 1702, when out of an Ecton population of about four hundred no fewer than fifty-one men—about half the householders in the village—were affluent enough to cast a vote: Northampton Mercury, *Northamptonshire Poll Books, 1702–1831* (Northampton, 1832), p. 27, at Northants RO.
12. "Meddlers with the Bible": W. J. Sheils, *The Puritans in the Diocese of Peterborough* (Northampton, 1979), pp. 13–18.
13. The Catesbys and Puritanism at Whiston and Ecton: H. I. Longden, *The Visitation of Northamptonshire, 1681* (London, 1935), pp. 43–44; V. A. Hatley and B. A. Bailey, *Church of St Mary the Virgin, Whiston* (Northampton, 1988); will of Isabel Catesby, proved February 16, 1581, at NAK, PROB 11/63/103; lands of Thomas Catesby, 1592, listed in his postmortem inquisition, NAK, C142/232; and Sheils, *The Puritans in the Diocese of Peterborough,* pp. 128–30. The Yelvertons, whose estate lay in the parish of Easton Maudit, Northamptonshire: Longden, *The Visitation of Northamptonshire, 1681,* pp. 43–44; Gyles Isham, *Easton Maudit and the Parish Church of St Peter and St Paul* (Northamptonshire Record Society, 1994), pp. 2–7; J. E. Neale, *The Elizabethan House of Commons* (London, 1963), pp. 343–49 and 362–63; and *ODNB.*

14. On Samuel Foster: *ODNB*. He was the son of the Puritan clergyman Francis Foster, who in 1605 was fired by the authorities from his post at Whiston during James I's purge of Puritans from the Church of England. Samuel's ancestry is confirmed by Francis Foster's will, proved July 25, 1622, at Northants RO (Archdeaconry Wills, AV/50/23). Also see Hatley and Bailey, *Church of St Mary the Virgin, Whiston,* and Sheils, *The Puritans in the Diocese of Peterborough,* Chapter 6.
15. John Palmer's career in the clergy: H. I. Longden, *Northamptonshire and Rutland Clergy from 1500* (1938–52), Vol. 10, pp. 155–56. Palmer's long friendship with the Catesbys and the Yelvertons is documented in his letter book (see note 7 to the next chapter) and in the Hatton-Finch Papers, BL, Add. Mss. 29,556 and 29,557.
16. Palmer worked with a third astronomer, the physician John Twysden (1607–1688), whose ties to the Yelvertons were still closer. In 1630, his sister Anne Twysden had married Sir Christopher Yelverton, who chose Palmer as rector at Ecton. Brief accounts of Foster, Palmer, and Twysden can be found in E. G. R. Taylor, *The Mathematical Practitioners of Tudor and Stuart England* (Cambridge, UK, 1954), pp. 206 and 212–13. Observations at Ecton and Easton: from *Observationes Eclipsium,* in Samuel Foster, *Miscellanea: sive lucubrationes mathematicae* (London, 1659); and John Palmer's *The Catholique Planisphere* (London, 1658), pp. 209–13, including recollections of Palmer's early life.
17. Description of Thomas Franklin: *BFSA (1717).* Discovered by chance on a London bookstall in 1851, John Palmer's account books were given to the Victorian sage Thomas Carlyle, who sent them on to a friend in Boston, where they have been ever since: Massachusetts Historical Society, Microfilm Reel P. 295. The second book refers to land agency and scrivening work done for the Palmers and the Catesbys by Thomas Franklin Jr. in the 1670s. The pages relating to Thomas Senior in the first book show him owing tithes as the owner of two "yardlands" at Ecton, meaning about twenty-eight acres of land altogether (the size of a "yardland" varied from one village to another: Hall, *The Open Fields of Northamptonshire,* p. 79), which fits in with the figure Benjamin Franklin gives in his autobiography. Thomas Senior also rented half a yardland from John Palmer. For Thomas Franklin Junior's holding of land at Ecton ca. 1700, see note 14 to Chapter 3.
18. "Ingenuity" in the 1650s: Slack, *The Invention of Improvement,* p. 93.
19. Walter Blith: Ibid., pp. 106–8. Ingenuity and improvement in Northamptonshire: John Morton, *The Natural History of Northamptonshire,* pp. 61–63, 382–97, 486, and 495. Morton's sources included Thomas Palmer, John Palmer's successor as rector at Ecton.
20. Cultural roots of the Industrial Revolution: Joel Mokyr, *The Enlightened Economy: An Economic History of Great Britain, 1700–1850* (New Haven, 2009), Chapters 3 and 5; and J. Mokyr, Michael Kelly, and Cormac Ó Gráda, *Precocious Albion: A New Interpretation of the British Industrial Revolution* (University College, Dublin, School of Economics Working Papers, 2013).
21. Flooding by the Nene: Morton, *The Natural History of Northamptonshire,* p. 337. Examples of Thomas Franklin Jr.'s scrivening practice survive in the county archives at Northampton, in the form of legal documents that he drew up and witnessed. The file of his letters relates to his work as land agent for Thomas Hackett of North

Crawley, Buckinghamshire, who bought an estate at Ecton in 1678: Centre for Buckinghamshire Studies, Aylesbury, file D-X464/4.

22. Bagley's bell foundry: Morton, *The Natural History of Northamptonshire,* p. 65; Michael Lee, "Henry Penn, Bellfounder, 1685–1729," in *Northamptonshire Past and Present* (2004), pp. 42–46. After the death of Thomas Franklin's business client Thomas Hackett in 1689, Henry Bagley bought Hackett's estate at Ecton for £1,380, further evidence that his bell-casting business was large and successful. Bagley and Thomas Franklin were very close, witnessing each other's wills in 1697. See BL, Additional Charters 24,144; and Northants RO, Archdeaconry Wills.
23. Importance of apprenticeships in English industrial and scientific history: Mokyr, *The Enlightened Economy,* pp. 116–21. High wages in London: Robert C. Allen, *The British Industrial Revolution in Global Perspective* (Cambridge, UK, 2009), Chapter 2.

Chapter Two: Coats of Many Colors

1. In his family memoir of 1717, Benjamin Senior said that Josiah was apprenticed in Banbury, which was not correct. Benjamin Franklin repeated the mistake in his autobiography. As a result, Josiah's London apprenticeship has been overlooked by previous Franklin biographers, because they had no reason to search for evidence about him in the archives from the capital. Josiah's apprenticeship and those of his brothers Samuel, John, and Benjamin are recorded in the Dyers' Company registers at London's Guildhall Library, Mss. 8171.1 and 8167.1. They show that Josiah was indentured as an apprentice dyer in London on June 22, 1671, six months before his fourteenth birthday, his employer being one Tobias Yates. As for Joseph Franklin, he was indentured to a member of the Armourers' Company, Joseph Titcomb, who ran a joinery business: Guildhall Library, Ms. 12,080/1. Cost of apprenticeships: Richard Grassby, *The Business Community of Seventeenth Century England* (Cambridge, UK, 1995), pp. 65–70; and Roger A. Feldman, *Recruitment, Training and Knowledge in the Dyers' Company, 1649–1826* (PhD thesis, London School of Economics, 2005), Chapter 2. The reference to Samuel's good looks and ingenuity comes from *BFSA (1717)*. Also see note 14 to Chapter 2.
2. English silk industry: Linda Levy Peck, *Consuming Splendor: Society and Culture in Seventeenth Century England* (Cambridge, UK, 2005), pp. 85–111.
3. Benjamin Franklin Sr., *Dyeing and Coloring,* printed in Colonial Society of Massachusetts, *Transactions,* Vol. 10, 1904–1906 (Boston, 1907), pp. 206–25. English dyeing trade: Anon., *The Whole Art of Dying, In Two Parts* (London, 1705); Eric Kerridge, *Textile Manufactures in Early Modern England* (Manchester, 1985), pp. 163–68; but best of all is Sir William Petty's report of his observations among the London dyers in the 1660s, *An Apparatus to the History of the Common Practices of Dyeing,* in Thomas Sprat, *The History of the Royal Society of London for the Improving of Natural Knowledge* (London, 1667), pp. 284–306. Sprat's book is a huge compendium of sources for the cult of ingenuity and "improvement" in Restoration England.
4. Josiah Franklin on his mother: Josiah to Benjamin Franklin, May 26, 1739, *BFP 2,* p. 231.

5. Palmer in 1648–9: A. G. Matthews, *Calamy Revised* (Oxford, 1934), Appendix 1.
6. John Palmer and Sir Henry Yelverton: John Palmer's letter book, 1640–1679, Bodleian Library, Oxford, England, Ms. Eng. lett 210; also, the Yelverton entry in B. D. Henning, ed., *History of Parliament, 1660–1690* (London, 1983), Vol. 3. Historical context: Tim Harris, Paul Seaward, and Mark Goldie, *The Politics of Religion in Restoration England* (Oxford, 1990), Harris's introduction; and Ronald Hutton, *The Restoration: A Political and Religious History of England and Wales, 1658–1667* (Oxford, 1985).
7. Sir Henry Yelverton on Thomas Franklin Sr.: Yelverton to Palmer, January 2, 1662, in Palmer's letter book at the Bodleian, with Yelverton's comment about England being "torn in pieces." Only one of the Franklins was an orthodox Anglican. This was Thomas Junior, who served two terms as churchwarden at Ecton (Northants RO, Archdeacon's Visitation Book No. 6). Later he fell out with the Palmers and by the time of his death in 1703 he was thinking of leaving the official church: *BFSA (1717)*.
8. John Palmer as archdeacon: His letters to Joseph Henshaw, Bishop of Peterborough, 1665–1667, at BL, Add. Ms. 22, 576. Palmer's correspondence with the Royal Society in the 1660s: A. R. and M. B. Hall, *The Correspondence of Henry Oldenburg* (Madison, WI, 1967), Vol. 4, pp. 3–4, 34–35, 71–73, 82–83, 202–3, and 224–25.
9. Conventicles: John Palmer, *An Account of the Conventicles,* August 11, 1669, Northants RO, Fermor Hesketh Baker Papers, 708, fols. 73–75; Yelverton to Palmer, January 2 and January 16, 1662, in Palmer's letter book; and *ODNB*. Also: David L. Wykes: *The Church and Early Dissent: The 1669 Return of Nonconformity for the Archdeaconry of Northampton in Northamptonshire Past & Present,* Vol. 8 (1991–92), pp. 197–208). The principal dissenting preacher who connected the Northampton-Wellingborough area with the capital was the ejected Presbyterian minister Vincent Alsop (1630–1703): *ODNB*.
10. Benjamin Senior's poems are in the two manuscript volumes of his Commonplace Book (*BFSCPB*), preserved at the American Antiquarian Society in Worcester, Massachusetts. The book appears to be a fair copy made in his old age in the 1720s in Boston from earlier manuscripts. Apart from "The Reflection," many of his other poems contain autobiographical details, especially "The Report." Also very useful is his list of other papers which were copied by his son Samuel, but which have not survived, because the titles allow us to trace the Franklin family's connections in England; and—in Vol. 2—Benjamin Senior's chronological account of his medical history and religious experiences.
11. Thomas Vincent and his younger brother Nathaniel: Matthews, *Calamy Revised,* pp. 502–3; *ODNB;* Benjamin Senior's preface to Nathaniel Vincent, *A Discourse on Forgiveness in Three Sermons,* printed in Boston in 1722 by James Franklin; and Nathanael Taylor, *A Funeral Service Occasioned by the Death of the Late Nathaniel Vincent* (London, 1697), Dedicatory Preface.
12. Whig politics of Nathaniel Vincent and the Dyers' Company: See Chapter 3, note 1.
13. The Popish Plot and the Exclusion Crisis: Tim Harris, *Restoration: Charles II and His Kingdoms* (London, 2006), Chapter 3. For the consequences all of this had in America, the classic account is still Bernard Bailyn's masterpiece, *The Ideological Origins of the American Revolution* (Cambridge, MA, 1967 and 1992), especially Chapter 2.

14. The Child family: Landholdings and tithe payments in John Palmer's account book at the MHS, and the Child family wills at Northants RO. Thomas Franklin witnessed the will of Ann Child, spinster, in October 1631. In January 1744, at the age of eighty-six, Josiah wrote a letter to a possible kinsman in England in which he said that he had lived with his brother John for eleven years (Tourtellot, *Benjamin Franklin,* p. 26). This is at variance with his London apprenticeship record, which clearly shows that Josiah was in the city in 1678 when he reached the end of his indentures. However, it may be that the eleven years included a period of rooming with his brother in London before John left the capital for Banbury. In the Freedom Book of the Dyers' Company, Josiah signed his name as "Josias," but there can be no doubt that this is our Josiah Franklin. The handwriting precisely matches later specimens of his signature collected in New England archives by Nian-Sheng Huang: see note 9 to Chapter 3.
15. Textiles at Banbury: Kerridge, *Textile Manufactures in Early Modern England,* pp. 63–65. The Franklins: *BFSA (1717).*
16. The clergyman who came to comfort Benjamin Senior was the eminent Presbyterian Richard Steele (1629–92): *ODNB.* His presence at the sickbed shows us just how close the Franklins were to the leading figures of the dissenting movement in London. Not only that: Steele may also have helped to shape the values that Benjamin Franklin would expound in the 1730s–50s in *Poor Richard's Almanack* and *The Way to Wealth.* Mr. Steele wrote two widely read books, *The Tradesman's Calling* and *The Husbandman's Calling,* which celebrated "diligence" in business as a Christian virtue.
17. Politics and religion at Banbury: J. S. W. Gibson, ed., *Baptism and Burial Register of Banbury, Part Two, 1653–1723* (Banbury Historical Society, 1968), pp. viii–xi; and Alan Crossley, ed., *A History of the County of Oxford, Volume Ten, Banbury Hundred* (London, 1972), pp. 71–89 and 89–95.
18. Samuel Welles: Matthews, *Calamy Revised,* p. 520; and his will, proved September 24, 1678, NAK, PCC, PROB 11/357/493. Most of what we know about Welles comes from Benjamin Franklin Sr. In May 1705, he sent a brief account of Welles's life to the dissenting historian Edmund Calamy, who included the material in his biographical dictionary of the ejected ministers of 1662. Benjamin Senior's letter to Calamy was reprinted in *The Gentleman's Magazine* in 1784 (Vol. 54, p. 248). The Doyley family: Harleian Society, *Visitations of Oxfordshire* (London, 1871), pp. 226–27; will of Edward Doyley, proved May 15, 1675, at NAK, PCC, PROB 11/347/538; and Mary Clapinson, ed., *Bishop Fell and Nonconformity: Visitation Documents from the Oxford Diocese, 1682–3* (Oxfordshire Records Society, 1980), pp. 1–2, 44, and 48.
19. Benjamin Senior's employers in the 1680s and 1690s were the Light family, prominent members of the Dyers' Company and generous donors to the Presbyterian clergy: will of Anthony Light, proved June 28, 1686, at NAK, PCC, PROB 11/383/414. Will of Dorothy Doyley Welles, with a bequest of £80 to Benjamin and Hannah Franklin: proved November 24, 1688, NAK, PCC wills, PROB 11/393/298. The Doyley family's connections are documented in W. D. Bayley, *A Biographical., Historical, Genealogical and Heraldic Account of the House of D'Oyly* (London, 1845), pp. 26–33 and 46–48.

They were especially close to Oliver Cromwell's spiritual counselor, Dr. John Owen, who until his death in 1683 led a congregation that included Hannah Franklin's cousin Ursula Doyley.

Chapter Three: Coming to America

1. Samuel Shute: *ODNB*. The principal sources for my description of the events of 1682–83 are the daily journal kept by the dissenting clergyman and Whig journalist Roger Morrice, in Mark Goldie et al., eds., *The Entring Book of Roger Morrice, 1677–1691* (2007), Vol. 2, pp. 342–78, with many references to Shute and Nathaniel Vincent; Narcissus Luttrell, *A Brief Historical Relation of State Affairs* (Oxford, 1857), pp. 245–72; Gary De Krey, *London and the Restoration, 1659–83* (Cambridge, UK, 2005), Chapter 7; and the State Papers of Charles II at NAK. Also: Tim Harris, *Restoration: Charles II and His Kingdoms* (London, 2005), Chapter 5.
2. Lists of dissenters: Clapinson, ed., *Bishop Fell and Nonconformity* (Oxfordshire Records Society, 1980), pp. xxx–xxxiv; and Bishop Lloyd of Peterborough, *Account of the Present State of the Bishopric*, 1683, at Bodleian Library, Rawlinson Ms. D.1163.
3. James West's son Robert West: *ODNB;* for his New Jersey connection, John E. Pomfret, *The New Jersey Proprietors and Their Lands, 1664–1776* (Princeton, 1964), pp. 36–42. The Raritan settlement (otherwise known as Perth Amboy): *Proposals by the Proprietors of East Jersey . . . for the Building of a Town on Ambo Point* (London, 1682). The dominant role of the West family in the politics of Banbury can be seen from the material collected in J. S. W. Gibson and E. R. C. Brinkworth, eds., *Banbury Corporation Records: Tudor and Stuart* (Banbury Historical Society, 1977), pp. 222–52, with biographical details on pp. 326–27 and a West family tree. The Wests first came to local prominence during the English Civil War, when Aholiab West—James West's elder brother—served as mayor of Banbury between 1644 and 1646, with support from Parliament. Aholiab was mayor again in 1655–56, when he made common cause with Samuel Welles in suppressing the Quaker movement in the town: Alfred Beesley, *History of Banbury* (London, 1841), pp. 451–54 and 625n. James West then served as mayor three times between 1657 and 1681, while Aholiab's son John West held the office in 1677–78 and 1690–91, when John Franklin was one of the town's constables. The Franklin family's acquaintance with the Wests is documented in Benjamin Senior's Commonplace Book (*BFSCPB* 2), which refers to epitaphs composed by Samuel Welles for one of James West's sons. These epitaphs formed part of the Welles family papers, which were in the possession of Benjamin Senior's son Samuel Franklin in Boston.
4. *Nathaniel Vincent's Letter to His Congregation,* dated June 24, 1683, and published as a broadsheet in London.
5. The Rye House Plot: Richard L. Greaves, *Secrets of the Kingdom: British Radicals from the Popish Plot to the Revolution of 1688–89* (Stanford, 1992), Chapters 4–6, especially pp. 186–96.
6. Loading of ships for America in the summer of 1683: London Port Book (Exports),

at NAK, E190/1170/1, with entries relating to the *Richard* between June 21 and August 4, and the *Endeavour* between August 14 and August 25.

7. Charles II's attack on the colonial charters: Ronald Hutton, *Charles II* (Oxford, 1989), pp. 439–41.
8. Banbury Charter: Gibson and Brinkworth, *Banbury Corporation Records,* pp. 233–35. Dyers' Company: Mark Knights, "A City Revolution: The Remodelling of the London Livery Companies in the 1680s," in *English Historical Review* 112, no. 449 (November 1997): 1146–48. October arrival date: Justin Winsor, *Memorial History of Boston* (Boston, 1881), Vol. 2, pp. 270–71.
9. Samuel Willard: J. L. Sibley, *Sibley's Harvard Graduates,* Vol. 2, 1659–77 (Cambridge, MA, 1881), pp. 13–36, with the description of him as a moderate on page 17. Josiah Franklin's early years in America: Nian-Sheng Huang's excellent article "Franklin's Father Josiah: Life of a Boston Tallow Chandler, 1657–1745," in *Transactions of the American Philosophical Society,* New Series 90, no. 3 (2000): 12–85, which assembles the references to Josiah in Boston archives and Professor Huang's amplification in his "Franklin's Boston Years, 1706–1723," in David Waldstreicher, ed., *A Companion to Benjamin Franklin* (Oxford, 2011).
10. The Folgers: Tourtellot, *Benjamin Franklin,* pp. 101–8; Lemay 1, p. 27; but the best source is now Jill Lepore's *Book of Ages: The Life and Opinions of Jane Franklin* (New York, 2013), Chapters 3 and 4.
11. Historical context: J. M. Sosin, *English America and the Restoration Monarchy of Charles II* (Lincoln, NE, 1980), Chapter 14.
12. John Franklin as constable, and the return of the Banbury Whigs: Gifford and Brinkworth (1977), pp. 244–49. John Franklin's property: Oxfordshire History Centre, Oxford, FC VIII/6, quitclaim dated January 9, 1689, and his will, proved May 20, 1692 (Banbury Peculiar Wills, Pec.38/5/5-6). Together with *BFSA (1717),* the Banbury probate file—containing a bundle of material relating to the execution of the will—documents not only the consequences of John Franklin's death, but also his friendship with Banbury's civic leaders. On Franklin's English cousins and his attempts to help them: see the genealogy in *BFP I,* pp. li–lii, and the comprehensive portrait of Franklin in the 1760s and 1770s in George Goodwin, *Benjamin Franklin in London: The British Life of America's Founding Father* (New Haven, CT, 2016), pp. 111–114.
13. Charles Montagu, Earl of Halifax (1661–1715): *ODNB.* His wife was Anne, Countess of Manchester, born Anne Yelverton, the sister of the Sir Henry Yelverton of the 1660s who had been so close a friend of Archdeacon Palmer. Thomas Franklin Junior as tax inspector: William A. Shaw, ed., *Calendar of Treasury Papers* (London, 1931), Vol. 9, p. 267; Treasury Reference Book, 1689–1693, at NAK, T4/6, p.163; Treasury Money Book, T53/10, pp. 469–70; and Treasury Warrant Book, T54/13, pp. 102–3. On the taxes that he collected: E. A. Reitan, "From Revenue to Civil List, 1689–1702: The 'Revolution Settlement' and the Mixed and Balanced Constitution," in *Historical Journal* 13 (1970): 571–88. Thomas Franklin as tax commissioners' clerk: noted in his burial record, January 7, 1703 (not 1702, the date given in error by Franklin in his autobiography), in the Ecton parish register at Northants RO. Benjamin

Senior overstates his rank by saying that Thomas was one of the commissioners, and not their clerk. This is another indication that *BFSA (1717)* cannot always be relied upon for accuracy.

14. The quarrel between Thomas Franklin and the Palmers in the 1690s makes for entertaining reading. Another John Palmer, the archdeacon's son, now held the post of rector, entitled to the tithes of Ecton, but reluctant to perform the duty of collecting them. Thomas Franklin took a lease on the tithes, gave the rector £200 a year, assessed the tithe payers for a much larger sum, and then kept the difference. It was a cunning scheme, but Mr. Palmer thought he had been swindled. In 1698 Palmer called in his lawyers, and when the case came to the Court of Chancery it revealed the abrasive side of Thomas Junior. Determined to keep what was his, he refused to answer the writ, went on felling trees in the rector's woods, and threatened to take the tithes by force next harvest time, or so it was alleged. When the judge heard that, he issued an injunction against Mr. Franklin, who had to obey: Chancery lawsuit (1698–99), *Palmer v. Franklin,* at NAK, C5/138/27; and Chancery Entry Book (1698-B), at C33/292, pp. 81, 367, and 452. In his legal defense, dated May 1699, Franklin describes himself as a "*gentleman,*" after calling himself a yeoman when he signed his will in September 1697 (Northants RO, Archdeaconry Wills, W.180, will of Thomas Franklin, proved April 17, 1703). According to Benjamin Senior, Thomas had built a fortune of £2,000 by the time of his death *(BFSA 1717),* but again this figure has to be treated with caution. Thomas Junior's will indicates that at his death he owned only two yardlands at Ecton (presumably the same as those his father had occupied) and two tracts of pasture, making a total of no more than about thirty-five or forty acres at the most.
15. Defoe's background and the *Essay upon Projects:* Paula R. Backscheider, *Daniel Defoe: His Life* (Baltimore, 1989), pp. 34, 7–8, and 67–71. His origins and early life had close affinities with those of Josiah Franklin and Benjamin Senior. Born in Northamptonshire in 1660, three years after Josiah, Defoe was the son of a tallow chandler who also worshipped at dissenting chapels in London, as did Defoe himself. Indeed it is almost certain that in their youth Daniel Defoe and the Franklin brothers occcasionally attended the same congregations. The Defoe family's pastor was Samuel Annesley (1620–96), another of the ejected Puritan clergymen of 1662. Annesley and the Vincent brothers (the Franklin mentors) were closely associated in the capital as radical preachers who defied the law against conventicles: De Krey, *London and the Restoration, 1659–83,* p. 120. Defoe was also an admirer of the work of the London Presbyterian friend of the Franklins Richard Steele: see note 16 to Chapter 2. Finally: Defoe was acquainted with Thomas Franklin's patron, Charles Montagu, Lord Halifax, and indeed the *Essay Upon Projects* may have been intended to win Defoe his own post on the Treasury's payroll.

Chapter Four: His Happy Childhood

1. Boston at the time of Franklin's birth: *Boston Newsletter,* December 31, 1705–January 7, 1706; the opening chapters of G. B. Warden's *Boston: 1689–1776* (New York, 1970),

Chapter 2; Michael G. Hall, *The Last American Puritan: The Life of Increase Mather, 1639–1723* (Middletown, CT, 1988), pp. 326–38; and generally, Gary B. Nash, *The Urban Crucible: Social Change, Political Consciousness and the Origins of the American Revolution* (Cambridge, MA, 1979), Chapter 3.

2. Joseph Dudley, the carriers, and Cotton Mather's pamphlet: M. Halsey Thomas, ed., *The Diary of Samuel Sewall* (New York, 1973), Vol. 1, pp. 532–35 and 539–40; and Cotton Mather, *A Memorial of the Present Deplorable State of New England* (Boston, 1707), p. 7.
3. The Holmes family: James and S. G. McConnell, *Fasti of the Irish Presbyterian Church, Part II* (Belfast, 1951), Entry 288A.
4. In December 1705, the month before Franklin was born, Massachusetts passed a law—the "Act for the Better Preventing of a Spurious and Mixt Issue"—that forbade marriage or fornication between white people and either "Negroes or mulattoes." Although Judge Sewall managed to insert a clause allowing African American slaves to marry each other without their masters' consent, they had no right to keep their children. Although masters could legally free their slaves, in practice this was unlikely to occur because a law of 1703 made it conditional on the master posting a £50 bond to guarantee that they did not fall into poverty and become a burden on the public purse. The town authorities were also given the power to press a freed slave into forced labor: *The Acts and Resolves . . . of the Province of Massachusetts Bay, Volume I* (Boston, 1869), pp. 519 and 576–79; and Sewall, *Diary*, Vol. 1, p. 532. On Benjamin Franklin and slavery: David Waldstreicher, "Benjamin Franklin, Capitalism and Slavery," in Waldstreicher, ed., *A Companion to Benjamin Franklin*, pp. 215–27; and Professor Waldstreicher's *Runaway America: Benjamin Franklin, Slavery, and the American Revolution* (New York, 2004), especially pp. 17–25, pp. 32–36, pp. 79–83, and pp. 125–34, charting the evolution of Franklin's attitudes to the subject until the end of the 1740s.
5. Pierre-Jean-Georges Cabanis, *Notice sur Benjamin Franklin*, in *Oeuvres posthumes de Cabanis* (Paris, 1825), pp. 219–28; and Franklin to Mme Brillon, November 10, 1779, *BFP 31*, pp. 69–77.
6. The Mill Pond and its surroundings: Nancy S. Seasholes, *Gaining Ground: A History of Landmaking in Boston* (Cambridge, MA, 2003), pp. 73–76. Despite all the landfill and the modern buildings, it is still just possible, with the aid of Ms. Seasholes's fine book and some patience, to trace on foot the layout of the area as Franklin knew it: in particular, the line of the creek that emptied the pond can be found along Salt Lane. Also very helpful is a Boston classic, Annie Haven Thwing's *The Crooked and Narrow Streets of the Town of Boston, 1630 to 1822* (Boston, 1920).
7. The Franklin miffiness, and the fish barrel: Lepore, *Book of Ages*, pp. 19–20.
8. Toland: quotations from John Toland, *Christianity Not Mysterious* (London, 1695–96), pp. xxx and 6. On the "deistical controversy": the leading historian is Jonathan Israel, in his *Radical Enlightenment: Philosophy and the Making of Modernity* (Oxford, 2001), especially Chapters 18 and 24, and his *Enlightenment Contested: Philosophy, Modernity and the Emancipation of Man* (Oxford, 2006), pp. 202–14 and 344–55. For a more concise treatment, see John Redwood, *Reason, Ridicule and Religion: The Age of Enlightenment in England, 1660–1750* (London, 1976), especially Chapters 1 and 2; and Margaret C. Jacob, *The*

Newtonians and the English Revolution, 1689–1720 (Hassocks, Sussex, UK, 1976), Chapters 5 and 6.

9. Cotton Mather, *Reason Satisfied and Faith Established* (Boston, 1712), p. iii.
10. Pierre Bayle: Israel, *Radical Enlightenment,* pp. 331–41, and Israel, *Enlightenment Contested,* pp. 66–71, 145–53, and 264–77. However, the best introduction to Bayle's career is still the 1729 biography by Pierre Des Maizeaux, *The Life and Works of Mr Bayle,* in Vol. 1 of *The Dictionary Historical and Critical of Mr Peter Bayle, Second Edition* (London, 1734). In 1742, Franklin and his friends at the Library Company of Philadelphia listed this ten-volume edition of Bayle in the library's catalogue.

Chapter Five: Mr. Pemberton's Method

1. Benjamin Senior's misadventures are recorded in his long autobiographical poem, *The Reflection,* in *BFSCPB 1,* and in his *Short Catalogue of the Afflictions wherewith it hath pleased God . . . to Exercise Me,* in Vol. 2.
2. Samuel Franklin indentured as a London cutler's apprentice, August 25, 1702: Cliff Webb, ed., *London Livery Company Apprenticeship Registers* (London, 2000), Vol. 35, p. 42.
3. Samuel Wright: Backscheider, *Daniel Defoe,* pp. 362–64; and Wright's entry in *ODNB.* After Nathaniel Vincent's death, Wright became Benjamin Senior's favorite preacher and a personal friend. In 1713, the old man wrote an acrostic poem in the preacher's honor to accompany a gift of candles: *BFSCPB 1.*
4. Ebenezer Pemberton: Biographical sketch in Clifford K. Shipton, ed., *Sibley's Harvard Graduates,* Vol. 4, 1690–1700 (Cambridge, MA, 1933), pp. 107–13); Benjamin Colman's funeral sermon, in Ebenezer Pemberton, *Sermons and Discourses on Several Occasions* (London, 1727), pp. 274–310; and M. Halsey Thomas, ed., *The Diary of Samuel Sewall, 1674–1729* (New York, 1973), Vol. 2, p. 796 (August 18, 1715).
5. Pemberton's library: *A Catalogue of Curious Books Belonging to the Late Learned Ebenezer Pemberton* (Boston, 1717).
6. Sir Henry Yelverton on the latitudinarians: Letters to Archdeacon Palmer, July 5, 1662, and January 20 and February 2, 1670 (see note 7 to Chapter 2). John Tillotson and the latitudinarian movement: Nicholas Tyacke, "From Laudians to Latitudinarians," in G. Tapsell, ed., *The Later Stuart Church, 1660–1714* (Manchester, 2013), pp. 49–57; and *ODNB.*
7. Tillotson on reason: Sermon 28, "Objections Against The True Religion Answer'd," in John Tillotson, *Works . . . Containing 54 Sermons* (London, 1720), p. 296. Pemberton's Old South sermons: Pemberton, *Sermons and Discourses on Several Occasions,* and (for his preaching on Isaiah) handwritten notes taken by Edward Bromfield, a member of Josiah Franklin's prayer meeting: MHS, Ms. N-1936. The sermons on Isaiah were given in March and April 1714 when Benjamin Franklin was eight. The closest echoes of John Tillotson are in the homily dated April 25. On Tillotson's influence in New England, see Norman Fiering, "The First American Enlightenment: Tillotson, Leverett and Philosophical Anglicanism," in *The New England Quarterly* (September 1981), with a discussion of Pemberton and Colman and the Brattle Square church on pp.

320–22 and 329–31. Also: Mark A. Noll, *America's God: From Jonathan Edwards to Abraham Lincoln* (Oxford, 2002), Chapter 2; and for Franklin's admiration of John Tillotson, see *BFP 3*, pp. 405-7.

8. James's visit to London: Lemay 1, pp. 54–56.
9. On Storke: William I. Roberts III: "Samuel Storke: An Eighteenth Century London Merchant Trading to the Colonies," in *Business History Review* 39, no. 2 (Summer 1965), pp. 147–170.
10. *"An agreeable miscellany:"* Nathaniel Mist's *Weekly Journal or Saturday's Post,* April 26, 1718. On Mist and the weekly journals generally: James Sutherland, *The Restoration Newspaper and Its Development* (Cambridge, UK, 1986), pp. 32–37, 212–13, and 229–30; and Jeremy Black, "The Press, Party and Foreign Policy in the Reign of George I" in the journal *Publishing History* (1983), Vol. 13, pp. 23–40. For evidence that James Franklin corresponded with Nathaniel Mist: *Weekly Journal or Saturday's Post,* July 20, 1723. It contains a detailed report on the attempt in the summer of 1722 by the Massachusetts Provincial Council to censor the *Courant.* The item is so sympathetic to James Franklin that he or one of his fellow writers of the *Courant* must have been the author.

Chapter Six: For the Love of Books

1. Context of *The Spectator:* Brian Cowan, "Mr Spectator and the Coffeehouse Public Sphere," in *Eighteenth Century Studies* 37, no. 3 (Spring 2004): 345–66, with a full analysis of Addison's ideas about literary style, gentility, and "politeness."
2. Benjamin Senior on Elizabeth Franklin: His poem "An Acrostick Elegie on his son Samuel Franklin," dated March 29, 1720, in *BFSCPB 2*, especially the very forthright stanzas 9–14.
3. Bishop Jonathan Shipley to Franklin, September 22, 1782, *BFP 37*, pp. 129–30.
4. For a discussion of the way adolescents channel their instincts into philosophizing, see a classic of psychoanalysis, Anna Freud's *The Ego and the Mechanisms of Defence* (London, 1993), pp. 158–65, on "intellectualization at puberty."
5. Tryon's biography: *Some Memoirs of the Life of Thomas Tryon, late of London, Merchant* (London, 1705), with an account of his mystical beliefs on pp. 29–32.
6. Tryon's ideal republic: *The Way to Health* (1683), pp. 70–128. Chapter 14 deals with the evils of flesh eating. His open letter to the Quakers was titled *The Planter's Speech to his Neighbours and Countrymen of Pennsylvania, East & West Jersey* (London, 1684).
7. Plutarch and vegetarianism: *Plutarch's Morals, Translated from the Greek* (London, 1691), Vol. 5, pp. 234–49. A copy of this edition of Plutarch was included in a book sale in Boston in October 1719 for which James Franklin printed the catalogue.
8. Franklin's knowledge of the work of Samuel and John Clarke can be authenticated as follows. In his autobiography, Franklin says that "some books against Deism fell into my hands: they were said to be the substance of sermons preached at Boyle's lectures." This specific phrase —"substance of sermons preached at Boyle's lectures"—appears on the title pages of only three books published in England in the early eighteenth century, each of which was the printed text of lectures given in a series endowed by the pioneer chemist, Sir Robert Boyle. One of these books—

Physico-Theology, by William Derham, who gave the Boyle lectures in 1711–12—can be ruled out because it did not refer to the deistical controversy. The other two were Samuel Clarke's Boyle lectures of 1704, published in 1705 as *A Demonstration of the Being and Attributes of God: More Particularly in Answer to Mr. Hobbs, Spinoza, and their Followers*, and reprinted in 1716 and 1719; and John Clarke's *An Enquiry Into The Cause and Origin of Evil* (given as the Boyle Lectures in 1719, and then published in 1720). Franklin must have read one or the other, or he may have read both. On the Boyle Lectures and the Clarkes: John Redwood, *Reason, Ridicule and Religion* (London, 1976), pp. 103–14.

9. Shaftesbury's aesthetic religion: A. O. Aldridge, "Shaftesbury and the Deist Manifesto," in *Transactions of the American Philosophical Society*, New Series, Vol. 41, Part 2 (1951), especially pp. 330–33.
10. Franklin does not say which of Collins's works he read, but in the 1730s he owned a copy of the *Discourse of Free Thinking* (1713), which he mentions in a list in *The Pennsylvania Gazette* (December 12, 1734) of items he had lent out and wished to have returned. From his conversations with Cabanis it can be shown that his early reading must have focused on this book. In his account of Franklin's youth, Cabanis gives a brief list of topics—namely, "the divinity of Scripture, revelation, and mysteries"—that Franklin said he had seen discussed by Collins (Cabanis, *Notice sur Benjamin Franklin*, pp. 228–29). This list precisely matches the contents of Collins's *Discourse.* Cabanis also refers to two aphorisms of Sir Francis Bacon that Franklin liked to repeat, and these aphorisms were quoted and discussed by Collins on pp. 104–6 of the same book. For the best scholarly account of Collins's work and his relationship to Locke and Toland: James O'Higgins SJ, *Anthony Collins: The Man and His Works* (The Hague, 1970), pp. 3–6, 13–15, and Chapter 6 on the *Discourse* of 1713. Franklin also owned a copy of Collins's *Philosophical Inquiry Concerning Human Liberty* (1717), which is now at the Library Company of Philadelphia.
11. *"Absurdity"*: Collins, *Discourse of Free Thinking*, pp. 13–18. For an example of Franklin's use of the word in a similar way, see his *Defense of Mr Hemphill's Observations* (Philadelphia, 1735) where it appears six times. *"Pious fraud"*: Collins, *Discourse of Free Thinking*, pp. 92–93.
12. List of heroes: Collins, *Discourse of Free Thinking*, pp. 125–76.
13. Fate of Socrates: Ibid., p. 126.
14. Elisha Cooke Jr.: Clifford K. Shipton, *Sibley's Harvard Graduates*, Vol. 4, 1690–1700 (Cambridge, MA, 1933), pp. 349–56. But for this period of Boston history the work of Perry Miller is still indispensable: principally his beautifully written *The New England Mind: From Colony to Province* (Cambridge, MA, 1953), Books 3 and 4.
15. The Cooke-Mather antagonism: Kenneth Silverman, *The Life and Times of Cotton Mather* (New York, 1984), pp. 322–29.
16. Henry Care: There is an excellent modern biography, which places Care in his context and shows how important he was for the future of Anglo-American journalism, in Lois G. Schwoerer, *The Ingenious Henry Care, Restoration Publicist* (Baltimore, 2001). My quotations come from pp. 29 and 54. Care had a direct connection with New England via his close associate, the printer Benjamin Harris (1647?–1720). The two men stood trial together for libel in London in 1680. In 1686, Harris immigrated

to Massachusetts, where he fleetingly produced America's first newspaper, *Publick Occurrences,* before returning to England in about 1694. In the early 1700s, Harris published new editions of Care's *English Liberties.* In 2000, Keith Arbour produced some fascinating typographical evidence suggesting that James Franklin may have trained as a printer with Benjamin Harris in London. The question is not a trivial one, because if James Franklin did meet Harris, this would be another indication that the Franklins in Boston remained closely in touch with English metropolitan culture throughout Benjamin Franklin's boyhood. See Keith Arbour, "James Franklin, Apprentice, Artisan, Dissident, and Teacher," in *Papers of the Bibliographical Society of America* 94 (September 2000): 366–372; and Lemay 1, pp. 54–55.

Chapter Seven: THE NEW-ENGLAND COURANT

1. The epidemic: Amalie M. Kass, "Boston's Historic Smallpox Epidemic," in *Massachusetts Historical Review* 14 (2012), pp. 1–51. Monthly burial numbers for Boston: *Boston Gazette,* No. 121, March 12–19, 1722. Shute's clash with the House of Representatives: *Colonial State Papers (America and West Indies), 1720–1721* (London, 1933), pp. 329–30 and pp. 371–74. Political context: G. B. Warden's *Boston: 1689–1776* (New York, 1970), Chapter 5.
2. Attack on Cotton Mather: Kass, "Boston's Historic Smallpox Epidemic," pp. 28–29.
3. Among the many academic articles about the Dogood letters, one of the most illuminating is George F. Horner, "Franklin's Dogood Papers Re-examined," in *Studies in Philology* 37, no. 3 (July 1940), pp. 501–23, which explores their social and economic context in Boston. Equally excellent is James N. Green and Peter Stallybrass, *Benjamin Franklin: Writer and Printer* (Newcastle, DE, 2006), pp. 3–8. Once again one must also return to Perry Miller, in chapter 24 of his *The New England Mind: From Colony to Province.*
4. For a discussion of *Moll Flanders* that brings out more of the affinities between Franklin and Defoe, especially in their writing about women and families: Backscheider, *Daniel Defoe,* pp. 505–10.
5. Franklin to Samuel Mather, July 7, 1773, and May 12, 1784, *BFP 20,* pp. 286–88, and *BFP 42,* pp. 236–37.
6. Unlike many American scholars, I do not believe that Cotton Mather—or indeed the orthodox New England Calvinism to which he adhered—had any significant or lasting influence on Benjamin Franklin. The first point to make is this: that we cannot be precisely sure what Josiah and Abiah Franklin believed about the finer points of divinity or what they conveyed to the boy. They might not have been Matherites at all. From correspondence that passed between them and their youngest son in 1738 *(BFP* 2, pp. 202–4), when Mr. and Mrs. Franklin were worried by reports of Benjamin's unorthodox opinions, it is clear that Josiah and Abiah were staunch Bible Christians with generally Calvinist views and a firm faith in the Holy Trinity. But that does not mean that they had to agree with Cotton Mather about all the details of his creed: for example, they did not have to subscribe to Mather's doctrine of Double Predestination. The underlying issue here is that Josiah Franklin and his

brother Benjamin Senior were not New England Puritans at all. The two men were *London* Presbyterians, and their religious education occurred in England, not in Massachusetts. By the time Josiah Franklin left for America in the 1680s, as an adult of twenty-five, some Presbyterian ministers in London—including the most famous, Richard Baxter—had already abandoned the most rigid forms of Calvinist dogma, while retaining to the full the Puritan concern with Bible reading and personal piety. And when Benjamin Senior arrived in Boston from London in 1715, the theological situation in England was still more complicated and nuanced. We do not know for certain which side—or sides—the old man took in the many religious debates under way in the empire's capital. But one thing we can say for sure: that when Benjamin Franklin had his own printing firm in Philadelphia, he took next to no interest in the work of the Mathers. While his firm was publishing between 1728 and 1766, it reprinted only one of the Mather family's vast array of books: a set of sermons by Increase Mather titled *Soul Saving Gospel Truths,* which Franklin produced in 1743. And in the catalogue of Franklin's library published in 2006 by Edwin Wolf and Kevin J. Hayes, we find listed only three works by Cotton Mather: Franklin's boyhood copy of *Bonifacius;* the *Magnalia Christi Americana* of 1702, his history of New England, which seems to have been there primarily because it describes Franklin's grandfather, Peter Folger; and a brief tract from 1700, in which Mather writes an open letter to nonconformists in England. There is nothing else.

7. Shute's dispatch of October 29, 1722, in *Colonial State Papers (American), 1722–3* (London, 1934), pp. 157–58.
8. Issue 76 and John Toland: The relevant passage on p. 58 of Toland's *Christianity Not Mysterious* (1695–6), containing language very similar to the closing section of the principal item in *Courant* No. 76, is this: "The natural man, that is he that gives the swing to his appetites, counts divine things mere folly, calls religion a feverish dream of superstitious heads, or a politick trick invented by statesmen to awe the credulous vulgar." Action against the *Courant:* Worthington C. Ford, ed., *Journals of the House of Representatives of Massachusetts, 1722–3* (Boston, 1923), pp. 205 and 208–9.
9. By the 1720s, the political usage of the word "canvass" to mean "solicit a vote in an election" was firmly established in the English language. The first example recorded by the *Oxford English Dictionary* dates from 1681.

Chapter Eight: The Crusoe of the Delaware

1. Among the many echoes of *Robinson Crusoe* in Franklin's autobiography, consider the following passages. Early in the book, Defoe describes Crusoe's time in a small boat after his ship was wrecked off the coast of Norfolk in England: "While we were in this condition, the men yet labouring at the oar to bring the boat near the shore, we could see, when our boat mounting the waves we were able to see the shore, a great many people running along the shore to assist us when we should come near, but we made slow way toward the shore, nor were we able to reach the shore, till we were past the lighthouse at Winterton." In his account of his attempt to land on the beach in Brooklyn, Franklin writes this: "When we drew near to the island [the Brooklyn

end of Long Island] we found it was a place where there could be no landing, there being a great surf . . . so we dropped anchor and swung around toward the shore. Some people came down to the water edge and hallow'd to us, as we did to them. But the wind was high and the surf so loud, that we could not hear as to understand each other."

2. Over two days in the spring of 2015 I retraced Franklin's journey across New Jersey, chiefly by car but also on foot where possible, using the topographical maps published by the U.S. Geological Survey. For his route, see Lemay 1, pp. 221–23. For evidence about the landscape and the settlements in the area as they were in 1723: W. Woodford Clayton, *History of Union and Middlesex Counties* (Philadelphia, 1882), pp. 822–24 and 852–53; Wheaton J. Lane, *From Indian Trail to Iron Horse: Travel and Transportation in New Jersey, 1620–1860* (Princeton, 1939), pp.17–18, 36, and 42–43; and Peter O. Wacker, *Land and People: A Cultural Geography of Pre-industrial New Jersey* (New Brunswick, NJ, 1975), pp. 48 and 88–89.
3. Quaker farmers in the Crosswicks area: E. M. Woodward and J. F. Hageman, *History of Burlington and Mercer Counties, NJ* (Philadelphia, 1883), pp. 275–77, 286–89, and 352–56. This source mentions the Quaker meeting house, erected in 1706.
4. Bordentown and Dr. Browne: Woodward and Hageman, *History of Burlington and Mercer Counties, NJ*, pp. 452–61; *PG*, May 26, 1737; and Browne's will, in *Calendar of New Jersey Wills* (Somerville, NJ, 1918), Vol. 2, p. 68.
5. Descriptions of Pennsylvania in the 1720s: Quotations from Donald F. Durnbaugh, "Two Early Letters from Germantown," in *PMHB* 84, no. 2 (April 1960): 219–33. For the political economy of Pennsylvania at the time of Franklin's arrival, the sources I have found most useful are the closing chapters of Gary B. Nash, *Quakers and Politics: Pennsylvania, 1681–1726* (Princeton, 1968); Joseph E. Illick, *Colonial Pennsylvania* (New York, 1976), pp. 107–12; Alan Tully, *William Penn's Legacy* (Baltimore, 1977), pp. 53–57 and passim; and also the immensely valuable biographical dictionary, *Lawmaking and Legislators in Pennsylvania*, Vol. 2 (Philadelphia, 1997), edited by Craig E. Horle and others and referred to below as *LLP 2*. For an official account of Pennsylvania by the governor, see the September 8, 1721, Board of Trade report on the state of the colonies, in *Colonial State Papers (American and West Indies), 1720–1721* (London, 1933), pp. 418–21.
6. Dispute following William Penn's death: Charles P. Keith, *Chronicles of Pennsylvania* (Philadelphia, 1917), Vol. 2, pp. 633–37.
7. The Crooked Billet, and other locations visited by Franklin on reaching Philadelphia: Hannah Benner Roach, "Benjamin Franklin Slept Here," in *PMHB* 84, no. 2 (April 1960): 127–30.
8. Sauer's account of Pennsylvania in 1724: in Durnbaugh, "Two Early Letters from Germantown," p. 230. Sauer's origins: Donald F. Durnbaugh, "Christopher Sauer, Pennsylvania German Printer," in *PMHB* 82, no. 3 (July 1958): 316–23.
9. Keimer, his origins, and the Camisards: Samuel Keimer, *A Brand Pluck'd From The Burning* (London, 1718), pp. 2–9; Stephen Bloore, "Samuel Keimer," in *PMHB* 3, no. 4 (1930); and Hillel Schwartz, *The French Prophets: The History of a Millenarian Group in Eighteenth Century England* (Berkeley, 1980).

10. Keimer, *The London Post,* and Defoe: Backscheider, *Daniel Defoe,* pp. 376–78.
11. The best account of Mrs. Franklin is Jennifer Reed Fry's "'Extraordinary Freedom and Great Humility': A Reinterpretation of Deborah Franklin," in *PMHB* 127, no. 2 (April 2003), pp. 167-196.
12. In 1997, the Franklin scholar Professor Leo Lemay began a project to transcribe and annotate the Franklin account books, for which later writers owe him a debt of gratitude. In the form of searchable PDF files, the complete transcriptions can be found on the University of Delaware Library website at http://udspace.udel.edu/handle/19716/2354.
13. Franklin to Deborah, September 6, 1758, *BFP* 7, pp. 138–46, with a family tree. Franklin's cousin: Benjamin Tyler (1700?–1760), whose will, proved on February 17, 1761, is at the Lichfield Diocesan Registry Office (LDRO). It shows that Tyler's closest friend was Peter Capper, a brass and copper merchant who was also a founding investor in the Birmingham Canal in 1768. Capper was a business associate of Matthew Boulton, the most famous Birmingham manufacturer of the eighteenth century, who financed the steam engines designed by James Watt.
14. On Deborah Read's family history, the only reliable published source is Francis J. Dallett, "Doctor Franklin's In-Laws," in *Pennsylvania Genealogical Magazine* 21 (1960): 297–302. Unfortunately, the surviving records from seventeenth-century Birmingham are far from satisfactory. However, from what remains it appears that Deborah's forebears had connections with the area's earliest industrialists. The key figure is her great-grandfather Abraham Cash, a shoemaker. At LDRO Cash's will, proved October 1, 1707, shows as one of his executors Samuel Banner, a leading Birmingham ironmaster. Abraham's granddaughter Anne Cash married into the Weston family, who belonged to a consortium that in 1694 won a contract to supply the army with muskets: W. H. B. Court, *The Rise of the Midland Industries, 1600–1838* (Oxford, 1938), pp. 142–43. Birmingham ca. 1700: Marie Rowlands, "Society and Industry in the West Midlands at the End of the Eighteenth Century," in *Midland History* 4 (1977): 49–60; and M. J. Wise, "Birmingham and Its Trade Relations in the Early Eighteenth Century," in *University of Birmingham Historical Journal,* 2 (1949–50): 53–79. Joseph White's trade as a whitesmith: his and Deborah Cash's marriage license, July 25, 1673, also at Lichfield.
15. Caleb Cash in Philadelphia: manuscript notes in the Cash/Leacock family Bible, at APS, ref 220.52 B471.
16. Thomas Rutter, Samuel Nutt, and the early iron and steel industry in Pennsylvania: The best brief introductions are the essay "Legislators, the Assembly and the Iron Industry, 1715–1775," in Craig Horle, ed., *Lawmaking and Legislators in Pennsylvania,* Vol. 3, 1757–1775 (House of Representatives of Pennsylvania, 2005), pp. 32–40; and A. C. Bining, *Pennsylvania Iron Manufacture in the Eighteenth Century* (Harrisburg, PA, 1938). The library of the Historical Society of Pennsylania (HSP) contains a wealth of relevant material. For Rutter and Nutt, see the typescript paper by Daniel A. Graham, "Thomas Rutter I (ca. 1660–1730) of Germantown, PA and the Birth of the Pennsylvania Iron Industry" (1996). On William Penn's attempt to persuade the Quaker ironmasters of the English West Midlands to invest in his colony: see

M. W. Flinn, *Men of Iron: The Crowleys in the Early Iron Industry* (Edinburgh, 1962), pp. 114–15. The Quaker merchants from Pennsylvania who visited the Birmingham area included William Penn's agent in the colony, James Logan, who hoped (in vain) to marry into the Crowley family, the most successful English ironmasters of the period; and Penn's close and wealthy friend, Isaac Norris Sr. (1671–1735), who was in England from 1706 to 1708. I think it is possible that John and Sarah Read traveled to America with Norris on his return journey, since the Reads certainly knew the Norrises well. When Isaac Norris's daughter—also a Deborah—died in 1767, Mrs. Franklin recalled that they had played together as small children. As she wrote to her husband: "She was one of my first play maites and I raly loved her" (quoted in Reed Fry, "'Extraordinary Freedom and Great Humility': A Reinterpretation of Deborah Franklin"). If I am correct, then we can fix 1708 as the date of Deborah Read Franklin's arrival in Philadelphia, meaning that she was born in England.

17. John Read's housebuilding: *AWM*, August 18, 1720; and Benner Roach, "Benjamin Franklin Slept Here," pp. 131–33.
18. John Leacock and Francis J. Dallett Jr., "John Leacock and the Fall of British Tyranny," in *PMHB* 78, no. 4 (October 1954): 456–57; and the sources in note 14 above.
19. Economic growth between the 1720s and 1740s: James G. Lydon, "Philadelphia's Commercial Expansion, 1720–1739," in *PMHB* 91, no. 4 (October 1967), pp. 401–418; and James T. Lemon, *The Best Poor Man's Country: A Geographical Study of Early Southeastern Pennsylvania* (Baltimore, 1972).

Chapter Nine: Forgetting Boston

1. Quaker merchant: Thomas Lawrence of Philadelphia, writing to Samuel Storke, January 17, 1724, in Lawrence's letter book (1718–1725), at Historical Society of Pennsylvania, Amb. 54. In general, the extensive collections of colonial letters from the 1720s to the 1740s at the HSP—especially those of Lawrence, James Logan, the Isaac Norris family, and John Reynell—are a superb resource for anyone writing about Franklin's early life and seeking to place his career in its historical context.
2. John Smith, clockmaker, *The Curiosities of Common Water* (London and Philadelphia, 1723); and Thomas Chalkley, *Letter To a Friend in Ireland* (London, 1720, and Philadelphia, 1723).
3. Keimer's *Parable*: *AWM*, December 17–24, 1723. *Free Gift*: *AWM*, January 7–14, 1724; and Thomas Woolston, *A Free Gift to the Clergy, Or the Hireling Priests of What Denomination Soever* (London, 1722, and Philadelphia, 1724), with the references to blockheads, dunces, etc. on p. 25 of the Philadelphia edition. The book ended with an allusion to a coarse English proverb about apples and horse turds, in which Woolston compared dissenting ministers to the latter. In London Woolston went on to become a popular author of anticlerical pamphlets expounding his very unorthodox views about Christian theology, until at last in 1729 he was sent to jail for blasphemy.
4. Sir William Keith: By far the best account of Keith is David Haugaard's, in Horle

et al., *Lawmaking and Legislators in Pennsylvania* (Philadelphia, 1997), Vol. 2, pp. 561–89, from which my quotations come unless noted otherwise.

5. Spotswood's western policy and his iron business: Leonidas Dodson, *Alexander Spotswood, Governor of Colonial Virginia, 1710–1722* (Philadelphia, 1932), pp. 227–33 and 296–98. Keith's admiration of Spotswood: Sir William Keith, *History of the British Plantations in America* (London, 1738), Vol. 1, pp. 173–74.
6. Keith's speech of January 22, 1723: In Gertrude Mackinney, ed., *Pennsylvania Archives, Eighth Series* (Harrisburg, PA, 1931–35), Vol. 2, pp. 1474–77.
7. Consequences of paper money: Theodore Thayer, "The Land-Bank System in the American Colonies," in *Journal of Economic History* 13, no. 2 (Spring 1953): 145–59.
8. Excitement aroused by the Schuyler copper mine: Isaac Norris Sr. to Henry Gouldney, April 9, 1722, in HSP, Norris family letter book, 1716–1735, Norris Papers, collection No. 454, Vol. 2. As Norris puts it: "people here are bending their thoughts to get suddenly rich—mines, ore, gold, silver, copper are full in everybody's mouth, since Schuyler's success." The Schuyler mine: Wayne Bodle, "'Such a Noise in the World': Copper Mines and an American Colonial Echo to the South Sea Bubble," in *PMHB* 127, no. 2 (April 2003): 131–65.
9. "His designs . . .": James Logan to Springett Penn, November 12, 1722, in Logan's letter books, as transcribed by Deborah Norris Logan, Vol. 3, p. 271, at APS, B L82. As yet, there is still no full-length biography of James Logan, which is understandable. He left behind an enormous corpus of papers, chiefly housed at HSP, on which a researcher could spend an entire career. Nash, *Quakers and Politics*, p. 268, has a succinct appraisal of the man, but the principal secondary work is still Frederick B. Tolles's condensed account, *James Logan and the Culture of Provincial America* (Boston, 1957). The most attractive route to an appreciation of Logan lies by way of a tour of Stenton, his country house in northwest Philadelphia, open to the public and maintained by the Colonial Dames of Pennsylvania. It has an excellent guidebook (2014) by the curator, Laura C. Keim. For Logan's Whiggish views and his loathing of Tories and Jacobites, see his letters to George Barclay, December 3, 1733, and Alexander Arscott, May 1, 1734, in James Logan's letter books, HSP, Coll. 0379, Vol. 8.
10. Keith and French at New Castle: Richard S. Rodney, "Delaware Under Governor Keith 1717–1726," in *Delaware History* (Wilmington, DE, 1948–49), Vol. 3, pp. 12–19; and Constance J. Cooper, ed., *350 Years of New Castle, Delaware: Chapters in a Town's History* (New Castle Historical Society, 2001), pp. 41–56. A visit to New Castle's historic district is another enjoyable way to experience Franklin's colonial environment.
11. *Onania:* Advertised for sale by Phillips in *The New-England Courant,* May 4–11, 1724.
12. John Franklin (1690–1756): His will, January 22–24, 1756, mentioning his two-volume set of Ephraim Chambers's *Cyclopedia, or Universal Dictionary of the Arts and Sciences; Boston Evening Post,* October 6, 1755; and Jill Lepore, *Book of Ages: The Life and Opinions of Jane Franklin* (New York, 2013), pp. 96–98.
13. Samuel Vernon: C. Louise Avery, *Early American Silver* (New York, 1930), pp. 100–103; and regarding Vernon's role as a pillar of the Congregational Church: Sydney V.

James, *The Colonial Metamorphoses of Rhode Island* (Hanover, NH, 2000), pp. 171–72 and 290. A measure of Vernon's importance in Rhode Island was this: that between 1729 and 1736 he served four times as a member of the elected assembly's upper house: J. R. Bartlett, ed., *Colonial Records of Rhode Island,* Vol. 14 (Providence, 1859).

14. Keith and Spotswood: James Logan to Joshua Gee, October 1, 1724, in Logan's letter books, at APS (B L82), Vol. 3. Spotswood arrived in England in November 1724 (*Weekly Journal & Gazetteer,* November 28) and far from being disgraced he was given a senior military post in Scotland. Disease on the *London Hope:* Isaac Norris to Joseph Pike, August 8, 1724, in Norris Family Papers, Coll. 454 at HSP, Vol. 2.
15. "Scandal and impertinence": Quoted in Walker Lewis, "Andrew Hamilton and the He-Monster," in *WMQ* 38, no. 2 (April 1981): 288. The most comprehensive appraisal of Andrew Hamilton is Craig W. Horle's account of his career in *LLP* 2, pp. 416–48.
16. "The celebrated . . .": Thomas Davies, *Memoirs of the Life of David Garrick Esq* (London, 1780), Vol 1, p. 224, with a character sketch of James Ralph on pp. 224–41. For an introduction to Ralph: Elizabeth R. McKinsey, "James Ralph: The Professional Writer Comes of Age," in *Proceedings of the American Philosophical Society* 117, no. 1 (February 1973): 59–78. With regard to Ralph's origins: The only genealogical detail that has so far been found is the marriage of a James Ralph—this is probably but not certainly our man—in Elizabethtown, New Jersey. His spouse, Rebecca Ogden, was the daughter of Jonathan Ogden (1639–1732), a member of the town's First Presbyterian Church: see William Ogden Wheeler, *The Ogden Family in America* (Philadelphia, 1907). However, this source says nothing about Ralph's birth or parentage. What we do know is that he had a sister in London: see Alan D. McKillop, "James Ralph in Berkshire," in *Review of English Literature, 1500–1900* 1, no. 3 (Summer 1961), pp. 43-51, in which McKillop draws upon letters written by Ralph in 1726 to Strickland Gough, a Presbyterian minister, and now preserved at the British Library in London. A friend of Samuel Billingsley, a London bookseller who published Ralph's poetry in 1727–28 (BL, Add. Ms. 4291, fol. 208), Gough belonged to a group of liberal, scientifically minded Presbyterian clergymen from the Bristol and Taunton areas of Somerset in western England. Their names and their ideas can be found in Nicholas Billingsley, *A Sermon Occasion'd by the death of . . . Hubert Stogdon* (London, 1728); see also the Gough and Billingsley entries in *ODNB.* Given that Bristol and Philadelphia had close trading connections, it seems likely that James Ralph came from the same region, and that he knew these ministers before going to America to work as a clerk.
17. "Agreeable, instructive . . .": Davies, *Memoirs of the Life of David Garrick Esq,* Vol. 1, p. 241.
18. Onion and Russell: Karl Pearson, *The Life, Letters and Labours of Francis Galton* (Cambridge, England, 1914), Vol. 1, p. 38n.
19. Thomas Denham: for his birth at Bristol, England (September 1689), and parentage, see Society of Friends Registers, NAK, files RG6/1650 no. 252, and RG6/1423, p. 131. Denham's career: Frederick B. Tolles, *Meeting House and Counting House: The Quaker Merchants of Colonial Philadelphia* (New York, 1963), p. 249n; *AWM,* April 6–13, 1721; July 5–12, 1722; October 3–10, 1723; and Denham's account book, at HSP.
20. Failed tobacco crop: Thomas Lawrence to Edward Foy, October 20, 1724, in Law-

rence's letter book at HSP. The London newspapers for that fall and winter refer many times to the bad Atlantic weather.

21. Walpole in 1722–26: J. H. Plumb, *Sir Robert Walpole: The King's Minister* (London, 1960), Chapters 2 and 3; and G. V. Bennett, *The Tory Crisis in Church and State, 1688–1730* (Oxford, 1975), pp. 223–91.
22. John Dunton, *Religio Bibliopolae, or the Religion of a Bookseller* (London, 1728), p. 1.

Chapter Ten: Little Britain

1. Little Britain, Smithfield, St. Bartholomew's Hospital, and the surrounding area: Edward Hatton, *A New View of London or an Ample Account of that City* (London, 1708), Vol. 1, pp. 141–49, 164–65, and 759–61; and John Mottley, *A Survey of the Cities of London and Westminster* (London, 1733–35), Book 1, p. 180, Book III, pp. 619–29 and 748–53. Appearance of the houses: Washington Irving, "Little Britain," in *The Sketch Book of Geoffrey Crayon, Gent* (New York, 1884), pp. 339–41; written by Irving in 1820 after a visit to London. However, to see London as Franklin knew it the indispensable resource is the array of pre-1914 photographs in Philip Davies, *Lost London, 1870–1945* (London, 2009), with pictures of Smithfield and the area around St. Bartholomew's Church and the hospital on pp. 42–49. The images come from the splendid photographic library at the London Metropolitan Archives. Franklin's lodgings at the Golden Fan: the site can be identified from Franklin's comment that the building was next door to John Wilcox's bookstore. In the Little Britain rent book for 1724–25 at the St. Bartholomew's Hospital Archives (file HB4/84), Wilcox is listed as a tenant on the south side of the street and to the east of Pilkington Place (also known as Pelican Place or Court). This means that the Golden Fan backed onto the churchyard of St. Botolph's, Aldersgate.
2. "Perpetual emporium . . .": A comment by Roger North, quoted in Walter Thornbury, *Old and New London* (London, 1889), Vol. 2, p. 225. The book trade and Little Britain: James Raven, *The Business of Books: Booksellers and the English Book Trade, 1450–1850* (New Haven, 2007), pp. 167–68.
3. Dickens on Smithfield: *Great Expectations,* Chapter 20, in which Pip visits Mr. Jaggers's law office in Little Britain. Gin shops: *London, What It is, Not What It Was* (London, 1725), pp. 8–16.
4. William Hogarth's upbringing in Smithfield, and the themes of his early work: Ronald Paulson, *Hogarth: The Modern Moral Subject, 1697–1732* (Cambridge, UK, 1992), Chapters 1 and 8, with references to his mother and sister on pp. 232–33. Like Paula Backscheider's biography of Daniel Defoe, Paulson's penetrating account of Hogarth provides an illuminating context in which to view Franklin's formative period. Franklin's apparent friendship with Hogarth: John Nichols, *Biographical Anecdotes of William Hogarth* (London, 1785), pp. 93–94. Nichols says that on the day Hogarth died in 1764, he received "an agreeable letter" from Franklin (who was in America at the time), and that the painter had just drafted a reply when he suffered his last seizure.

I see no reason to doubt the truth of Nichols's story. Three years later, Hogarth's widow wrote to Franklin asking for his support for a bill in Parliament aimed at helping engravers such as Hogarth and their families to defend their copyright. As regards Franklin's knowledge of Hogarth's work, he was certainly aware of it by 1739 at the very latest, because his Philadelphia shop accounts show that in April of that year he sold a Hogarth print to the Swedish American painter Gustavus Hesselius. Also, the 1741 catalogue of the Library Company of Philadelphia includes the edition of Samuel Butler's satirical poem *Hudibras* illustrated by Hogarth and published in 1732.

5. Tories in Farringdon Without: Anon, *The Art of Managing Popular Elections* (London, 1724); and *Daily Journal,* December 27, 1723, March 30, 1724, and March 29, 1725. Political allegiances of printers: John Nichols, *Literary Anecdotes of the Eighteenth Century* (London, 1812), Vol. 1, pp. 289–312; and *Daily Post,* November 23–28, 1724, showing members of the Stationers' Company who voted for the Tory candidate in a parliamentary by-election. Fewer than half of the printers in London were Whigs, the remainder being Tory, Jacobite, or simply unreliable. The City Elections Act: A. J. Henderson, *London and the National Government, 1721–1742* (Durham, NC, 1945), Chapter 4.
6. Riddlesden act: Maryland Historical Society, *Proceedings and Acts of the General Assembly of Maryland, 1727–9* (Baltimore, 1916), Vol. 36, p. 569: with many references in other volumes of the same series. The British press followed Riddlesden's career closely, with scores of stories about him appearing in 1723, when he was in Newgate prison awaiting transportation (for the second time) to the colonies. His life of crime had apparently begun during the reign of Queen Anne, when he stole a silver candlestick from the Chapel Royal: see for example *Daily Post,* January 28, 1723.
7. The *Samuel: AWM,* January 5–12, 1725.
8. Robert Wilks: Robert W. Lowe, ed., *An Apology for the Life of Mr Colley Cibber, Written by Himself* (London, 1889), Vol. 2, pp. 225–31; Samuel Johnson, "The Life of Richard Savage," in *Lives of the Poets* (Everyman edition, London, 1925), Vol. 2, pp. 73–75. Harlequin Sheppard: *Weekly Journal or Saturday's Post,* December 5, 1724.
9. Samuel Palmer: his manuscript treatise *On the Practical Art of Printing* (ca. 1729), at BL, Add. Ms. 4386; H. R. Plomer, *A Dictionary of the Printers . . . in England etc., 1680–1725* (Oxford, 1922), pp. 228–29; and the sources in notes 6 and 7 to Chapter 11 below.
10. Quotations from William Wollaston, *The Religion of Nature Delineated* (London, 1724 on the title page, but actually 1725), pp. 7, 73, and 122. Wollaston's opening chapters in particular are very sophisticated, showing that he was a powerful thinker with a style that looks forward to British philosophers of the early 1900s. In places the book's techniques of argument (but not its conclusions) strikingly resemble those of G. E. Moore's *Principia Ethica* of 1903.
11. Defoe and Wollaston: Maximilian E. Novak, "Defoe, the Occult, and the Deist Offensive During the Reign of George I," in J. A. Leo Lemay, ed., *Deism, Masonry and the Enlightenment* (Newark, DE, 1987), pp. 98–100.
12. Franklin to Benjamin Vaughan, November 9, 1779, quoted in the introduction to Franklin's *Dissertation* in *BFP 1,* p. 57.
13. For example: See the article on "necessity" by "Diogenes" in *The British Journal,*

December 29, 1722. The author was probably John Trenchard, one of those responsible for *Cato's Letters.*

14. Mandeville and fatalism: Presentment by the Tory-dominated Middlesex Grand Jury, July 3, 1723, condemning the second edition of Bernard Mandeville's *The Fable of the Bees;* reprinted in F. B. Kaye's edition of the *Fable* (Oxford, 1924), Vol. 1, pp. 383–86; and also see *The British Journal,* July 13, 1723; *Evening Post,* July 13–16; and Mandeville's self-defense in *The London Journal,* August 10. Attacks on Spinoza: Jonathan I. Israel, *Radical Enlightenment: Philosophy and the Making of Modernity, 1650–1750* (Oxford, 2001), Chapter 8 and pp. 459–64.
15. French parallels to Franklin's *Dissertation:* Jonathan I. Israel, *Enlightenment Contested: Philosophy, Modernity and the Emancipation of Man, 1670–1752* (Oxford, 2006), pp. 712–36. The relevant sections of John Locke are in Book 4, Chapter 3 of his *Essay Concerning Human Understanding.*
16. The career and the ideas of Franklin's friend John Lyons can be pieced together from a wide variety of sources, published and unpublished. He came from King's Lynn in Norfolk, which may be significant because this was the borough for which Sir Robert Walpole sat in Parliament. This might account for what seem to have been Lyons's close connections with the Whig leadership, who dominated the affairs of the county. Lyons's Norfolk origins: John Lyons, *The Principles of a Rationalist* (London, 1721), title page, saying that he came from "Lynn Regis"; and a Chancery lawsuit, *Lyons v. Moor* (1720), NAK, C11/2650/30, which also gives some details of John Lyons's marriage to a widow who had inherited some land nearby in Lincolnshire. His explosive scheme for preventing disease: John Lyons, *A Prevention of the Plague* (London, 1743); *Daily Journal,* December 1, 1721; and *Applebee's Weekly Journal,* December 2. The record of his subsequent examination by a senior government official, Charles Delafaye, is in the State Papers of George I, at NAK, SP35/29/37-40, December 1721. With regard to Lyons's imprisonment in Newgate in 1723, there is a long series of references in the State Papers between April 19 and August 7 of that year, chiefly NAK, SP35/42/184-5; SP35/43 Part 1/42; and SP35/44 pt 1/102. This last reference is a letter from Lyons in Newgate, addressed to the secretary of state, Lord Townshend, who was also Walpole's brother-in-law. The letter complains about Lyons's treatment in prison and it is the source of my quotation. Lyons's release and his friendship with Richard Mead: John Lyons, *The Infallibility of Human Judgement,* fourth edition (London, 1723), Postscript, pp. 247–49. Lyons's later career as a propagandist, tax collector, and informant for Sir Robert Walpole: letters from John Lyons to Walpole, October 15, 1734, and August 16, 1739, at Cambridge University Library, Cholmondeley (Houghton) Papers, Ch (H) Corr/2356 and 2912. In some modern biographies of Franklin or editions of his autobiography, John Lyons is referred to as "William" Lyons. This is incorrect. There was no William Lyons.
17. Pemberton's ingenuity: James Wilson, ed., *A Course of Chemistry . . . formerly given by Dr Henry Pemberton* (London, 1771), Biographical Preface, with my quotation coming from pp. iii–iv.
18. *A Harlot's Progress:* Paulson, *Hogarth,* Chapters 8–10. On the identity of Mrs. T: see note 19.

19. Among James Ralph's friends in London was a young physician, Thomas Dale, a translator of scientific books who moved in the same circles as Richard Mead. In the 1730s Dale set up a practice in Charleston, South Carolina, from where he wrote letters home to another friend, Thomas Birch, later the secretary of the Royal Society, who also knew Ralph well. On December 19, 1736 (BL, Birch Papers, Add. Ms. 4304, fols. 65–67), Thomas Dale wrote these words to Mr. Birch: "I have seen some extracts of *The Prompter* [a critical magazine for theatergoers] by the manner and style I take Ralph to have a hand, pray let's know what he does now and how he lives, whether still with Astraea, & what's gone with the women and children—I don't remember I ever mentioned that some people here who knew Jenny Wilkins thought this a good place for her as a milliner or sempstress if you see her please tell her."

    "Astraea" was the fictitious name that James Ralph gave in 1729 to the dedicatee of his poem *Clarinda, or the Fair Libertine*. Dale's letter appears to suggest that Ralph had a series of relationships with women who bore him children, one of whom was a milliner, Jenny Wilkins, who might well be identical with Franklin's Mrs. T. One final point is worth making. A very sociable fellow, Thomas Birch served as a connecting link between Franklin and many of the leading writers and thinkers in England. In his diary for 1738, we find Birch dining with the poet James Thomson on September 7 and with William Hogarth on October 30. He had dinner with James Ralph on January 27, 1739. Fast-forward to Franklin's arrival in London in the summer of 1757, and we see him dining with Birch five times during his first two months in the city. One wonders whether they also discussed the fate of the women who fell for Ralph. Birch's diary with lists of his dinner companions is at BL, Add. Ms. 4478c.

Chapter Eleven: The Papists of Duke Street

1. Duke Street and Lincoln's Inn Fields: A. C. B. Urwin, "The Public Trustee Office: A History of the Site" (typescript dated 1973, at the Guildhall Library, London); and Sir John Summerson, *Georgian London* (London, 2003), pp. 16–17.
2. Catholics in London and the Sardinian Chapel: Edwin H. Burton, *The Life and Times of Bishop Challoner* (London, 1909), Vol. 1, pp. 69–81; and Eamonn Duffy, "Richard Challoner: A Memoir," in Duffy, ed., *Challoner and His Church: A Catholic Bishop in Georgian England* (London, 1981), pp. 6–11; and regarding Catholics on the stage, see the biography of Susanna Maria Cibber (1714–66) in *ODNB*. The ward of Farringdon Without, where Samuel Palmer's printing house was located, had a remarkably high number of Roman Catholic residents. At the time of Walpole's tax on Catholics in 1723, the assessors counted twenty-five suspected Papists in the ward, while the average number in each of the other city wards was only four: London Metropolitan Archives (LMA), CLA/047/LR/02/04/059, August 1723.
3. I have established the identity of Franklin's landlady from tax records; from the list of Catholics who refused the oath of allegiance; and from newspaper advertisements. The manuscript sources are at the LMA: Westminster sewer rate book,

1723, LMA, WCS/666, pp. 19–21, showing Mrs. Elizabeth Holt as a tenant of John Richardson at the eastern end of Duke Street (north side); and the list of recusant Papists, April 21, 1718, MR/R/F/026. The newspaper sources, which refer to Mrs. Holt's Italian warehouse and describe her merchandise, are the *Daily Post,* November 17, 1725; *Daily Courant,* May 29, 1727; and *Daily Post,* June 21, 1727.

4. Anti-Catholicism in Boston: Thomas H. O'Connor, *Boston Catholics* (Boston, 1998), pp. 9–10. Roman Catholics in colonial Pennsylvania: Joseph L. J. Kirlin, *Catholicity in Philadelphia* (Philadelphia, 1909), pp. 23–26, 39–41, and 81–83.
5. In the April 1718 roll of recusant Papists at the London Metropolitan Archives, the Holborn names include two spinsters, Martha Beck and Elizabeth Sherwood, alongside Mrs. Holt and her daughter. One of these spinsters may have been Franklin's maiden lady. It seems to me that the more likely candidate is Miss Sherwood. During the 1640s there was a Catholic gentry family of that name from Somerset who also lived in Holborn. On the wider significance of Franklin's acquaintance with Roman Catholics in London: Kerry S. Walters, *Benjamin Franklin and His Gods* (Urbana, IL, 1999), pp. 70–2.
6. John Watts and the Tonsons: Hazel Wilkinson, "Benjamin Franklin's London Printing 1725–6," in *Proceedings of the Bibliographical Society of America* 110, no. 2 (2016): 150–52 and 174–80.
7. Work in the press room: Joseph Moxon, *Mechanick Exercises on the Whole Art of Printing, 1683–4* (Oxford, 1962), Chapter 24, "The Press Man's Trade." Work rate and output per hour: James Mosley, "The Technologies of Printing," in Michael Suarez SJ and Michael Turner, eds., *Cambridge History of the Book in Britain* (Cambridge, UK, 2009), Vol. 10, 1695–1830, pp. 179–82.
8. "Constant and methodical . . .": Moxon, *Mechanick Exercises on the Whole Art of Printing, 1683–4,* p. 303.
9. Rules and practices of printing Chapels in London: Ibid., pp. 323–29.
10. Thomas Denham's business: See note 4 to the next chapter.
11. Ackers and Wygate: D. F. McKenzie, ed., *Stationers' Company Apprentices, 1701–1800* (Oxford, 1978), pp. 1–2, 34, and 258.
12. Wygate was apprenticed in 1721 to James Bettenham, a nonjuror who printed books with Jacobite tendencies. For Bettenham's connection with Mist, see James Sutherland, *The Restoration Newspaper and Its Development* (Cambridge, England, 1986), p. 215. Wygate's family: parish register of Thornbury, Gloucestershire, with John Wygate's baptism dated March 15, 1706; and the will of his mother, Anna Wygate, proved January 20, 1737, in which she left him only £300: NAK, PROB 11/687/197. That sum would have been only just enough in 1737 to maintain a gentleman in London for eighteen months.
13. James Salter: *ODNB;* and *A Catalogue of The Rarities To Be seen at Don Saltero's Coffee House in Chelsea* (London, 1733), with his piece of asbestos listed on page 10.
14. Career of Charles Ackers: D. F. Mackenzie and J. C. Ross, *A Ledger of Charles Ackers, Printer of the London Magazine* (Oxford, 1968), introductory essay, pp. 1–28; and for remarks on his character: Isaac Kimber, *Sermons* (London, 1756), pp. xiv–xv. Kimber

was a Baptist minister whom Ackers befriended, employing him as a proofreader. Caslon and Benjamin Franklin: C. William Miller, *Benjamin Frankin's Philadelphia Printing, 1728–1766* (American Philosophical Society, 1974), pp. xxxii–xxxiv. Franklin's business connection with Ackers is evidenced by a note in one of his account books: Lemay 2, pp. 268 and 496n.

15. *The London Magazine:* Notice in *The Daily Journal,* May 10, 1732.

Chapter Twelve: Seaweed, Sickness, and the Junto

1. A very handsome book, beautifully illustrated, the second volume of Sir Hans Sloane's *Voyage to the Islands* appeared in London in the spring of 1726. On pages 341–48, it contains Sloane's journal of his voyage from Jamaica in 1689, with points of similarity to Franklin's account of his trip on the *Berkshire.*
2. Wollaston and "equivocal generation": William Wollaston, *The Religion of Nature Delineated* (London, 1724–25), pp. 90–92. Also, for contemporary debate about the issue: Jacques Roger, *The Life Sciences in Eighteenth Century French Thought* (Stanford, 1997), pp. 354–66; and Edward G. Ruestow, "Leeuwenhoek and the Campaign Against Spontaneous Generation," in *Journal of the History of Biology* 17, no. 2 (Summer 1984), pp. 225–248.
3. Keimer's almanac: Jacob Taylor, *A Complete Ephemeris for the Year 1726* (Philadelphia, 1725), with Sarah Read named on the title page as one of the retailers who sold it. Titan Leeds the sea captain: *AWM,* May 24–31, 1722.
4. Thomas Denham's account book, 1726–28: HSP, Am. 9055, from which a profile of his business can be created. The longest entries relate to Denham's ship's chandlering clients, including a Quaker shipowner, Daniel Flexney, who later became one of the busiest transatlantic merchants in London, frequently referred to in the English press and in the mercantile records at HSP. Since Flexney continued in business until his death in 1748, this connection alone would probably have sufficed to make the firm of Denham & Franklin a powerful force in Philadelphia; and so if the firm had survived, Franklin might never have printed another word. Denham's friendship with Plumstead is documented in Denham's will, proved July 29, 1728, on microfilm at HSP. Plumstead was one of his executors.
5. Winter of 1726–27 and the epidemic: Letters of Isaac Norris Sr. to Joseph Pike, February 12 and May 10, 1727, in his letter book, Norris Family Papers, Coll 454 (Vol. 2), HSP.
6. Benjamin Senior's closing years: Notes in Vol. 2 of his Commonplace Book (BFSCPB), with his list of relevant psalms. My quotation is from Psalm 119, v. 71. The death notice: *New England Weekly Journal,* March 27, 1727.
7. George Webb at Balliol: Joseph Foster, *Alumni Oxonienses 1715–1886* (Oxford, 1891), p. 1516. The Webb family papers, with details of their estates, are at the Wiltshire and Swindon History Centre, Chippenham, England.
8. Discovered by the Philadelphia historian George W. Boudreau, Scull's Junto notes were first published in July 2007 in Professor Boudreau's paper, "Solving the Mys-

tery of the Junto's Missing Member: John Jones, Shoemaker," in *PMHB* 131, no. 3, (July, 2007), pp. 307–17. The originals are in Scull's notebooks at HSP.

9. William Coleman: Whitefield Jenks Bell Jr., *Patriot Improvers: Biographical Sketches of Members of the American Philosophical Society* (APS, 1997), Vol. 1, pp. 15–19. Despite his very close friendship with Franklin, Robert Grace remains an obscure figure. The principal source is Mrs. Thomas P. James, *Memorial of Thomas Potts Jr* (Cambridge, MA, 1874), pp. 375–91, but like many family histories written in the nineteenth century it may be unreliable. For example, it contains an implausible genealogy making Robert Grace's father out to be an Irish Jacobite nobleman who had fled into exile with James II and served as a soldier of fortune in Europe before going to Barbados. More likely, he came from a Grace family of clergymen in Staffordshire, England: see Henry Sanders, *History and Antiquities of Shenstone* (London, 1794), pp. 92–97, referring to a Robert Grace "who married and settled in America." The Graces also had a brass foundry in Birmingham. The reason why his origins may be significant is simply this: that Grace was Franklin's principal contact in the Pennsylvania iron and steel industry, and the man who arranged the casting of Franklin's iron fireplace. In the 1730s, Grace spent several years traveling in Europe studying metallurgy, returning in the spring of 1737.

10. William Parsons: There is a biographical sketch in *LLP* 2, pp. 801–8, but it chiefly deals with his career after 1741, when he became surveyor general of Pennsylvania. For his shoemaking and for his earlier surveying work, the sources are his account book (1723–26), and his field books from 1730 to 1737, among the William Parsons Papers at HSP (Collection No. 470). His calculations of the width of the Delaware are in Notebook No. 4, pp. 83–86, from 1736–37. Also useful is the unpublished book by Anthony F. Wallace, "William Parsons, Proprietary Agent, 1701–1757" (ca. 1940), in typescript at APS, Ms B P 252.

11. The case for making Cotton Mather the inspiration for the Junto rests on pp. 167–74 of his *Bonifacius, or Essays to Do Good* (which of course Franklin knew) in which Mather recommended the formation of neighborhood "societies of good men" for fostering morality and civic virtue. The problem here is that—as Mather says himself—he borrowed this idea from England, where many towns and cities had created local Societies for the Reformation of Manners. By the 1720s these societies were a familiar feature of public life in London, producing annual reports of their progress and also commissioning sermons from leading clergymen. The principal publisher of these sermons and reports in 1724–25 was a printer and bookseller, Joseph Downing, who operated from Bartholomew Close, where at that time Franklin worked for Samuel Palmer. And so it is just as plausible to argue that Franklin was directly influenced by the London model. However, the closest English parallels with Franklin's Junto are definitely to be found in Locke and *The Spectator:* see below.

12. Scull's Junto poem: Printed in Nicholas B. Wainwright, "Nicholas Scull's Junto Verses," in *PMHB* 75 (1949): 82–84. For Addison's description of a weekly club, see Essays 8 and 9 of *The Spectator,* March 9–10, 1711. It seems to me that anyone who

reads these essays will recognize them as a far more likely inspiration for the Junto than Mather's *Bonifacius.*

13. We can be sure that the Junto members knew *Gulliver's Travels,* because in September 1729 Joseph Breintnall wrote an article for *The American Weekly Mercury* referring to the book: specifically to Part IV, featuring the Houyhnhnms and the Yahoos.
14. John Locke, *Rules of a Society,* in Locke, *A Collection of Several Pieces* (London, 1720), pp. 358–62; and Dorothy Grimm, "Franklin's Scientific Institution," in *Pennsylvania History* 23, no. 4 (October 1956): 439–43.
15. Bustill, Pearson, Decow, etc: William Whitehead, ed., *Documents Relating to Colonial New Jersey, 1720–1737* (New Jersey Historical Society, 1882), Vol. 5, pp. 278–82; and Edwin Tanner, *The Province of New Jersey, 1664–1738* (New York, 1908), pp. 550–51 and 689–702.
16. The book was William Sewel's *History of the Rise, Progress, and Increase of the Christian People called Quakers,* first published in London in 1718.
17. Baird: *AWM,* May 19–26, 1726, and June 19–26, 1729; and T. Scharf, *History of Philadelphia* (Philadelphia, 1884), p. 201.
18. Franklin on Thomson: Franklin to William Strahan, February 12, 1745, *BFP 3,* pp. 13–14. The precise date at which Franklin first read *The Seasons* is impossible to determine, but it must have been no later than the early 1730s because in his memoirs Franklin quotes some lines from *Winter,* which he used at that time as a personal prayer. *Winter* first went on sale in London in April 1726, three months before Franklin left for America.
19. Thomson's *Seasons* and Sir Isaac Newton: For a recent account of Thomson's scientific poetry, see Philip Connell, "Newtonian Physico-Theology and the Varieties of Whiggism in James Thomson's The Seasons," in *Huntington Library Quarterly* 72, no. 1 (March 2009), especially pp. 20–23. Thomson's political stance was also very close to Franklin's.

Chapter Thirteen: Citizen Franklin

1. For a chronology of James Ralph's poetic career, the best source is the diary of his friend Thomas Birch at BL, Add. Ms. 4478c, fols. 4–10. London newspaper references: *Evening Post,* February 13–15, 1728; and *London Journal,* May 11, June 1, and September 14, 1728. On the politics of *The London Journal:* N. R. Hanson, *Government and the Press, 1695–1763* (Oxford, 1936), pp. 111–15, with a mention of Ralph on p. 120. But the best thing to do is to read the poems themselves and those of Alexander Pope—and to see *The Beggar's Opera.*
2. Pope on Ralph: *The Dunciad Variorum* of 1729, Book III, lines 159–60, and the notes going with them. Attacks on Ralph: *Grub Street Journal,* May 28 and July 30, 1730, April 20, 1732, and (a reply by Ralph) May 24, 1733.
3. On his relationship with Fielding: Martin C. Battestin, *Henry Fielding: A Life* (London, 1989), pp. 151–53; and on Ralph's humiliation: Samuel Johnson's life of Alexander Pope, in *Lives of the Poets* (Everyman edition, London, 1925), Vol. 2, p. 177. In

the same volume is Dr. Johnson's deeply moving life of the doomed poet Richard Savage, which takes us into the heart of the milieu that Ralph and Franklin inhabited in the London of the 1720s. James Ralph's begging letters from the late 1730s are in Birch's papers at the BL, Add. Ms. 4317, fols. 99, 100, 102, 104, and 106. "I am now really at my last resource.... I am very serious when I say I am without money entirely and without any prospect of being otherwise": just one example.

4. *BFP 1*, pp. 111–39.
5. For the source of these quotations, see the next note.
6. For the immigration and paper money debates of 1728–29, the principal source is the official journal of the Pennsylvania General Assembly, in Gertrude MacKinney, ed., *Pennsylvania Archives*, Series 8, Vol. 3 (Harrisburg, PA, 1931), pp. 1909–63. In what follows I have also drawn upon Leo Lemay, "Franklin's Suppressed 'Busy Body,'" in *American Literature* 37, no. 3 (November 1965): 307–11; and Keith Arbour, "Benjamin Franklin's First Government Printing," in *Transactions of the American Philosophical Society*, New Series 89, no. 5 (1999), pp. 1–90. For the political context of the 1720s and 1730s, see Alan Tully, "Benjamin Franklin and Pennsylvania Politics," in Waldstreicher, ed., *A Companion to Benjamin Franklin*, especially pp. 104–11. As Professor Tully says: "Classic though it is, Franklin's autobiographical narrative hardly supplies the most accurate guide to his early life." Quite so. For an example of an attack on the Triumvirate: Anon, *A Revisal of the Intreagues of the Triumvirate* (Philadelphia, 1729), which includes on p. 4 the accusation that Andrew Hamilton was a "blasphemer" who had read an "atheistical libel" to the assembly.
7. For Pennsylvania-Lenape relations, the book I have found most helpful is Steven Craig Harper, *Promised Land: Penn's Holy Experiment, the Walking Purchase and the Dispossession of the Delawares, 1600–1763* (Bethlehem, PA, 2006), with broader context supplied by Daniel K. Richter, *The Ordeal of the Longhouse: The Peoples of the Iroquois League in the Era of European Colonization* (Chapel Hill, NC, 1992), pp. 270–75. Nicholas Scull's role as a frontier envoy and surveyor can be traced through the *Minutes of the Provincial Council of Pennsylvania*, Vols. 3 and 4 (Harrisburg, PA, 1840 and 1851).
8. The Wagon Road: Carl Bridenbaugh, *The Colonial Craftsman* (Chicago, 1961), pp. 22–24.
9. "Consummate networker": Walter Isaacson, *Benjamin Franklin: An American Life* (New York, 2003), p. 55.
10. William Allen: See the biographical essay in the perennially helpful *LLP 3*, especially pp. 232–34, dealing with his business interests. Durham: Benjamin F. Fackenthal, *The Durham Iron Works in Durham Township* (Bucks County Historical Society, PA, 1922) in the Fackenthal collection of material about the Pennsylvania iron industry at the Spruance Library, Mercer Museum, Doylestown, PA.
11. Hamilton's speech, August 10, 1739: MacKinney, ed., *Pennsylvania Archives*, Vol. 3, pp. 2505–8. On the economic history of Pennsylvania, and the central importance of the Keystone State for the economic history of the United States as a whole, see Thomas M. Doerflinger's invaluable *A Vigorous Spirit of Enterprise: Merchants and Economic Development in Revolutionary Philadelphia* (Chapel Hill, NC, 1986), especially pp. 74–77,

97–22, and 136–64. Without the kind of insights that Doerflinger provides, it is impossible to understand what Frankin and his friends and neighbors were trying to achieve in the colony after 1730.

Chapter Fourteen: Years of Success

1. For examples of Bradford's attacks on Hamilton and Franklin's response, see the crossfire between the two newspapers in the files of *The American Weekly Mercury* and *The Pennsylvania Gazette* at election time in September–November 1733.
2. Franklin to Sarah Franklin Davenport, June ?, 1730, *BFP 1,* p. 171.
3. *The Morning Post,* June 1, 1779.
4. Hugh Roberts: *LLP 2,* pp. 892–99.
5. George Roberts: Quoted in Sheila J. Skemp, "William Franklin: His Father's Son," in *PMHB* 109, no. 2 (1985): 147–48.
6. Quotations: From William Smith, *A Sermon Preached In Christ Church, Philadelphia, Before the Provincial Grand Master . . . On Tuesday June 24th 1755* (Philadelphia, 1755).
7. Membership in the 1730s: *Liber B* of St. John's Lodge, Philadelphia, at HSP, file Am. 327. Early history of Freemasonry in America: Mark A. Tabbert, *American Freemasons: Three Centuries of Building Communities* (New York, 2005), pp. 33–36.
8. British Freemasonry: Ric Berman, *The Foundations of Modern Freemasonry* (Eastbourne, UK, 2011), Chapters 2 and 3. For examples of the public dissemination of information about masonic membership and rituals: London *Universal Spectator and Weekly Journal,* December 5, 1730; and (probably by Martin Clare) *A Defence of Masonry* (1730), reprinted in James Anderson, *The New Book of Constitutions of the . . . Free and Accepted Masons* (London, 1738), pp. 216–30.
9. *BFP 1,* pp. 192–93.
10. James Logan's use of the Franklinian phrase "ways to get wealth" occurs in his September 1723 *Charge Delivered from the Bench to the Grand Jury,* printed by Andrew Bradford, also including Logan's list of virtues. I take the view that the influence of James Logan, the freethinking Quaker, was far more significant in the shaping of Franklin's career than the cultural legacy the latter received from New England Calvinism.
11. *BFP 1,* pp. 191–92. On Joseph Morgan: Whitfield J. Bell Jr., "The Reverend Joseph Morgan, an American Correspondent of the Royal Society, 1732–1739," in *Proceedings of the American Philosophical Society* 95, no. 3 (June 1951).
12. The Logan Memorandum: Joseph E. Johnson, "A Quaker Imperialist's View of the British Colonies in America, 1732," in *PMHB* 60, no. 2 (April 1936), especially pp. 125–27.
13. Thomas Hopkinson and his background: G. E. Hastings, *The Life and Work of Francis Hopkinson* (Chicago, 1936), pp. 8–12; London *Flying Post,* May 3–5, 1716; London *Daily Courant,* October 23, 1721; and Matthew Hopkinson's Piccadilly leases dated 1716, at Westminster City Archives, England, files 0097/023-5.
14. South Carolina in the 1730s: M. Eugene Sirmans, *Colonial South Carolina: A Political History, 1663–1763* (Williamsburg, VA, 1966), pp. 164–83.
15. On Franklin's printing partnerships: Ralph A. Frasca, *Benjamin Franklin's Printing*

Network: Disseminating Virtue in Early America (Columbia, MO, 2006), pp. 58–75 and passim.

16. The best brief account of the origins and development of *Poor Richard* is in James N. Green and Peter Stallybrass, *Benjamin Franklin: Writer and Printer* (Newcastle, DE, 2006), Chapter 6.
17. Improvements in Philadelphia: Jessica Choppin Roney, *Government by a Spirit of Opposition: The Origins of American Political Practice in Colonial Philadelphia* (Baltimore, 2014), pp. 55–62.

Chapter Fifteen: The Devil's Instrument

1. *BFP 1*, pp. 194–99.
2. *AWM*, September 20–27, 1733.
3. *PG*, October 11, 1733; and *BFP 1*, pp. 333–38.
4. *AWM*, January 22–29, 1734. On Hamilton's alleged atheism, also see note 6 to Chapter 13.
5. These quotations come from Franklin's Preface to the pro-Hemphill pamphlet, *A Letter to a Friend in the Country* (September 1735), in *BFP 2*, pp. 66–67. This volume of the Franklin papers reprints all the pro-Hemphill material he published.
6. Mr. Andrews: Biographical sketch in Clifford K. Shipton, *Sibley's Harvard Graduates*, Vol. 4, 1690–1700 (Cambridge, MA, 1933), pp. 219–25. For a narrative of the Hemphill affair, and for the state of Presbyterian churches in the colony, the most important source (apart from the pamphlets that appeared pro and con Mr. Hemphill) is the minute book of the Synod of Philadelphia, September 1729–September 1736, published in *Records of the Presbyterian Church in the U.S.A.* (Philadelphia, 1841), pp. 90–117. It lists the synod's members including the lay elders. For an account of the affair that reviews the academic literature, see Bryan F. LeBeau, *Jonathan Dickinson and the Formative Years of American Presbyterianism* (Lexington, KY, 1997), pp. 45–63; also, Melvin H. Buxbaum, *Benjamin Franklin and the Zealous Presbyterians* (Philadelphia, 1975), Chapter 2. Neither book places the Hemphill case in its wider, transatlantic context.
7. Growing congregation: Marriage register, at the Presbyterian Historical Society in Philadelphia (F/MI/46/P477r), showing the number of weddings increasing from an average of about twenty per annum in the early 1720s to about seventy each year in the mid-1730s.
8. Ulster schism: Peter Brooke, *Ulster Presbyterianism: The Historical Perspective, 1610–1970* (Dublin, 1987), pp. 81–96; and I. R. McBride, *Scripture Politics: Ulster Presbyterianism and Irish Radicalism in the Late Eighteenth Century* (Oxford, 1998), Chapters 1 and 2. The most famous New Light preacher was the Reverend John Abernethy of Belfast, who in 1719 preached a highly controversial sermon—*Religious Obedience Founded on Personal Persuasion*—whose title captures the flavor of the movement to which he and Samuel Hemphill belonged.
9. Scots-Irish settlers: Richard K. MacMaster, "Searching for Order: Donegal Springs, Pennsylvania in the 1720s and 1730s," in Warren R. Hofstra, ed., *Ulster to America: The*

Scots-Irish Migration Experience, 1680–1830 (Knoxville, TN, 2012), pp. 51–76; and Patrick Griffin, "The People with No Name: Ulster's Migrants and Identity Formation in Eighteenth Century Pennsylvania," in *WMQ* 58, no. 3 (July 2001): 590–96.

10. Logan to the Reverend James Kirkpatrick, August 2, 1729, in Logan's letter books, Vol. 4, p. 223, at the American Philosophical Society. Kirkpatrick was a leading New Light minister in Ulster and a close associate of John Abernethy (see note 8 and *ODNB*).
11. Hemphill had entered Glasgow University in April 1716, but it is not clear whether he graduated: *Records of the University of Glasgow from its Foundation until 1727* (Glasgow, 1854), Vol. 3, p. 49.
12. The Vance letter and Hemphill's Ulster background: *Records of the General Synod of Ulster, 1691–1820* (Belfast, 1897), Vol. 2, pp. 189 and 208–9. Also: Strabane Presbytery Minutes (1723–1740), at Public Record Office of Northern Ireland, CR3/26/2/1, Ac 17173, showing Hemphill subscribing to the Westminster Confession on March 4, 1729.
13. Pemberton Junior: Biographical sketch in Clifford Shipton, *Sibley's Harvard Graduates,* Vol. 6 (1713–1721) (Cambridge, MA, 1942), pp. 535–46.
14. "Silly women," etc.: From Franklin and Hemphill, *A Defence of the Rev. Mr Hemphill's Observations* (Philadelphia, October 1735), in *BFP* 2, pp. 125–26. Scornful comments about Andrews: pp. 40–41.
15. Hemphill's plagiarism: "Obadiah Jenkins," *Remarks Upon the Defence of the Rev. Mr Hemphill's Observations* (Philadelphia, 1735–36), pp. 17–20. This pamphlet was apparently coauthored by Pemberton and by Jonathan Dickinson, the first president of the College of New Jersey, which later became Princeton University.
16. *BFP* 3, p. 398.
17. In their material (*BFP* 2, p. 65), Hemphill and Franklin quoted from a "lay sermon" given to an audience of lawyers in London in 1733 by the radical Whig Thomas Gordon, one of the writers for *The London Journal.* Gordon's attacks on the Anglican clergy were part of an anticlerical campaign in the press and in Parliament in the mid-1730s to which (for his own devious reasons) Walpole gave a degree of official support: see T. F. J. Kendrick, "Sir Robert Walpole, the Old Whigs and the Bishops, 1733–1736," in *Historical Journal* 11, no. 3 (1968), pp. 421–445. An avid reader of the London newspapers—too avid, perhaps—Franklin could easily have jumped to the conclusion that in England freethinkers such as he were about to win a decisive victory over the Anglican establishment. So he tried to copy Gordon and pursue a similar kind of anticlerical campaign in Pennsylvania, but with the Presbyterians as his target. In fact the issues at stake in London and Philadelphia were very different, and anyway Thomas Gordon and his allies were defeated when Walpole called a halt to their activities. I do not think that Franklin understood just how cynical Walpole could be in his political exploitation of religious controversies. Another example of Franklin's borrowings from Gordon: *PG,* September 21, 1733.
18. Wissahickon and the early paper industry in Pennsylvania: James N. Green, *The Rittenhouse Mill and the Beginnings of Paper Making in America* (Philadelphia, 1990); John Bidwell, "Printers' Supplies and Capitalization," in David D. Hall, ed., *The History of*

the Book in America (Chapel Hill, NC, 2000), Vol. 1, pp. 176–77; and C. William Miller, *Benjamin Franklin's Philadelphia Printing, 1728–1766* (Philadelphia, 1974), pp. xxxviii–xli). The first rag advertisement in the *Pennsylvania Gazette:* April 11, 1734.

19. Miller, *Benjamin Franklin's Philadelphia Printing, 1728–1766,* pp. 56–61.
20. Charles Coleman Sellers, *Benjamin Franklin in Portraiture* (New Haven, 1962), pp. 8–13 and 21–22.
21. *BFP* 2, pp. 173–78.
22. The Rees affair: *BFP* 2, pp. 198–202.
23. Franklin to his parents, April 13, 1738, *BFP* 2, pp. 202–4.

Chapter Sixteen: War and Mr. Whitefield

1. John Kinsey: Biographical sketch in *LLP* 2. On the political watershed ca. 1739 and the conflicts of the early 1740s: Alan Tully, *William Penn's Legacy: Politics and Social Structure in Provincial Pennsylania, 1726–1755* (Baltimore, 1977), pp. 23–37.
2. War with Spain: The best source is a forgotten classic from the 1930s: Richard Pares, *War and Trade in the West Indies* (Oxford, 1936), Chapters 1–3. Also useful is Robin Harding, *The Emergence of Britain's Global Naval Supremacy: The War of 1739–1748* (Woodbridge, Suffolk, UK, 2010), pp. 9–25.
3. "Troublesome times" and "dead trading:" Letter book of John Reynell, Vol. 4, 1738–41, at HSP, October 12 and December 15, 1739.
4. International situation: Tim Blanning, *Frederick the Great: King of Prussia* (London, 2015), pp. 74–90.
5. For George Whitefield's career, the best handbook is still the biography by Luke Tyerman, *The Life of the Reverend George Whitefield* (London, 1890), because although Tyerman's judgments may be dated he supplies a wealth of detail, carefully documented. His account of Whitefield's American mission of 1739–41 is in Vol. 1, pp. 307–458. Also: Frank Lambert, "Subscribing for Profits and Piety: The Friendship of Benjamin Franklin and George Whitefield," in *WMQ* 50, no. 3 (July 1993): 529–54. As always, Mark Noll's *America's God* (Oxford, 2002) is essential, placing the Great Awakening in its wider context. So is Patricia Bonomi's *Under the Cope of Heaven: Religion, Society and Politics in Colonial America* (Oxford, 2003), especially pp. 158–70. However, in writing about Whitefield and Franklin I have mostly gone back to the primary sources, principally the *Journals* of Whitefield himself and his friend William Seward and the newspapers of the period.
6. Charles Wesley: November 5, 1737, quoted in Tyerman, *The Life of the Reverend George Whitefield,* Vol. 1, p. 89. Vomiting: W. Jay, *Memoirs of the Life and Character of the late Rev. Cornelius Winter* (London, 1809), p. 26.
7. Edmund Gibson, *The Bishop of London's Pastoral Letter, August 1st 1739* (London, 1739), especially pp. 10–16.
8. "Partition wall": Tyerman, *The Life of the Reverend George Whitefield,* Vol. 1, p. 189.
9. Whitefield's first visit to Philadelphia: George Whitefield, *A Continuation of the Rev. Mr Whitefield's Journal from his Embarking after the Embargo* (Philadelphia, 1740), daily entries, November 3–25, 1739, pp. 118–47.

10. William Seward: *General Evening Post,* May 8–10, 1735; *Daily Gazetteer,* December 16, 1738; *Weekly Miscellany,* August 25, 1739, and November 1, 1740; *ODNB;* and Tyerman, *The Life of the Reverend George Whitefield,* Vol. 1, pp. 163–68.
11. Whitefield profile: *AWM,* December 27–30, 1739.
12. Whitefield and Seward in Philadelphia, April–May 1740: William Seward, *Journal of a Voyage from Savannah to Philadelphia etc, 1740* (London, 1740), daily entries, April 14–May 8, pp. 4–29; and George Whitefield, *A Continuation of the Rev. Mr Whitefield's Journal, after his Arrival in Georgia* (London, 1741), daily entries, April 14–May 11, 1740, pp. 18–37.
13. The Stono Rebellion: Peter H. Wood, *Black Majority: Negroes in South Carolina from 1670 Through the Stono Rebellion* (New York, 1974), Chapter 12.
14. Lewis Timothy's cruelty: Ibid., pp. 245–47. On Franklin and slavery: Lemay 2, pp. 277–280; and the references in note 4 to Chapter Four above.
15. Archibald Cummings, *Faith Absolutely Necessary: Two Sermons* (Philadelphia, 1740), Preface, pp. iii and x–xii.
16. Obadiah Plainman and Tom Trueman: *Pennsylvania Gazette,* May 15, May 22, and May 29, 1740; and *AWM,* May 15–22, 1740.
17. *PG,* June 12, 1740.
18. English Methodists in the eighteenth century: J. C. D. Clark, *English Society, 1660–1832* (Cambridge, UK, 2000), pp. 484–85.
19. Franklin at the 1787 Convention: Michael Klarman, *The Framers' Coup: The Making of the United States Constitution* (New York, 2016), pp. 194–95.
20. Casualties in the Caribbean: Richard Harding, *Amphibious Warfare in the Eighteenth Century: The British Expedition to the West Indies, 1740–2* (Woodbridge, Suffolk, UK, 1991), pp. 114–16 and 137.
21. Winter of 1740–41: John Reynell, February 19, 1741, from his letter book, Vol. 4, at HSP.
22. *BFP* 2, pp. 419-446; and Samuel T. Edgerton Jr., *The Myth of the Franklin Stove,* in the journal *Early American Life* (June 1976).
23. Parliament and American iron: *House of Commons Journals,* Vol. 22 (1732–37), pp. 849–54; and Vol. 23 (1738–41), pp. 107–18. Joseph Farmer, James Logan's friend from Birmingham, England, was a gunsmith as well as an ironmaster, and one of the early investors in the Principio ironworks in Maryland. Farmer had been to America, studied the colonial iron industry, and acted as Logan's advisor in 1726 when the Durham Iron Company was in process of formation. Farmer's evidence to Parliament was dated April 20, 1737. His friendship with Logan: Logan to Farmer, October 15, 1733, in Logan Papers, Vol. 8, HSP.
24. The Pennsylvania long rifle: Henry J. Kauffman, *The Pennsylvania-Kentucky Rifle* (Morgantown, PA, 1960), Chapter 2; and Joe Kindig Jr., *Thoughts on the Kentucky Rifle* (Wilmington, DE, 1960), pp. 25–28. The inventor of the rifle is thought to have been Martin Meylin, who took up residence in 1711 on land rented from Andrew Hamilton: Samuel E. Wenger, *Pequea Settlement 1710* (Lancaster, PA, 2010), pp. 48–50. A stone building reputed to be Meylin's gun shop can still be found on Long Rifle Road in Amish country four miles from Lancaster. In this part of *Young Benjamin Franklin,* I am indebted to Gary B. Nash and his book *First City: Philadelphia and the Forg-*

ing of Historical Memory (Philadelphia, 2002), in which—on pp. 55—Professor Nash makes the point that the Franklin fireplace was a hybrid of English and German craft traditions. My reading of *First City* in 2014 prompted me to make a series of visits to the Mercer Museum and its research library, where I developed the ideas in this section.

25. *BFP 3*, p. 429; and Henry Chapman Mercer, *The Bible in Iron: Pictured Stoves and Stoveplates of the Pennsylvania Germans* (Doylestown, PA, 1961), pp. 29–31. A decorated fireback made at Durham in 1728 can be seen in James Logan's house at Stenton. Numbers of German immigrants: Marianne Wokeck, "The Flow and the Composition of German Immigration to Philadelphia, 1727–1775," in *PMHB*, Vol. 105, No. 3 (July 1981), pp. 260–1. German culture in Pennsylvania: Aaron S. Fogleman, *Hopeful Journeys: German Immigration, Settlement and Political Culture in Colonial America, 1717–1775* (Philadelphia, 1996).
26. Branson's ironworks: Coventry Account Books, 1727–33, at HSP, Collection 212, Vol. 379. In the 1720s, Branson principally sold bar or pig iron or made farming tools or wagon parts. By 1733, as the economy prospered, deepening the demand for local manufactures, he had extended his product range to include pots and pans and sash weights for windows. The Coventry works sold bar iron to Mordecai Lincoln, whose homestead was fifteen miles away. In Philadelphia, Branson served on grand juries and acted as collector and trustee of donations for Whitefield's orphanage in Georgia: George Whitefield, *A Further Account of God's Dealings* (Philadelphia, 1746), endnote.
27. The Warwick Furnace and the Franklin fireplace: Warwick Furnace Papers, 1726–75, MSC 149, in the Fackenthal Collection at the Spruance Library at the Mercer Museum. The key document is a lease and inventory of the furnace, December 17, 1741, signed by Robert Grace, which refers to the molds for the fireplace and stipulates the annual output. Robert and Rebecca Grace: *PG*, May 29, 1740. Mrs. Grace was the granddaughter of Thomas Rutter, the colony's first ironmaster. Her first husband was the son of Samuel Nutt, who for many years had been Branson's partner in the Coventry works and founded the Warwick Furnace in 1736.
28. *BFP 2*, pp. 419–46.
29. Problems with the fireplace: see Edgerton (1976) cited in note 22.
30. Franklin's heat experiments, and his reading in the 1730s: I. Bernard Cohen, *Franklin and Newton: An Inquiry into Speculative Newtonian Science and Franklin's Work in Electricity as an Example Thereof* (Philadelphia, 1956), Part 3, Chapter 7, especially pp. 216–22.
31. On "Fire:" W. J. 's Gravesande, *Mathematical Elements of Natural Philosophy*, trans. J.-T. Desaguliers (sixth edition, London 1747), Vol. 2, pp. 63–64; and Robert F. Schofield, *Mechanism and Materialism: British Philosophy in an Age of Reason* (Princeton, 1970), pp. 80–87.
32. Newton's "electric spirit": Richard S. Westfall, *Never At Rest: A Biography of Sir Isaac Newton* (Cambridge, England, 1983), pp. 745–48 and 790–93.
33. Franklin, Logan, and Logan's treatise on ethics: Franklin to Logan (1737?), *BFP 2*, pp. 184–85; Logan to Thomas Story, May 12, 1736, and November 15, 1737, in Norman Penney, ed., *The Correspondence of James Logan and Thomas Story, 1724–1741* (*Bulletin of the*

Friends' Historical Society, Philadelphia, 1916), pp. 57–60 and 64–65; and James Logan, *Of the Duties of Man as may be Deduced from Nature*, ed. Philip Valenti (Philadelphia, 2013), pp. 151–52.

34. Jean-François Gauvin, *Le cabinet de physique du château de Cirey*, in Judith P. Zinnser and Julie Candler Hayes, *Émilie du Châtelet: Rewriting Enlightenment Philosophy and Science* (Oxford, 2006); and Mme du Châtelet, *Dissertation sur la nature et la propagation du feu* (second edition, Paris, 1744), pp. 91–92, 95, and 118. The marquise was a close friend of the principal French researcher into electricity, Charles Du Fay, keeper of the Jardin du Roi in Paris. She also studied Newton's *General Scholium* of 1713, in which he referred to his "electric spirit." Mme du Châtelet died far too young, in childbirth in 1749 while in her early forties. One of the might-have-beens of Franklin's career is this: if the marquise had lived to read his electrical essays, would the two have met, and what would have been the consequences?

Chapter Seventeen: A Change of Life

1. Zinzendorf: C. William Miller, *Benjamin Franklin's Philadelphia Printing, 1728–1766* (Philadelphia, 1974), pp. 150–60; Donald F. Durnbaugh, "Pennsylvania's Crazy Quilt of German Religious Groups," in *Pennsylvania History* 68, no. 1 (Winter 2001); and Fogleman, *Hopeful Journeys*, pp. 107–22.
2. Properties: Deeds dated July–August 1741, in *BFP* 2, pp. 310–11.
3. The ballad: *BFP* 2, pp. 352–54; and Lemay 2, pp. 271–75.
4. Lawrence Henry Gipson, *Lewis Evans* (Philadelphia, 1939), pp. 1–7 and 14.
5. Election riot: *PG*, October 7, 1742; and John Reynell to Daniel Flexney, November 20, 1742, in Reynell's letter book, Vol. 5, HSP.
6. Clymer's fire: *PG*, January 13, 1743.
7. The fire engine came from Richard Newsham's workshop in Cloth Fair, London, just around the corner from the printing shop at St. Bartholomew the Great, where Newsham started to manufacture his "new invented perpetual water engine to quench fire" in 1721: *Applebee's Weekly Journal*, November 4 1721.
8. Indian affairs in 1743, including McKee's testimony and a full account of its consequences: *Minutes of the Provincial Council of Pennsylvania*, Vol. 4, 1736–1745 (Harrisburg, PA, 1851), pp. 630–69.
9. European situation: Blanning, *Frederick the Great*, pp. 81–90 on "the European state system in 1740."
10. Franklin's early coverage of Sibbald's exploits: *PG*, April 8, May 20, December 21, 1742; and March 17, April 21, and October 6, 1743. *Poor Richard*: *BFP* 2, p. 367.
11. Bartram, Collinson, Grace, and Franklin: E. and D. S. Berkeley, *The Correspondence of John Bartram, 1734–1777* (Gainesville, FL, 1992), pp. 43, 49, 63–64, 79, 99, 106, 188–89, and 214.
12. *BFP* 2, pp. 378–83. The standard account of the society's early days is still Carl Van Doren, "The Beginnings of the American Philosophical Society," in *Proceedings of the American Philosophical Society* 87 (1944): 437–62, but Van Doren did not see the

connections between the society and the crisis in Indian affairs in 1743. In general, and despite the brilliance of his writing, Van Doren had a tendency to neglect the wider political and economic circumstances of Franklin's work in Philadelphia. On the new sophistication of material culture in Pennsylvania in the early 1740s: Mark Reinberger and Elizabeth McLean, *The Philadelphia Country House: Architecture and Landscape in Colonial America* (Baltimore, 2015), pp. 70–78.

13. Franklin and maps: Joyce Chaplin, *The First Scientific American: Benjamin Franklin and the Pursuit of Genius* (New York, 2006), pp. 117–21.
14. The Onondaga mission: John Bartram, *Observations made by John Bartram . . . in his travels from Pennsylvania to Onondaga* (London, 1751; reprinted, Rochester, NY, 1895).
15. Bartram's earlier maps: Bartram to Peter Bayard?, ca. March 1742, *CJB*, p. 188; and Bartram to Peter Collinson, July 6, 1742, *CJB*, p. 200.
16. Franklin to Jane Mecom, July 28, 1743: *BFP* 2, pp. 384–85.
17. Cambuslang: L. Tyerman, *The Life of the Revd. George Whitefield* (London, 1890), Vol. 2, Chapter 1.
18. Franklin to Jane Mecom, July 28, 1743, *BFP* 2, p. 384–85.
19. Spencer's description: *London Evening Post*, April 14–16, 1743. Genealogical records from Scotland contain a reference to an Archibald Spence born at Jedburgh on July 10, 1700, the son of a tobacco spinner, and this is probably our man.
20. London career of Spencer, and lectures by Desaguliers: *London Evening Post*, March 16–18, 1736, December 1–4, 1739, February 26–28, 1741, and November 19–21, 1741; and *Daily Advertiser*, November 29, 1742. His career and reputation in America: J. A. L. Lemay, "Franklin's 'Dr Spence': The Reverend Archibald Spencer (1698?–1760), MD," in *Maryland Historical Magazine* 59, no. 2 (June 1964): 199–216. Spencer obtained his medical degree from St. Andrews University in October 1739 by providing testimonials from two physicians who belonged to the Royal Society: William Stukeley, often regarded as the founder of British archaeology, and Robert Taylor, who was one of the king's doctors: St. Andrews University Library, Special Collections, UY 350/28.
21. Details of Spencer's American lectures: I. Bernard Cohen, "The Mysterious 'Dr Spence,'" in his *Benjamin Franklin's Science* (Cambridge, MA, 1990). His brick church—All Hallows—is still standing at South River, Maryland, not far from Annapolis. With the help of the Sunday congregation I tried in vain to find his grave in the churchyard; and so it may be that Archibald Spencer lies buried beneath the floor of the building.
22. Electrical experiments in the 1730s, and the life and work of Du Fay: Fontenelle, "Éloge de Du Fay," in *Histoire de l'Académie Royale des Sciences, 1739* (Paris, 1741); Henri Becquerel, *Notice sur Charles-François de Cisternay Du Fay* (Paris, 1893); and the superb modern account by J. L. Heilbron, *Electricity in the Seventeenth and Eighteenth Centuries: A Study of Early Modern Physics* (Berkeley, CA, 1979), Vol. 1, Chapters 8 and 9.
23. Just as there is no full-length modern scholarly biography of James Logan, the same is true in the case of Cadwallader Colden. The most recent study is John M. Dixon's book, *The Enlightenment of Cadwallader Colden: Empire, Science, and Intellectual Culture in British New York* (Ithica, NY, 2016), but it is relatively brief. Colden's correspondence was

published by the New-York Historical Society a century ago, but without adequate annotation or commentary. The relevant volumes are *The Letters and Papers of Cadwallader Colden,* Vol. 1 (1711–1729) (NYHS, 1917); Vol. 2 (1730–1742) (NYHS, 1919); and Vol. 3 (1743–1747) (NYHS, 1920).

24. American science in the 1730s: Raymond S. Stearns, *Science in the British Colonies of America* (Urbana, IL, 1970), pp. 502–14, with also a brief account of Colden's work on pp. 491–97.

Chapter Eighteen: Colden, Franklin, and the Two Frontiers

1. Colden to Peter Collinson, May 1742 and November 13, 1742, *CCP 2,* pp. 257–63 and 277–83.
2. Colden to William Douglass, ca. 1728, *CCP 1,* pp. 272–73.
3. Colden on "benevolence": Cadwallader Colden, *History of the Five Indian Nations* (New York, 1727), p. v; and Colden to Collinson, November 13, 1742, as note 1 above.
4. Bartram to Collinson, September 5, 1742, *CCP 2,* p. 202.
5. *BFP 2,* pp. 385–88.
6. Rutherfurd to Colden, April 19, 1743, *CCP 3,* pp. 17–21.
7. John Rutherfurd: *BFP 3,* p. 90; Rutherfurd of Edgerston papers, National Library of Scotland, Acc. 7676, Bundles 22–23 and 36; NAK, SP 41/13./102; and biographical sketch in R. Sedgwick, ed., *History of Parliament, 1715–1754* (London, 1970). His father-in-law was Sir Gilbert Elliot, Lord Minto, a close friend of the philosopher David Hume. Minto was a leading advocate of "improvement" in Scottish agriculture and also one of the originators of the Edinburgh New Town of the 1760s and 1770s. Rutherfurd's command in New York: *House of Commons Journal* (1742), Vol. 24, p. 356; and S. M. Pargellis, "The Four Independent Companies of New York" in *Essays in Colonial History Presented to C. M. Andrews* (New Haven, 1931), pp. 100–103.
8. Bartram to Colden, June 26, 1743, *CCP 3,* pp. 23–24.
9. Because most of these letters were unpublished, they have to be recovered from the manuscript journals of the Royal Society, Vols. 17–19 at RoySoc, covering the years 1736–45.
10. Colden's 1738 report: K. G. Davies, ed., *Calendar of State Papers (Colonial)* (London, 1969), Vol. 44, pp. 130–36.
11. Rutherfurd to Colden, January 10, 1743, *CCP 3,* p. 2.
12. Franklin to Jane Mecom, June? 1748, *BFP 3,* p. 303.
13. William Strahan ca. 1743: His account book, at BL, Add. Ms. 48,800, showing how he built his business; and *ODNB.* In Strahan's accounts, the Whitefield-related entries begin in August 1739 and reach their peak early in 1744. His correspondence with Franklin: *BFP 2,* pp. 383–84, 409–13, 416–17; and *BFP 3,* pp. 13–14.
14. Philadelphia on June 11: Alexander Hamilton, *Hamilton's Itinerarium of 1744* (St. Louis, 1907), pp. 28–30.
15. Privateers: Carl E. Swanson, "American Privateering and Imperial Warfare, 1739–1748," in *WMQ* 42, no. 3 (July 1985): 357–82; and A. P. Middleton, "The Chesapeake Convoy System, 1662–1763," in *WMQ* 3, no. 2 (April 1946): 192–94.

16. Examples of Franklin's coverage of Sibbald and the *Wilmington: PG,* September 27, October 18, and November 8, 1744.
17. The *Mercury: London Daily Post,* March 7, 1744; and *PG,* June 21. Strahan's advice: Strahan to Hall, March 9 and June 22, 1745, *BFP* 2, p. 409n.
18. Bartram to Colden, April 29, 1744, in *CJB,* pp. 237–38.
19. James Alexander: Henry McCracken, *Prologue to Independence: The Trials of James Alexander, American, 1715–1756* (New York, 1964), pp. 67–72 and 85–89. On Alexander's role as the defender of landlords' rights in New Jersey, see Brendan McConville, *These Daring Disturbers of the Public Peace: The Struggle for Property and Power in Early New Jersey* (Philadelphia, 2003), pp. 32–36 and Chapters 5–7. After James Alexander was named as New Jersey's surveyor general in 1718, he delegated the work involved to a deputy, Franklin's old Burlington friend Isaac Decow, who held the post until his death in the 1740s: see note 15 to Chapter 12.
20. Hatred of Colden: For example, *A Letter From Some of the Representatives in the Late General Assembly* (New York, 1747), pp. 28–30, describing him as "this artful crafty and designing man."
21. *BFP* 2, p. 415, and *BFP* 3, p. 54 (*PG,* March 5, 1745).
22. James Alexander to Colden, November 12, 1744, *CCP* 3, pp. 82–83; and Colden to Gronovius, December 1744, *CCP* 3, p. 91.
23. Franklin's diplomatic letter to Colden, October 25, 1744, *BFP* 2, pp. 417–18.
24. *BFP* 2, pp. 446–48.
25. The Berlin Academy: Theodor Schieder, *Frederick the Great* (London, 2000), pp. 42–43 and 258; and Ronald S. Calinger, "Frederick the Great and the Berlin Academy of Sciences, 1740–1766," in *Annals of Science* 24, no. 3 (1968): 239–51.
26. German experiments: Heilbron, *Electricity in the Seventeenth and Eighteenth Centuries,* Vol. 1, pp. 261–75.
27. Quotations from "An Historical Account of the Wonderful Discoveries, Made in Germany etc, concerning Electricity," in *The Gentleman's Magazine,* April 1745. This was a translation from a German essay by Albrecht von Haller: see J. L. Heilbron, "Franklin, Haller and Franklinist History," in *Isis* 68, no. 4 (December 1977): 539–49.
28. Manteuffel and Wolff on the polyp and electricity: Katharina Middell and Hans-Peter Neumann, *Briefwechsel zwischen Christian Wolff und E. C. von Manteuffel* (Leipzig University, 2012), Vol. 1, letters 136 (July 27, 1743) and 147–50 (December 1743). Significance of the polyp: Jonathan I. Israel, *Enlightenment Contested* (Oxford, 2006), pp. 745–77.
29. *Journal Book of the Royal Society,* Vol. 19 (1742–45) at RoySoc, JBO/19, pp. 64–79, 81–82, 109–12, 375–76, and 379–80. Collinson to Colden: *CCP* 3, pp. 109–10.

Chapter Nineteen: A Calling Found

1. Franklin to his parents, September 6, 1745, *BFP* 2, pp. 413–14; Franklin to Edward and Jane Mecom, 1744–45, *BFP* 2, p. 448.
2. The Louisbourg expedition: Julian Gwyn, ed., *The Royal Navy and North America: the Warren Papers, 1736–52* (Navy Records Society, London, 1973), pp. xix–xxvi and 83–115.

3. *Notes on Assembly Debates, BFP 3*, pp. 14–17.
4. Franklin to his brother, May ?, 1745, *BFP 3*, pp. 26–27.
5. Franklin to Strahan, February 12, 1745, *BFP 3*, pp. 13–14.
6. Thomson and science in *The Seasons:* Alan D. McKillop, *The Background of Thomson's Seasons* (Minneapolis, 1942), Chapter 2 and pp. 170–71.
7. Colden on "animal spirits": Roy N. Lokken, "Cadwallader Colden's Attempt to Advance Natural Philosophy Beyond the Eighteenth Century Mechanistic Paradigm," in *Proceedings of the American Philosophical Society* 122, no. 6 (1978): 366–69; and Franklin to Colden, August 15 and November 28, 1745, *BFP 3*, pp. 33–38 and 46–49.
8. John Wygate's career: *London Gazette*, December 3, 1737, listing him as a fugitive debtor; Christopher Middleton, *A Vindication of the Conduct of Captain Christopher Middleton* (London, 1743), many references, especially pp. 138–41; and Wygate's short obituary in the *Penny London Post*, March 21–24, 1746. Wygate and HMS *Hind:* muster book of the *Hind*, NAK, ADM 36/1501 and 1502; and the captain's log, 1744–46, ADM 51/4219, recording his death in January 1746.
9. Lease: *BFP 3*, pp. 50–52.
10. *PG*, June 12, 1746; and Lemay 2, p. 354.
11. *BFP 3*, pp. 74–79.
12. Whitefield's Culloden sermon: *Britain's Mercies and Britain's Duty, Represented in a Sermon preached . . . on Sunday August 24th 1746* (Philadelphia, 1746).
13. Military and political situation in New York: Rutherfurd to Colden, June 26, 1746, *CCP 3*, pp. 218–19; Patricia U. Bonomi, *A Factious People: Politics and Society in Colonial New York* (New York, 1971), pp. 140–58; and Michael Kammen, ed., *William Smith Jr.'s History of the Province of New York* (Cambridge, MA, 1972), Vol. 2, pp. 74–77. Franklin covered these events in detail: for example, *PG*, June 5 and 19, July 10 and 31, September 11, and October 30, 1746.
14. Colden to Gronovius, May 30, 1746, *CCP 3*, pp. 209–11.
15. Discovery of the Leiden jar, and its dissemination in 1745–46: Joseph Priestley, *The History and Present State of Electricity, with Original Experiments* (London, 1775), Vol. 1, pp. 102–9; and Heilbron, *Electricity in the Seventeenth and Eighteenth Centuries*, Vol. 2, pp. 309–23.
16. London *General Advertiser*, April 18, 1746.
17. Abbé Nollet, *Essai sur l'électricité des corps* (Paris, 1746), pp. 194–96 and 202n.
18. Cadwallader Colden, *An Explication of The First Causes of Action in Matter and of the Cause of Gravitation* (New York, 1745–46), pp. 24–28; and *BFP 3*, pp. 84–93.
19. Archibald Home: *BFP 2*, pp. 407–9. Baxter's book: *An Enquiry into the Nature of the Human Soul, Wherein the Immateriality of the Soul is Evinced from the Principles of Reason and Philosophy* (London, 1737); and for a discussion: John W. Yolton, *Thinking Matter: Materialism in Eighteenth Century Britain* (Minneapolis, 1983), pp. 94–100.
20. Collinson's trunk of books and letter to Breintnall, May 1746: James N. Green, "Peter Collinson, Benjamin Franklin and the Library Company," in *Library Company of Philadelphia Annual Report*, 2012, pp. 18–20. The *Carolina* and the *Friendship:* Collinson to Bartram, April 23, 1746, *CJB*, pp. 274–75; London *General Advertiser*, May 20 and June 5; Franklin to Strahan, September 25, *BFP 3*, pp. 82–83; and *PG*, October 16, all from 1746.

21. Timing of Franklin's visit to Boston: Lemay 2, pp. 316–17. Publication date of the *American Magazine & Historical Chronicle: Boston Evening Post,* November 10, 1746, referring to the article titled "Electrical Phenomena Produc'd at Paris and the Apparatus Described." Of the nineteen items in the October issue, every one was lifted verbatim from the British monthlies.
22. Le Monnier's full-length account of his experiments appeared as *Recherches sur la communication de l'électricité* in the 1746 edition of the *Histoire et mémoires de l'Académie Royale des Sciences.* The condensed version by Father Needham was dated July 4, 1746, and addressed to Martin Folkes, president of the Royal Society. After appearing in the July *Gentleman's Magazine* (Vol. 16, pp. 371–74), it was separately published in London at the end of September, before its formal reading at the Royal Society on October 23: see *London Evening Post,* September 27–30, 1746, and John Turberville Needham, "A Letter . . . Concerning some New Electrical Experiments Lately Made at Paris," in the Royal Society's *Philosophical Transactions* 44 (1746–47), pp. 247–63. See also Heilbron, *Electricity in the Seventeenth and Eighteenth Centuries,* Vol. 2, pp. 316–21; and Lemay 3, pp. 65–67. Their account of the beginning of Franklin's experiments differs from mine by leaving out the decisively important influence of Le Monnier.
23. Franklin as sales agent for the *American Magazine: Boston Weekly Newsletter,* January 20, 1743.
24. Franklin to Strahan, January 4, 1747, *BFP* 3, pp. 107–8; Bartram to Professor Gronovius in Leiden: December 15, 1746, *CJB,* p. 283; Bartram to Collinson, March 2, 1747, *CJB,* p. 285. Heilbron, *Electricity in the Seventeenth and Eighteenth Centuries,* Vol. 2, Chapter 11, argues that Franklin began his electrical experiments in the winter of 1745–46, but this cannot be correct because (see note 20) Collinson did not send the tube until April of the latter year.
25. Franklin to Thomas Darling, February 10, 1747; and Logan to Franklin, February 23, 1747, *BFP* 3, pp. 110–13. Logan mentions a "printed piece" that Collinson sent him the previous summer referring to electrical experiments made by the French scientist the Comte du Buffon. In fact, Buffon had not yet begun his own electrical work. However, in Paris he had seen the trials by his friend Le Monnier and he had discussed them with Father Needham, who mentioned their conversations in his article of July 1746. And so this article must have been the "printed piece" that Logan had seen.

Epilogue: An Uneasy Spirit

1. *BFP* 3, p. 186.
2. For the eighteenth century's love of "variety," the best sourcebook is James Boswell's *Life of Samuel Johnson,* where time and again he praises Dr. Johnson's variety of knowledge and conversation: or indeed Johnson's own essay "Variety Necessary to Happiness," No. 80 of *The Rambler* (1750).
3. Colden admired *Plain Truth* so much that he lifted whole paragraphs from it and included them in his patriotic "Address to the Freeholders of New York," published

in *The New-York Gazette* of January 18, 1748. On Colden's political vision of a unified empire in America with the colonies making common cause in matters of defense and Indian affairs: Paul Tonks, "Empire and Authority in Colonial New York: The Political Thought of Archibald Kennedy and Cadwallader Colden," in *New York History* 91, no. 1 (Winter 2010), pp. 25–44.

Sources and Further Reading

For nearly seventy years after it appeared in 1938, Carl Van Doren's biography of Franklin led a crowded field as the most attractive single volume account of his adventures. Even now, when Van Doren has found himself displaced from bookstore shelves by Walter Isaacson's *Benjamin Franklin: An American Life* (2003), his book retains its charm as a rare combination of scholarship, accessibility, and elegant prose. For anyone coming to Franklin for the first time, the best place to begin is with his memoirs in Joyce Chaplin's annotated Norton edition (2012), followed perhaps by a viewing on video of one of Isaacson's sparkling lectures about Franklin and then by a reading of his or Van Doren's book.

Neither Isaacson nor Van Doren delve as deeply as they might into Franklin's scientific work, but we have two sound guidebooks to this complicated topic: Joyce Chaplin's *The First Scientific American* (2006), and Bernard Cohen's superb introductory essay to his edition of *Benjamin Franklin's Experiments*. Cohen was one of the Harvard University pioneers of the history of science. Although his essay dates back to the early days of that academic discipline (it was published in 1941), Cohen still provides the clearest description of Franklin's achievements with electricity.

When readers venture beyond overviews of Franklin's life and work, they can soon feel overwhelmed by the sheer quantity of material about him and by a host of differing interpretations of this multifarious human being and his diverse career. On average, in each year of the twenty-first century so far, scholarly journals have published more than thirty articles with "Benjamin Franklin" in the title. New books appear with equally daunting frequency.

Fortunately, Professor David Waldstreicher has laid a trail through the forest by editing an excellent collection of essays by historians and Franklin scholars—*A Companion to Benjamin Franklin* (2011)—that gives us a composite portrait of the man with the benefit of the best recent research. The book also provides a program for inquiry into questions that remain unanswered about his place in the wider history of the eighteenth century. The first four chapters, by Nian-Sheng Huang, George Boudreau, Sheila Skemp, and

Jonathan Dull, contain in eighty pages a concise, chronological analysis of the principal issues at stake in each decade of his life. The remainder of the book comes at Franklin from almost every relevant angle—political, religious, social, economic, and literary—with clear signposts for readers who wish to explore each area more thoroughly.

Other than those mentioned above, the books about Franklin and his era that I have found most rewarding are as follows. Looming over the landscape like a scholarly sierra we have Leo Lemay's immense biography, left unfinished at his death in 2008. Three volumes appeared, taking the story as far as Franklin's departure for London in 1757. Each one is a treasure store of diligent research. As a university professor of English, Lemay lays too heavy a stress on Franklin's achievements as a writer and journalist, rather than his science, and his account of Franklin's politics makes the young Franklin sound too much like a New Deal Democrat, more egalitarian than Franklin really was in the 1720s and 1730s. But taken as a whole, Lemay's book is as important as the vast Yale edition of Franklin's papers. No biographer can do without them.

The same is true of Bernard Cohen's *Franklin and Newton* from 1956, with its painstaking analysis of the roots of his electrical work. Next on my list come Edmund Morgan, with his extended essay *Benjamin Franklin* (2002), and Gordon Wood's *The Americanization of Benjamin Franklin,* first published in 2004, which helped to shape my ideas about Franklin's yearning for the status of a gentleman.

Too many writers about Franklin and his era fall at the first hurdle, by failing to convey any sense of life as it really was in colonial America or Georgian England. This could never be said about Jill Lepore. From 2013, her *Book of Ages: The Life and Opinions of Jane Franklin* gives us the Franklins without clichés, nostalgia, or sentimentality, but better still is Professor Lepore's disturbing book about the early 1740s, *New York Burning: Liberty, Slavery, and Conspiracy in Eighteenth-Century Manhattan.* To help me make my way around the Philadelphia of Franklin's early manhood, I turned most of all to Gary B. Nash, and especially the opening chapters of his book *First City: Philadelphia and the Forging of Historical Memory* (2002), with its brief but excellent account of artisan culture in the town.

As a path of entry into Franklin's world, I can also recommend a book about someone else: Ronald Paulson's masterpiece *Hogarth,* especially the first volume, subtitled *The Modern Moral Subject, 1697–1732,* published in 1992. Anyone who looks at it will soon see why I find in William Hogarth's life, his pictures, and his obsessions so many parallels with the young Benjamin Franklin's career and attitudes. Last but most enjoyable, I have to mention Stacy Schiff. Although her *A Great Improvisation: Franklin, France, and the Birth of America* (2005) deals with a much later epoch in Franklin's life, it surpasses every other Franklin book (including Van Doren's) in its literary quality.

However, on many occasions while working on *Young Benjamin Franklin: The Birth of Ingenuity* I have had to operate without modern writers to help me. The decisive moment in my research took place in 2014 at the Guildhall Library in London, England, where I found the apprenticeship records of his father, Josiah. This was entirely unexpected—I was merely looking for a little extra detail about Josiah's brothers—since hitherto it has always been thought that Josiah Franklin trained as a silk dyer in the English country town of Banbury. My discovery that Josiah actually learned his trade in the capital meant that I felt obliged to check and verify from primary sources every statement about the Franklin family's origins that I found in earlier biographies or indeed in Franklin's memoirs.

Later I spent several days in Worcester, Massachusetts, at the American Antiquarian Society, a wonderfully tranquil haven of scholarship, examining the Commonplace Book of his uncle Benjamin, an item long overdue for publication. While reading it, I formed the view that biographers have tended to pass over too quickly the environment from which Franklin and his family emerged, all too often making them out to be people who came from almost nowhere. From material in the archives on both sides of the Atlantic, and especially those in Northamptonshire, London, and Pennsylvania, I have tried to redress the balance by putting Franklin firmly back into the context of his time. My endnotes to this book record the sources on which I have drawn.

Index

Page numbers in *italics* refer to illustrations.

Illustration Credits

In Text

ii Frontispiece (Jean-Antoine Houdon's bust of Franklin): Philadelphia Museum of Art, 125th Anniversary Acquisition. Purchased with a generous grant from The Barra Foundation, Inc., matched by contributions from the Henry P. McIlhenny Fund in memory of Frances P. McIlhenny, the Walter E. Stait Fund, the Fiske Kimball Fund, and with funds contributed by Mr. and Mrs. Jack M. Friedland, Hannah L. and J. Welles Henderson, Mr. and Mrs. E. Newbold Smith, Mr. and Mrs. Mark E. Rubenstein, Mr. and Mrs. John J. F. Sherrerd, The Women's Committee of the Philadelphia Museum of Art, Marguerite and Gerry Lenfest, Leslie A. Miller and Richard B. Worley, Mr. and Mrs. John A. Nyheim, Mr. and Mrs. Robert A. Fox, Stephanie S. Eglin, an anonymous donor, Mr. and Mrs. William T. Vogt, and with contributions from individual donors to the Fund for Franklin, 1996–162–1

30–1 Wenceslaus Hollar's map of London. London Metropolitan Archives (City of London).

40 Josiah Franklin's freedom record, 1678. The Worshipful Company of Dyers and Guildhall Library (City of London).

47 Broadsheet engraving of the Rye House Plot © The Trustees of the British Museum.

55 Thomas Franklin Jr. as a tax inspector. National Archives, Kew, England.

62 Judge Samuel Sewall, painted by Nathaniel Emmons. Collection of the Massachusetts Historical Society.

69 John Bonner's map of Boston. Library of Congress.

108 Cotton Mather, by Peter Pelham. Library of Congress.

132 Philadelphia house on Chesnut and 2nd Streets. Philadelphia Museum of Art, gift of Harvey S. Shipley Miller and J. Randall Plummer, 2010–212–2.

138 Slate Roof House, Philadelphia. Free Library of Philadelphia/Bridgeman Images.

151 Sir Isaac Newton's letter. National Archives, Kew, England.

155 Vernon's tankard. Metropolitan Museum of Art, New York, gift of Sylvester Dering, 1915.

166 William Hogarth's shop card for his mother and sister. Courtesy of the Lewis Walpole Library, Yale University.
189 William Hogarth's shop card for Mrs. Elizabeth Holt. Courtesy of the Lewis Walpole Library, Yale University.
228 The Distressed Poet by William Hogarth. Library of Congress.
278 A page from the Franklin shop accounts: American Philosophical Society.
286 Enthusiasm Displayed. Library of Congress.
304 Edward Marshall's rifle. From the collection of the Mercer Museum of the Bucks County Historical Society.
305 left: James Logan's Iron Fireback from Stenton. Courtesy of the National Society of the Colonial Dames of America in the Commonwealth of Pennsylvania at Stenton, Philadelphia.
305 right: German stove plate with David and Goliath. Yale University Art Gallery, Mabel Brady Garvan Collection.
308 Early example of a Franklin fireplace. From the collection of the Mercer Museum of the Bucks County Historical Society.

Color Insert

1 Great Map of Ecton, 1703. Map 2115, © Northamptonshire Record Office, England.
3 (top) Bartholomew Close. London Metropolitan Archives (City of London).
3 (bottom) The Oxford Arms, Warwick Lane. London Metropolitan Archives (City of London).
4 (top) Seventeenth-century houses. London Metropolitan Archives (City of London).
4 (bottom) Sardinian Embassy, Lincoln's Inn Fields. London Metropolitan Archives (City of London).
5 (top) Don Saltero's Coffee House, Chelsea. London Metropolitan Archives (City of London).
5 (bottom) Peter Cooper's panorama of Philadelphia. Library Company of Philadelphia.
6 (top) From William Hogarth's The Harlot's Progress. Metropolitan Museum of Art, New York.
6 (bottom) From Hogarth's Industry and Idleness. Metropolitan Museum of Art, New York.
7 (top left) James Logan, by Gustavus Hesselius. Courtesy of the Philadelphia History Museum at the Atwater Kent, the Historical Society of Pennsylvania Collection.
7 (top right) Andrew Hamilton, by Adolf Ulrick Wertmüller. Courtesy of the Philadelphia History Museum at the Atwater Kent, the Historical Society of Pennsylvania Collection.
7 (bottom) William Allen, by Robert Feke. Courtesy of Independence National Historical Park.
8 (top) Cadwallader Colden, by John Wollaston. Metropolitan Museum of Art, New York, bequest of Grace Wilkes, 1932.

8 (bottom left) Deborah Read Franklin, by Benjamin Wilson. American Philosophical Society.

8 (bottom right) Benjamin Franklin, by Robert Feke. Harvard University Portrait Collection, bequest of Dr. John Collins Warren, 1856; and photograph by Imaging Department © President and Fellows of Harvard College.

A NOTE ABOUT THE AUTHOR

NICK BUNKER is the author of *Making Haste from Babylon: The* Mayflower *Pilgrims and Their World* and *An Empire on the Edge: How Britain Came to Fight America,* the latter of which won the 2015 George Washington Prize. In the same year, *An Empire on the Edge* was a finalist for the Pulitzer Prize for History. Educated at King's College, Cambridge, and Columbia University, he worked as a reporter for the *Liverpool Echo* and the *Financial Times,* where he was one of the writers of the Lex Column. After leaving journalism, he was a stockbroker and investment banker, principally for the HongKong and Shanghai Banking Corporation. For many years he served on the board of the Freud Museum, based in the house in Hampstead, London, where Sigmund Freud died in 1939. Nick Bunker now lives with his wife, Susan, and their otterhound, Champion Teckelgarth Mercury, in Lincolnshire, England.

A NOTE ABOUT THE TYPE

The text of this book was set in Centaur, the only typeface designed by Bruce Rogers (1870–1957), the well-known American book designer. A celebrated penman, Rogers based his design on the roman face cut by Nicolas Jenson in 1470 for his Eusebius. Jenson's roman surpassed all of its forerunners and even today, in modern recuttings, remains one of the most popular and attractive of all typefaces. The italic used to accompany Centaur is Arrighi, designed by another American, Frederic Warde, and based on the chancery face used by Lodovico degli Arrighi in 1524.

Composed by North Market Street Graphics, Lancaster, Pennsylvania
Printed and bound by Berryville Graphics, Berryville, Virginia
Designed by Michael Collica